Why does "judgment according to deeds" produce no discernible theological tension for Paul, the apostle of justification by faith? For students of his writings, *paradox, incoherence,* or *eschatological tension* come more readily to mind.

Paul felt no such theological tension because there was none – neither within his own soteriology, nor in that of the Judaism from which he learned to speak of "judgment according to deeds." For both, salvation is wholly by God's grace *and* the saved will be repaid (i.e., saved or condemned) in accordance with what they have done. Thus, Paul can promise eternal life to those who "do good," while threatening wrath upon the disobedient (Rom. 2:6–11), and without undermining justification by faith

This thorough examination of second temple and Pauline texts interacts with recent discussions of "covenantal nomism," justification, and the "new perspective" on Paul to explore the Jewishness of the apostle's theology.

SOCIETY FOR NEW TESTAMENT STUDIES

MONOGRAPH SERIES

General editor: Richard Bauckham

105

PAUL, JUDAISM, AND JUDGMENT ACCORDING TO DEEDS

Paul, Judaism, and Judgment According to Deeds

KENT L. YINGER

Fuller Theological Seminary

CAMBRIDGE
UNIVERSITY PRESS

PUBLISHED BY THE PRESS SYNDICATE OF THE UNIVERSITY OF CAMBRIDGE
The Pitt Building, Trumpington Street, Cambridge CB2 1RP, United Kingdom

CAMBRIDGE UNIVERSITY PRESS
The Edinburgh Building, Cambridge CB2 2RU, UK http://www.cup.cam.ac.uk
40 West 20th Street, New York, NY 10011–4211, USA http://www.cup.org
10 Stamford Road, Oakleigh, Melbourne 3166, Australia

First published 1999

Printed in the United Kingdom at the University Press, Cambridge

Typeset in 10/12 Times   [CE]

A catalogue record for this book is available from the British Library

Library of Congress cataloguing in publication data

Yinger, Kent L.
    Paul, Judaism, and judgment according to deeds / Kent L. Yinger.
        p.   cm. – (Monograph series / Society for New Testament Studies; 105)
    Includes bibliographical references and index.
    ISBN 0 521 63243 9
    1. Bible. N.T. Epistles of Paul – Cricitism, interpretation, etc.
2. Judgment of God – Biblical teaching. 3. Bible. O.T. – Theology.
4. Bible. N.T. Epistles of Paul – Relation to the Old Testament.
5. Bible. O.T. – Relation to Epistles of Paul. I. Title.
II. Series: Monograph series (Society for New Testament Studies); 105.
BS2655.J74Y56   1999
234–dc21   98–30667   CIP

ISBN 0521 63243 9 hardback

To Jack and Wanda Yinger

CONTENTS

PREFACE

"Justified by grace through faith" ... "Judged according to works." While this study focuses only upon the second part of what is often perceived as a Pauline paradox, it ultimately hopes to suggest why these two thoughts produced no apparent theological tension in the writings of Paul. That, of course, does not mean that they produced no existential tension. As the reader will see, divine judgment according to deeds has regularly conveyed both challenge and consolation. Precisely how it does this is a major part of this book.

Thanks are in order first of all to Professor Andrew T. Lincoln, without whose encouragement and guidance as adviser during my doctoral studies this investigation would probably never have been undertaken. His suggestions and challenges along the way made the dissertation upon which this book is based a much better product than it would have otherwise been. Dr. R. Barry Matlock and Dr. John A. Ziesler gave much needed encouragement to proceed with the publication of this material. The entire period of research and writing would have been impossible without the understanding and flexibility shown by my wife Debi. Dr. Rodney K. Duke reviewed an early draft of chapter 1 and offered critique that led to several significant changes. I wish also to record my thanks to my former employer during a major period of writing, OC International, Inc., and in particular to its president, Dr. Larry Keyes, for generously allowing a flexible work load and occasional leaves of absence from my duties while living in Germany and in the US.

Finally, thanks are in order to Dr. Margaret E. Thrall and Dr. Richard J. Bauckham, former and current General Editors respectively of the Society for New Testament Studies Monograph Series, for their willingness to accept this work into the series, and to the fine editorial staff of the Cambridge University Press.

Much of the work done on this topic remains in untranslated German works. To aid the reader, I have given my own English translations in most cases.

ABBREVIATIONS

Most abbreviations of primary and secondary sources correspond to standard usage and will not be reproduced here. The reader should consult the *Society of Biblical Literature Membership Directory and Handbook* (Decatur, GA: Society of Biblical Literature, 1994), 223–242, the *Catholic Biblical Quarterly* (revised each October), or the instructions website of the *Journal of Biblical Literature* (http://shemesh.scholar.emory.edu/scripts/SBL/Archive/INSTR.HTM).

Additional abbreviations are as follows:

CTM	*Concordia Theological Monthly*
EB	Expositor's Bible
EETh	Einführung in die evangelische Theologie
ET	English translation
MeyerK	H. A. W. Meyer (ed.), Kritisch-exegetischer Kommentar
NIDNTT	C. Brown (ed.), *New International Dictionary of New Testament Theology*
NumenSup	Supplements to *Numen*
PLJP	E. P. Sanders, *Paul, the Law, and the Jewish People*
PPJ	E. P. Sanders, *Paul and Palestinian Judaism*
TANZ	Texte und Arbeiten zum neutestamentlichen Zeitalter
TPINT	Trinity Press International New Testament

INTRODUCTION

Why study "judgment according to deeds?"

Particularly since the Protestant Reformation, interpreters of Paul have pondered over the meaning of judgment according to deeds in the light of justification by faith alone. According to Romans 2:7 God will repay with eternal life those who do good, but in Romans 3:28 "a person is justified by faith apart from works."[1] Yet in spite of the immense effort expended by scholars to resolve this puzzle, no consensus or even large-scale agreement on how to relate these two elements in Paul's thought has been reached. Nevertheless, students of the apostle's writings return to this theme again and again, demonstrating its importance for an understanding of his theology.[2]

This book seeks to shed light on one important but somewhat neglected component in that debate: *divine judgment according to deeds*. Although some important preliminary work has been done in the past few decades,[3] most treatments have given relatively little attention to a first-hand study of the use and meaning of this motif in Jewish sources prior to Paul. The studies referred to even today

---

[1] Apart from an historic Protestant aversion to any overemphasis on "works," the two terms ("deeds" and "works") can hardly be distinguished in meaning and will be used interchangeably.

[2] See, for instance, Matthias Kinghardt, "Sünde und Gericht von Christen bei Paulus," *ZNW* 88 (1997), 56–80.

[3] E. P. Sanders, *Paul and Palestinian Judaism: A Comparison of Patterns of Religion* (Philadelphia: Fortress, 1977; hereafter *PPJ*, see subject index "Reward and Punishment"); R. Heiligenthal, *Werke als Zeichen, Untersuchungen zur Bedeutung der menschlichen Taten im Frühjudentum, neuen Testament und Frühchristentum* (WUNT 2/9; Tübingen: J. C. B. Mohr, 1983), 143–164, 172–184, 234–264; S. Travis, *Christ and the Judgment of God: Divine Retribution in the New Testament* (Foundations for Faith; Basingstoke: Marshall, Morgan and Scott, 1986), 5–29; D. W. Kuck, *Judgment and Community Conflict: Paul's Use of Apocalyptic Judgment Language in 1 Corinthians 3:5–4:5* (NovTSup 66; Leiden: E. J. Brill, 1992), 38–95.

by most when commenting on this issue are either in German, have a different focus, or are only suggestive in scope. No monograph has been devoted to a thorough examination of the motif of divine judgment (or recompense) according to deeds in pre-Pauline Jewish sources, and that in spite of the fact that it is precisely the language of judgment according to deeds which is most often felt to be in direct conflict with Paul's teaching on justification by faith.

Thus, one of the major goals of this study is to examine carefully the terminology and rhetorical functions of recompense according to deeds in relevant Jewish texts. Paul's use will then be examined against the same background in order to ascertain the degree of terminological and functional continuity or discontinuity. Does he evince proximity to use in the Scriptures, to that in apocalyptic writings, in sectarian circles? Does he significantly modify the traditional wording or rhetorical function(s), and, if so, does this give any hint as to his own particular theological understanding of the motif?

Studies of judgment and justification written prior to the 1970s were generally reliant upon an understanding of Judaism represented by names such as Weber, Strack-Billerbeck, and Bousset.[4] These suggested a radical *discontinuity* between Paul and his Jewish upbringing in regard to a doctrine of divine recompense. Whereas Judaism was thought to be a religion of works in which salvation had to be earned by accumulating more good works than bad in one's lifetime, in Paul justification (and thus judgment) was by grace apart from works.

This debate over Paul's relationship to Judaism has received new impetus from the work of E. P. Sanders, who raises the possibility of greater *continuity* between Paul and Judaism on the point of judgment according to works.

> Paul's view is typically Jewish ... the distinction between being *judged on the basis of deeds* and punished or rewarded at the judgment (or in this life), on the one hand, and being *saved by God's gracious election*, on the other,

---

[4] F. W. Weber, *Jüdische Theologie auf Grund des Talmud und verwandter Schriften* (2nd edn.; Leipzig: Dörffling & Franke, 1897); H. L. Strack and P. Billerbeck, *Kommentar zum Neuen Testament aus Talmud und Midrasch* (4 vols.; Munich: 1922 [hereafter *Str-B*]), esp. Exkursus 20: "Das Gleichnis von den Arbeitern im Weinberg Mt 20,1–16 u. die altsynagogale Lohnlehre" (IV.484–500); W. Bousset and H. Gressmann, *Die Religion des Judentums im späthellenistischen Zeitalter* (3rd edn.; HNT 21; Tübingen: J. C. B. Mohr, 1926).

was the general view in Rabbinic literature ... Salvation by grace is not incompatible with punishment and reward for deeds.[5]

Though Sanders himself argues that Paul and Palestinian Judaism represent two differing "patterns of religion," he also admits they evince no essential difference in regard to the relationship between grace and works. A reevaluation of judgment according to works in both Paul and second temple Judaism is necessary to determine whether Paul's understanding of judgment as well as of the relationship among the concepts faith – obedience – salvation – judgment might not be much closer to Jewish views than previously allowed. Perhaps Mark Seifrid is correct in suggesting that the resolution of the "inherent but invisible connection" in Paul between justification and sanctification may only be achieved by a reexamination of the background of such a connection in Judaism.[6]

Thus, another goal of this study will be to examine the place, theologically, of judgment according to deeds within the larger soteriological pattern(s) represented in the various sources. Of course, a full-scale study of their soteriological views is beyond the scope of this book. Therefore, I will be somewhat more reliant at this point on the findings of others. Sanders' basic insight into the pattern of Palestinian Jewish religion ("covenantal nomism") has been adopted as a working hypothesis, but has been tested constantly against the texts studied. For clarification, "covenantal nomism" means that salvation is not earned by human initiative or merits, but is granted freely by means of God's election and the giving of the covenant. One "gets in" by grace. Within this covenantal relationship, however, obedience to God's will (the Law) is required. Works are the condition of maintaining one's status within the saved. One "stays in" by obedience.[7]

In adopting this hypothesis, I am not unaware of the challenges that have been raised against Sanders as to the relation of grace and works in Judaism and in Paul. Laato, for instance, contrasts Jewish synergism with Pauline monergism. Paul's pessimistic anthropology demands both a radical doctrine of *sola gratia* and the rejection of Judaism's optimistic anthropology in which the

[5] *PPJ*, 517; see also 515–518, 543.
[6] *Justification by Faith: The Origin and Development of a Central Pauline Theme* (NovTSup 68; Leiden: E. J. Brill, 1992) 46.
[7] See *PPJ*, esp. 75, 236, 422.

freedom and ability of the human will remain intact.[8] This rejection
of Pauline continuity based upon Jewish synergism has been voiced
by others as well.[9] While there may well be more variety in second
temple Judaism than Sanders' "pattern" indicates, these critics
have not succeeded in demonstrating that the grace–works axis in
Judaism generally is any more synergistic or meritorious than in
Paul. Both entry into and continued (and final) enjoyment of
salvation find their *cause* in God's grace and mercy; the condition
for the maintenance and final enjoyment of the same is human
obedience.[10]

Finally, ongoing debate regarding δικαιοσύνη θεοῦ [the righteousness of God] raises anew the question of the relationship
between Pauline justification by faith and Christian obedience, and
thus, of justification and judgment. For example, the movement
away from a strictly forensic-judicial perspective in favor of "Heil-
setzende Macht" [saving power] which includes transformational
categories virtually collapses justification and sanctification.[11]
Without claiming to provide a fresh analysis of this issue, these
developments will nevertheless have to be kept in mind as possibly
providing new avenues for defining the relationship between justification and judgment.

---

[8] T. Laato, *Paul and Judaism: An Anthropological Approach* (trans. T. McElwain;
South Florida Studies in the History of Judaism 115; Atlanta: Scholars Press, 1995),
167.

[9] Examples include D. A. Carson, *Divine Sovereignty and Human Responsibility:
Biblical Perspectives in Tension* (New Foundations Theological Library; London:
Marshall, Morgan & Scott, 1981), 45–109; R. H. Gundry, "Grace, Works, and
Staying Saved in Paul," *Bib* 66 (1985), 1–38; and C. F. D. Moule, "Jesus, Judaism,
and Paul," *Tradition and Interpretation in the New Testament: Essays in Honor of
E. Earle Ellis* (ed. G. Hawthorne; Grand Rapids: Eerdmans, 1987), 43–52.

[10] Though maintaining points of criticism, examples of the general acceptance of
this fundamental thesis of Sanders include J. Neusner, "The Use of the Later
Rabbinic Evidence for the Study of Paul," *Approaches to Ancient Judaism*, vol. II
(ed. William Scott Green; Brown Judaic Studies 9; Atlanta: Scholars Press, 1980), 48,
50; J. D. G. Dunn, "The New Perspective on Paul," *BJRL* 65/2 (1983), 95–97; and
W. D. Davies, *Jewish and Pauline Studies* (Philadelphia: Fortress Press, 1984), 17–23
and 308, n. 27; idem., *Paul and Rabbinic Judaism: Some Rabbinic Elements in Pauline
Theology* (4th edn.; Philadelphia: Fortress Press, 1980), xxix.

[11] E. Käsemann, "Gottesgerechtigkeit bei Paulus," *ZTK* 58 (1961), 367–378 (ET
= *New Testament Questions of Today* [1969], 168–182). M. T. Brauch provides an
overview, "Appendix: Perspectives on 'God's righteousness' in recent German
discussion," in E. P. Sanders, *PPJ*, 523–542. For a critical response, see M. Seifrid,
Justification by Faith, 37–77.

Method and procedure

The study of the motif in Judaism prior to Paul has value in its own right, apart from its significance for understanding Paul's letters. Thus, part one will be devoted to an examination of the pertinent Jewish literature. The attempt will be made to avoid imposing Pauline categories on this literature, or only combing it for parallels to Paul's use. In comparing one literary motif across several bodies of literature I will investigate its linguistic characteristics and rhetorical functions as well as its theological significance. Attention will be given especially to identifying the vocabulary and rhetorical functions which are typical in order to provide a basis for determining to what extent Paul's use is or is not continuous with that of second temple Judaism. Further, the theological significance of the motif within the soteriological pattern of each individual writing will be explored, and related motifs noted (e.g., divine impartiality, two-ways contrast, weighing of deeds). Thus by the end of part one we should have formed a clear picture of the form, function and content of divine judgment according to deeds in second temple Judaism.

Part two will then turn to the Pauline texts and will follow a similar procedure, but with greater detail in the exegetical analysis. The same issues of form, function, and content will guide the study, but in addition special attention will be given to the relationship between Paul's use and that discovered in second temple Judaism. In particular, at what points do the form and function of the motif in Paul show continuity or discontinuity with common Jewish use? Is there evidence of his having modified the tradition in ways which hint at his (differing) understanding of its meaning within his own soteriological pattern? Or, lacking indications of significant change in form and function, does judgment according to deeds function for him theologically in the same way that it does in the Jewish sources? What is the meaning of this judgment motif for the believer's justification or salvation?[12] The concluding chapter will summarize these results and will suggest an understanding of

---

[12] Sanders' objections to certain types of motif-comparison (*PPJ*, 1–24, esp. 12–18) can be avoided, it seems to me, by attempting to understand the motif in each instance within its own soteriological pattern before attempting any comparison. Examples of the approach I am using to understand a particular motif are J. Bassler, *Divine Impartiality: Paul and a Theological Axiom* (SBLDS 59; Chico, CA: Scholars Press, 1982), see esp. 1–4; R. Scroggs, *The Last Adam: A Study in Pauline Anthropology* (Philadelphia: Fortress Press, 1966), xxiii; and Davies, *Paul and Rabbinic Judaism*.

judgment and justification in Paul which has been made plausible by the foregoing analysis.

In order to keep the amount of pertinent material within reasonable limits, I will confine myself to *divine recompense to those within the religious community*. Thus the focus is not upon intra-community (human) judgment or judgment upon outsiders. Primary texts to be considered will be those using the terminology of "judgment (or recompense) according to deeds," or texts alluding to a divine judgment-recompense in connection with deeds.[13]

As witnesses to the pre-Pauline Jewish use of the motif I will examine the Jewish Scriptures (both the MT and the LXX), the OT Pseudepigrapha, and the DSS.[14] Rabbinic texts will be cited occasionally for comparison, but the current state of research into this literature suggests that a defensible reconstruction of first-century CE rabbinic perspectives is still a task for the future.[15] Greco-Roman views of judgment will be noted only briefly since Paul's use of the particular motif under consideration stems by common consent from Jewish sources. Evidence for Paul's use of the motif will be taken from the undisputed Paulines, and from Colossians.[16]

The longstanding debate: judgment and justification in Paul[17]

As noted above, attempts to understand judgment in Paul have traditionally approached the subject in terms of defining and

---

[13] See the next chapter for further definition of the semantic field.

[14] On the omission of Philo, cf. C. Roetzel, *Judgement in the Community: A Study of the Relationship between Eschatology and Ecclesiology in Paul* (Leiden: E. J. Brill, 1972), 14, n. 1; and Heiligenthal, *Werke als Zeichen*, 273–278.

[15] K. Müller, "Zur Datierung rabbinischer Aussagen," in *Neues Testament und Ethik: FS R. Schnackenburg* (ed. H. Merklein; Freiburg: Herder, 1989), 551–587.

[16] On the authenticity of Colossians, see chapter 7. The motif is found in 2 Thessalonians only at 1:6 ("it is indeed just of God to repay with affliction those who afflict you"), but applied to enemies of the gospel, thus not meeting this study's criteria for primary motif-texts. The occurrence in Eph. 6:8 ("whatever good we do, we will receive the same again from the Lord") may be safely overlooked, since it is so similar to Col. 3:24 and would make little difference to my conclusions. 2 Tim. 4:14 may also be mentioned here, being one of the few instances in the Pauline corpus where the motif is used to pronounce a sentence of divine punishment upon a named individual: "Alexander the coppersmith did me great harm; the Lord will pay him back for his deeds." Elsewhere such statements are generally left conditional ("if you") or more oblique in their reference ("whoever").

[17] A good survey can be found in Kuck, *Judgment and Community Conflict*, 1–7. Older reviews include H. Braun, *Gerichtsgedanke und Rechtfertigungslehre bei Paulus* (UNT 19; Leipzig: J. C. Hinrich'sche, 1930), 14–31; C. Haufe, *Die sittliche Rechtfertigungslehre des Paulus* (Halle: VEB Max Niemeyer, 1957), 37–68; and R. C.

resolving the theological paradox or tension perceived to exist between the twin Pauline affirmations of judgment and justification. Writers on this topic may be organized broadly into two basic groups, those for whom the tension between judgment and justification is ultimately unresolvable, and those who propose a resolution. To the first group belong those who see Paul's thought on this subject as incoherent or ultimately illogical.

Gillis Wetter, for example, is particularly concerned to focus on Paul's relation to his prior Jewish world of thought.[18] Specifically, to what degree did the apostle retain Judaism's emphasis on retribution? For Wetter, the discontinuity on this point is stark indeed. Paul "does not proclaim retribution with punishment and reward as did the Jews, but he calls out to everyone: God has rescued us from retribution."[19] Although divine recompense still works in the world, it has no more effect upon the Christian. Grace in Paul replaces Jewish retributive thinking. While explainable psychologically, "Every attempt to express Paul's eschatology as a coherent system is utterly impossible; the elements he places side by side *cannot be united.*"[20]

Herbert Braun adds that it is particularly in paraenetic contexts that Paul's use of judgment must be deemed inconsistent.[21] On the one hand, the judgment (of Christians) is integral to Paul's doctrinal system, and is no "unüberwundener jüdischer Rest" [unexpunged remnant of Judaism]. This judgment according to works is the same judgment as is in view in justification by faith (i.e., no "second" justification). Paul maintains a dominant note of hope, certain of a positive outcome, though with occasional notes of uncertainty or even warning of loss. Its outcome for believers is salvation (not simply gradations of blessedness), and is according to works.

On the other hand, judgment is subservient to justification by faith. This is in sharpest contrast to Judaism. For the apostle, justification assures the eschatological verdict with a certainty which cannot be overturned by disobedience, even in the light of grave sinning. But this means, particularly in paraenetic contexts,

Devor, *The Concept of Judgment in the Epistles of Paul* (Ph.D. Diss., Drew University, 1959), 95–150.
[18] Gillis P. Wetter, *Der Vergeltungsgedanke bei Paulus: Eine Studie zur Religion des Apostels* (Göttingen: Vandenhoeck & Ruprecht, 1912).
[19] Ibid., 173.
[20] Ibid., 154 (my emphasis).
[21] Braun, *Gerichtsgedanke und Rechtfertigungslehre.*

that Paul's use of judgment must be deemed inconsistent. Texts
which allow a double possibility of behavior as well as of outcome
for Christians (salvation or damnation) reflect this inconsistency;
they are *an unreflected paraenetic use of Paul's Jewish traditions.*
Braun ties this to Paul's mode of "unsystematic Jewish thinking."

Somewhat similar is Nigel Watson who argues that judgment
and justification conflict in Paul because they are "directed to
different addresses."[22] Justification texts speak to overscrupulous
legalists, while judgment warnings aim at the presumptuous. Yet
both these poles are fully Pauline (not simply a Jewish remnant),
and can be understood properly only from within a sort of
dialectical preaching. Paul did not draw these various elements
from a single, and to him coherent, system. The result is that
"nothing else remains for us but to remain under the contradiction
and to see it through."

Finally, to this group may be added two authors who dispute
that there is any tension to be resolved; at least Paul does not
appear to have felt any. Not that Paul's thought exhibits any
logical harmony; instead, the very possibility of paradox is
removed by sealing off statements on justification and on judgment
from one another. Calvin Roetzel (*Judgement in the Community*)
believes the perceived impasse is caused largely by trying to
interpret Paul's statements on judgment against the backdrop of a
theology of justification by faith. His alternative is to give greater
attention to the occasional nature of the texts, and to highlight
eschatology and ecclesiology as the primary conceptual back-
grounds upon which to understand Paul's statements about judgment.

Roetzel challenges a prevailing assumption that Paul is best
understood in juxtaposition or contrast to his Jewish background.
A brief analysis of judgment in the post-exilic prophets, Jewish
apocalyptic literature, Qumran and rabbinic materials, leads to the
conclusion that Paul's thought is in essential continuity with the
eschatological framework found in all but the rabbinic materials.
The major discontinuity is located in the apostle's christology. The
cross of Christ means that the Eschaton (including judgment and
salvation) is already present, while the still outstanding parousia

[22] Nigel M. Watson, "Justified by Faith; Judged by Works – An Antinomy?"
NTS 29 (1983), 209–221. The "problem texts" are: Rom. 2:1–16; 14:7–12; 1 Cor.
3:1–17; 4:1–5; 5:1–5; 6:9–11; 9:24–27; 11:27–34; 2 Cor. 5:9–10; Gal. 5:19–21; and
6:7–10.

simultaneously necessitates an "eschatological reservation" for believers in all these matters. This tension is rooted in the nature of the church which lives between the cross and parousia. Thus, Paul can say believers already enjoy salvation and freedom from wrath, yet, without contradiction, warn them that they must still face judgment and attain salvation. Roetzel's rationale for de-coupling justification and judgment statements is two-fold: (1) the latter have a corporate focus (i.e., are not addressing the issue of individual justification by faith), and (2) the apostle can speak of judgment without reference to faith or justification.

Ernst Synofzik is not satisfied with Braun's arbitrary dismissal of certain paraenetic texts.[23] Paul could indeed place judgment and justification in theological relation to one another, which indicates that the apostle did not perceive them to be incompatible. Rather, Paul's judgment statements stem from preexisting Jewish or early Christian traditions, and he uses these pieces of tradition strictly as *Argumentationsmittel* [rhetorical devices]. This can be an encouragement to endure, an admonition to Christian responsibility before God, or a warning of consequences. By thus *restricting* Pauline intention to a rhetorical employment of such traditional *Argumentationsmittel*, their conceptual significance can be minimized, relieving Paul (and his interpreters) of the need to seek harmonization. Although Paul utilizes such judgment sayings, he rejects (or at least rhetorically sidesteps) the Jewish theology (= legalism) supposedly implicit in them.[24] While Braun and others dismiss such difficult sayings as an inconsistency, Synofzik answers – this is just rhetoric.[25]

---

[23] Ernst Synofzik, *Die Gerichts- und Vergeltungsaussagen bei Paulus. Eine Traditionsgeschichtliche Untersuchung* (GTA 8; Göttingen: Vandenhoeck & Ruprecht, 1977).

[24] The term "legalism" can denote different things: (i) emphasis on the letter rather than the spirit of the law; (ii) belief in salvation by obedience to the law rather than by the grace of God or by faith; or (iii) undue stress on legal details without balancing considerations of justice or mercy (D. T. Kauffman, *The Dictionary of Religious Terms* [Westwood, NJ: Revell, 1967], 287). For clarity these could be termed "literalism" (i) and "casuistry" (iii), with "legalism" reserved for definition (ii) above.

[25] In spite of the rich insights and methodological advance represented by this book, its conclusion is based on an unproven assumption; namely, once the paraenetic purpose of a particular judgment statement has been identified, one can safely ignore the associated conceptual matter. One wonders if it could not be equally argued that Paul takes up such eschatological judgment sayings as motivation for his paraenesis precisely *because* they were part of the conceptual worldview of both the apostle and his readers.

Turning now to those who seek some logical resolution of the tension between Paul's judgment and justification statements, it is possible to divide this group further into three basic approaches. First, some seek to *redefine Paul's judgment statements* so as to reduce the tension. D. E. Kühl argues, more theologically than exegetically, for a position that has played a major role in studies on judgment and justification in Paul.[26] The key lies in understanding saving grace to be exclusive of any sort of dependence on human activity. *Grace* is "the highest religious principle of the apostle."[27] For this reason, whatever might be the result of a future judgment according to deeds, it cannot be described with such terms as σώζεσθαι or σωτηρία. Judgment according to works does not conflict with justification by grace, because the former deals solely with reward, but it cannot affect salvation (see Braun's opposite position above). Justification, salvation, and eternal life are seen as guaranteed by grace, regardless of the outworking of grace in the moral life.

I may be permitted to point out a certain ambiguity in Kühl's position regarding the place and importance of works in the lives of the justified. On the one hand, faith is to evidence itself in the moral life, and walking in the Spirit is everywhere the expectation. The author can even affirm in this vein, when speaking of vice-catalogs (1 Cor. 6:9–10), "Whoever acts in this way is no Christian at all, but a pagan."[28] Yet, commenting on 1 Corinthians 3:15, he concludes that salvation and participation in life are "certain, even when the sum total of one's behavior must be judged in the final assize to have been worthless."[29] However important works might be in the process of salvation, they are not a necessity or condition for its ultimate attainment. If one asks how Paul logically related grace and works, Kühl contends that Paul simply didn't sense a need to draw the connection between these two circles of thought, since it was the strength of the apostle's position to tolerate absolutely no hint of deviation from his chief principle, the sole supremacy of grace in matters of salvation.

In a similar fashion, Richard Devor asserts that justification by faith leads to salvation, while judgment according to works deter-

---

[26] D. E. Kühl, *Rechtfertigung auf Grund Glaubens und Gericht nach den Werken bei Paulus* (Königsberg i.Pr.: Wilh. Koch, 1904).

[27] Ibid., 6.

[28] Ibid., 25.

[29] Ibid., 26.

mines the grade of glory within the sphere of salvation, appealing to Jewish views of varied rewards for the elect to buttress this latter idea.[30] He is careful to note that justification is not thereby an automatic guarantee of salvation. The seriousness of judgment for the elect in Paul is reinforced by an examination of Jewish views, whereby Devor concludes that Paul was "an atypical Pharisee" (in that he showed some concern over the outcome of judgment for the elect) and thus closer to the stream of Judaism one associates with the Dead Sea Scrolls. He then contrasts Paul's view of righteousness to Judaism's, concluding that it is the "gift character" of justification that distinguishes Paul from a Judaism which sought to earn righteousness. "That which the Jew labored to acquire, that which he would lay hold of by his own right, is now given, freely, as a gift. This is *the complete and direct inversion of his previous conception*. As a Pharisee he had once believed that righteousness could be earned; it could even be claimed. But it was never a free gift."[31]

By far one of the most influential monographs on the subject of judgment and justification in Paul is that by Luise Mattern.[32] She opens by differentiating the views of Jewish apocalyptic and rabbinic literature on judgment. Paul shows certain similarities to Jewish apocalyptic thought, but in the last analysis Mattern concludes that the apostle's notion of judgment is "not Jewish."[33] Turning to Pauline texts, she finds that the apostle does bring together judgment and justification language, but only when he wants to stress the impossibility of the justified falling under this judgment. This corresponds with apocalyptic views, and means that for Paul a Christian cannot be subject to the final judgment, which is the execution of wrath on the unrighteous. Since Paul obviously does speak often of Christians being judged by God, this leads to Mattern's fundamental assertion that there must be two different judgments envisioned by the apostle: a last judgment which simply separates Christians from non-Christians on the basis of faith resulting in the destruction of the unbelievers; and an evaluative judgment for Christians only, dealing with their "work" (sg.) and having no relation to salvation or damnation, but only judging the

---

[30] Devor, *Concept of Judgment*.
[31] Ibid., 330 (my emphasis).
[32] *Das Verständnis des Gerichtes bei Paulus* (ATANT 47; Zurich/Stuttgart: Zwingli, 1966).
[33] Ibid., 215.

level of obedience and resulting in reward. In this way she relieves Paul of the charge of inconsistency by cleanly separating justification by faith and judgment according to works. Paul's doctrine of justification (versus Judaism's view of salvation through works of obedience to the Law) becomes an interpretive key which leads to sharp discontinuity with Jewish views of judgment.

If Kühl, Devor, and Mattern resolve the tension by softening Paul's judgment statements, the next group does so by *redefining justification*. Though brief, the lecture delivered by Karl Donfried in 1974 is important as a concise attempt to apply the insights of E. Käsemann and K. Kertelge on justification to the question of last judgment in Paul.[34] Specifically, justification is misunderstood when viewed predominantly or exclusively as God's already received gift to the individual (as in R. Bultmann). Rather justification has both "a present and a future dimension – it is a matter of promise and expectation" and "recaptures man for the sovereignty of God."[35] This yields a consistent pattern in Paul's letters: (1) *justification* is an initiating event, which is actualized and made concrete through (2) *sanctification* (= a present process), leading to (3) *salvation* (= a future gift, already anticipated and partially experienced in justification and sanctification and clearly dependent upon them).

Occasional references to salvation as a present reality are not a contradiction since they condition this salvation upon continued obedience ("if you hold it fast," 1 Corinthians 15:2). As to judgment upon Christians, "Paul expects a last judgment for Christians which can have different results: salvation for the Christian who has been obedient in faith and wrath for the one who has been disobedient to his calling in Christ."[36] Thus, for Donfried this means that justification is better understood as "the beginning of a process," the initial entry onto the path of life which must be "actualized in sanctification" and "consummated with salvation."

Christoph Haufe goes much further and eliminates the *sola fide* of justification altogether.[37] He is primarily concerned with the relationship between grace and reward, and sees the chief difficulty

---

Karl P. Donfried, "Justification and Last Judgment in Paul," *Int* 30 (1976), 140–152.
[35] Ibid., 141.
[36] Ibid., 147.
[37] Haufe, *Die sittliche Rechtfertigungslehre*.

to lie in the Protestant understanding of grace as excluding all conditions or requirements (see Kühl above), and of faith as the opposite of human activity, work, or achievement. Through Christ's death and resurrection (thus through grace) God has relativized the Jewish requirement of sinless obedience and replaced it with a new norm that is attainable, an *Evangeliums-Gesetz* [law of the gospel] or *Gnadenrecht* [order of grace]. Ultimately, salvation by grace means God has adjusted the condition so that it is now something within human reach, a life of obedience to the best of one's ability (with the Spirit's aid of course). In this way "reward" retains its full biblical content (= salvation), and the causal relationship between work and reward is maintained, yet without thereby losing the central place of grace in both establishing, enabling and completing this "possibility of salvation." Haufe has resolved any tension with grace by eliminating the *sola fide* as the ground of present and of future justification. Faith itself is no longer "reckoned as righteousness," but instead becomes a confident hope that God's new and gracious possibility of salvation through moral effort will indeed lead to the desired verdict – justified (= sanctified). Thus, common to this second approach to resolving the tension is a subordination of the "already" of justification by faith to the "not yet" of future justification.

A third approach accepts that both justification by faith and judgment according to works deal with the final verdict of righteousness for eternal life. The latter is complementary to the former because of the expectation that those justified by faith will also become (perfectly) righteous in behavior. *Judgment confirms justification.* For Floyd Filson this means attempting to understand Paul's thought against his Jewish-Pharisaic background.[38] "The Pharisee Saul was most certainly an adherent of the view that God recompenses men – to some extent now, fully at the great judgment – on the basis of their conformity to his law. There is ample reason to believe that Saul held this view in a legalistic, superficial, casuistical form, and that with all good intentions and effort he could not escape a suppressed, smouldering sense of lack and inadequacy."[39] Following the Damascus road experience, there was "a reorganization of his ideas to the extent that God's grace became central instead of God's recompensing activity, but this was

[38] Floyd V. Filson, *St. Paul's Conception of Recompense* (UNT 21; Leipzig: J. C. Hinrichs'sche, 1931).
[39] Ibid., 8.

merely a shifting of emphasis and not an abandonment of the recompense principle."[40]

Paul's expectation of essential post-baptismal sinlessness allows him to look toward the final judgment according to works with an assurance based upon "the feeling that the Christians will, in the vast majority of cases at least, pass the judgment successfully."[41] For Christians who sinned without forfeiting their Christian status Paul expected some sort of gradation in the sentence pronounced, generally an inferior place or privilege in the Kingdom. For those who persisted in deliberate sin, however, he clearly threatened the loss of eternal life. This optimistic perfectionism has a biographical explanation. Paul experienced a thoroughgoing moral renewal through God's grace, thus enabling him to perceive harmony between justification by grace and judgment by works. (Of course, Filson admits that two thousand years of Christian history, including much Christian sinning, make this solution seem less workable for contemporary interpreters.) Filson's presentation would appear to make justification essentially a term of initiation, without clear connection to the verdict of the last judgment. Although he rejects such a limiting of the impact of justification to an initiatory act, it is difficult to see how he can properly avoid this.[42]

Lastly, the careful study by David Kuck, although not actually directed towards this particular issue and dealing with only one Pauline passage (1 Cor. 1–4), has made a significant contribution to the problem of judgment and justification in two respects.[43] Relying heavily on the insights of social and rhetorical analysis for NT studies, Kuck is especially concerned to interpret the judgment sayings in the social context of the Corinthian church conflicts. An accurate assessment of such judgment texts must inquire first as to their function for the hearers, before turning to their function in Paul's theology. Second, Kuck has recognized that any advance in

---

[40] Ibid., 14.

[41] Ibid., 90. Central to this contention, as well as to his later discussion of judgment on believers, is his adoption of Paul Wernle's conclusion that the benefits of Christ's death avail only for pre-baptismal sins; hence the converted must remain blameless thereafter (*Der Christ und die Sünde bei Paulus* [1897]).

[42] To this third category one might also possibly reckon John Calvin, *Institutes of the Christian Religion* (2 vols.; ed. John T. McNeil; trans. Ford Lewis Battles; LCC 20/21; Philadelphia: Westminster, 1960), Bk. III.16:1–3, 18:1–4. It would, in fact, seem typical of reformational exegesis to turn the judgment according to deeds in Rom. 2 into a judgment over faith or unbelief (H. Braun, *Gerichtsgedanke und Rechtfertigungslehre*, 19–20, 22–23).

[43] Kuck, *Judgment and Community Conflict*.

understanding Paul's judgment texts will require a renewed first-hand look at the traditions which influenced his language and thought. Thus, a large part of his book is devoted to "The Functions of Divine Judgment in Jewish Texts" (38–95) as well as "in Greek and Roman Traditions" (96–149).

Conclusions

While most writers on this subject may be grouped under the rubrics of "incoherence" or "harmony," there is certainly nothing resembling consensus or even large-scale agreement on this issue; and the fact that scholars return to it again and again demonstrates its importance for understanding Paul's theology. What is remarkable in all of this is that the very thing which so exercises the modern interpreter of Paul – a seeming "tension" – seems to have caused the apostle himself almost no apparent theological discomfort. We find no lengthy explanations or qualifications when judgment according to deeds is mentioned in his letters. He would appear to sense no theological struggle between justification and judgment, nor does he seem to fear misunderstanding (i.e., the introduction of synergism or works-righteousness into salvation), although we know he was sensitive to potential or actual misunderstandings of his message (cf. Rom. 3:1–8; 6:1–23).

This observation regarding Paul's own lack of tension on this matter is not particularly novel.[44] Proponents of Pauline incoherence, of course, argue that he simply never put two and two together on this matter, and failed to perceive the inherent contradictions of his own teaching. This cannot be excluded *a priori*, but the fact that Paul does on occasion show awareness of their interrelationship certainly means that it should be a solution of last resort.[45] Hence, a key question guiding the study must be: Why does the apostle appear to sense no serious tension between judgment according to deeds and justification by faith?

My thesis is that Paul's use of this motif – terminologically, rhetorically, and theologically – demonstrates fundamental

---

[44] See, for instance, Filson, *St. Paul's Conception of Recompense*, 130; Roetzel, *Judgement in the Community*, 177–178; Synofzik, *Die Gerichts- und Vergeltungsaussagen*, 11.
[45] Rom. 2:6–11 occurs, after all, within the argument for justification by faith. 1 Corinthians 4:4–5 and 6:9–11 bring together justification and judgment terminology. See also Gal. 6:7–8; Col. 1:22–23; and Phil. 2:12–13.

continuity with second temple Jewish sources, and this in spite of notable differences (e.g., the christological focus of judgment in Paul). As to *terminology*, while the roots of his usage are in the Scriptures, the influence of subsequent developments in the motif tradition are equally clear. Then, his repeated use of the motif and related judgment themes in the same *rhetorical* contexts found in the Jewish sources favors the assumption that Paul, though certainly not all his later interpreters, thought he was saying essentially the same thing on this point as were his predecessors. Finally, the fact that neither Paul nor second temple sources felt significant *theological* tension over this matter of judgment according to deeds within their soteriological pattern, raises at least the possibility that divine grace and human obedience were similarly interconnected in both patterns. A universal and eschatological divine judgment awaited all humanity, applicable to those within as well as without the people of God. Although a few texts hint at Paul's acceptance of the developing doctrine of varied eschatological rewards, in most instances this judgment results in eternal salvation or damnation. It will be according to one's deeds, and will not so much determine as *reveal* one's character and status as righteous or wicked.

PART ONE

Judgment according to deeds in Jewish literature

1

THE USE OF THE MOTIF IN THE JEWISH SCRIPTURES[1]

When speaking of God repaying each according to deeds, "the echo of Psalms and Proverbs recollects images of God that were in Paul's bones. We, belated rootless readers, can learn only through marginalia and concordances ... what Paul knew by heart: to quote the confession that God will render to each one according to his works is to trigger overtones in which God's omniscience and mercy play in counterpoint and blend."[2] However, even this restriction to "the echo of Psalms and Proverbs" is too narrow. Divine recompense according to deeds was a motif found in nearly all strata of the OT and itself part of the ongoing intertextual play aimed at better understanding the divine character and, among other things, the interplay between privilege and obligation in Israel, that is, between grace and works. These words about Paul could be said equally of those intertestamental writers to be studied in chapters two and three. For them too, the scriptural tradition of divine retribution according to deeds formed the foundation upon which they built their own usage and understanding.

For this reason, I will give somewhat more attention in this chapter to questions of form and function in order to describe adequately this foundation upon which later Jewish authors build. Due to the large number of texts involved an extensive exegetical analysis of each motif occurrence will be impossible. (A complete

---

[1] On Paul's use of versions of the Jewish Scriptures (e.g., LXX, MT), see C. D. Stanley, *Paul and the Language of Scripture: Citation Technique in the Pauline Epistles and Contemporary Literature*, (SNTSMS 69; Cambridge: Cambridge University Press, 1992); J. Barr, "The Interrelation of Hebrew, Aramaic and Greek," *The Cambridge History of Judaism*, vol. II (ed. W. D. Davies and L. Finkelstein; Cambridge: 1989), 110–114; and D.-A. Koch, *Die Schrift als Zeuge des Evangeliums: Untersuchungen zur Verwendung und zum Verständnis der Schrift bei Paulus* (BHT 69; Tübingen: Mohr, 1986), 48–57, 59, 78.

[2] R. Hays, *Echoes of Scripture in the Letters of Paul* (New Haven: Yale University Press, 1989), 42–43.

listing may be found in Appendix I.) Instead I will group texts according to function, focusing on representative passages in each grouping with more cursory reference, where needed, to others in each group.

In addition to the above, a number of further questions will guide this investigation. (i) Does this divine recompense address the people of God or the enemies of the righteous, the individual or the community? Since my thesis concerns Paul's use of this motif in relation to (Christian) believers, primary attention will rest upon passages indicating a judgment/recompense upon those belonging to the people of God, in both negative (punishment) and positive (blessing) senses. (ii) What related motifs occur in connection with divine recompense according to deeds (e.g., revealing of hidden deeds, weighing, divine omniscience or impartiality)? (iii) Are there indications as to how the writers (or the community) understood the relationship between this divine recompense according to deeds and one's participation in the covenant community? In particular, how do Yahweh's merciful faithfulness [חסד], his covenant, and recompense according to deeds relate, and what part do human obedience, faith, and repentance play in their interaction? In general, how is the motif related to soteriology and eschatology within the OT writings? (iv) Did the LXX translators introduce to the motif new conceptual elements? Did they eschatologize a previously this-worldly, temporal model? Did they individualize passages with a community reference? Is a greater degree of synergism present in the LXX? Thus the chapter's central aim is to examine the motif's semantic form and the rhetorical purposes for which it was employed, and to discover how divine recompense according to deeds functioned theologically within the larger soteriological perspective(s) of the Jewish Scriptures.

A working definition of the semantic field

The analysis will be limited to texts exhibiting each of the following elements:[3]

---

[3] Roman Heiligenthal (*Werke als Zeichen*, 148–151) refers to "the three ever-recurring fundamental elements of this semantic field" which he identifies as:

   (a) θεός/κύριος + δίδωμι (or related verbs) + κατά,
   (b) Object: ἔργον/πρᾶξις (or related terms),
   (c) Personal Object: ἕκαστος/ἄνθρωπος (or "him/her," "them," etc.).

(a) God functions explicitly or implicitly as the *subject* of the recompensing activity. While I will have occasion to refer to texts with a human or an impersonal subject, this will only be for purposes of comparison, since my main concern is with possible influences on *divine* recompense according to deeds in Paul.

(b) *A verbal component* expresses the divine *recompensing activity*, whereby a considerable variety in terminology is present.

(c) Reference is made to human *deeds*, again utilizing a broad range of terminology. I will seek to note along the way whether differences in number (*work* versus *works*) or terminology (e.g., *way, work of one's hands, righteousness*) bear any significance. The reference to human deeds can be related syntactically to the verbal component in the form of:

    (i) a **standard** (e.g., God recompensed him *according to his deeds*): in which case it is usually introduced by κατά (Heb. ־כ), or

    (ii) a **direct object** (e.g., God repaid him *his deeds*).

(d) In most instances there is also reference to the *person* or *group to whom* or *upon whom* the divine recompense is directed (e.g., God brought his evil deeds *upon his head*).

As thus defined, and with the exception of the Pentateuch, the motif is found across the various genres of OT literature, occurring in the LXX nearly seventy times (see Appendix I).[4]

Observations on wording and syntax[5]

The motif in its Greek (LXX) form cannot be properly understood without reference to its use in the Hebrew Bible. Three Hebrew

---

However, κατά is not required in the motif, and Heiligenthal's inclusion of this criterion unnecessarily restricts his analysis.

[4] Translations of motif-texts are generally the author's own; other passages are cited according to the NRSV unless noted.

[5] The only other extended treatment of this motif is found in R. Heiligenthal (*Werke als Zeichen*, 143–164, "Die Vergeltung nach den Werken in der LXX und den anderen griechischen Übersetzungen des AT"). He fails, however, to examine the entire range of this motif in the OT since his focus on ἔργον [work] limits the semantic field to (ἀντ)αποδίδωμι + κατά + ἔργον/πρᾶξις and closely related words (see also n. 3 above). See also F. Horst, art. "Vergeltung: II. Im AT," *RGG*, VI.1343–1346; P. D. Miller, Jr., *Sin and Judgment in the Prophets: A Stylistic and*

verbs predominate: שוב (Hiphil = "(re)turn," 18x); נתן (Qal = "give," 12x); and שלם (Piel = "(re)pay, recompense," 13x).[6]

In spite of differences in nuance, the terms are largely interchangeable in the context of this motif.[7] The use or absence of "according to …" (־כ) is also more a matter of style than of significant change of meaning,[8] as is, generally, the choice between singular or plural nouns. Thus Yahweh can recompense according to one's "deed" or "deeds,"[9] "sin" or "sins,"[10] and can judge equally according to one's "way" or "ways."[11] In some cases the choice between singular or plural "works" was determined by the noun itself,[12] or by the use of a set phrase.[13] In the MT the use of the singular for the motif predominates slightly.[14]

The LXX translators followed their Hebrew *Vorlage* fairly closely in the case of this motif. Three verbs, all forms of δίδωμι ("give"), predominate.[15] While not entirely synonymous, the choice between ἀνταποδίδωμι ("repay, recompense") and ἀποδίδωμι ("return, give back") appears to have been more a matter of

Theological Analysis (SBLMS 27; Chico, CA: Scholars Press, 1982); and the following chapters conveniently collected in *Um das Prinzip der Vergeltung in Religion und Recht des Alten Testaments* (ed. K. Koch; Wege der Forschung 125; Darmstadt: Wissenschaftliche Buchgesellschaft, 1972): H. Gunkel, "Vergeltung im Alten Testament," 1–7; K. Koch, "Gibt es ein Vergeltungsdogma im Alten Testament?" 130–180; J. Scharbert, "Das Verbum PQD in der Theologie des Alten Testaments," and "ŠLM im Alten Testament," 278–299, 300–324.

   [6] Additional verbs used include שפט ("judge," 7x, all but one in Ezekiel), פקד ("visit," 4x), גמל and עשה ("recompense" and "do (to)," 3x each), and מצא ("cause to find," 2x).

   [7] So, for instance, Ps. 28:4b where נתן [give] and שוב [return] stand in synonymous parallelism; or 1 Kgs. 8:32, Ps. 18:20, and 18:24 where God "gives," "recompenses" [גמל] and "returns" "according to one's righteousness," all with only minor shifts in meaning.

   [8] See for instance Isa. 59:18, or 2 Chr. 6:23. In some cases the use or absence of "according to" is determined by the choice of verb (e.g., עשה and גמל both normally require ־כ).

   [9] Prov. 24:12; Hos. 12:2b.

   [10] Jer. 16:18; Ps. 103:10.

   [11] Ezek. 33:20; 36:19. The singular "according to one's way" in Ezek. 36:19 stands in parallelism with "according to deeds."

   [12] Thus עלילות and מעללים (both "practices") are only found in the plural form, while גמול ("dealing, recompense, due") is always singular.

   [13] As in the "fruit (sg.)" or "evil (sg.) of one's deeds (pl.)," or the "work (sg.) of one's hands (pl.)."

   [14] Excluding set phrases (e.g., "work (sg.) of one's hands (pl.)") the singular occurs 39 times, the plural 29 times.

   [15] In addition: κρίνω, 9x (6x for שפט, 3x without Hebrew original); ἐκδίκω, 4x (3x for פקד, 1x for שפט); ποιέω, 3x (always for עשה); and once each ἀποστρέφω (שוב), ἀποτίνω (שלם), ἀφανίζω (צמה), ἐκχέω (נטש) and εὑρίσκω (מצא).

Hebrew Vorlage

	שׁוּב	נתן	שׁלם	גמל
Greek Verb				
ἀνταποδίδωμι (22x)*	10x		8x	3x
ἀποδίδωμι (12x)*	7x	2x	2x	
δίδωμι (10x)		10x		

*Both ἀνταποδίδωμι and ἀποδίδωμι occur once each without an extant Hebrew original.

translational taste than of theological meaning.[16] The same motif is being employed whether God is said to "give," "return," "repay," or "recompense" according to one's deeds. Although κρίνειν [judge] and ἐκδίκειν [take vengeance, punish] bring in a more juridical nuance, their synonymous parallelism with other non-juridical expressions of the recompense motif demonstrates that the same basic conception of a divine recompense according to deeds stands behind all the expressions.[17] The use or omission of κατά [according to] generally follows the MT,[18] so that essentially the same idea is present whether God is said to recompense "one's deeds" or "according to one's deeds." Likewise the use of singular and plural nouns appears to be dictated for the most part by the Hebrew original. There does seem to be a slight tendency to prefer the plural τὰ ἔργα [works] following κατά, but changes in number need not point to any theological bias (see below).[19] Overall the use of singulars versus plurals for the motif is evenly balanced in the LXX.[20] The use of ἕκαστος [each] is relatively infrequent and mirrors the Hebrew original, so that the notion of an increasing

[16] According to Büchsel, ἀνταποδίδωμι differs mainly in that "the thought of recompense in ἀποδίδωμι is strengthened by the prefix ἀντί-" (*TDNT* 3.169). The Greek MS tradition contains numerous instances of substitution between ἀπο- and ἀνταποδίδωμι (e.g., Jer. 32:19; Lam. 3:64; 2 Sam. 22:25; Ps. 94:23).

[17] Ezek. 7:3, 8 [LXX, verses 7, 5], 27; Hos. 4:9; 12:2 [LXX, verse 3].

[18] Exceptions: (adding) Ps. 94:23; Prov. 19:17; Jer. 23:2; Ezek. 7:27; (omitting) Ezek. 7:3, 8, 9; 33:20.

[19] Changing singular to plural: Ps. 28:4 (twice); 62:13; Prov. 24:12; Lam. 3:64. Changing plural to singular: Jer. 32:19; Ezek. 7:9; 18:30; cf. also 1 Macc. 7:42. Most such changes can be explained on the basis of style, context (Jer. 16:18; change from singular to plural "sins" due to plural "ways and unrighteous acts" in verse 17), perception of a collective singular in the original (see below), or perhaps uncertainty regarding the pointing of the MT.

[20] Excluding set phrases, singular = 34x; plural = 34x.

individualization of the doctrine of divine recompense by the LXX is unfounded.[21]

Thus one finds an axiom capable of great terminological variety available to a speaker or writer who might wish to make reference to God's recompense according to deeds:

> Give them according to their deeds
> and according to the evil of their works;
> according to the deeds of their hands give to them,
> return to them their recompense.   (Ps. 28:4 [LXX, 27:4])

> who gives to each according to his/her deeds. (Prov. 24:12)

> therefore I shall give your way upon you.
> (Ezek. 7:4 [LXX, 7:8])

> and I shall doubly recompense their unrighteous acts and their sins.   (Jer. 16:18)

> to give his/her way upon his/her head ...
> to give him/her according to his/her righteousness.
> (1 Kgs. 8:32)

The possible significance of singular versus plural ("work/ works")

Paul's understanding of "work(s)" has not infrequently been contrasted with that of Judaism. It is asserted that the latter speaks primarily of "judgment according to *works* (pl.)": "Every person does good and evil deeds, and the judgment is determined according to the majority."[22] Paul, on the other hand, "no longer employs the plural, as though good and evil works could be added up. 'Work' is no longer the work of the law; instead, it encompasses the entirety of one's life's work."[23] Thus, while Judaism purportedly stressed a multiplicity of unrelated *Einzelleistungen* [individual achievements] in judgment, and was prone to adding or weighing

---

[21] Job 34:11; Ps. 62:12 [LXX, 61:13]; Prov. 24:12; Jer. 17:10; 32:19 [LXX, 39:19]; Ezek. 18:30; 33:20; also Sir. 16:14. R. Heiligenthal speaks somewhat misleadingly of "the regularly occurring ἕκαστος" (*Werke als Zeichen*, 150, n. 30).

[22] L. Mattern, *Das Verständnis des Gerichtes*, 141, cf. 141–151. See also R. Bultmann, *Theologie des Neuen Testaments* 8th edn.; (Uni-Taschenbücher 630; Tübingen: J. C. B. Mohr (Paul Siebeck), 1980), 283–284, 316–317, 525; and H. Braun, *Gerichtsgedanke und Rechtfertigungslehre*, 50–53.

[23] E. Schweizer, *RGG* (3rd edn.), II. 1406.

the same, Paul differentiated consciously between "works" and "work." For him judgment "is not pronounced upon one's performance whether good or bad – a Christian has no 'works' ... – but upon the Christian's participation in God's 'work' ".[24]

In point of fact, the OT shows scarce interest in a single isolated "deed," but neither is recompense seen as applying to a multiplicity of unrelated actions. Rather, the easy interchange between singular and plural "deeds" is grounded in a holistic view of human deeds. One's deeds are regarded as a unity revealing the "way" upon which one walks.

> I will give your way [ὁδόν, sg.] upon you,
> and your detestable practices [βδελύγματα, pl.] shall be in
> your midst.   (Ezek. 7:4)

Likewise one's heart and kidneys (= the seat of thoughts and desires) are made known in one's actions:

> I, the Lord, search hearts and prove kidneys,
> to give to each according to his/her ways [ὁδούς, pl.]
> and according to the fruit of his/her actions [ἐπιτηδευ-
> μάτων, pl.]   (Jer. 17:10)

This rejection of a fundamental distinction between the use of "deed" and "deeds" in the motif corresponds to the OT's holistic attitude in general towards obedience.[25] This is confirmed as well by the heavy use of terms and phrases with a collective meaning, whereby a singular noun represents a multiplicity of human deeds: "according to my way" or "righteousness," "the evil (sg.) of one's deeds," "the cleanness (sg.) of one's hands," etc.

Of course, the biblical texts do know the difference between a single "work" and a multitude of "works." They make, however, no *theological distinction* between the two of the sort so often asserted. While an occasional deed "out of character," as it were, is to be reckoned with (for which repentance, the sacrificial system, and forgiveness provide the remedy), the OT expects a generally

---

[24] Mattern, *Das Verständnis des Gerichtes*, 151. For a critique of this view of "work/works" in Paul, see pp. 158–159 below.

[25] See W. Eichrodt, *Theology of the Old Testament*, 2 vols. (trans. J. A. Baker; OTL; Philadelphia: Westminster, 1961 [orig. *Theologie des Alten Testaments* 6th edn., 1959]), I.93; II.289, 303, 328, and esp. chap. 21, "The Fundamental Forms of Man's Personal Relationship with God."

consistent pattern of behavior or deeds giving visible testimony to one's true character as either righteous or wicked.

Retribution: an innovation of the LXX?

In his influential article, "Gibt es ein Vergeltungsdogma im Alten Testament?" [Is There a Doctrine of Retribution in the OT?], Klaus Koch argued that the legal-juridical ideas evoked by such terms as "recompense," "retribution," and "punishment" were first introduced by the LXX.[26] Building on the Hebrews' "synthetische Lebensauffassung" [synthetic view of life], he contended for what he termed "schicksalwirkende Tat(sphäre)" or "Tun-Ergehen-Zusammenhang" as characteristic of the Hebrew Bible. That is, a deed and its consequences are organically connected, so that the deed produces a sphere or a fate surrounding the doer, which will eventually, and almost automatically, return to that person for good or evil.[27] Thus:

> they sow the wind, and they shall reap the whirlwind.
> (Hos. 8:7)

> one's mischief returns upon one's own head,
> and one's violence descends upon one's crown.   (Ps. 7:16)

> one who digs a pit will fall into it,
> if one rolls a stone, it will roll back upon that person.
> (Prov. 26:27)

> evil comes to the one who searches for it.   (Prov. 11:27)

Although God watches over this process, his intervention would be termed an activation of this process of deed-consequence, rather than a retribution or punishment meted out according to some external measure of justice. The Hebrew שׁלם (Piel) means not *vergelten* [to recompense] but *vollenden*, i.e., to bring the deed-consequence connection to fulfillment. Thus, rather than speaking of Yahweh's punishment and retribution, it is said:

---

[26] *ZTK* 52 (1955), 1–42. Reprinted in *Um das Prinzip der Vergeltung in Religion und Recht des Alten Testaments* (ed. K. Koch; Darmstadt: Wissenschaftliche Buchgesellschaft, 1972), 130–180; a shortened English translation can be found in *Theodicy in the Old Testament* (ed. J. L. Crenshaw; Philadelphia: Fortress Press, 1983), 57–87. Citations follow the pagination in *Um das Prinzip*.
[27] Ibid., 132–133, 160–161.

Whoever is kind to the poor lends to the Lord,
and the Lord will *complete* [יְשַׁלֵּם] that one's deed.

(Prov. 19:17)

I will visit upon them their ways,
and *turn* their deeds *back* [אָשִׁיב] upon them. (Hos. 4:9b)

In addition, according to Koch, the Hebrew Bible did not have any term for punishment. The connection between a deed and its consequence was expressed not by terms with a legal-judicial flavor, but only in ways pointing to an organic and immanent deed-consequence relationship. A doctrine of retribution, according to Koch, was first introduced by the LXX which had too little understanding of the organic process just described, and which (mis)translated שׁוּב and שׁלם with the legal-juridical terminology of ἀπο- or ἀνταποδίδωμι [recompense, bring retribution].

It is certainly to Koch's credit that he so convincingly demonstrated the presence of this organic deed-consequence connection throughout the OT, and we will observe in the exegetical sections to follow its significant role in the motif of divine recompense according to deeds. However, his attempt to separate this cleanly from all legal-juridical background and, thus, to deny the presence of "retribution," must be judged unsuccessful.[28] Among the criticisms are the following. (1) Koch omits passages clearly showing a retribution extrinsic to the deed itself,[29] and destruction as resulting from Yahweh's wrath.[30] (2) Prophetic judgment statements evidence a strongly judicial background and terminology.[31] (3) Koch's

---

[28] Notable proponents of Koch's thesis include G. von Rad, *Theologie des Alten Testaments* (Einführung in die evangelische Theologie; Munich: Chr. Kaiser Verlag, 1957), I.263–265, 382–384; and J. Becker, *Das Heil Gottes: Heils- und Sündenbegriffe in den Qumrantexten und im Neuen Testament* (SUNT 3; Göttingen: Vandenhoeck & Ruprecht, 1964), 13–19. Most, however, take a more critical stance. See, for example, E. Pax, "Studien zum Vergeltungsproblem der Psalmen," *Studii biblici Franciscani* (Liber Annuus XI; Jerusalem: 1960), 56–112; F. Horst, "Recht und Religion im Bereich des Alten Testaments," *Um das Prinzip*, 181–212; J. G. Gammie, "The Theology of Retribution in the Book of Deuteronomy," *CBQ* 32/1 (1970), 1–12; O. Eckart, "Die 'synthetische Lebensauffassung' in der frühkönigli-chen Novellistik Israels: Ein Beitrag zur alttestamentlichen Anthropologie," *ZTK* 74 (1977), 371–400; Miller, *Sin and Judgment*, esp. 121–139.

[29] E.g., plagues on the Egyptians, disease (Num. 11:33), drought (Jer. 14:1–7), famine (Ezek. 5:12, 16), earthquakes, lightning. Cf. Travis, *Christ and the Judgment*, 8–9.

[30] Deut. 7:4; 9:8, 19, 25; Num. 16:21; Ezek. 22:31; 43:8.

[31] See C. Westermann, *Grundformen prophetischer Rede* (5th edn., BEvT 31; Munich: Chr. Kaiser, 1978), esp. 130–136.

contention that terms such as פקד and שלם do not carry any sense
of "punishment," "recompense," or "retribution" has been
refuted.[32] (4) There is an emphasis in many passages on *correspondence* of deed and effect rather than organic *consequence*.[33] While I
thus reject Koch's thesis that it was the LXX terminology which first
introduced retribution into the OT, it will remain a task of the
ensuing exegetical sections to determine what, if any, changes in the
understanding and use of the motif were introduced by the Greek
translators (e.g., an eschatologizing of the concept?).

On the origin of the motif[34]

The motif of divine recompense according to deeds does not have
the character of a specific form [*Gattung*], for which one might
expect a single *Sitz im Leben*. Rather it "belongs to the storeroom
of materials available to the prophet, poet, or speaker," and
probably arose from "multiple settings, sources, or contexts for this
pattern of speech."[35] One of these probable sources was the
"general literary usage of poetic justice and irony," found almost
universally in myths, legends and novels of various locales, in
which the doers' fate corresponds to their deeds.[36] A second source
was almost certainly the curses of the covenantal tradition. This
(often verbal) correspondence of sin and punishment can be seen in
the OT,[37] in the parity style of other international diplomatic
communications, and in widespread futility curses in which the
punishment is the frustration of the intention of a sinful action.[38] A

---

[32] See Scharbert, "Das Verbum PQD," and "ŠLM" in Koch, ed., *Um das Prinzip*;
G. Andre, *Determining the Destiny: PQD in the Old Testament* (ConBOT 16; Lund:
CWK Gleerup, 1980).

[33] See Miller, *Sin and Judgment*, 121–137.

[34] The following depends heavily on the groundbreaking work done by Patrick
Miller, "Source and Setting of the Correspondence Pattern," *Sin and Judgment*,
97–110.

[35] Ibid., 97–98. Similar recompense ideas and terminology (though not always
"according to deeds") were apparently widespread throughout the ancient Near
East, being found in Akkadian and Aramaic literature, though not in Ugaritic (H.-J.
Fabry, *Die Wurzel ŠUB in der Qumran-Literatur* [BBB 46; Cologne/Bonn: Peter
Hanstein, 1975], 185–187).

[36] Miller, *Sin and Judgment*, 98.

[37] Cf. Josh. chap. 7 (esp. verse 25); Hos. 4:4–6; Deut. 28:47–48 (note the
repetition of "serve"); 31:16–18 (note the repetition of "abandon" and "evil" in
both stipulation and curse). See also N. Lohfink, "Zu Text und Form von Os
4,4–6," *Bib* 42 (1961), 303–332.

[38] Cf. Lev. 26; Deut. 28; Amos 5:7, 10–11; Isa. 5:8–10.

third source was the *lex talionis*, broadly understood rather than solely in its specific form *"x for x."*[39] Here the religio-legal principle of *talio* was applied by the prophetic messenger of Yahweh's heavenly court to a king or nation. There was a flexibility of expression possible, yielding three different categories of logical relationship between sin and punishment:

(i)   indication of a general correspondence or appropriateness between crime and punishment,
(ii) precise talionic correspondence,
(iii) the instrument or means of the crime becomes the object of the punishment.[40]

A functional typology and analysis of motif passages

By a functional typology I mean the *rhetorical purpose(s)* for which the motif is employed.[41] This should not be confused with divisions of classical rhetoric (epideictic, etc.). This functional typology can be applied easily to both later Jewish and Pauline writings, enabling comparison of motif usage across various bodies of literature without ignoring contextual considerations. Although not completely exclusive of one another, the categories are sufficiently discrete to provide clear-cut groupings.

(1) Praising God's manner of dealing with humanity.
(2) Justifying God's dealings with humanity.
(3) Appealing to God to intervene on behalf of the righteous.
(4) Pronouncing a benediction or prayer-wish.
(5) Motivating the righteous to obedience.
(6) Comforting and assuring the righteous (i.e., that God will correct seeming injustices).
(7) Pronouncing sentence upon the disobedient.
(8) Summoning the disobedient to repentance.

---

[39] Reference here and elsewhere is to the *lex* (or *ius*) *talionis* in which wrongdoers suffer precisely the same injury which they inflicted upon the victim. Thus "life for life, eye for eye, tooth for tooth" (Exod. 21:23–35; Lev. 24:18–20; Deut. 19:21).

[40] See Miller, *Sin and Judgment*, 108–110.

[41] The term "functional typology" has been borrowed from D. W. Kuck who, without much explanation, suggests four categories:

(i)   Moral recompense within the life of an individual or nation,
(ii) Announcement of God's decision to recompense his people,
(iii) Appeals to the higher court of God's judgment,
(iv) Israel and the nations in God's judgment (*Judgment and Community Conflict*, 38–53).

Praising God's manner of dealing with humanity

Jeremiah 32:19

Although this use overlaps to some degree with texts seeking to justify Yahweh's dealings with humanity, Jeremiah 32:19 (LXX, 39:19) employs the motif primarily as a means of ascribing praise to God. The saying occurs within Jeremiah's prayer (verses 17–25), uttered after he has obeyed the Lord's instructions and purchased a field in Anathoth, a sign of Yahweh's intention to restore Israel (verse 15). Having regularly preached Yahweh's fierce judgment against a faithless people, Jeremiah is understandably disturbed by this seeming divine change of heart. His prayer climaxes with the question in verse 25: If it is according to your will and purpose to destroy Israel, why then are you now having me give a sign of hope by buying this field?

With conventional language Jeremiah recites Yahweh's character as one who "shows steadfast love to the thousandth generation, but repays the guilt of parents into the laps of their children after them" (verse 18). The prophet recounts God's deeds of lovingkindness in the mighty deliverance from Egypt and the giving of the land (verses 20–23a). However, Israel did not obey God's commands, and reaped disaster (verse 23b). Thus mercy has been succeeded by repayment of sins. Now, however, this is all called into question by the sign of Yahweh's intended mercy. Is he no longer willing or able to repay sins?

The motif of divine recompense according to deeds is here taken up as a supporting argument in praise of Yahweh's consistent justice, "to give to each according to his/her way" (MT = "ways," pl.). In this context the reference is to punishment only, since blessings are presented as based on Yahweh's mercy (cf. verses 18a, 20–22) rather than according to deeds. Jeremiah connects this motif with that of divine omniscience,[42] perhaps in order to reaffirm that the apparent divine reversal in attitude could not be due to God's failure to note any of sinful Israel's ways. Both motifs are connected terminologically by the word "way," a further indication that "*wicked* ways" are meant in the light of Yahweh's own depiction of Israel's consistently wicked ways in verses 29–35. Already we see something that will reappear at many points;

---

[42] "whose eyes are open to all the ways of mortals," verse 19b.

namely, the application of this motif in its negative (= punishment) aspect to the people of God.

This text raises some fascinating questions related to the interplay between God's mercy and his recompense according to deeds. Jeremiah's citation of the traditional character description of Yahweh as "doing mercy, and repaying sin" (verse 18) suggests already a certain dialectic between these two aspects of Yahweh's dealings with humanity.[43] The prophet understood Israel's wicked ways as bringing Yahweh's mercy toward the nation to an end, and God's actions toward them now as operating strictly on the basis of recompense according to deeds. Yahweh's response in verses 36–44, while not negating the operation of his burning anger in recompense, nevertheless stops it from being his last word to the nation. While the recompense exhibited in the destruction and deportation of the nation certainly goes far beyond any corrective chastisement (cf. verse 33 for this idea), it can still be followed at a corporate level by renewed חסד. Even this renewed mercy, however, is not without reference to behavior, being closely tied to a renewal of the nation's conduct (cf. verse 39). This text also confirms the presence of legal-juridical ideas in the motif prior to the LXX, discernible here in the covenantal language of "provoking Yahweh to anger" by idolatry (verses 29, 30, 31).

As to the fate of individuals within the nation who die during the exhibition of God's fierce anger, the text is ambiguous. Unlike the nation, such individuals do not appear to enjoy a renewed hope. For them retribution would seem, indeed, to be the last word. Perhaps Yahweh's unquenchable anger is directed toward the unrepentant individuals within the community, in order that a repentant remnant may once again enjoy his mercy.

Justifying God's dealings with humanity

Judges 1:7

Of the four passages found in this category, two occur as the explanatory conclusion to narratives about God bringing

---

[43] See W. L. Holladay, *Jeremiah 2: Chapters 26–52* (Hermeneia; Philadelphia: Fortress Press, 1989) 217. In the light of this verse, Heiligenthal can hardly be correct to assert that "there is as yet no apparent connection between the idea that God repays according to deeds and that he deals in mercy and forgiveness" (*Werke als Zeichen*, 153).

punishment upon evildoers. Judges 1:4–7 recounts Judah's victory over the Canaanites and Perizzites, including the capture of Adoni-bezek, whose thumbs and big toes are consequently cut off. As a conclusion to this brief episode, Adoni-bezek's words are:

> Seventy kings with their thumbs and big toes cut off used to pick up scraps under my table; as I have done, so God has paid me back.   (Judg. 1:7)

In this case the *standard* of recompense is expressed by the related phrase "as I have done." Miller has demonstrated that Adoni-bezek's statement is a development of a talionic formulation such as is found in Leviticus 24:17–21. However, rather than the impersonal "it shall be done to him" of Leviticus, Judges 1:7 advances to the identification of God as the active party. "The correspondence [of deed and consequence] is perceived as a part of divine justice, not simply human vengeance."[44] This text demonstrates the double-sided character so common in judgment statements (i.e., both organic consequence and divine retribution), and is of interest, further, in showing a non-Israelite as subject to Yahweh's punishing retribution according to deeds.

Ezekiel 36:19

Ezekiel 36 concerns Israel's restoration following the exile in Babylon. This restoration, however, is purely a matter of God's gracious initiative, not Israel's obedience.[45] In verses 16–19 the displacement of the people is explained as due to their own sins, which called down Yahweh's wrath and just judgment, and even in exile the nation has not ceased to sin (verses 20–21). Thus verse 19b comes within a subsection explaining that Israel's deportation was due to her own sins (= "their way" [ὁδός], verse 17b), and the motif is applied to the people of God as justification and explanation for Yahweh's (past) punishment of them with destruction and deportation to Babylon:

---

[44] *Sin and Judgment*, 94.
[45] However, this prevenient grace does not render Israel's subsequent obedience less important (cf. verses 23b, 27). If Israel's sin and exile as just recompense have meant anything, it is that *future maintenance of the covenant blessings is contingent upon obedience.* "Then you shall remember your evil ways...and you shall loathe yourselves for your iniquities and your abominable deeds" (verse 31).

according to their way and according to their sin I have judged [ἔκρινα] them.

Apart from two occurrences in the deutero-canonical literature[46] the motif is found with the verb "judge" [שׁפט/κρίνω] only seven times, all in Ezekiel. However, it would be a mistake to think that Ezekiel originated the combination of divine judgment and recompense according to deeds.[47] In Ezekiel 36:19 God's judgment of his people is an expression of his *wrath* (verse 18). Israel's election and God's mercy are no protection from his just recompense, even for the people of God. However, as in Jeremiah 32:19, divine punishment of the nation is not the last word, but is embedded within a greater promise of grace and restoration following judgment. Here judgment and grace (i.e., restoration) are related sequentially without the latter rendering the former impotent.

Conclusion

When used to justify God's actions, the motif is made to refer exclusively to his *punishing* activity, particularly to justify his vengeance upon his own people (Zech. 1:6; Ezek. 36:19). This raises the issue of the relationship of God's (punitive) judgment to his gracious saving or restoring activity. In neither of the two texts addressed to the nation of Israel does God's recompense according to deeds lastingly nullify the covenant relationship. Ezekiel 36:19 relates grace and recompense in a sequential manner (after punishing he restores), not restricting the validity of either for the people of God, but giving ultimacy in this instance to God's saving activity. The fate of particular individuals at given stages of God's dealing with the nation is not considered in these passages. Where it is applied to specific individuals (Judg. 1:7; Job 34:11), the motif has reference to physical punishments or chastisements.

---

[46] Sir. 16:12; 1 Macc. 7:42.

[47] The language of judgment is found in the immediate context of the motif quite a number of times; 1 Kgs. 8:32 (= 2 Chr. 6:23), Ps. 94:2, Isa. 66:16, Jer. 51:9, Hos. 5:1, Joel 3:2, 12, Sir. 35:25, cf. also Eccl. 12:14. Thus, in spite of the relative infrequence of the phrase "to *judge* according to one's deeds," the combination of divine "judgment" and "recompense according to deeds" was already an accomplished fact in the Jewish Scriptures. See R. Heiligenthal (*Werke als Zeichen*, 150), who still wishes to call "judgment according to works" a "later conception."

Appealing to God to intervene on behalf of the righteous

Psalm 28:4

Psalm 28 reflects the situation of one falsely persecuted and hence taking refuge in God's sanctuary. The petitioner fears being carried away with the wicked (verse 3) and thus utters this cry for mercy (verses 2, 6), consisting of both protection for the innocent sufferer (verse 3) and divine recompense (punishment) upon the oppressors (verses 4–5).

> Give to them according to their works,
> and according to the evil of their practices;
> according to the works of their hands give to them,
> repay to them their conduct.   Ps. 28:4 (LXX, 27:4)

תֶּן־לָהֶם כְּפָעֳלָם וּכְרֹעַ מַעַלְלֵיהֶם]
[כְּמַעֲשֵׂה יְדֵיהֶם תֵּן לָהֶם הָשֵׁב גְּמוּלָם לָהֶם

[δὸς αὐτοῖς κατὰ τὰ ἔργα αὐτῶν
καὶ κατὰ τὴν πονηρίαν τῶν ἐπιτηδευμάτων αὐτῶν.
κατὰ τὰ ἔργα τῶν χειρῶν αὐτῶν δὸς αὐτοῖς,
ἀπόδος τὸ ἀνταπόδομα αὐτῶν αὐτοῖς.][48]

A great variety of nouns for the standard of recompense were clearly at the disposal of one wishing to utilize this motif. In this case all the terms are in reference to *evil* deeds or practices, and the LXX shows a preference for the plural κατὰ τὰ ἔργα in place of the singular כְּפָעֳלָם and כְּמַעֲשֵׂה. The final noun, ἀνταπόδομα, is normally rendered "repayment, reward, retribution, recompense" in Greek literature,[49] and when used as here with ἀπο- or ἀνταπο-δίδωμι yields the somewhat tautologous "repay them their repayment." I have translated it with "conduct," since this noun regularly renders in the motif the Hebrew גְּמֻל,[50] which refers generally to "ethically relevant action" or "the dealing(s) of a person which affect another person pleasantly or unpleasantly."[51]

---

[48] Where particularly illuminating, the Hebrew and Greek texts will be reproduced, but usually only of the motif-phrase itself rather than of the entire verse(s).

[49] BAGD, 72.

[50] Ps. 28:4d; 94:2; Isa. 66:6; Jer. 51:6; Lam. 3:64; Joel 3:4, 7. An exception is Prov. 19:17 with δόμα.

[51] K. Seybold, art. גמל, *TWAT*, vol. 2, cols. 24–35. See for instance 1 Sam. 24:17 [MT, verse 18]: "You have treated me well [גְּמַלְתַּנִי הַטּוֹבָה], but I have treated you badly [הָרָעָה גְּמַלְתִּיךָ]."

Earlier attempts to include *retribution* within the meaning of the word itself have been abandoned, but the idea of recompense may be retained if indicated by the context. When the "dealing" occurs in return for some previous action, it insinuates "*repay* good or evil."[52] When used in the motif of "returning" or "repaying" one's *dealing(s)* (i.e., conduct) it most often has reference to a negative recompense (= punishment).[53]

The recompense in Psalm 28:4 appears to be this-worldly and not eschatological, but can result in death (verses 1, 3, 5), whereas the preservation of the righteous from this fate is part of Yahweh's protection and salvation of his anointed one and his people (verses 8–9). The appeal for recompense is an appeal for God to punish the supplicant's enemies, the "workers of evil, who speak peace with their neighbors, while mischief is in their hearts" (verse 3). This mention of "neighbors" makes it likely that the enemies are fellow Israelites, while their recompense consists in lasting destruction (verse 5) and exclusion from the salvation awaiting the righteous (verses 3, 9).

Excursus: "Eschatological" in recompense statements

It cannot be my intent to settle the ongoing debate as to the presence or absence of eschatology and (proto-)apocalypticism within this body of literature.[54] Nor need I enter into that dispute since my goal in this study is to explain *Paul's* use of the motif, including his use of the tradition from the Jewish Scriptures. Therefore I will restrict my use of this term to *that which pertains to the Eschaton, the radically new and discontinuous age of salvation.* Thus I am asking such questions as:

- Are rewards and punishments seen to be distributed in a new era, one discontinuous with the present world order, and thus part of an ultimate and lasting state of salvation

---

[52] Gen. 50:15; Ps. 7:4 (MT: verse 5); 28:4; 94:2; 137:8.

[53] Isa. 3:11; 35:4; 59:18; 66:6; Jer. 51:6; Obad. 15; Joel 3:4, 7. In this sense also Yahweh is termed "God of recompense" [אֵל גְּמֻלוֹת] (Jer. 51:56).

[54] In addition to the important articles on "Old Testament Eschatology" in *RGG* (A. Jepsen, II.655–662) and the *ABD* (D. L. Peterson; II.575–579), see esp. the collection of essays on the subject in *Ex Auditu* 6 (Papers from the North Park Symposium on Theological Interpretation of Scripture, Oct. 12–14, 1990; Theme: Prophetic and/or Apocalyptic Eschatology, 1990), and *Eschatologie im Alten Testament* (ed. H. D. Preuß; Wege der Forschung 480; Darmstadt: Wissenschaftliche Buchgesellschaft, 1978).

or damnation, or were they part of corporate or individual experience in this world and its history?

- Is a recompense-scene envisioned as taking place at the end of or beyond this present cosmic and historical order?
- Does the recompense occur post-mortem for the individual or the community?

With this restriction of the term to its later, apocalyptically informed, meaning, it is obvious that I will find less of eschatological recompense than might be the case if I were to employ a definition more appropriate to the OT writings themselves. My goal once more, however, is to see whether eschatological divine recompense according to deeds *as Paul understood it* may be found in the Jewish Scriptures. If indeed it proves to be scarce, it will need to be asked whence came the apostle's eschatological interpretation of these OT recompense statements? And this question will lead to the writings of second temple Judaism whose interpretations moved more strongly in eschatological and apocalyptic directions.

1 Kings 8:32 (= 2 Chronicles 6:23)

Another example of the motif used in an appeal to Yahweh occurs in Solomon's prayer of dedication of the temple in Jerusalem (1 Kgs. 8:23–53). The setting involves a legal dispute among covenant members in Israel necessitating an oath before the altar (verse 22). God is called upon to judge his people Israel, in the sense of "adjudicating" between the guilty and the innocent. This divine judgment is described as taking two courses:

(i)   destroying (NRSV: condemning) the lawless[55]
      by giving his/her way on his/her head,
(ii) and justifying the righteous
      by giving to him/her according to his/her righteousness.[56]

As always in divine judgment the result is more than a mere *declaration* of guilt or innocence, but includes as well the *execution* of the appropriate sentence; in this case, possibly a self-maledictory curse which could result in physical harm or exclusion from the

---

[55] The parallel in 2 Chr. 6:23 reads "recompensing [שוב/ἀποδίδωμι] the wicked."
[56] The NIV's "and so establish his innocence" obscures the meaning and presence of the motif.

community.[57] Here is a clear instance of the motif connected with divine "judgment" in which it is Yahweh's determination and initiative which must set the organic *Tun-Ergehen-Zusammenhang* in motion. Of further interest is the intersection within this text of the language of judgment with that of justification, so that judgment according to deeds is not dreaded as inimical to but in fact welcomed as leading to the justification of the righteous.[58]

Conclusion

When used in prayer-appeals the motif can be directed against the wicked or oppressors outside of Israel (Lam. 3:64; 1 Macc. 7:42; Sir. 35:24), or against the wicked within the covenant community itself (2 Sam. 3:39; 1 Kgs. 8:32; Ps. 28:4). In some of the instances the divine recompense is a divine judgment. In most cases, the desired result of such divine recompense is nothing less than destruction, divine vengeance, wrath and curse, and in Psalm 28 exclusion from the salvation which awaits the righteous. In the one appeal where the motif is applied positively to the people of God (1 Kgs. 8:32), the language of judgment and justification intersected, so that judgment according to deeds actually resulted in justification for the innocent. In such instances, judgment and justification produce no theological tension since both are concerned with a determination of the same righteousness.

Pronouncing a benediction or prayer-wish

Ruth 2:12

Closely related to the previously discussed use is that as benediction or prayer-wish, found only in Ruth 2:12. In response to Ruth's demonstration of kindness, Boaz states:

> May the Lord repay your deed,
> And may your reward be full.
>
> יְשַׁלֵּם יהוה פָּעֳלֵךְ]
> [וּתְהִי מַשְׂכֻּרְתֵּךְ שְׁלֵמָה
>
> [ἀποτείσαι κύριος τὴν ἐργασίαν σου,
> καὶ γένοιτο ὁ μισθός σου πλήρης[59]]

---

[57] See Exod. 22:7–12; Num. 5:4–31.
[58] LXX: τοῦ δικαιῶσαι δίκαιον.
[59] The LXX adds "before the Lord God of Israel" (παρὰ κυρίου θεοῦ Ισραηλ).

Ruth's "deed" was to leave her own land and people (verse 11) so as to remain with Naomi and live with "a people that [she] did not know before." This stress on her leaving one "people" for another highlights the covenant ideas present in the context,[60] which are then underscored by Boaz' words: "under whose wings you have come for refuge." Thus the motif of divine recompense of deeds is used here to wish the covenant blessing upon one who has willingly entered into the covenant people. The recompense is seen, in fact, as a "wage"[61] earned or deserved through such entry into Yahweh's covenant people. There would appear to be no tension involved at this juncture in combining covenantal ideas with economic conceptions. As I will note elsewhere, Yahweh's gracious electing and sustaining of his people are not in tension with his "repayment" of their covenant obedience.

Motivating the righteous to obedience

Proverbs 19:17

Proverbs 19:17 urges the listener to "be kind to the poor," one of the chief characteristics of the wise and righteous person in the wisdom literature.

> Whoever is kind to the poor lends to the Lord,
> and according to his/her gift he will repay him/her.

Whereas elsewhere this particular pious behavior is motivated by the desire to honor God and thereby receive blessing, here alone the motivation is explicitly found in the expectation of a divine repayment. Even more remarkable is the expression (found only here in

---

[60] Note the similarity to the account of Abram's migration to the promised land (Gen. 12:1–5; cf. R. L. Hubbard, Jr.; *The Book of Ruth* [NICOT; Grand Rapids: Eerdmans, 1988], 165 and footnotes).

[61] Gk. μισθός [wage]; also ἀποτείσαι [make compensation, repay a debt; cf. BAGD, 101; LSJ, 223]. The Heb. משכרת (collective) is used apart from Ruth 2:12 only in patriarchal narratives for "the wages of a servant" (Gen. 31:7, 41; 29:15). The related שכר (also collective singular) is also taken from the economic sphere referring to "hire" or "wages" for services rendered (e.g., Gen. 30:28, 32, 33; Exod. 2:9; 1 Kgs. 5:20), and then applied by extension to Yahweh's reward to those who serve him (Gen. 15:1; Num. 18:31; Isa. 40:10; 62:11 [eschatological "wages" for the daughter of Zion!]; Jer. 31:16). While "reward" is an appropriate translation in some contexts, this should not eliminate the "wage" connotations of the term. Contrast Cleon Rogers' comment which has obvious theological motivation but little linguistic support: "God never hires his servants; they work for him freely out of love and thanksgiving and he rewards them for faithfulness out of his grace" (*Theological Wordbook of the Old Testament* [ed. R. L. Harris; Chicago: Moody, 1980], 878).

the OT) that such an act constitutes "lending to Yahweh." While this repayment is not conceived of as an act of Yahweh as judge, the imagery of "lending" and "repayment" clearly moves beyond the confines of Koch's *Tun-Ergehen-Zusammenhang* and does indeed suggest a belief in divine retribution, or, more precisely, retributive reward.[62] The motivation itself consists not so much in a calculable reward as in the assurance that one's righteous deeds will not be forgotten. Readers of later Jewish texts should keep this in mind and not jump too quickly to the conclusion that divine repayment of each good or evil deed breathes a spirit of petty calculation.

Proverbs 24:12[63]

Verses 11–12 constitute a unit addressed to one who has occasion and ability to "rescue those taken away to death." As such, it is an admonition to members of the covenant people toward right behavior. Verse 12 motivates this admonition via a warning against excusing oneself from such a duty on behalf of the needy by pleading ignorance:

> If you say, "Look, I did not know this" –
> Know that the Lord knows the hearts of all,
> and he who formed breath for all, he knows all things,
> who repays to each according to his/her deeds.[64]
> [וְהֵשִׁיב לְאָדָם כְּפָעֳלוֹ]
> [ὃς ἀποδίδωσιν ἑκάστῳ κατὰ τὰ ἔργα αὐτοῦ]

---

[62] *Pace* S. Travis who acknowledges the presence of "retributive punishment" in the OT while contending that "the complementary idea of retributive reward is absent, or nearly so" (*Christ and the Judgment*, 8, cf. also 8–13). The language of "debt" and "repayment" in texts such as 1 Sam. 24:19, Prov. 11:18, 19:17, 25:22, Ruth 2:12, Sir. 11:21–22, and 51:30, moves beyond Travis' "inherent (i.e., non-retributive) rewards," especially when this is in a balanced formulation opposite what even Travis acknowledges to be retributive punishment. See further Kuck, *Judgment and Community Conflict*, esp. 38–43.

[63] Brief reference may be made here to Prov. 24:29, which is not included above since *human* and not *divine* recompense is in view:

> Do not say, "I'll do to them as they have done to me;
> I'll pay them back for what they did."

Although this appears at first sight to be a rejection of the principle of corresponding recompense, it is actually only a rejection of its *false use*, of acting unjustly toward another in a spirit of revenge, and thus akin to the maxim "two wrongs do not make a right." See Wm. McKane, *Proverbs: A New Approach* (OTL; Philadelphia: Westminster, 1970), 574–575.

[64] MT: "Does not he who weighs hearts perceive it?
Does not he who keeps watch over your soul know it?
Does he not return to each according to his/her deed?

This text illustrates the connection between the motifs "God knows (Heb. weighs) the hearts," "God knows all things," and divine recompense according to deeds. Thus the recompense motif functions to warn presumptuous sinners that none of their deeds will be overlooked, since God weighs hearts and knows all things. As in Proverbs 19:17, the recompense is left undefined, since the certainty (rather than the nature) of negative consequences is sufficient as a warning. As to *when* God will recompense such deeds, the text gives no information. In spite of Egyptian parallels to the "weighing of hearts" at a post-mortem judgment,[65] this text should probably be interpreted in the light of other Israelite wisdom sayings referring to consequences in this life. Thus righteous behavior is motivated by a warning that omission of the same will result in negative consequences for the doer, understood as a divine recompense.

Ecclesiastes 12:14[66]

Although the syntax does not conform precisely to the pattern I have established for the motif, I include a discussion of Ecclesiastes 12:14 under this category of passages due to its close conceptual relationship to the motif:[67]

> For God will bring every act into judgment,
> every hidden deed, whether good or bad.
>
> [כי אח־כל־מעשׂה אלהים יבא במשׁפט
> על כל־נעלם אם־טוב ואם־רע]
>
> [ὅτι σὺν πᾶν τὸ ποίημα ὁ θεὸς ἄξει ἐν κρίσει
> ἐν παντὶ παρεωραμένῳ
> ἐὰν ἀγαθὸν καὶ ἐὰν πονηρόν.]

Verse 14 functions as the concluding motivation or reason for

---

[65] Whatever the original connections, they play no role any longer in the Greek versions, which have eliminated the "weighing" motif. On the Egyptian background of this and other judgment motifs, see J. Gwyn Griffiths, *The Divine Verdict: A Study of Divine Judgement in the Ancient Religions* (Studies in the History of Religions 52; NumenSup; Leiden: E. J. Brill, 1991), 102–242, esp. 224–225, 239–242.

[66] "There is a broad consensus that 12:9–14 is an addition to the book of Ecclesiastes" and "can be termed an epilogue or postscript." (R. E. Murphy, *Ecclesiastes* [WBC 23A; Dallas, TX: Word, 1992], 124).

[67] Instead of a verb of recompense, we have יבא במשׁפט/ἄξει ἐν κρίσει.

obedience. One should fear God and obey him, because he brings every deed into judgment, even the secret deeds, both good and evil.[68] The mention of "secret deeds" [נעלם][69] alludes to the related motif of God as the knower of human secrets.[70] Nothing in the text demands an eschatological judgment scene. As in most other texts, the time, place and precise nature of the recompense are left ambiguous. The knowledge that God will assuredly reward or punish one's behavior is considered sufficient to motivate proper action.

Sirach 11:26; 16:12, 14; 17:23

The deutero-canonical book of Sirach utilizes the motif of divine recompense according to deeds four times to motivate the righteous to obedience.[71] That this was understood fundamentally as a *dual recompense* (i.e., punishment for the wicked; blessing for the righteous) is made especially clear in Sirach 16:12–14:

> Great as his mercy, so also is his chastisement;
> he will judge a person according to his/her deeds.
> The sinner will not escape with plunder,
> and the patience of the godly will not be frustrated.
> He makes room for every act of mercy;
> each will receive in accordance with his/her deeds.
> [וכל אדם כמעשיו ימצא]
> [ἕκαστος κατὰ τὰ ἔργα αὐτοῦ εὑρήσει]

The larger context (15:11–16:23) aims to motivate the wise member of the covenant to choose obedience and fidelity to God's

---

[68] See Paul's similar formulation, "in order that each may receive the things done in the body, whether good or bad" (2 Cor. 5:10b).

[69] The term is used for guilt of which one is unaware (Lev. 5:2–4; 4:13), or which remains hidden from others (Num. 5:13), for concealed wisdom (1 Kgs. 10:3; Job 28:21; 2 Chr. 9:2), or for hypocrites, i.e., those who "conceal themselves" (Ps. 26:4). The thought here is of deeds of (dis)obedience to Torah (Eccl. 12:13, "keep His commandments") concealed from public view and knowledge, which, however, are known to God's penetrating gaze.

[70] See especially Prov. 24:12–14; Jer. 17:9–10; and additional references in Kuck, *Judgment and Community Conflict*, 43, nn. 22–23.

[71] Originally composed in Hebrew about 180 BCE, this work circulated for the most part in Greek, being translated first by ben Sira's grandson around 125 BCE (P. W. Skehan and A. A. Di Lella, *The Wisdom of Ben Sira* [AB 39; New York: Doubleday, 1987], 8–10).

will (15:15–17). The duality of God's dealings with his people
(mercy and reproof) is noted in verse 12a, followed by the
statement of retributive principle in verse 12b, understood as divine
judgment (κρινεῖ).

Verse 13 makes the dual purpose of this motif explicit: (1) to
warn presumptuous sinners that they will not escape; and (2) to
comfort the godly who must often wait patiently through hardship
for the reward of their obedience. In Sirach, as in the rest of the
LXX, this comfort is addressed to Jews only, or to those who
choose to live under Israel's covenant God. The warning, on the
other hand, can be addressed as a judgment sentence on the
consistently unfaithful in Israel or to heathen nations.[72] Equally,
however, this warning can be addressed to the covenant people as a
stern but hopeful call to repentance.

> Afterward he will rise up and repay them,
> and he will bring their recompense on their heads.
> Yet to those who repent he grants a return,
> and he encourages those who are losing hope.
> Turn back to the Lord and forsake your sins.
>
> (Sir. 17:23–25a)

In such cases, the listeners are generally not viewed as hardened
impenitents or apostates, but as backsliders, whose laxity could (if
continued) place in jeopardy their standing in the divine favor.
Sirach 17 is particularly interesting for its softening of a strict
doctrine of retribution according to works. Israel's sinning is
viewed almost as an inherent inevitability arising from human
limitations and frailty:[73]

> For not everything is within human capability, since
>   human beings are not immortal.   (Sir. 17:30)

And for this reason, the divine recompense according to deeds is
superseded for the penitent by mercy and forgiveness:

---

[72] Sir. 35:23a, 24; see also the use of the motif to pronounce sentence upon the
disobedient (below).

[73] This is attested further by the stress on "creation from the earth" (17:1, 11c
[v.1.], 21 [v.1.: "knowing how they are formed"]), the penchant towards transgression
(17:16 [v.1.: "Their ways from youth tend toward evil, and they are *unable* to make
for themselves hearts of flesh in place of their stony hearts"]), human limitedness
(17:2, 30–32; 18:8–10), and God's forgiving patience with such frail creatures
(18:11–14).

> How great is the mercy of the Lord,
> and his forgiveness for those who return to him!
>
> (Sir. 17:24)

As will become more common in later Jewish literature, "punishment" according to deeds is here reduced to "chastisement" for Israel's sins:

> Israel, as his firstborn, he cares for with chastisement (παιδεία)[74]
>
> But the Lord, being good and knowing how they are formed, neither neglected them nor left off sparing them (i.e., from judgment).[75]

In the Hebrew original of these sayings this divine recompense was not understood eschatologically, but occurred in this life and was perceived most clearly at one's end:[76]

> Do not say, "I have enough, and what harm can come to me now?"
> In the day of prosperity, adversity is forgotten,
> and in the day of adversity, prosperity is not remembered.
> For it is easy for the Lord on the day of death
> to repay each person according to his/her ways.
>
> [להשיב לאדם כדרכיו]
>
> [ἀποδοῦναι ἀνθρώπῳ κατὰ τὰς ὁδοὺς αὐτοῦ]
>
> An hour's misery makes one forget past delights,
> and *at the close of one's life one's deeds are revealed.*
> Call no one happy before their death;
> by how he/she ends,[77] a person becomes known.
>
> (Sir. 11:24–27)

---

[74] Sir. 17:18a (v.l.). This is spoken in explicit contrast to God's treatment of other nations (verse 17).

[75] Sir. 17:21 (v.l.). This is added after "their sins are before the Lord," i.e., softening the sense of wickedness, so that God "spares" them from punishment, instead disciplining.

[76] 1:13; 9:12; 14:12; 14:16–17; 18:24. On Sirach's "eschatology" see Skehan and Di Lella, *Wisdom of Ben Sira*, 83–87.

[77] Following the MT. The LXX reads "and through offspring a person becomes known."

At issue is fidelity to the covenant:

> Stand firm in your covenant (ἐν διαθήκῃ σου)
> and busy yourself in it
> and grow old in your work (ἐν τῷ ἔργῳ σου).   (verse 20)

The wise person will not presume upon current blessings as an excuse for laxity in obedience, but will remember that God can easily reverse such blessing, even if only at the very end of one's life. This motivation (i.e., one's "end" will reveal one's true happiness or condition) is also found widely in Greek sayings such as that of Aeschylus (525–456 BCE): "Only when man's life comes to its end in prosperity can one call that man happy."[78] Both here and in Sirach, the recompense is envisioned as earthly delights or sufferings.

The Greek translation of Sirach, on the other hand, does make definite allusion to post-mortem retribution.[79] It associates this theme with several related motifs: God's knowledge of every human action (including hidden deeds),[80] and the "revealing" of deeds at the hour of recompense (11:27b).

Conclusion

The use of the motif in Motivation-texts belongs to Israel's wisdom tradition.[81] As such it is directed, as would be expected for this genre, to the covenant people, and envisions the recompense as undefined sufferings or blessings in this life (post-mortem categories are introduced in the LXX of Sirach). It is the *certainty* rather than the precise nature of the reward/punishment which is felt to motivate. There is clearly a *dual recompense* envisioned in these texts (i.e., both reward and punishment), functioning to encourage the righteous to persevere in doing good, and to warn the presumptuous against laxity in obedience. As elsewhere, especially in warning texts the divine recompense is related to God's omniscience, including knowledge even of hidden deeds. The Jews' privileged standing in Yahweh's covenant mercy is not felt to be incompatible with the demands for covenant obedience.

---

[78] Agamemnon, 1.928, citation in Skehan and Di Lella, *Wisdom of Ben Sira*, 241.

[79] See Di Lella's comments on the eschatological additions or modifications at 7:17b and 48:11b (Skehan and Di Lella, *Wisdom of Ben Sira*, 86, 201–202, 531–532, 534).

[80] 15:19b; 17:15, 19–20.

[81] "Wisdom stands or falls with the validity of the doctrine of recompense" (E. Würthwein, *TDNT*, 4.711).

Comforting and assuring the righteous

Psalm 18:20, 24 (= 2 Samuel 22:21, 25)

The motif occurs ten times with this function, predominantly in the Psalms. The nature of the comfort can take several forms, including the comforting knowledge that one's occasional sins will *not* be recompensed.

Psalm 18:20, 24 could be easily misunderstood as a relapse into Jewish-nomistic self-righteousness, not unlike caricatures of (legalistic) first-century Judaism:

> The Lord will repay[82] me according to my righteousness,[83]
> and according to the cleanness of my hands he will repay me.
> For I have kept the ways of the Lord,
> and have not wickedly departed from my God.
> For all his judgments are before me,
> nor have I turned aside from his righteous decrees.
> I will be blameless before him,
> and I will keep myself from lawlessness.
> The Lord will repay me according to my righteousness,
> and according to the cleanness of my hands in his sight.

This, however, is not an introspective assertion of sinless perfection, but rather a declaration of loyalty to the covenant. The above-cited words reflect the "Torah liturgy" recited by worshipers entering the temple:

> O Lord, who may abide in your tent?
> Who may dwell on your holy hill?
> Those who walk blamelessly, and do what is right,
> and speak the truth from their heart;
> who do not slander with their tongue,
> and do no evil to their friends,
> nor take up a reproach against their neighbors . . .
>
> (Ps. 15:1–3)

---

[82] Both in verses 20 and 24 the LXX has replaced an original reference to *past* recompense with a verb in the *future* tense; and in verse 23, *past* blamelessness becomes a vow of *future* behavior; cf. also verses 17, 19 (where future rescue is mentioned amidst past deliverance), 25–29. For the significance of this, see below.

[83] Both here and in verse 24 the parallel text in 2 Samuel reads the plural כצדקתי. It would appear that no significant difference is intended between the use of "my righteousness" versus "my righteousnesses" in the Hebrew use of the motif.

In this manner those entering the temple professed their faith in the provisions and protection of the covenant:

> Citizenship on Zion is only for the *ṣādîq*, the Israelite who lives according to the precepts of the covenant of Yahweh... Thus [Ps. 18:]20ff. draw a picture of the *ṣādîq* who is adjusted to the covenant and admitted to the sanctuary...The emphasis on obedience over against the thorah and the profession of a righteous life are basically a reference to the declaration of loyalty on the part of the worshiper usually given upon entering the sanctuary.[84]

Thus the motif does not speak of moral introspection and error-free behavior, but rather reflects liturgical traditions about general loyalty to the covenant.

The assertion that the divine recompense will be "according to my righteousness" reflects the psalmist's conformity to the covenant demands of Yahweh, not in terms of moral perfection, but in contrast to those who "depart from God," "despise his decrees," and do not "keep his ways" or "keep themselves from sin" (verses 21–23). "Cleanness of hands" speaks of the integrity of one's conduct within the framework of this covenant relationship, and especially of avoidance of idolatry.[85] As throughout the OT, the *ṣādîq* is one whose behavior demonstrates *consistency with Yahweh's covenant demands*. "Despite divergence on details, and on the history of the root, there is something of a consensus that righteousness is covenant-behaviour, or loyalty to the covenant"; it is "activity which befits the covenant," and thus "everything (including inward disposition) which fits the requirements of the covenant in a given situation is then 'normal' or righteous."[86] Provision is made for occasional transgressions through the system of sacrificial atonement and through repentance,[87] showing that one's standing as "righteous" and "obedient" before God can be maintained in spite of occasional covenant violations.

It is therefore not a question of a protestation of innocence

---

[84] H.-J. Kraus, *Psalms 1–59: A Commentary* (trans. H. C. Oswald; Minneapolis: Ausgburg, 1988), 262, see also 227 on "Torah-liturgy."

[85] Cf. Ps. 24:4; 1QS IX, 15.

[86] J. A. Ziesler, *The Meaning of Righteousness in Paul* (Cambridge: Cambridge University Press, 1972), 39–40. He points especially to Gen. 18:19; Ps. 15; and Ezek. 18 as showing this covenant connection.

[87] See W. Eichrodt, *Theology of the Old Testament*, II.443–483.

which, prompted by self righteousness, gives an account to God of the king's own deserts, but of an affirmation of faith in the covenantal faithfulness of God, which may be experienced by those who in obedience to God's ordinances keep their faith in him. That it is at all possible to do so is not credited to human merit but is a gift of the grace of God who has instituted the Covenant and its ordinances for the benefit of his people.[88]

In the MT this motif is included as part of a long litany of God's *past acts of deliverance* on behalf of the supplicant. The LXX of the Psalm, on the other hand, places the divine recompense in the future.[89] This may be an example of what M. Reiser calls the LXX's "tendency to eschatologize," particularly in the Psalms.[90] In any case, the use of future verbs (ῥύσεται, ἀνταποδώσει, etc.) certainly opened the way for the later eschatological understanding of divine recompense such as one sees in Paul.[91]

As for the theological import of the motif under consideration, loyal members of the covenant community could look upon the divine recompense according to deeds as providing assurance and consolation. They could rejoice in this belief which meant (future) deliverance in times of trouble. Statements such as Psalm 18:20–24, then, do not express self-righteousness, nor do they tend toward synergism, but thankfully affirm confidence in the covenant relationship, which at one and the same time is completely an act of divine grace, and yet conditional upon the loyal obedience of those within this elect community.[92]

Psalm 103:10

In quite a different fashion Psalm 103:10 (LXX, 102:10) employs a variation on the motif to comfort the righteous and reassure them of God's gracious conduct toward them:

[88] A. Weiser, *The Psalms* (ET: trans. H. Hartwell; OTL; Philadelphia: Westminster, 1962), 192–193.

[89] Cf. n. 82 above.

[90] *Jesus and Judgment: The Eschatological Proclamation in Its Jewish Context* (trans. Linda M. Maloney; Minneapolis: Fortress Press, 1997), 24–25, 32–38.

[91] E.g., Rom. 2:6; 1 Cor. 3:8, 14, 4:5; Col. 3:24–25.

[92] On this covenantal interplay between divine grace and human obedience in the OT, see R. M. Fuller, *A Pauline Understanding of Rewards: Its Background and Expression in First Corinthians* (Diss. Fuller Theological Seminary, 1991), esp. 16–107.

> He has not treated us according to our sins,
> nor recompensed us according to our iniquities.

If Psalm 18 rejoiced in God's recompense according to the obedient conduct of the covenant people, this text rejoices that the principle of recompense is overturned or ignored in particular cases; namely, when the sins (plural!) of the righteous are considered. The tenet of divine retribution according to deeds is not being universally declared null and void in the case of Israelites; rather, this striking negation of recompense has application only to those who "fear him" (verses 11b, 13b, 17) and otherwise "keep his covenant and remember to do his commandments" (verse 18). For these, the principle of divine recompense according to evil deeds is overturned, being replaced by the forgiveness of sins, removal of transgressions far from the doer, and fatherly compassion (verses 3, 8, 12, 13). Clearly this abrogation of divine retribution has reference only to the *occasional transgressions* of those who otherwise walk faithfully in Yahweh's statutes, and who do not commit such sins haughtily, but have come to recognize and repent of their errors which arise not out of a heart aimed at disloyalty, but out of the frail and transitory character of human existence.[93] It may, however, be noted from this text that a *strict* doctrine of dual retribution whereby *every* good or evil deed must receive its corresponding reward or punishment is not characteristic of the OT. Rather, within the provisions and demands of the covenant relationship, divine compassion and forgiveness can allow for a flexible application with regard to the occasional sins of the elect, yet without leading to a general abrogation of the principle. This should be kept in mind when approaching Paul.

Psalm 94:23

Thus far writers have used the motif to comfort the righteous inasmuch as their covenant integrity will be rewarded (Psalm 18) and their occasional sins will *not* be recompensed (Psalm 103). Psalm 94 presents another way of comforting, namely by assurance that the wicked oppressors will be repaid for their sins:

[93] See verses 14–15. "But take heed, warns the psalmist: this love is not to be wilfully abused. Its recipients must respond with respectful awe, vv. 11, 13, 17... The activity of God, v. 6, must find an echo of obedient activity in their lives. חסד is essentially a two-way relationship of obligation" (L. C. Allen, *Psalms 101–150* [WBC 21; Waco, TX: Word, 1983], 22).

> And he will give back to them their sin,
> and according to their evil the Lord our God will destroy
> them.   Ps. 94:23 (LXX, 93:23)

The people of God are being crushed by the violence and injustice of the wicked. Therefore, appeal is made to "the God of vengeance" and "judge of the earth" to "give to the proud what they deserve" (verses 1–2). The psalm concludes with an expression of firm certainty in the Lord as one's refuge and help, who will correct these injustices and recompense the wicked according to their deeds.[94] In this case, the divine recompense is further described as a future "destruction[95] according to their evil." Though likely not understood originally as referring to an eschatological judgment and recompense, the use of the future tense in verse 23 and the theophanic language of verses 1–2 would have recommended such an interpretation to later Jewish readers, so that such recompense could easily be viewed as eschatological divine vengeance. Interestingly in this instance, the comforting destruction of the wicked probably has reference not to non-Israelites, but it is the "foolish ones *among the people* (ἐν τῷ λαῷ)" (verse 8) who will experience God's judgment.[96]

Conclusion

If my interpretation of the above texts is accurate, three complementary aspects of the interplay between grace, obedience and divine recompense according to deeds have been highlighted:

(1) the divine recompense brings encouragement to the righteous that they will be blessed as promised within the covenant;

(2) this applies equally to the righteous who repent from occasional sins, in which case any supposed strict understanding of retribution is superseded by divine forgiveness; but

---

[94] A similar use of the motif is found in Isa. 59:18 and Ps. 62:12 (LXX, 61:13), though in this latter instance a dual recompense is to be understood as the basis of comfort: reward to the righteous, retribution to the wicked.

[95] Gk. ἀφανιεῖ = Attic form of ἀφανίζω: destroy, ruin.

[96] Also clearly the case in the use of the motif in the MT of Isa. 66:6 (cf. verse 5: "Your own people who hate you"). The LXX, however, has modified verse 5 so as to avoid identifying "brothers" (= Jews) with those who hate the righteous and who experience the coming divine retribution.

(3)   such comfort is not extended to those within the nation (or
      without) whose ways are characterized by wickedness and
      unrighteousness without repentance; to them divine recom-
      pense according to deeds will mean divine vengeance and
      exclusion from salvation.

Pronouncing sentence upon the disobedient

Most frequently in the prophetic literature of the OT the motif
occurs in order to threaten and condemn the consistently disobedient, and especially the faithless people of God,[97] sometimes (but
not always) including a summons to repentance which bears a note
of continued hope. Ignoring Sirach for the moment, this particular
function is also largely limited to the prophetic literature, whereas
its function to comfort the righteous and encourage them to
obedience is largely absent from this same literature.[98] We will
want to pay particular attention in this group of passages to the
soteriological implications of these judgment threats directed
against members of the elect community.

In saying this, the fluidity of the categories being applied to
these texts becomes obvious. A "summons to repentance" obviously contains an element of "encouragement to obedience."
However, these categories are still distinct in that the encouragement is directed to those whom the speaker views as walking in
Yahweh's ways, and needing such motivation only due to some
form of opposition. The "threat" and "summons" on the other
hand address those viewed as living in defiance of the covenant
demands.

Jeremiah 17:10

The prophet Jeremiah has an obvious affinity for this motif, using
it six times as a threat[99] and twice more with different functions,[100] and can employ it with considerable terminological

[97] A sentence upon Jews: Jer. 16:18; 17:10; 21:14; 23:2; Ezek. 7:3, 4, 8, 9, 27;
24:14; Hos. 4:9; 12:2, 14; a sentence upon other nations: Jer. 25:14, 51:6, Joel 4:4, 7,
and Obad. 15.
[98] Exceptions are Isa. 59:18 and 66:6.
[99] Jer. 16:18; 17:10; 21:14 (not in the LXX, but found in the MT, Hexapla,
Aquila, and Theodotion); 23:2; along with 25:14 and 51:6 which are directed at
foreign nations.
[100] Jer. 32:19; 50:29.

variety.[101] Jeremiah 17:10 brings together the motif with the concepts of "trust in Yahweh" and of the deceitful human "heart." As part of a larger indictment of Judah's sin (17:1–13)[102] there appears a wisdom saying (verses 5–8) pronouncing a curse on those who trust in "mortals" or "flesh" (= "whose *hearts* turn away from the Lord," verse 5) and blessing on those who trust in God. Jeremiah's response (verse 9) is a confession of the insidious character of the human heart, which is sick beyond cure and unknowable to human understanding. As a response to Jeremiah's exclamation, God speaks:

> I, the Lord, test the heart
> and examine the mind (lit. "kidneys"),
> to give to each according to his/her ways,
> according to the fruit of his/her deeds.

Interestingly in this text, the divine recompense according to deeds is based upon Yahweh's examination of one's *inner* thoughts and affections, rather than strictly observable actions, and, in context, refers to God's determination of one's "faith" [πέποιθεν/ בטה, verse 7]. The fascinating interplay of trust, heart, and deeds in this passage testifies to an understanding of human works and obedience far removed from any externalism. Rather, trust in Yahweh, which already marks one as belonging to the "blessed" and the "righteous," and which is a reality of the unseen heart, is the ultimate basis of the divine examination.[103] At the same time it is understood that this inner reality *must of necessity* be worked out in one's behavior, one's "ways." Thus there can be ultimately no disparity between a blessing (or curse) based on trust, and a recompense according to deeds.

Jeremiah 23:2

This text contains the prophet's oracle of woe against the shepherds of Israel. The correspondence between sin and punishment is quite clear:

---

[101] Verbs: שלם, 4x; ותן and פקד, 2x each; עשׂה, 1x. For the standard or object of recompense he uses ten different nouns or expressions.

[102] The strongest indictment of Judah is omitted in the LXX (verses 1–4). Is this simple haplography (W. Holladay, *Jeremiah 1: Chapters 1–25*, 484), or did the translator desire to soften the severity of judgment upon Judah?

[103] For possible influence from the Egyptian motif of "weighing the heart," see above, n. 65.

You have scattered them, that is, my flock, and driven them away and have not tended [פקדתם] to them.
So I will tend [פקד] to you for the evil of your deeds.[104]
[ἰδοὺ ἐγὼ ἐκδικῶ ἐφ᾽ ὑμᾶς κατὰ τὰ πονηρὰ ἐπιτηδεύματα ὑμῶν.]

"Because the shepherds did not *pāqad* the people in a positive way, Yahweh will *pāqad* the shepherds in a negative way."[105] This verb does not of itself signify "punishment" meted out after some legal-juridical determination of wrongdoing; its sense is "to attend to, visit, investigate" someone or something with a view toward either blessing or harming. When used with "evil" as the direct object, however, it takes on the sense of "visiting evil upon someone," and hence to "punish" in a judicial-retributive sense.[106] Thus, the LXX's ἐκδικέω ("take vengeance") is an appropriate translation. As in a couple of other instances, the motif is employed here as a threat to counter failure in proper leadership, especially abuse of position and privilege.[107]

Ezekiel 7:8–9, 27

Ezekiel's considerable usage of the motif[108] is of interest for a number of reasons, not least because he is often isolated as the one who initiated an individualizing of the doctrine of retribution in Jewish thought, moving from a national or collective application (i.e., retribution upon Israel's enemies and then upon the unrighteous in Israel) to one in which each individual stood independently before God to be judged.[109] Furthermore, Ezekiel's predilection for the verb "to judge" [שפט/κρίνειν/ἐκδικείν] in the motif is both

---

[104] Translation from Miller, *Sin and Judgment*, 68.

[105] Ibid. Along with the word play using פקד (not reproduced in LXX), Miller notes an additional correspondence between the *shepherds'* [רעים] failure to properly *shepherd* [הרעים] the flock of God, which brings punishment for the *evil* [רע] they have done.

[106] See A. Gunnel, *Determining the Destiny: PQD in the Old Testament* (ConBOT 16; Lund: CWK Gleerup, 1980), who translates "to determine the destiny of…" (241). What is said of the use with a direct object applies equally to use with the preposition ־ב (Jer. 21:14; Hos. 12:3).

[107] See Jer. 21:14; Hos. 4:9. Note also Paul's use of the motif against leaders in 1 Cor. 3:5–17, Rom. 14:10–12, and 2 Cor. 11:15.

[108] As a threat: 7:3, 4, 8, 9, 27; 18:30; 33:20; as justification: 36:19.

[109] See on this subject B. Lindars, "Ezekiel and Individual Responsibility," *VT* 15 (1965), 452–467.

unusual[110] and instructive for the development of the idea of "*judgment* according to deeds."

Following his proclamation of punishment upon the countryside (chapter 6), he then warns of the end [קֵץ/πέρας] coming upon the "land of Israel" (7:2), both inside and outside the city walls (verses 15, 23). This divine judgment is given universal (verse 2) and eschatological scope (LXX, verse 10). Ezekiel "makes Israel form up along with the other nations who are ripe for judgment. That spells a very effective attack upon the pride of the chosen people, who throw away their preferential position through the contempt they show for their God."[111] God will pour out his wrath and anger upon the nation,[112] neither sparing nor showing mercy (verses 4, 9). Such unsparing judgment is explained as due to God's recompense according to deeds.

The motif occurs here in two nearly identical forms (verses 3b-4 and 8b-9) with only minor differences between the two (substitution of εκδικέω for κρίνω and sg. "way" for "ways"). They probably represent two similar oracles delivered separately but here brought together by the redactor, or perhaps testify to textual confusion. The juxtaposition of "judging" and "giving upon you all your deeds" shows again how the juridical and organic conceptions of recompense have been combined by this time.

> Soon now I will pour out my wrath upon you; I will spend my anger against you.
> I will judge you by your ways
> and bring upon you all your detestable practices.
> My eye will not spare you, neither will I show mercy,
> for your ways I will bring upon you,
> and your detestable practices shall be in your midst;
> and you will know that it is I the Lord who strikes the blow.   Ezek. 7:8–9 (LXX, 7:5–6)

Whereas I have noted numerous instances of divine mercy super-seding this operation of recompense to Israel, here it is explicitly stated that God will *not show mercy* (οὐδὲ μὴ ἐλεήσω). As I have suggested earlier, the difference in the divine attitude (mercy/no

[110] Elsewhere in the motif only in Sir. 16:12 and 1 Macc. 7:42; cf. also 1 Kgs. 8:32 (= 2 Chr. 6:23) and Eccl. 12:14.

[111] W. Eichrodt, *Ezekiel* (ET; trans. C. Quinn; OTL; London: SCM, 1970), 102.

[112] Verses 3, 8; cf. also verses 12b, 19, and verse 22 ("I will avert my face from them").

mercy) can be traced to the difference between a fundamental and ongoing turning from Yahweh (as here), and a disobedience which may still be viewed as reversible, occasional, a failure not indicative of one's way in general. The prophets give no clearly defined line by which one could infallibly determine which of these two situations is present; rather the determination lies with God, who alone can see the hidden things of the heart and who acts not in submission to principles of retribution but in sovereign freedom.

The oracle closes on a note of total calamity, with the people seeking in terror for some word of hope (verses 25–26). But this is in vain, for neither prophet, priest, king, nor prince will be able to help on the day of God's just recompense:

> The ruler will wear destruction, and the hands of the
> people of the land will be paralyzed;
> according to their ways I will do to them,
> [... מדרכם[113 אעשה אותם]
> [κατὰ τὰς ὁδοὺς αὐτῶν ποιήσω αὐτοῖς]
> and in their judgments I will take vengeance on [MT:
> "judge"] them.[114]
> Then they will know that I am the Lord.   Ezek. 7:27

Thus, after a long period of chastising judgments, during which God was patient and did *not* deal with the people according to their sinful ways, he now judges them to be fundamentally "unwilling," "hardened and obstinate" (3:7), and so will begin to deal with them according to the principle of recompense.

Hosea 4:9

In the midst of a lawsuit (ריב) against Israel, and particularly against her priests, Hosea prophesies:

> And it will be: Like people, like priest;

---

[113] מדרכם: probably just an alternative way of expressing "for ... " or "on the basis of ... " (G. A. Cooke, *The Book of Ezekiel* [ICC; Edinburgh: T. & T. Clark, 1970] 88). In any case, the LXX has understood it as כדרכם.

[114] NIV: "and by their own standards I will judge them." The LXX phrase (καὶ ἐν τοῖς κρίμασιν αὐτῶν ἐκδικήσω αὐτούς), however, is not an instance of the recompense motif. These judgments are the words and visions being sought from earthly authorities (verses 25–26), not the sinful deeds of the people. This is a case of prophetic irony (cf. W. Zimmerli, *Ezechiel* [2nd edn.; BKAT 13/1; Neukirchen: 1979], 179). Cf. also 23:24.

I will take vengeance upon him for his ways,
And his deeds I will recompense to him. Hos. 4:9

וּפָקַדְתִּי עָלָיו דְּרָכָיו[
וּמַעֲלָלָיו אָשִׁיב לוֹ]
[καὶ ἐκδικήσω ἐπ᾽ αὐτὸν τὰς ὁδοὺς αὐτοῦ
καὶ τὰ διαβούλια[115] αὐτοῦ ἀνταποδώσω αὐτῷ.]

It was a prophetic innovation to apply this imagery of an Israelite lawsuit to the covenant relationship between Yahweh and Israel, with Yahweh becoming both prosecutor and judge.[116] Many divine lawsuit texts omit both a defense and a verdict, a rhetorical means of forcing the listeners to draw their own conclusions about their catastrophic situation so that they will repent. Such usage reveals the *personal* character of divine recompense and "the undogmatic, unsystematic way of thinking, in religious matters, of the Old Testament. All is ultimately left to...the Supreme Judge and Ruler, whose judgement is righteous, but unpredictable, and inscrutable for human understanding, whose ways are not ours. He is a person, not a system or an order."[117] In general, the prophetic lawsuits involve a battle against apostates within the nation in order to preserve the remnant for salvation.

Hosea's lawsuit arises because of the covenant unfaithfulness of both people and priests.[118] The epigrammatic "like people, like priest" may have been a popular saying with an originally positive sense designed to highlight the privileged position of the priestly class. If so, the sense is here ironically reversed. Both priest and people will be judged upon the same basis, and thus the motif functions to avert the abuse of privilege.

The outcome of this particular judgment is Yahweh's rejection of these priests (4:6), and destruction and ruin upon both priest and people.[119] In Hosea 12:2 and 14, where the motif occurs again in a lawsuit, the language suggests that the wicked in Israel are viewed

[115] διαβούλια = "debatings, deliberations" (LSJ, 390). This word translates מעצות [intrigues] at Ps. 5:10 and Hos. 11:6. Perhaps the similar מעלליו was misread by the translator or his Hebrew text.

[116] See K. Nielsen, *Yahweh as Prosecutor and Judge: An Investigation of the Prophetic Lawsuit (Rib-pattern)* (JSOTSup 9; Winnona Lake, IN: Eisenbrauns, 1978) 74; and B. Gemser, "The Rib or Controversy Pattern in Hebrew Mentality," *Wisdom in Israel: FS H.H. Rowley* (VTSup 3; Leiden: E. J. Brill, 1955), 124–137.

[117] Gemser, "The Rib or Controversy Pattern" in *Wisdom in Israel*, 137.

[118] 4:1, 6, 7, 10–18.

[119] 4:5–6, 14b. See Miller (*Sin and Judgment*, 9–15) for the exact correspondence between sin and punishment in Hosea 4.

as the "rebellious" covenant violators of Deuteronomy 32 whose lot will be rejection, vengeance and fiery wrath. Whereas blood-guilt which was accidental could be removed by Yahweh (Josh. 20:1–9), this defrauding of God himself and covenant unfaithfulness will not be removed, and the rebellious will be cut off from the covenant provisions, experiencing instead its curses and a return to conditions as in the wilderness wandering.[120] Yet even in this ultimate threat there remains a note of hope for the remnant who repent.[121]

Summoning the disobedient to repentance

This final category is closely related to the foregoing. It differs, however, in that the threat is more strongly *conditional* due to the greater emphasis on a call to repentance.

Ezekiel 18:30

Chapter 18 is a disputation dealing with the charge by the people of Israel that Yahweh is not just or fair.[122] Thus the prophet pronounces that:

(i)   the individual who sins will die (verses 1–4), and
(ii) the righteous person will live (verses 5–9).

Further, this status (righteous or wicked) cannot be passed on to the succeeding generation, for

(iii) the wicked offspring of a righteous person will die (verses 10–13), while
(iv) the righteous offspring of a wicked person will live (verses 14–20).

Finally, even the wicked who repent will live (verses 21–23), while the righteous who turn to wickedness will die (verse 24). Thus Yahweh is just in his treatment of the people (verses 25–29). This just treatment is confirmed by the prophet's citation of the motif immediately prior to the call to repentance (verses 30b–32).

> Therefore, I will judge you, each one, O house of Israel according to his/her ways.

[120] Hos. 2:11–13; 9:15–17.
[121] 12:6; 14:1–9.
[122] "Yet you say, 'The way of the Lord is unfair'" (verse 25; cf. also verse 29). On the whole chapter see especially the treatment by W. Eichrodt, *Ezekiel*, 231–249.

Neither according to *another's* behavior, nor even according to one's own *previous* actions (assuming a change of ways) will God judge the individual. Rather so long as death has not put an end to opportunity, one can begin to walk in a new "way" according to which judgment will be determined.

The individualization of the recompense doctrine is striking, and, not surprisingly, has resulted in the very common view that in Jeremiah and Ezekiel one sees the first beginnings of a consciousness that the *individual* (not only the community) is subject to the deity's favor and anger.[123] However, as Rankin has demonstrated, this can hardly be correct. That Ezekiel did wish his hearers to make an individual application of his prophecy seems unambiguous by the inclusion of "each" [אִישׁ/ἕκαστος] in the motif of divine recompense. However, allowing for development and modification, it is clear that religious individualism of this kind had characterized Israelite religion throughout its recorded history.[124] Individual accountability in matters of human judicial administration was never in dispute;[125] and a personal-individual relationship to the deity was clearly expressed in Isaiah's call, the many Psalms reflecting an individual's plight, and numerous other tales.[126] That Yahweh rewards and punishes on an *individual*, not only communal, basis was already well known by the time of Jeremiah and Ezekiel.

On the other hand, there is no need to deny the presence of what is commonly termed "corporate solidarity." The prophecy of chapter 18 was intended as a corrective to a *false application* of this latter concept. The proverb quoted at the beginning of the chapter ("The parents have eaten sour grapes, and the children's teeth are set on edge," verse 2) expresses a certain fatalism among the people and their leaders. Ruin and death can no longer be averted because they are being punished for the sins of past generations; thus the efficacy of a reformation of ways is also doubted. Ezekiel challenges

---

[123] Overview of positions in *Ezekiel 18 and the Rhetoric of Moral Discourse in the Book Ezekiel* by Gordon H. Matties (Diss. Vanderbilt University, 1989), esp. 195–217.

[124] O. S. Rankin, *Israel's Wisdom Literature: Its Bearing on Theology and the History of Religion* (Edinburgh: T. & T. Clark, 1954 [orig. 1936]), esp. 53–76. See also Gammie, "The Theology of Retribution in the Book of Deuteronomy," 1–12.

[125] See for instance 2 Kgs. 14:1–6. Cf. also Lindars, "Ezekiel and Individual Responsibility," 452–467.

[126] E.g., Hannah and Eli in 1 Sam. 1:9–10, 17 and the strange tale in Exodus 4 regarding Zipporah's action.

this error, asserting that a change in ways, toward good or evil, both on an individual and on a corporate level, can indeed work a change in the divine–human relationship and in the outcome of divine judgment.

However, the central rhetorical thrust of this passage is not so much to justify Yahweh's actions to the people as it is to summon them to repentance. Precisely *because* each will be judged according to his/her own ways, the prophet immediately calls them to repent (verses 30b–32). Raitt may be correct that these verses are not an oracle of doom, but instead constitute a distinct prophetic speech-form, a "summons to repentance."[127] Unique to this *Gattung* is that "both threat of judgment and promise of salvation are incorporated under a predominant motif of admonition," resulting in a "tension" between doom and hope conditioned upon the people's response, and a "planned ambiguity" regarding the fate of those addressed.[128]

This does not mean, however, that the threat of judgment is merely an *Argumentationsmittel*. Barring repentance, they will surely die,[129] referring to premature death for the individual and premature extinction on the collective level, and connoting being cut off from Yahweh's favor and protection within the covenant.[130] On the other hand, Ezekiel's *aim* is clearly to move the wayward to repentance and thus to life, so that the motif functions within this larger context *both* as a threat of imminent divine punishment and as a motivation to the errant to save themselves by repentance.

This text gives further insight into the theological content of the motif. While quite a number of various sins or righteous acts are listed, no single one of them is viewed as bringing judgment or vindication.[131] Rather, *together* they mark an individual as "wicked," as "one who sins"; or as "righteous," that is, as one who "follows my statutes and is careful to observe my ordinances, acting faithfully – such a one is righteous" (verse 9). Thus, once again, the divine judgment has as its criterion the life of an individual (or group) seen as a whole. "Ezekiel does not consider

---

[127] T. M. Raitt, "The Prophetic Summons to Repentance," *ZAW* 83 (1971), 30–49. Cf. Amos 5:4–5; Zech. 1:2–6.

[128] Ibid., 33.

[129] "Why will you die, O house of Israel?" verse 31b. See also verses 4b, 13b, 18, 20a, 24b, 26b.

[130] See L. Wächter, *Der Tod im Alten Testament* (Arbeiten zur Theologie II/8; Stuttgart: Calwer, 1967), esp. 205.

[131] See esp. verses 5–9, 11–13, 15–17.

here the case of the person who commits only minor sins or only one serious crime.... For the sake of clear and consistent casuistic reasoning, he is considering persons as totally good or as totally evil at the moment of their judgment. There is no calculation of how much good or how much evil anyone has done."[132]

But this also means, as is evident in this passage, that the verdict is not a future eventuality currently unknowable to the individual. The identification of the wicked and the righteous is outlined in this chapter in a way that allows Ezekiel, and presumably his hearers, to recognize who is who right now. At issue, therefore, in this judgment, is not so much a verdict, nor even the sentence, but the *execution* of the same, resulting in life or death. This judgment according to deeds does not carry a note of uncertainty with regard to the verdict or sentence, as if one were anxiously waiting to discover whether one is to be considered by God righteous or wicked. Any anxiety it may occasion is caused more by the certainty of its execution than uncertainty as to the verdict.

Finally, this text also reveals that the works which identify one as righteous or wicked are not necessarily the sum of *all* one's deeds in a lifetime. To repent and change one's ways is tantamount to "getting a new heart and a new spirit" (verse 31) and results in one's previous deeds no longer being "remembered" in judgment (verses 22, 24), i.e., they will no longer be considered.

Ezekiel 33:20

Ezekiel 33:20 occurs in a context almost identical to that outlined for chapter 18 above. The exiled people of Israel, burdened under their sins, see no hope in Yahweh ("How then can we live?" verse 10) and question his justice (verses 17, 20). "It is not fair: is God so unjust as either to overlook earlier moral commitment ... or to welcome back diehard sinners?"[133] On the pastoral front, Ezekiel must speak a message of grace promising forgiveness through repentance to those despairing of hope (verses 11, 14, 16, 19), while at the same time guarding against this message of grace being misused to promote moral indifference and a false sense of security (verses 12b–13, 18).

The prophetic word closes with the motif of judgment according

[132] W. H. Brownlee, *Ezekiel 1–19* (WBC 28; Waco, TX: Word, 1986), 290.
[133] L. C. Allen, *Ezekiel 20–48* (WBC 29; Dallas, TX: Word, 1990), 146.

to deeds, demonstrating once again its remarkable flexibility, functioning here simultaneously as warning, summons, encouragement, and justification.

> I will judge you, each one, according to his/her ways.
>
> [איש כדרכיו אשפוט אחכם]
>
> [ἕκαστον ἐν ταῖς ὁδοῖς[134] αὐτοῦ κρινῶ ὑμᾶς.]

Particularly as a warning and summons to repentance, this passage shows much similarity to Paul's employment of the motif in Romans 2. Like that text, Ezekiel 33:20 is addressed to those who "trust in their righteousness" (verse 13), summoning them to repent, and warning of a two-fold outcome in judgment in terms of "life" and "death." Without suggesting direct literary dependence, it would appear that Paul's use of the motif as a warning to the complacent and falsely self-confident people of God, who may trust in status and righteous performance, has clear prophetic precedent.

Summary

The motif of divine recompense according to deeds is widespread within the writings and the prophets of the Jewish Scriptures. Its absence from the Pentateuch may be coincidental, or it may indeed be present *in nuce* through the *lex talionis* and other correspondence patterns which were its predecessors.

In addition, the motif could be made to function in a great variety of ways: as praise or justification of God, as comfort for the righteous, or as warning to the disobedient (both within and without the covenant community). This widespread and varied usage counsels against insisting on linking Paul's use to any single scriptural text, unless there is unambiguous evidence for such. Rather, it should occasion no surprise to find in Paul "echoes of Scripture" as he draws from the "storeroom of materials" available to one steeped in biblical tradition.

This widespread use of the motif along with its flexible application to a broad range of rhetorical situations also suggests that divine recompense according to deeds has already become in the OT an important theological axiom for Judaism. Thus, the varying situation of the hearers can call forth varying applications and formulations. Especially when confronted with the wayward people

---

[134] Several MSS read κατὰ τὰ ὁδούς (Codex A, Lucian, Syrian).

of God, whose deeds are beginning to mark them as disloyal to God and his covenant, the motif assumes a hortatory function, motivating to (renewed) obedience via encouragement of reward and warning of punishment. In more extreme cases this assumes the form of a summons to repentance. The application as a warning to the errant and presumptuous people of God is the major function of the motif in this literature. Where God determines that the boundary between faith and apostasy has been crossed, the motif expresses the divine sentence of wrath. I also noted the association of this motif with others which illuminate how it was understood. Divine recompense according to deeds deals with the heart (Prov. 24:12), and with hidden deeds (Eccl. 12:14; Sir. 17:15, 19–20) which will be revealed (Sir. 11:26–27). Further, God's omniscience (Prov. 24:12) assures that "every deed both good and evil" will be included in this judgment (Eccles. 12:14). Although "*judgment* according to deeds" is not as frequently attested as "*recompense*," it is firmly established within the Jewish Scriptures as an equivalent formulation. However, the rather late development of an eschatological perspective, noticeable mainly in the prophets and the LXX, means that such a judgment should not at this stage be confused with the later apocalyptic judgment scenarios.

Since this study is concerned to discover whether Paul's particular way of relating justification and judgment may have antecedents in his Jewish background,[135] the question may be posed: How do the Jewish Scriptures relate salvation to recompense according to deeds? The exegetical observations above have suggested that divine recompense according to deeds functions within the general pattern of soteriology found in the Jewish Scriptures.[136] The invitation to, and the provision for, life within God's covenant

---

[135] For a position opposite to that argued here, see H. Braun, *Gerichtsgedanke und Rechtfertigungslehre*, 6–8. He characterizes OT religion as collective (versus individual), this-worldly, and legalistic.

[136] The depiction of OT soteriology in this section follows Eichrodt's analysis in his *Theology of the Old Testament*. There has been, and continues to be, considerable debate as to whether there exists any "center" of OT theology, and just what that "center" might be (cf. D. G. Spriggs, *Two Old Testament Theologies: A Comparative Evaluation of the Contributions of Eichrodt and von Rad to our Understanding of the Nature of Old Testament Theology* [SBT 2nd. ser., 30; London: SCM, 1974]; J. Goldingay, *Theological Diversity and the Authority of the Old Testament* [Grand Rapids: Eerdmans, 1987]; G. Hasel, *Old Testament Theology: Basic Issues in the Current Debate* [4th edn.; Grand Rapids: Eerdmans, 1991]). However, as for Eichrodt's description of the fundamental relationship between Yahweh and Israel in terms of "covenant," there seems to be less debate (cf. Spriggs cited above, esp. 11–33).

favor and protection (= *salvation*) proceeds solely from God's grace. However, as would be natural in an ancient Near Eastern covenant arrangement, entry into and continuance in this gracious covenantal relationship requires walking in God's *ways*. This was not seen as *earning*[137] a covenant status one did not yet have, but as the only proper response of love and trust in the covenant God who had already bestowed life in fullness. One's works of obedience are not viewed as *merits*, each to be recompensed in atomistic fashion, but instead are the observable manifestations of the covenant loyalty of the unseen heart.[138] One's deeds are thus viewed as a unity, the *way* upon which one is going. It is this *way*, the *work of one's hands*, which normally forms the basis or standard for the divine recompense. Behavior demonstrating a fundamental inward disposition of covenant loyalty brings promise of continued partici- pation in the covenant blessings; consistently disloyal behavior – the curses of the covenant. The requisite obedience (righteousness) was never viewed as *flawless perfection*, but might be better described by such terms as *consistency*, *integrity*, and *authenticity* of action.[139] A radical understanding of retribution, whereby *all* one's deeds without exception are brought together and judged by weighing good against evil deeds does not characterize the OT. Mercy could be applied as God determined, and repentance could bring a new beginning, a clean slate as it were. Provision was made for occasional failure,[140] and divine patience provided for correc- tive chastisement upon the seriously wayward to bring them to repentance and a renewed commitment to God's *way*.

Nevertheless, the threat of divine retribution remains a real one, for both the elect nation and for groups or individuals within the covenant community. For those whose *ways* consistently reveal unbelief and disloyalty, who presume upon covenant lovingkind- ness, "throw off the yoke," and are unrighteous, there awaits as repayment only wrath, anger, destruction, and death. Or expressed

---

[137] Though even the economic language of "earning" could be employed in this context (Ruth 2:12; Prov. 19:17).

[138] Note Jeremiah 17 (pp. 50–51 above) where works manifest one's faith, and such unseen matters form the basis of divine judgment.

[139] On "perfection" in the OT, see H. K. La Rondelle, *Perfection and Perfec- tionism: A Dogmatic-ethical Study of Biblical Perfection and Phenomenal Perfec- tionism* (Andrews University Monographs 3; Berrien Springs, MI: Andrews University Press, 1971), 51–158.

[140] On "atonement" and "forgiveness" see Eichrodt, *Theology of the Old Testa- ment*, II.443–483.

in other terms, apostasy is possible, and will be punished with God's wrath and the loss of covenantal blessings (= salvation).[141] Yet in spite of its reality, the boundary between apostasy and fidelity is nowhere legislated in unambiguous fashion, since it is a matter not of legal boundaries but of the human heart and of sovereign divine freedom. Hence questions as to the quantity of transgressions necessary to activate God's wrath are pointless. The sinner cannot check in any legal code to determine his/her status with God.

In short, these texts suggest a soteriology fully committed to the centrality of divine grace, yet stressing equally and without contradiction or tension the necessity of human obedience.[142] Salvation, while not earned by human righteousness, is certainly not undemanding in regards to the same. Righteousness is both a status to be received by grace, and a behavior to be maintained.[143] This dynamic understanding of righteousness will have to be kept in mind when studying subsequent Jewish material so as to avoid a too-facile charge of synergism. Thus, overlooking for the moment the eschatological and christological differences, a dialectic of salvation/judgment, already/not yet, grace/works is present in the Jewish Scriptures. Having said this, however, it is good to remind ourselves that these same Scriptures present us not primarily with a system of retribution – a set of principles by which one can always ascertain or predict God's (re)action – but with a living and personal God whose freedom to forgive, as well as to destroy, cannot be subjugated to any doctrine of retribution.

---

[141] See Eichrodt, "Covenant-Breaking and Judgment," ibid., I.457–471.

[142] Far from tension, one's deeds can bring assurance of salvation.

[143] Thus, "usually the forensic and ethical (i.e., status and behaviour) are inseparable" (J. A. Ziesler, *The Meaning of Righteousness in Paul*, 43).

2

THE USE OF THE MOTIF IN THE OLD TESTAMENT PSEUDEPIGRAPHA

Earlier studies of Jewish theology in the so-called intertestamental period generally drew upon tannaitic and pseudepigraphical sources indiscriminately, seeking to present a composite position. This approach falsely assumed that later rabbinic traditions accurately portrayed "normative" Judaism in the first century CE.[1] Instead, it is now generally recognized that Judaism of the first century was a religion encompassing much more creative variety than the later rabbis might suggest. The OT Pseudepigrapha are a major documentary source of Jewish thought for the period 200 BCE to 100 CE, and thus for the NT era.

A complete listing of passages is found in Appendix II. The relevant texts are conveniently collected in *The Old Testament Pseudepigrapha* edited by James H. Charlesworth,[2] whose translations are used below unless otherwise indicated. Within this corpus I have limited attention to those works which may be considered Jewish and may be dated no later than the end of the first century CE.[3]

In addition to offering an exegesis of texts containing the recompense motif, they will be placed within their respective rhetorical and theological contexts through a discussion of the

---

[1] Representative of this older approach are P. Volz, *Die Eschatologie der jüdischen Gemeinde* (Hildesheim: Georg Olms Verlagsbuchhandlung, 1966; repr. of *Jüdische Eschatologie von Daniel bis Akiba* [2nd edn.; Tübingen: J. C. B. Mohr, 1934]); and Bousset and Gressmann, *Die Religion des Judentums*. For criticism see J. Neusner, "The Use of the Later Rabbinic Evidence" in Scott Green, ed., *Approaches to Ancient Judaism*, II.43–63; and K. Müller, "Zur Datierung rabbinischer Aussagen" in Merklein, ed., *Neues Testament und Ethik*, 551–587.

[2] 2 vols; New York: Doubleday, 1983 (hereafter *OTP*).

[3] See J. H. Charlesworth, *The Old Testament Pseudepigrapha and the New Testament* (SNTSMS 54; Cambridge: Cambridge University Press, 1985), 41–44. The Testament of the Twelve Patriarchs, though often used by others as background material for the NT, is considered by Charlesworth too questionable as a pre-Christian Jewish source.

soteriology and doctrine of judgment in each document considered. Of particular interest will be the following questions. Do we note any development or change in the use of the motif in this period? Has the wording been modified? Are the same functions in evidence as in the OT? Is there a diminishing application to Israel and a correspondingly greater emphasis on the condemnation of the Gentiles? How is divine recompense/judgment according to deeds related to the salvation or damnation of Jews? Do we find tendencies toward an atomization of deeds, toward a more legalistic, perfectionistic conception of righteousness? Does the covenant still form the basis of soteriological thought? How is this all related to the Torah?

Jubilees

Jubilees 5:11

Composed in Palestine in the mid-second century BCE, this work is probably from the Hasidic or Essene branch of Judaism but prior to the establishment of the Qumran sect.[4] Chapter five is a retelling of the biblical Flood account, intertwined with the story of the imprisonment of the Watchers and the punishment of their children. As a conclusion to this account, the motif is cited (verse 11) to explain or justify God's action. This particular judgment is ultimately prototypical of the future universal judgment (verses 13–16) which is likewise according to deeds (see on verse 15 below). In its role as a model of the future judgment, verse 11 functions also as a warning to motivate the righteous to faithfulness.[5]

> And he wiped out every one from their places and not one of them remained whom he did not judge according to all his wickedness.[6]

---

[4] O. S. Wintermute (*OTP*, II.43–44). Theories of later redaction are less relevant since they uniformly view chapter 5 as original; see, for instance, G. L. Davenport, *The Eschatology of the Book of Jubilees* (SPB 20; Leiden: E. J. Brill, 1971), 10–18.

[5] This understanding of the past-tense references in verses 10–11 alleviates the need for emendation to future tenses (suggested by R. H. Charles, *The Book of Jubilees or the Little Genesis* [London: 1902], 44–45, note). Against emendation, see Davenport, *Eschatology*, 48, n. 3.

[6] The fragmentary Greek and Syriac MSS (themselves translations of a non-extant Hebrew text) do not contain Jub. 5:11, 15; thus, English translations are reliant on Ethiopic MSS.

God's punishing judgment did not overlook any of their evil deeds. As elsewhere the motif stresses the certainty and thoroughness of divine judgment according to deeds.[7] This particular judgment is preliminary to the final judgment and is non-eschatological, though it is also prototypical of the eschatological judgment.

Jubilees 5:15

Verses 12–19 focus on the new era resulting after the flood.[8] Having wiped out the corrupted angelic offspring, God "made for all his works a new and righteous nature so that they might not sin in all their nature forever, and so that they might all be righteous, each in his kind, always" (verse 12). This is not speaking of an eschatological era of sinlessness, but of a new (post-Flood) beginning for humanity with the *possibility* of righteousness.[9] Verses 13–14 speak then of the (basis of) judgment for this new generation of humanity, followed by the motif, though in a slightly different form.

> He will judge concerning every one: the great one according to his greatness and the small one according to his smallness, and each one according to his way.

Quite unusual here is the admission of differing standards of judgment according to smallness or greatness.[10] The author hints in verse 13 at differing rules of conduct for various groups of humanity (and of all creation).[11] "And the judgment of all of them [God's works] has been ordained and written in the heavenly tablets without injustice. And (if) any of them transgress from *their way* with respect to *what was ordained for them to walk in*, or if they do not walk in it, the judgment for *every (sort of) nature and every kind* has been written." Thus in verse 15 the "great" and the

---

[7] Note the inclusion of "all" in the motif and the stress on "all of them" in verses 12–19.

[8] Not "a prophecy of the new creation" (E. P. Sanders, *PPJ*, 381, n. 36). In favor of a non-eschatological interpretation, see K. Berger (*Das Buch der Jubiläen* [JSHRZ II/3; ed. W. G. Kümmel, *et al.*; Gütersloh: G. Mohn, 1981], 351, n. 12b), and n. 5 above against emendation to future tenses. This makes for a slight disturbance in the chronology of the chapter, since the destruction of corrupt humanity at the Flood must be assumed but will not be recounted until verses 19ff. (though envisioned already at verse 4).

[9] Cf. verses 17–18.

[10] Cf. also Wis. 6:6–8. See P. Volz, *Eschatologie der jüdischen Gemeinde*, 289–290.

[11] Likewise verse 12b; and 7:21. Cf. also 1QS III,15–17.

"small" each have their own standard of judgment specific to their nature, and only in this way can judgment according to deeds be "without injustice." This sounds something like Paul's argument for differing standards of judgment (upon Jews and Gentiles) in Romans 2:12–16.

Verse 14 stresses the exhaustiveness of this judgment, "there is nothing excluded."[12] This is followed in verse 16 by the motif of divine impartiality, proving God is a righteous judge for both small and great. Interestingly, verse 19 qualifies this impartiality in judgment. After mentioning the forgiveness available to repentant Israelites (verses 17–18) the author continues, "But to any who corrupted their way and their counsel before the Flood, he did not show partiality, except Noah alone, for *he showed partiality to him* for the sake of his sons, whom he saved from the waters of the Flood (and) for his sake because his heart was righteous in all of his ways just as it was commanded concerning him." This implies that the post-Flood forgiveness of errant Jews *does* amount to a certain degree of partiality on God's part toward his covenant people, since it is both contrasted with God's impartial judgment of Jew and Gentile alike before the Flood, and foreshadowed in the partiality shown to Noah. The condition of repentance, however, preserves this partiality from being viewed as unfair favoritism.

Within the larger rhetorical thrust of the chapter this use of the judgment motif functions as a warning intended to motivate faithful obedience to the way which God has ordained for each of his works. Such obedience is viewed as entirely within human capability due to the post-Flood renewal which brought to each "a new and righteous nature" (verse 12). The author's implicit assumption in verses 12–16 is that both the demand of obedience and the warning of eschatological judgment apply equally to the Gentiles ("all his works," verse 12).[13] However, this remains only implicit, since his real concern is with Jewish faithfulness.

In any case divine mercy in judgment consists here in the forgiveness of sins *for the repentant Israelite*. "If they return to him in righteousness, he will forgive all of their sins and he will pardon all of their transgressions" (5:17–18). Judgment according to deeds demands not perfect obedience but covenant faithfulness, including

---

[12] I.e., "from liability before the judgment mentioned in vs. 13" (O. S. Wintermute, *OTP*, II.65, n. *e*).

[13] Cf. Davenport, *Eschatology*, 49. On the attitude of the rest of the book of Jubilees towards Gentiles, see Sanders, *PPJ*, 374–375.

turning back to God's path when one has strayed.[14] Although the precise result of this judgment for unrepentant Israelites is not detailed in verses 12–16, the implication of verses 17–18 is that they will not experience divine mercy and forgiveness, but instead will join the Watcher angels and their offspring in the "judgment to be executed upon all of those who corrupted their ways and their deeds before the Lord" (verse 10). The exclusion of faithless members of the covenant from the promised blessings is a theme recurring throughout the book.[15]

Judgment and salvation in Jubilees

Thus, judgment according to one's way concerns fundamentally one's adherence to the covenant and commandments of God. In it God "executes judgment with all who transgress his commandments and despise his covenant" (21:4b). Specific transgressions are certainly in view; yet it is not individual sins, atomistically conceived, which merit judgment, but rather the underlying turning from God and rejection of his covenant.[16] Forgiveness of sins and mercy are necessary to salvation, with condemnation in judgment limited to those who "corrupt their way" and do not "return from all their error." In spite of some language which might suggest a certain moral perfectionism in the book, the righteous are those in Israel who consistently (but not necessarily perfectly) observe the covenant and commands of God. In this covenantal sense, some sins are so flagrant that they can be termed mortal, excluding all possibility of repentance and forgiveness.[17] The motif is not used in Jubilees in reference to a rewarding judgment for righteousness. Rather it always has the punishment of the disobedient in view.

---

[14] Sanders, *PPJ*, 375–380.

[15] Cf. 2:27; 6:12–14; 15:32–34; 21:21–24 ("mortal sin," verse 22); 30:21–23; 36:9–11 ("eternal reproach and execration and wrath and torment and indignation" on the Israelite who "desires to harm his brother"); 41:26. See further Davenport, *Eschatology*, 77–79.

[16] On the centrality of the "covenant" to Jubilees, see J. C. Endres, *Biblical Interpretation in the Book of Jubilees* (CBQMS 18; Washington DC: 1987), esp. 226–233. This covenantal view stands against an older scholarly tradition which saw in this document "the glorification of legalistic Judaism" (R. H. Charles, *Eschatology: The Doctrine of a Future Life in Israel, Judaism and Christianity (A Critical History)* [New York: Schocken Books, 1963 (orig. 1899)], 236).

[17] Cf. 21:22; also 2:27; 6:12; 30:7; 33:13, 18 ("let them not commit a sin worthy of death"); 36:8–11; 49:8–9. On the other hand, sins of ignorance can be forgiven (22:14). See further, Sanders, *PPJ*, 368–370; and on righteousness in Jubilees, 380–383.

1 Enoch[18]

1 Enoch is preoccupied with "the great day of judgment" (or "day of great judgment").[19] Charles, in fact, found four differing ideas of judgment in this composite work.[20] A thoroughgoing systematization of the various eschatologies of judgment has not been achieved, which is not surprising in the light of 1 Enoch's composite nature. Often this is an eschatological and universal judgment upon every individual, involving the transformation of earth and heaven.[21] At some points, however, the judgment is viewed as destruction wreaked by the righteous themselves upon the wicked at the end of the age, or prior to the messianic kingdom.[22] The righteous, or elect, who have suffered injustice during earthly existence, may expect eternal life as a result of divine mercy in judgment.[23] In fact, it is the general pattern in Enoch that the righteous may expect mercy and no judgment, whereas the wicked experience judgment with no mercy at all.[24] As Sanders notes, "While the righteous are also said to be recompensed in the final judgment for their labours (103.3), the author characteristically thinks that the reward of the righteous in the resurrection will not be earned by works, but be given by the mercy of God; even the righteous man's continuing uprightness in the new life will be by grace."[25]

Thus, although the righteous are certainly characterized as such by their righteous conduct, and their salvation is manifestly related

[18] In spite of its composite nature, there is now general agreement that all the individual sections (excepting the Similitudes, chapters 37–71) are Jewish and pre-date Christian times. The Similitudes are not critical to this study, and are variously assigned anywhere from the first to the fourth century CE (E. Isaac, "Enoch," in *OTP*, I.6–7).

[19] 10:7; 22:11; 25:4; 54:6; 62:3 ("that day"); 84:4; 91:15; 94:9; 98:10 ("day of destruction"); 99:15; 100:4; 104:5.

[20] *The Book of Enoch or 1 Enoch* (rev. ed.; Jerusalem: Makor, 1912) 84, footnote on 45:2. S. Aalen notes that in addition to 1 Enoch, a *two-stage judgment* (i.e., both an immediately post-mortem *and* a final universal judgment) can be found in Wis. 4:7; 3:3; 3:1; 4:19 ("St. Luke's Gospel and 1 Enoch," *NTS* 13 [1966], 6–9).

[21] 10:12; 16:1; 22:4, 8; 25:4; 27:2; 45:4–5; 72:1; [83:7]; 91:9, [14], 15, 16; 97:5; 103:8 (post-mortem); 104:5. In addition to Charles (cited above), helpful discussions of judgment in 1 Enoch are given by E. P. Sanders, *PPJ*, 352–358, 361–362; and G. E. W. Nickelsburg, Jr., *Resurrection, Immortality, and Eternal Life in Intertestamental Judaism* (HTS 26; Cambridge: Harvard University Press, 1972), 112–130.

[22] 95:3, 7; 96:1; 98:12.

[23] 62:16; see also chap. 58.

[24] 5:5; 27:3–5; 45:6; 60:6, 25; [62:11–12]; 81:4; 94:10; 104:5; see also chap. 50.

[25] *PPJ*, 356; with reference to 92:4–5 for this last point.

to "walking in the ways of righteousness,"[26] *the clear impression is that a judgment according to deeds is not expected for them.* That judgment day is, instead, a "day of covenant for the elect" (60:6). They are resurrected and rewarded with everlasting life in the new age free of evil.[27] The reader should note here a developing dichotomy between judgment according to deeds (for sinners, including sinners within Israel) and the rewarding of the righteous by mercy.[28] Furthermore the beginnings of an individual judgment occurring immediately after death appear alongside the older conception of a last judgment upon nations or groups.[29]

The wicked of all generations are likewise removed from Sheol, but to judgment. All their deeds, even secret sins, have been recorded on tablets, and will be "revealed" in heaven, and read aloud.[30] Thus "sinners shall be judged for their sins," and their actions "weighed in a balance."[31] Hence, for 1 Enoch, the last judgment is especially "the day of tribulation and pain" *for sinners.*[32] While the language of organic consequence is not lacking, it is clearly the forensic imagery which has come to the fore by this time.[33] Yet this does not imply a formal judgment scene with the interrogation of witnesses, etc. In spite of the forensic elements, the verdict is predetermined, and the judgment consists largely in the finalizing of the sentence and execution of the punishment.[34]

1 Enoch 95:5 and 100:7

With this larger judgment context of the book now in view, the investigation turns to the only two references to the motif:

[26] 91:19; 94:1–5; 99:10.

[27] 103:3–4, 7–8; 108:11–12; see also chap. 51.

[28] Reference to a positive recompense according to deeds might be found in 103:3: "much good will be given to you in recompense for your toil" (cf. M. A. Knibb, *The Ethiopic Book of Enoch: A new edition in the light of the Aramaic Dead Sea Fragments* [vol. 2; Oxford: Clarendon, 1978], 240). However, the wording is suspect ("replacement," not "recompense" [L. Goldschmidt, *Das Buch Henoch: aus dem Aethiopischen in die ürsprünglich hebräische Abfassungssprache* (Berlin: Richard Heinrich, 1892) 67]), as is the text (omitted in the Greek MSS [C. Bonner, *The Last Chapters of Enoch in Greek* (SD 8; London: Christophers, 1937), 64]).

[29] See Bousset and Gressmann, *Die Religion des Judentums*, 293–294.

[30] 49:4; 61:9; 81:2; 97:6–7; 98:6–8; 104:7; cf. also 96:4: "hearts reprimand" sinners as a "witness against you, as a record of your evil deeds" (= conscience; cf. Rom. 2:14–15).

[31] 38:1; 41:1; 61:8; 63:9; 95:4.

[32] 54:6; 55:3; 96:2.

[33] 90:23–24.

[34] Reiser, *Jesus and Judgment*, 50–69.

> Woe unto you who reward evil to your neighbors!
> For you shall be rewarded in accordance with your deeds.
>
> (95:5)

> Woe unto you, sinners, when you oppress the righteous
>   ones, in the day of hard anguish, and burn them with
>   fire!
> You shall be recompensed according to your deeds.[35]
>
> (100:7)

Although both verses constitute a sentence of judgment upon sinners, it is commonly acknowledged that the "announcement of the sinners' judgment is given as a reason for the righteous to 'fear not',"[36] just as the announcement of the reward of the righteous comforts them and encourages endurance (104:2). This primary intent to comfort and encourage the righteous may help to explain why in 1 Enoch, as well as in Jewish apocalyptic literature generally, judgment according to works focuses primarily on punishment for the wicked while proclaiming mercy to the righteous. It is not so much the correction of the errant, but solace for the suffering which prompts these statements.[37]

Reference in both instances is to the final eschatological punishment of the wicked, perhaps carried out by the righteous themselves (95:3). While heathen oppressors are undoubtedly included, there are clear indications that the wicked *within Israel* are equally the objects of this damnation. It is because of their mistreatment of their "neighbors" (95:5; also 99:11, 15) and "honored brother" (100:2) that they are recompensed by God. Their Jewishness is further confirmed by the fact that they "alter the words of truth" and "pervert the eternal law (v.l. "covenant")" (99:2).[38]

Yet, as in the OT, it is not individual transgressions *per se* which cause these apostate Israelites to experience God's damnation. Rather, the deeds manifest that they are "wicked in [their] hearts"

---

[35] Isaac's MS *A* reads: "Their deeds shall be recompensed."

[36] G. W. E. Nickelsburg, "The Apocalyptic Message of 1 Enoch 92–105," *CBQ* 39 (1977), 312; cf. 95:3, 5; 96:1; 97:1.

[37] The issue of the sins of the righteous and the necessary repentance from such is touched upon (5:8), but remains peripheral to the document's central concern. See J. C. VanderKam, *Enoch and the Growth of an Apocalyptic Tradition* (CBQMS 16; Washington DC: Catholic Biblical Association of America, 1984), 173.

[38] Cf. also 46:7b-8. Sanders identifies "sinners" as both apostate Israelites (collaborators) and Gentile oppressors (*PPJ*, 352–354); cf. also Volz, *Eschatologie der jüdischen Gemeinde*, 18–19.

(104:9) and "do not fear the Most High" (101:9), while those who
are accounted righteous fear God and "walk in the path of his
righteousness" (99:10; 101:1).[39] It would appear that the use of the
motif to threaten fundamentally disloyal members of the covenant
community with ultimate destruction was very much alive just prior
to the common era. Yet while acknowledging this fact, one should
also note that this is not, strictly speaking, an individual judgment,
but the sentencing and punishment of a group ("sinners") for the
comfort and encouragement of the righteous.

In spite of the centrality of the judgment theme in this book, the
recompense motif occurs only rarely. It was apparently one among
many prophetic and wisdom motifs which the apocalyptic writer,
as a compiler of existing traditins, used in the attempt to provide a
necessary eschatological framework to his ethical exhortation, since
he saw no more improvement of the lot of the righteous in this
life.[40] Its use is, perhaps, motivated in part by the attitude of the
"sinners" who fear no recompense after death. "As we die, so do
the righteous die. *What then have they gained by their deeds?*
Behold, like us they died in grief and in darkness, and *what have
they more than we?* From now on we have become equal. What will
they receive or what will they see forever?" (102:6b-8b; also 104:7)

Unfortunately the two motif passages are not extant in their
Hebrew or Aramaic form, and only 100:7 is found in a single Greek
translation: ὅτι κομιεῖσθε κατὰ τὰ ἔργα ὑμῶν.[41] The use of
κομιεῖσθε [receive (back); i.e., one's pay, wages, or reward] occurs
here for the first time in the motif, but will become more common
in the NT.[42] In both instances of the motif the correspondence
pattern is emphasized, bringing assurance to the godly (and
warning to the wicked) that the wickedness of the wicked will not
be forgotten as the latter assume, but repaid in kind.[43] This note of
the *certainty* of recompense is further reinforced in 100:10: "And
now, do know that your deeds shall be investigated." The certainty

---

[39] On the unity of deeds and faith in 1 Enoch, see C. Münchow, *Ethik und Eschatologie: Ein Beitrag zum Verständnis der frühjüdischen Apokalyptik mit einem Ausblick auf das Neue Testament* (Göttingen: Vandenhoeck & Ruprecht, 1981), 34.
[40] Ibid., 41–42.
[41] Greek text from M. Black, *Apocalypsis Henochi Graece* (Leiden: E. J. Brill, 1970), 40; see also C. Bonner, *The Last Chapters of Enoch in Greek*, 51.
[42] Cf. 2 Cor. 5:10; Col. 3:25; Eph. 6:8 (alternate form: κομίζω). BAGD (442) suggests μισθόν as the understood subject in 1 En. 100:7; but see my comments on the meaning of this verb in 2 Cor. 5:10 (pp. 262–263).
[43] 95:5, 7; 100:7, 9.

of eschatological recompense is meant to restore the courage of the righteous in a violent situation which threatens their confidence in an orderly and just world.[44]

The Psalms of Solomon

Judgment and salvation in the Psalms of Solomon: an overview

God's *righteous judgments* are praised throughout these psalms.[45] Although this judgment can be worked out in this world and life (e.g., 4:14–22), it is more commonly conceived of in eschatological terms, leading to eternal life for the righteous and eternal destruction for sinners and hypocrites, and taking place on a universal scale.[46] One striking thing about this doctrine of judgment is its thoroughgoing covenantal background, and the centrality of chastisement or discipline as the lot of God's people.[47] Israel cannot ultimately be rejected in God's judgment (7:8), something which is grounded in God's eternal covenant with her.[48] Although a certain universalistic tendency is to be noted,[49] it is clear that faithful Israelites are treated differently than others, and this can be summed up in the words *mercy* and *discipline*. The Psalms of Solomon repeatedly stress God's mercy upon those who fear him, love him, obey him, and endure his discipline.[50] While such mercy can be understood as cleansing and forgiving, it is most commonly seen as corrective discipline

---

[44] See Kuck's depiction of the *Sitz* of 1 En. 1–36 (*Judgment and Community Conflict*, 71).

[45] E.g., 2:10; 5:1; 8:8, 24; 9:2.

[46] 2:31; 3:11, 12; 8:24; 9:2; 13:11; 15:10–13.

[47] Cf. G. Maier, *Mensch und freier Wille: Nach den jüdischen Religionsparteien zwischen Ben Sira und Paulus* (WUNT 12; Tübingen: J. C. B. Mohr, 1971), 320–324; and J. Schüpphaus, *Die Psalmen Salomos: Ein Zeugnis Jerusalemer Theologie und Frömmigkeit in der Mitte des vorchristlichen Jahrhunderts* (ALGHJ 7; Leiden: E. J. Brill, 1977), 83–107.

[48] 9:8–11; 10:4; 18:3.

[49] 5:15; 17:34b.

[50] 2:33; 4:25; 6:6; 7:6, 10; 8:27; 10:3; 13:12; 14:9; 15:13; 16:15; 18:5, 9. Braun finds two kinds of mercy – one undeserved and one earned – but he ignores the covenantal context of the statements and thus theorizes a false dialectic between grace and works ("Vom Erbarmen Gottes über den Gerechten: Zur Theologie der Psalmen Salomos," *Gesammelte Studien zum Neuen Testament und seiner Umwelt* [3rd edn.; Tübingen: J. C. B. Mohr, 1971], 8–69, esp. 18–35).

preempting condemning judgment.[51] By acceptance of such discipline upon their unintentional sins, the errant are brought back into the way of the Lord, their purity is restored or maintained, and they thus "prove God's judgments right."[52] Thus, for the devout, the day of judgment is in fact the "day of mercy."[53] The righteous are those who maintain faithful obedience to God's gracious covenant with Israel, though such obedience is nowhere understood as flawless perfection.[54] While judgment is expressly "according to deeds," this is not conceived as a legalistic measuring of merit, but such deeds *confirm* or *deny* one's status vis-à-vis God; they do not *create* such status.

By contrast, sinners will be punished without mercy, according to their actions. This applies in these psalms especially to the hypocrites and sinners *within* the covenant people, who reject discipline and depart from God's ways.[55] Even their secret sins will be exposed when they are "condemned by the thoughts of their hearts."[56] The hypocrites differ from the others in the nation, in that their sins are intentional and are of a fundamental nature, amounting to rejection of the commandments.[57] Thus their punishment is ultimate and eternal and amounts to exclusion from the elect's salvation.[58] Maier is probably correct that there is no resurrection unto judgment in the Psalms of Solomon. Rather, the righteous are raised not to judgment but to eternal life, while the wicked are judged and punished without being raised bodily.[59] Interestingly, the soteriological distinction between Jewish and non-Jewish sinners is removed much as in Paul's letters.[60] Both receive the same epithets (ἁμαρτωλός, ἄνομος) and are characterized by the same inward attitudes.

The foregoing outline of soteriology in the Psalms of Solomon

---

[51] 3:4; 7:3, 9; 8:26c, 29; 9:6–7; 10:1–4; 13:7, 8–10 (sins wiped away through discipline); 14:1; 16:4, 11; 17:42; 18:4, 7–8.

[52] 2:15; 3:3, 5, 7, 8; 4:8; 8:7, 26; 9:2; 10:3; 17:26–27; 18:4b.

[53] 14:9; 18:9 (= messianic era).

[54] See Schüpphaus, *Die Psalmen Salomos*, 101–102. On the sins and imperfections of the righteous, see 3:7; 8:29; 9:4, 7; 13:5, 10; 16:1, 3; 17:5. All such sins are unintentional (3:8; 13:7; 18:4).

[55] 4:1–3, 14–22; 8:8–22. On the definition of "sinners" and "righteous," see Schüpphaus, *Die Psalmen Salomos*, 94–105.

[56] 4:5, 7, 11b; 8:8; 9:3; 14:8; 17:25b.

[57] See Sanders, *PPJ*, 396, 400–406; and Maier, *Mensch und freier Wille*, 318–319.

[58] 3:11; 13:11; 14:9; 15:13b.

[59] *Mensch und freier Wille*, 295.

[60] See esp. D. Lührmann, "Paul and the Pharisaic Tradition," *JSNT* 36 (1989), 75–94.

differs markedly from an older but still prevalent interpretation as typical legalistic Pharisaism.[61] The identification of this theology with later first-century CE Pharisaism is being increasingly challenged by scholars, and it is better to characterize this work as an expression of early Palestinian hasidism.[62]

The Psalms of Solomon 2:7, 16, 25, 34–35

The second psalm justifies God's destruction of Jerusalem (verses 1–21) and implores him now to relent (verses 22–37), and in so doing utilizes the motif several times. After noting that God "did not interfere" (i.e., to protect Israel) when Pompey destroyed Jerusalem (2:1–2), the psalmist blames Israel for this judgment: "Because the sons of Jerusalem defiled the sanctuary of the Lord" (2:3–5).

> He did (this) to them according to their sins,
> so that he abandoned them to the hands of those who
> prevailed. (2:7)
> For you have rewarded the sinners according to their actions,
> and according to their extremely wicked sins. (2:16)

Although this certainly does not spell the final rejection of Israel as God's covenant people (cf. verses 22ff.), the judgment does not seem to be corrective, but is strictly punitive.[63] This generation of Jerusalemites must be removed far from God and his mercy and their memory obliterated from the earth, that the earth might know God's righteous judgments (2:10) and God be proved right (2:15). Their disobedience is so grave (verse 16) that the psalmist classes these Israelites with the sinners, whose judgment they now must share. As was the case in the OT, the motif is here associated with divine impartiality (verse 18: "God...will not be impressed by appearances"), aimed in this case most likely at the privileged Hasmoneans to support their classification with the sinners. Thus, the motif is applied to groups within the elect nation who are cut off from God and his covenant mercy forever by a disobedience so

---

[61] A classic expression of this view was put forth by Herbert Braun, "Das Erbarmen Gottes," 8–69.

[62] For example, J. O'Dell, "The Religious Background of the Psalms of Solomon," *RevQ* 3 (1961–1962), 241–257 (earlier literature is cited on pp. 252–254); and Schüpphaus, *Die Psalmen Salomos*, 127–137.

[63] Cf. verses 4, 7b, 8a, 17b, 21.

extremely wicked that it amounts to a fundamental breaking of the covenant.

Verse 22 marks a turning point, now imploring God to judge the heathen conquerors and relent in his punishment of Jerusalem. This is not due to any repentance on Israel's part, but solely because of the evil of the heathen (2:22–23). Lest Jerusalem be finished off (verse 23b), the psalmist appeals:

> Do not delay, O God, to repay to them on (their) heads.
>
> (2:25)

Although no "deeds" are included in this formulation, it undoubtedly reflects the Hebrew phrase – "to return *one's deeds* upon one's head."[64] Possibly by this time the original sense of organic consequences is yielding to a greater focus on punishment and vengeance, and the phrase means "to bring *punishment* on their head". The recompense is recorded in verses 26–27, probably a reference to Pompey's subsequent ignominious demise, and now interpreted as "eternal destruction in dishonor" (verse 31).

A concluding summons to praise (verses 33–37) highlights the differential treatment accorded sinners and the righteous:

> Praise God, you who fear the Lord with understanding,
> for the Lord's mercy is upon those who fear him with judgment.
> To separate between the righteous and the sinner
> to repay sinners forever according to their actions
> And to have mercy on the righteous (keeping him) from the humiliation of the sinner,
> and to repay the sinner for what he has done to the righteous.   (2:33–35)

As consistently in this psalm, repayment according to deeds is applied only to sinners, whereas the righteous are dealt with according to God's mercy (verse 36). Such a differentiation is not intended as an abrogation of the principle of recompense in the case of the righteous; rather it testifies to the centrality of divine mercy and empowerment in the salvation of the faithful (verse 36). The motif itself, however, is used solely in terms of punishment, and highlights especially the justice and certainty of God's judgment of the wicked as a form of comfort for the righteous.

---

[64] השיב על רואש (Becker, *Das Heil Gottes*, 28).

Ἀποδίδωμι is the preferred verb for the motif, though not exclusively.[65]

The Psalms of Solomon 17:8–9[66]

This same justice and certainty of divine judgment is brought out in the seventeenth psalm.

> You rewarded (lit. will reward) them, O God, according to
> their sins;
> it happened to them according to their actions.
> According to their actions,[67] God showed no mercy[68] to
> them;
> he hunted down their descendants, and did not let even one
> of them go.
> The Lord is faithful in all his judgments which he makes in
> the world.   (17:8–10)

Exactly as in the second psalm, the motif refers exclusively to punishment against sinners, again the Hasmoneans who rose up against the devout (verse 5), set up an arrogant and illegitimate monarchy in Jerusalem (verses 5–6), and were then overthrown by Pompey (verse 7). Though Jews, they have no part in the "promise" (verse 5b), but are "arrogant sinners," classed with the Gentiles in contrast to the "holy people" who will be gathered

---

[65] Ἀποδίδωμι: 2:16, 25, 34, 35; 17:8. Ποιέω: 2:7. Εὑρεθῆναι: 17:8b.

[66] PssSol. 9:5c does not conform to the motif-requirements, but is almost certainly a variation of the same:

> for the Lord's righteous judgments are according to the individual and the household [τὰ γὰρ κρίματα κυρίου ἐν δικαιοσύνῃ κατ᾽ ἄνδρα καὶ οἶκον].

The unusual κατ᾽ ἄνδρα καὶ οἶκον highlights individual accountability versus corporate responsibility, as in Ezek. 18. Thus the doing of righteousness lies in the responsibility and choice of the individual (or one's "house") in contrast to the view that the individual is subject (without personal choice) to the fate of the nation. Against the more common interpretation of verses 4–5 as containing a doctrine of free will (Maier) or *Werkoptimismus* (Braun), see Schüpphaus, *Die Psalmen Salomos*, 102–104, n. 257.

[67] Phrase omitted in several Greek MSS and in the Syriac version.

[68] All the Greek MSS read ἐλεήσει (future), but this is probably a corruption prompted by the future verb in verse 8a (R. Hann, *The Manuscript History of the Psalms of Solomon* [SBLSCS 13; Chico, CA: Scholars Press, 1982], 99). Svend Holm-Nielsen favors the future reading ("Die Psalmen Salomos" in JSHRZ [eds. Werner Georg Kümmel *et al.*; Gütersloh: Gütersloher Verlagshaus G. Mohn, 1974/1977/ 1983], vol. IV *Poetische Schriften*, nos. 1–3, 99, and notes.

under the messiah (verse 26). When God repays sinners according to their sins it occurs as a merciless hunting down of the wicked which is praised in verse 10 as his "faithfulness in judgment." Both here and in psalm 2 the judgment spoken of is historical (Pompey), though it is meant to be understood as typical of eternal judgment (cf. 2:31, 35). The result is in any case the exclusion from divine grace and salvation.

Sanders notes in these psalms a tension between rewarding the righteous "according to their deeds" and "according to God's mercy."[69] And it is true, as mentioned above, that the Psalms of Solomon generally refrain from speaking of judgment or recompense upon the righteous according to their deeds.[70] However, that this hesitance is due to some *theological tension* between grace and works (so Braun) is unlikely in the light of the covenant framework of these sayings. Rather, as Sanders himself concludes, the resolution may be more psychological than theological, arising from a proper attitude of humility on the part of the righteous. "When speaking *of God*, one can say that he is a just judge who rewards and punishes in accord with fulfillment and transgression. When speaking of one's own treatment by God, however, *particularly in the form of prayer to God*, one would hesitate to attribute good treatment by God to one's own merit. Before God, man can best hope for mercy."[71]

Joseph and Aseneth

Joseph and Aseneth 28:3

The date and provenance of this work are difficult to pinpoint. It was most likely composed between 100 BCE and 135 CE, with a majority of scholars choosing an Egyptian origin. The work is clearly Jewish, with some Christian interpolations, and "enhances our knowledge of Greek-speaking Judaism around the beginning of the present era."[72] Scholars remain divided as to its purpose and audience, viewing it either as a mission document addressed to

---

[69] *PPJ*, 393.

[70] 9:5 may be the exception. Cf. Braun, "Vom Erbarmen Gottes," 36.

[71] *PPJ*, 395. See also A. Büchler's rhetorical explanation (*Types of Jewish-Palestinian Piety from 70 B.C.E to 70 C.E.* [New York: KTAV, 1968], 168, n. 1).

[72] C. Burchard, *OTP*, II.187.

potential Gentile converts, or as a means of strengthening the faith of Jews and/or Gentile believers.[73] The motif occurs only once:

> And we have wickedly committed evil (things) against you and against our brother Joseph; and the Lord repaid us according to our works.   (28:3)

This text refers to God's intervention on behalf of Aseneth against her (Jewish) oppressors. The latter take up the motif as part of their confession of sin and plea for clemency. The divine repayment consists in their swords falling from their hands before they could attack Aseneth (27:11), and thus takes place on a mundane level. From this text it is clear that the motif has not been exclusively eschatologized, but can still be used to refer to divine interventions within this world. This understanding of the event as a divine retribution in the historical sphere[74] fits in well with the general thrust of the second part of this story (chapters 22–29): God's deliverance is promised to proselytes and is demonstrated by the fact that God is with his new convert, protecting her in mortal danger.[75] Thus the motif attests that God is indeed with Aseneth, protecting her by repaying her enemies according to their evil deeds against her. This use of the motif as a piece of narrative explanation comes closest to the category of justifying God, but, in its larger context, functions as a comfort to the righteous that God will indeed be with them protecting them.

Pseudo-Philo's Biblical Antiquities (LAB)[76]

LAB 3:10

Chapter 3 is a retelling of the Flood narrative (Gen. 6–9). In recounting God's promise never again to curse the earth in this way

[73] See G. W. E. Nickelsburg, Jr., "Joseph and Aseneth," *Compendia Rerum Iudaicarum ad Novum Testamentum* 2/2 (Leiden: E. J. Brill, 1984), 69–70 (to Gentile converts); C. Burchard, *OTP*, II.195 (to Jewish readers); and R. D. Chestnutt, "The Social Setting and Purpose of Joseph and Aseneth," *JSP* 2 (1988), 21–48.

[74] On the difficult eschatological conceptions of this work, see U. Fischer, *Eschatologie und Jenseitserwartung im hellenistischen Diasporajudentum* (*BZNW* 44; Berlin: Walter de Gruyter, 1978), esp. 106–112. It is possible that Joseph and Aseneth envisions an immediate post-mortem judgment for individuals, perhaps deriving less from apocalyptic than from Hellenistic influence (see R. Bauckham, "Early Jewish Visions of Hell," *JTS* n.s. 41 [1990], 355–385).

[75] 26:2; 27:10–11. See also G. W. E. Nickelsburg, Jr., "Joseph and Aseneth," 65–71.

[76] Harrington dates the work between 135 BCE and 100 CE (*OTP*, II.299). Only Latin translations are extant.

the statement is made that the promise is valid "until the appointed times are fulfilled," leading the author to insert a brief excursus pertaining to that future time when a (final) judgment will once again take place.

> But when the years appointed for the world have been fulfilled, then the light will cease and the darkness will fade away. And I will bring the dead to life and raise up those who are sleeping from the earth. And hell will pay back its debt, and the place of perdition will return its deposit *so that I may render to each according to his works and according to the fruits of his own devices*, until[77] I judge between soul and flesh. And the world will cease, and death will be abolished, and hell will shut its mouth. And the earth will not be without progeny or sterile for those inhabiting it; and no one who has been pardoned [lit. justified] by me will be tainted. And there will be another earth and another heaven, an everlasting dwelling place.
>
> (3:10)

Here is an instance of the motif plainly set within an eschatological judgment scene taking place at the end of this age and introducing the eternal age. A general resurrection to judgment may be envisioned, reminiscent of the language of Isaiah 26:19 and Daniel 12:2 (though see below). Up to this point, the dead have been kept in "chambers";[78] whereby already a division between the righteous and the wicked had taken place. The intermediate abode of the righteous is described as "the repose of the just" (28:10) whose lot there is "eternal life...in peace" (23:13) and who resemble the stars,[79] while the wicked are kept in darkness and fire.[80] Though one cannot be certain, the first phrase, with its reference to resurrection ("I will bring the dead to life and raise up those who are sleeping from the earth"), may pertain only to the righteous,[81] while the second phrase ("hell will pay back its debt,

---

[77] Or "inasmuch as," i.e., judgment is simultaneous to recompense rather than subsequent to it. Cf. G. Stemberger, *Der Leib der Auferstehung: Studien zur Anthropologie und Eschatologie des palästinischen Judentums im neutestamentlichen Zeitalter (ca. 170 v.Ch. – 100 n.Chr.)* (AnBib 56; Rome: Biblical Institute Press, 1972), 108.

[78] 15:5; 32:13.

[79] 33:5; cf. also Dan. 12:2–3.

[80] 15:5; 16:3; 23:6; 51:5; 63:4.

[81] So also 19:12.

and the place of perdition will return its deposit") refers to the wicked only.[82]

Although it is possible that the ensuing recompense according to deeds has both the righteous and the wicked in view, and thus a dual recompense,[83] it more likely has reference only to the punishment of the wicked, since the phrase "fruits of his own devices" hints at *evil* deeds.[84] Thus the wicked are brought forth from their dark chambers for the express purpose of receiving their final recompense from God. The standard against which they are measured is elsewhere termed the "everlasting Law" (11:2). The final result of this judgment upon all the wicked is nowhere made explicit, but is surely some form of destruction since it is modeled upon the Flood-judgment (3:1–9). The righteous, on the other hand, are resurrected directly to their "immortal dwelling place" (19:12–13) on the renewed and fruitful earth (3:10b). This is the "new age" (23:8), which is "without measure" (34:3), and which belongs to those who have been "justified" by God (3:10).[85]

If LAB is primarily a piece of Jewish apologetic literature designed to resolve Bible difficulties and other misconceptions about Judaism,[86] then the purpose of this eschatological insertion (3:10) will consist in averting any sense of moral laxity which might arise from a misinterpretation of God's promise never again to destroy mankind as he had at the Flood. Thus the writer qualifies that promise by the addition, "until the appointed times are fulfilled" (3:9b). The miniature apocalypse of 3:10 highlights the need for obedience in this age in the light of the final judgment according to deeds, at which time God will once again destroy the

[82] Cf. 33:3; for this idea of "restoring the deposit," cf. also 2 Bar. 21:23; 1 En. 51:1; 4 Ezra 4:41–43.

[83] A positive recompense is envisioned in 64:7 (see below).

[84] An exact equivalent is found at Jer. 6:19: "Hear, O earth; I am going to bring disaster on this people, the fruit of their schemes [מחשבה = evil schemes]." More common in the OT was the phrase "fruit of their *practices* [מעלל/ἐπιτήδευμα]" with reference to an evil way of life (cf. Jer. 17:10; 21:14; 32:19; Mic. 7:13; cp. Isa. 3:10). See also on 4:10 below.

[85] On "justified" in 3:10, see E. Reinmuth, "Beobachtungen zum Verständnis des Gesetzes im Liber Antiquitatum Biblicarum," *JSJ* 20/2 (1989), 161–162. See also 32:17. The eschatological end is called *tempus iustificationibus* (v.l.:*iustificatis*) *suis* [the time of his justifications] (see Reiser, *Jesus and Judgment*, 110 and n. 342).

[86] See the "Prolegomenon" by Louis Feldman in M. R. James, *Biblical Antiquities* (Translations of Early Documents 1: Palestinian Jewish Texts; New York: KTAV, 1971 [orig. London: 1917]), xxxiii–xlvii.

earth as at the Flood. A concern with moral laxity is confirmed by another insertion in the middle of verse 9. After citing the promise from Genesis noted above, the author has God continue, "But [i.e., in spite of this promise] when those inhabiting the earth sin, I will judge them by famine or by the sword or by fire or by death; and there will be earthquakes, and they will be scattered to uninhabited places. But no more will I destroy the earth by the water of the flood." Thus God's promise is given two more qualifications (against possible misunderstanding); namely, (a) God will continue to judge those who sin, even destroying them by death; and (b) the promise of no further destruction refers only to the repeated destruction of the earth by flood waters, leaving the way open for a future universal destruction. For any readers, and especially Jews, who may have fallen prey to such a misunderstanding, the text functions as an exhortation, a warning against disobedience in the light of coming judgment, and an encouragement to obedience in view of the resurrection of the just.

LAB 44:10

Although the precise idiom of recompense according to deeds is not utilized in 44:10, the pronounced correspondence pattern merits comment. Concluding a lengthy expansion of the OT account of the idolatry and punishment of the Ephraimite, Micah, and his mother, the author appends a general divine warning:

> but to every man there will be such a punishment that *in whatever sin he shall have sinned, in this he will be judged.* And if they have lied before me, I will command the heaven and it will deny them rain. And if anyone wished to covet the wife of his neighbor, I will command death and it will deny them the fruit of their womb. And if they will make a false declaration in my name, I will not hear their prayers. And when the soul is separated from the body, then they will say, "Let us not mourn over these things that we suffer; but because whatever we ourselves have devised, these will we receive."

Judgment (= punishment) will correspond to the particular form of one's sin. Although this form of judgment is announced to "the race of men," it is clear that Israelites are particularly in view (44:6–8). The last phrase of verse 10 stresses that this eschatological punishment[87] will be far worse than any earthly suffering they may have experienced, and functions as a warning to the wayward.

Sin in this case is "departing from the Lord" (44:6) characterized by transgression of the Decalogue (44:6–7). Harrington notes, "At the basis of Pseudo-Philo's views on God and humanity is the biblical notion of covenant."[88] He points especially to the "Deuteronomic concept of history (sin–punishment–salvation)" which he finds at 3:9–10; 12:4; 13:10; and 19:2–5. I might add, that which excludes the individual or nation from participation in salvation in LAB is a "heart turned away from God" (25:3; 26:2), or to "depart from His name" (21:10). Perfectionistic legalism would seem to be excluded by 25:7 which teaches that confession of sin with temporal destruction *may* (though not automatically) avert eternal condemnation.

LAB 64:7

This text does not contain the motif, but has an interesting reference to the day of judgment as "the time for being rendered the reward of my deeds." The words are spoken by Samuel upon being called forth (post-mortem) by the witch of Endor; and the section is, in part, an apologetic against necromancy.[89] The viewpoint that the deceased Samuel is *awaiting* the final day of recompense corresponds with what was discovered in LAB chapter 3 about the intermediate state. The coming day does not appear to carry any tone of anxiety or terror for the righteous Samuel, who knows that on that day the final recompense of his deeds will be rewarded him. As I surmised above, this may likely be due to the belief that the righteous do not actually go through the same judgment process which awaits the wicked. Though the motif is not used, this text demonstrates that the concept of a positive recompense according to deeds for the righteous was still prevalent.

---

[87] "when the soul is separated from the body," i.e., at death. Thus the last sentence ("Let us not mourn . . .") is ostensibly being spoken by the wicked in their intermediate chambers (cf. on 3:10 above) in view of what they are yet to receive at the final judgment ("these we *will* receive").

[88] *OTP*, II.301.

[89] C. A. Brown, *No Longer Be Silent: First Century Jewish Portraits of Biblical Women* (Louisville: Westminster/John Knox, 1992), 189.

2 Baruch

Written in Palestine following the destruction of the temple in 70
CE, this work shows close acquaintance with traditions known from
later Jewish rabbinical literature.[90] Although there can be no
question of any literary influence on Paul, many of the ideas
presented were probably current in Paul's day. With the cultic
center of Judaism removed, the central concern of 2 Baruch is "the
continued efficacy of the covenant which God made with His
people through Abraham and Moses."[91] Thus, the temple and
Jerusalem are relativized by being relegated to the present, passing
age, and true Jews are now those who follow God's law.[92]

2 Baruch 54:21

The single occurrence of the motif in this work appears in Baruch's
prayer as a descriptive element of God's rule over the world.

> For at the end of the world, a retribution will be demanded
> with regard to those who have done wickedly in accor-
> dance with their wickedness, and you will glorify the
> faithful ones in accordance with their faith.   (54:21)

In the light of the larger purpose of the work the intent will be to
motivate the righteous to continued faithful obedience to the Law. A
retribution will be demanded "at the end of the world" (= eschatological recompense)[93] and is understood as punishment on the wicked
"in accordance with their wickedness." Not surprisingly in this
work, the Law takes central place as the forensic norm of judgment.
The wickedness which brings eschatological judgment can be variously described as "sinning," "uncleanness" and "oppression"
which amount to "not remembering the Law," and "despising,"
"not knowing," "not loving," or "rejecting" God's Law.[94] These

---

[90] A. F. J. Klijn, *OTP*, I.616–617 (early second century CE).

[91] G. Saylor, *Have the Promises Failed? A Literary Analysis of 2 Baruch* (SBLDS
72; Chico: Scholars Press, 1984), 153.

[92] See esp. F. J. Murphy, *The Structure and Meaning of Second Baruch* (SBLDS
78; Atlanta: Scholars Press, 1985); and T. W. Willett, *Eschatology in the Theodicies
of 2 Baruch and 4 Ezra* (Journal for the Study of the Pseudepigrapha Supplement
Series 4; Sheffield: JSOT Press, 1989).

[93] 83:7; cf. also 21:8; 48:2; 54:1.

[94] 21:12; 48:38, 40, 47; 51:4; 54:14, 17. See further, C. Münchow, *Ethik und
Eschatologie*, 104–106.

last expressions of human failure, elsewhere termed "denial" (= unbelief; 59:2), caution one, however, against charging this author with some sort of externalistic legalism.[95] The same unity of internal attitude with external behavior is assumed here as in the OT.

In contrast to retribution upon the wicked, the faithful are said to be glorified "in accordance with their faith," rather than recompensed according to works. This corresponds to the same dichotomy we have noted elsewhere between judgment upon the wicked and mercy to the righteous.[96] It is not, however, evidence of any theological tension between grace and works, judgment and mercy. It is clear from verse 22 ("those who sin, you blot out among your own") that a judgment according to deeds applies equally to Israelites, making adherence to the Law the standard of recompense for Jews with the same consequences of rejection, condemnation and eternal punishment.[97] Just as the wicked exhibit a unity of unbelief and transgressions, so for the righteous faith stands not in contrast to works, but means to live according to the Law.[98] The author can say the righteous are saved "because of their works and for whom the Law is now a hope" (51:7), and can tie their future hopes to their store of good works (14:12). It is easy to see why Charles would argue that "faith" here equals *righteous behavior, a meritorious fulfillment of the law*.[99] However, "faith" in 2 Baruch is not a meritorious achievement, but consistently the inward attitude of submission and loyalty from which springs the corresponding behavior, just as in the OT.[100]

---

[95] *Pace* R. H. Charles, *The Apocalypse of Baruch* (London: Adam and Charles Black, 1896), lxix–lxx, lxxxi–lxxxiv.

[96] See above on PssSol. 2:34–35; 17:8–9; Jub. 5:11, 15; 1 En. 95:5; 100:7.

[97] For verse 22 as supporting such a doctrine of dual recompense, see W. Harnisch, *Verhängnis und Verheißung der Geschichte: Untersuchungen zum Zeit- und Geschichtsverständnis im 4.Buch Esra und in der syr. Baruchapokalypse* [FRLANT 97; Göttingen: Vandenhoeck & Ruprecht, 1969], 199–200.

[98] 54:5; see also 4 Ezra 6:27, 28; 9:7–8; 1 En. 47:8.

[99] R. H. Charles, *Apocalypse of Baruch*, 95, footnote. For a critique of Charles' arguments on this point, see Murphy, *Structure and Meaning*, 64–66.

[100] Note the use of the terms "faith" and "submit" in 54:4–5, which connect this passage to earlier ones (cf. 17:1–19:3; 48:19; and chaps. 41–43) in which "the recipients of God's revelatory consolation are identified as the few Jews and the proselytes who have remained loyal to their Mosaic heritage and who therefore represent 'Israel'" (Saylor, *Have the Promises Failed?*, 68). For the opposite view, that 2 Baruch is a legalistic work in contrast to the covenant theology of the OT, see Harnisch, *Verhängnis und Verheißung*, 213, 225–226.

Judgment in 2 Baruch: additional comments

Although 2 Baruch is generally less concerned with the externals and details of the judgment than with its content and criteria, it nevertheless teaches that the good works of the righteous constitute a store or treasure (14:12; 24:1), while the sins of the disobedient are recorded in books (24:1), and that even their secrets will be exposed in the judgment (83:3). Following a temporary messianic kingdom of earthly bliss[101] the souls of the righteous will be resurrected from their treasuries to their eternal rest (30:1–3; 54:16; 85:11, 15), while the wicked perish (30:4–5). Though not explicit, it is likely that 2 Baruch locates the judgment according to works following the temporary messianic kingdom rather than immediately post-mortem (30:1). The wicked are vigorously denied any hope of post-mortem repentance (85:12), whereas the righteous may expect forgiveness and pardon out of God's covenant mercy,[102] demonstrating once again that flawless obedience was not considered the necessary condition for righteousness.[103] In the attempt to redefine Judaism without its cultic center and to explain the punishment which befell the people, righteous and unrighteous alike, 2 Baruch focuses judgment upon the Jewish nation, but makes Torah-obedience the distinguishing factor cutting right through the nation. Thus, it is neither election nor external participation in the chosen nation which guarantees salvation, but (to use Paul's language) the "doers of the law will be justified."[104]

Summary

Wording and syntax

In spite of our limitation generally to English translations it has become sufficiently clear that the wording and syntax of the recompense motif in the pseudepigraphical writings continues the

---

[101] See Willett, *Eschatology in the Theodicies*, 112–118.

[102] 24:2; 75:1; 78:13; 85:8, 15.

[103] 85:2 speaks of "righteous prophets and holy men" who "trusted in their works." Whether or not this special class was credited with perfect obedience, they are contrasted with the present generation of righteous ones who need intercession and purging from their sins.

[104] Rom. 2:13. Thus, the issue of who is a *true Jew*, so evident in Paul's letter to the Romans, was very much a live one in 1st century Judaism, and 2 Baruch is in agreement with the apostle that election and national identity alone do not suffice.

OT tradition. The number of relevant texts is too small to permit far-reaching conclusions, but the following tendencies have appeared. The predominant form of the motif now includes a *standard* (*"according to..."*) rather than a direct object,[105] while passive constructions may be somewhat more common than in the OT.[106] Explicit *judgment* terminology, rare outside Ezekiel in the OT use of the motif, also occurs in these writings.[107] In fact, given the central importance of judgment conceptions to these writings, the motif might be better termed "divine *judgment* according to deeds," even where the verb is one of *repayment*.[108] Also similar to the OT usage is the easy interchange between singular and plural "deed(s)" without theological distinction.[109]

Function

All the major categories of our functional typology have been found in evidence in this literature.[110] This renders suspect a common verdict on this period; namely, that the prophetic announcement of God's judgment on Israel disappears altogether.[111] It is true that there is no occurrence of such a prophetic sentence against the nation as a whole; but 1 Enoch 95:5 and 100:7 clearly announce judgment-woes against a group of wicked Israelites, and numerous texts contain warnings which, if not heeded, are surely expected to lead to such a sentence upon the wicked *within Israel*.[112] It has been similarly thought by many that there is a diminishing use of judgment as applicable to Israel; that is, that judgment is made applicable only to the enemies of national Israel.[113] Quite the reverse is the case, since a majority of these

[105] Exceptions: PssSol. 2:25, (35).

[106] 1 En. 95:5; 100:7; PssSol. 17:8. Rare in the OT; see Obad. 15; Prov. 19:17 (LXX, v.l.).

[107] Jub. 5:11, 15; (PssSol. 9:5c).

[108] Note how often the recompense occurs within a judgment scene: 1 En. 95:5; 100:7; PssSol. 2:33–35; 17:8–10; LAB 3:10; (44:10); 2 Bar. 54:21. On the coalescing of "judgment" and "recompense according to deeds" during the intertestamental period, see Heiligenthal, *Werke als Zeichen*, 172–182.

[109] While the plural is the more common, the singular is found in PssSol. 2:35; Jub. 5:11, 15; 2 Bar. 54:21.

[110] See Appendix II. The functions as "wish/benediction" and "summons to repentance" are absent from this literature, but may be ignored since their occurrence in the OT is similarly sparse.

[111] So Kuck, *Judgment and Community Conflict*, 53.

[112] Cf. Jub. 5; PssSol. 2; 17; LAB 3:10 and comments on these texts above.

[113] So, for instance, H. Braun, *Gerichtsgedanke und Rechtfertigungslehre*, 8–11.

motif-texts have been shown to contain warnings to Israelites. In fact, and of considerable interest for Paul's use of the motif in Romans 2 and 1 Corinthians 3, we have seen repeatedly how these writers are deeply concerned to establish a distinction between the righteous and the wicked *within the nation of Israel*, and in this connection apply the motif of recompense according to deeds simultaneously to warn and to exhort.

Judgment is central in this literature[114]

Not merely one element among others, *judgment is the central issue in Jewish eschatology of this period and forms the main theme of many of its literary products.*[115] The explanation for this phenomenon will be best sought in the social-historical context of the writers and their communities, for whom the historical realm no longer held hope of improvement or justice. The coming age alone promised a reversal of the present evil reality, and the judgment constituted the central event of such a reversal.

However, this rooting of the centrality of the judgment theme in the social-historical matrix has a corresponding theological explanation. This pessimistic view of history as dominated by evil means that the fundamental issue for the apocalypses is the question of God's reassertion of power, or in language that sounds quite Pauline, the question of his righteousness. The eschatological judgment becomes, then, the centerpiece of the apocalypticist's answer. In this event God's power and righteousness are finally

---

[114] Luise Mattern's analysis of judgment in Jewish apocalyptic literature remains a good overview of the subject matter (*Das Verständnis des Gerichtes*, 9–35; she deals only with 1 Enoch, 4 Ezra, and 2 Baruch). However, her failure to understand the dynamic between faith and works in these writings leads to similar misunderstandings of Paul. She does not treat adequately the warnings of eschatological judgment according to deeds addressed to Jews, which reveal the theological relevance of such a final judgment unto salvation/damnation even for the people of God. This leads her then to an artificial distinction in Pauline statements on judgment: when judgment according to deeds deals with salvation/damnation, this excludes Christians; when it deals undeniably with Christians and their work(s), then it must be a different judgment, one dealing only with reward. Already in her treatment of Jewish apocalyptic literature one can see at work the artificial wall between faith and works which will skew her interpretation of Paul. "Salvation or damnation depends (solely!) on one's status as a 'Christian' or 'non-Christian'. The inferiority of a Christian's work cannot endanger that salvation" (110).

[115] "'Follow the law and expect the judgment.' That is, in short, the sum of Jewish piety" (Bousset and Gressmann, *Die Religion des Judentums*, 202; cf. also 192).

revealed and established. By this means, potential doubts or resignation caused by political or religious setbacks could be countered and Israel both comforted and exhorted to continued vigilance.[116]

Eschatological recompense is clearly prominent

Although divine judgment according to deeds can still be understood to operate within this historical realm as in the OT,[117] the definitive judgment according to deeds is being increasingly viewed as an event beyond or subsequent to this era.[118] Formulaic expressions such as "the great day of judgment" begin to carry a self-evident eschatological reference. This *eschatologizing* of the motif has not led, however, to any systematization of the whole concept, as evidenced by the coexistence of earthly-messianic and transcendent futures, or individual post-mortem and universal final judgments (see below).

Punishment is normally meant

> "Woe unto you, sinners, when you oppress the righteous ones, in the day of hard anguish, and burn them with fire! You shall be recompensed according to your deeds."
>
> (1 Enoch 100:7)

In fact, we found not a single instance of the motif being used to promise a positive reward to the righteous according to their deeds.[119] This does not, however, mean that there existed no belief in a retributive reward. A dual recompense is attested by LAB 64:7 and suggested by other texts.[120] Nevertheless, the consistent use of

---

[116] See Harnisch, *Verhängnis und Verheißung*, 19–88, 318–321; also P. Stuhlmacher, "Eindeutige Verkündigung," *EvT* 24 (1964), 493.

[117] Cf. JosAsen. 28:3; PssSol. 2:7, 16, 25, 34–35; 17:8–9.

[118] 1 En. 95:5; 100:7; 2 Bar. 54:21; (Jub. 5:10–11); LAB 3:10.

[119] LAB 64:7 is no exception since it does not use the motif. On 1 En. 103:3 and PssSol. 9:5c, see above, nn. 28 and 66 respectively.

[120] 2 Bar. 54:21b; PssSol. 9:5c. On the nature of "reward" in this literature, see Mattern, *Das Verständnis des Gerichtes*, 32–35; Kuck, *Judgment and Community Conflict*, 64–65, 95; and Volz, *Eschatologie der jüdischen Gemeinde*, 404–406. The idea of varying rewards for varying labor does not appear to be present, or if so, only in later texts; the reward is the eternal blessing, the heavenly paradise, eternal life.

the motif exclusively for punishment would suggest that this was its primary, if not sole, association during this period.

A dichotomy exists between the treatment of the righteous and the wicked

While the wicked are threatened with punishment according to their deeds, the righteous are promised mercy.[121] This dichotomy of treatment is further reinforced by the explicit denial to the wicked of any mercy in judgment[122] and the occasional assertion of "no judgment" at all for the righteous.[123] I noted above, however, that this contrast is not intended as an abrogation of the principle of just recompense in the case of the righteous, nor does it testify to a fundamental disharmony between grace and works in Jewish soteriology of the period. While the favorable judgment upon the righteous will indeed be according to their deeds, pious humility and a primary focus upon the fate of the wicked combined to produce an avoidance of the language of judgment according to deeds in the case of the righteous. This represents a change from the usage of the OT where the pious did not hesitate to plead their righteousness before God.[124]

Chastisement is prominent for the righteous

Although present in the OT, and developed further in the deutero-canonical writings, the idea that God's judgments upon the righteous take the form of chastisements or corrective discipline in this life becomes standard doctrine.[125]

> For the Lord will spare his devout,
> and he will wipe away their mistakes with discipline.
>
> (PssSol. 13:10)

Such temporal correction is contrasted explicitly with the fate of the wicked (verses 7, 11). These judgments are meant to turn

---

[121] See esp. PssSol. 2:34–35; 2 Bar. 54:21; also PssSol. 14:9; 18:9; 1 En. 60:6.

[122] 1 En. 5:5; 94:10; PssSol. 17:9.

[123] Cf. 1 En. 81:4 (though the MSS are confused at this point). Otherwise 1:8: "there shall be a judgment upon all, (including) the righteous."

[124] Cf. 1 Kgs. 8:32b; Ps. 18:20–24.

[125] 2 Bar. 13:8–10; 78:5–7; PssSol. 3:4; 7:9; 8:26, 29, 32; 10:1–4; 13:7–12; 14:1; 16:12–15; 18:4–5. See G. Bertram, art. παιδεύω, *TDNT*, V.603–612.

God's people from their sins and thus lead to forgiveness
(2 Baruch 13:9–10). They are part of God's mercy to his people and
preserve them from being judged according to their deeds (= punished) at the eschatological judgment.[126]

An intermediate state is prominent

In spite of great conceptual variety, it nevertheless remains generally true that these writers anticipated some sort of shadowy
existence for both the righteous and unrighteous dead during the
intermediate period.[127] For some writers this was merely a sort of
holding chamber, while for others a preliminary reward and
punishment was envisioned. In the case of righteous martyrs, both
the intermediate state and the final judgment could be bypassed,
with this special class of persons passing immediately to their
eternal reward.[128] Regardless of whether a judgment scene is
depicted in connection with this intermediate state (see the next
point), an immediate post-mortem *division* of humanity (saved/
damned) is everywhere assumed.

Both an immediate post-mortem division and a final judgment are envisioned

Logically one might expect such a post-mortem division to be
accompanied by a judgment scene, but such is only rarely the case:
"You yourselves know that they will bring your souls down to
Sheol ... Your souls shall enter into the great judgment; it shall be
a great judgment in all the generations of the world. Woe unto you,
for there is no peace for you!" (1 En. 103:7–8)
    Only around the end of the first century CE does irrefutable
evidence begin to appear of such a special judgment occurring for

---

[126] This thought is made explicit in the rabbinic literature. "He deals strictly with
the righteous, calling them to account for the few wrongs which they commit in this
world, in order to lavish bliss upon and give them a goodly reward in the world to
come" (Gen. Rab. 33:1; cited in Sanders, *PPJ*, 171).

[127] "Hence we may conclude that the universal tradition of Palestinian Judaism
always taught the doctrine of an intermediate abode for the righteous" (Charles,
Eschatology, 300). See further Volz, *Eschatologie der jüdischen Gemeinde*, 117–121,
256–271. Joseph and Aseneth seems to be the exception, since each individual enters
immediately at death into their eternal salvation.

[128] Nickelsburg, *Resurrection, Immortality, and Eternal Life*, 68–92.

each individual immediately following death and with reference to one's earthly works.[129] Prior to this it is nowhere made clear just *how* this post-mortem division and the assignment of souls to their various chambers occurs.[130]

Widely attested, on the other hand, is a last judgment, universal and introducing the age to come.[131] The preceding pages have noted at numerous points that the motif of judgment according to deeds normally occurs in such a context. There would seem to be little concern at this stage to harmonize these two conceptions, and the variety seen elsewhere regarding details of judgment is equally in evidence here. It is entirely possible that the growing emphasis on an immediate post-mortem fate is due to Hellenistic influence.[132]

Resurrection is occasionally mentioned in connection with judgment

Actually a general resurrection of all the dead unto judgment is extremely difficult to document in this literature. Only LAB 3:10 and 1 Enoch 51:2 come into question, but both admit of other interpretations.[133] In most instances, the language of resurrection is reserved for the righteous only, who are raised not to judgment, but directly to their eternal reward.[134] The wicked, on the other hand, are in some fashion brought forth from Sheol to face judgment, or proceed directly from Sheol to their eternal damnation. In 2 Baruch 85:15 this final destruction of the wicked is explicitly contrasted with the resurrection of the righteous, so that elsewhere it can be said of the wicked that after their time in Sheol they simply "the more waste away" (30:4).

---

[129] Cf. T.Abr. 12:1–18 (recension A); b.Ber. 28b. See M. Reiser, *Jesus and Judgment*, 127, 132–136, 148–150; also Bauckham, "Early Jewish Visions of Hell," 355–385.

[130] Reiser suggests that judgment occurs throughout one's lifetime, and is brought to completion at death (*Jesus and Judgment*, 148–149).

[131] See, for instance, LAB 3:10; 2 Bar. 30:1–5; 54:21; 1 En. 95:5; 100:7; Jub. 5:10.

[132] Aalen, "St. Luke's Gospel," 1–13; and U. Fischer, *Eschatologie und Jenseitserwartung*, 256–258.

[133] See above.

[134] LAB 19:12; 1 En. 103:4; 108:11–12; 2 Bar. 30:1–5; 85:15. On the Psalms of Solomon see above.

> The equality of Jewish and Gentile sinners in judgment is occasionally envisioned

Faithful Israelites receive preferential treatment from God, especially the mercies of atonement and forgiveness for unintentional transgressions. For those who have proven themselves *sinners* (i.e., who have rejected God's covenant and life according to his ways), however, judgment according to deeds applies without distinction to Jew and Gentile. Jubilees 5:12–16 applies the motif to "all [God's] works" (i.e., Jew and Gentile alike), and even suggests differing standards for various groups in order to assure impartiality. In the Psalms of Solomon Jewish sinners are treated no differently than the heathen in judgment, all being classed together as "sinners."

> The purpose of the judgment is more to reveal than to determine status

In no instance have we found the note of fearful uncertainty so often associated with judgment according to deeds in caricatures of legalistic Judaism.[135] As noted above divine judgment according to deeds usually meant punishment of the wicked and was not even applied to the righteous. For the latter it was instead a day "of mercy" or "of covenant," a day awaited without fear and at which they would receive their reward.[136] "The judgment never has the character of an examination or inquiry to determine who are the sinners and who the righteous; their separation is always presupposed."[137] Rather than being necessary to *determine* one's status as righteous or wicked before God, this judgment functions primarily to *reveal* this status publicly and to initiate the execution of the appropriate sentence. "I swear to you, sinners, by the Holy Great One, that all your evil deeds are revealed in the heavens. None of your deeds of injustice are covered and hidden" (1 En. 98:6–7).[138]

---

[135] As seen, for instance, in Bousset and Gressmann, *Die Religion des Judentums*, 392–393; also Volz, *Eschatologie der jüdischen Gemeinde*, 108–113.

[136] PssSol. 14:9; 18:9; 1 En. 60:6; LAB 64:7.

[137] Reiser, *Jesus and Judgment*, 157, cf. also 151.

[138] Cf. also 1 En. 97:6–7 where their sins will be "read aloud"; and 4 Ezra 14:35. On the revelatory nature of judgment in Jewish apocalyptic literature, see Mattern, *Verständnis des Gerichtes*, 23; and Heiligenthal, *Werke als Zeichen*, esp. 195–197, 234–264.

Such a public revealing is necessary due to the secret nature of many sins which must be exposed.[139]

But what of the imagery of "weighing deeds (or souls) in a scale" which seems to suggest a process of determining whether one is good or evil?[140] Unfortunately, older studies relied almost exclusively on rabbinic sources and assumed later rabbinic conceptions were also present in passages from Jewish apocalyptic literature. Such is not the case, and the weighing motif is actually fairly rare in this literature. Where it does occur, the image "should not be taken to imply an adding up or a weighing of individual deeds so that God may recompense men in strict proportion to their deeds, or so that he may decide their destiny according to whether good or bad deeds are more numerous ... In no instance is a *mixture* of good and bad deeds recorded and men's destiny determined by which are more numerous."[141] In 2 Baruch 41–42, in fact, there is a protest against any mechanical application of the weighing motif. "Their time will surely not be weighed exactly, and they will certainly not be judged as the scale indicates" (2 Bar. 41:6).

A collective focus is generally maintained

We have noticed no greater *individualization* of the motif than was already present in the Jewish Scriptures, although the development of an immediate post-mortem division late in the period under consideration opens the way to rabbinic teaching on a truly individual judgment. In the texts considered above, even where a single individual is in view, it is usually his/her membership in the *group* of the righteous or the wicked which is at issue. Thus, by and large one may still characterize all judgment conceptions for this period as collective.[142]

---

[139] 1 En. 49:4; 61:9; 63:3; 2 Bar. 83:3.

[140] 1 En. 41:1; 61:8; PssSol. 5:4; 2 Bar. 41:6; also 4 Ezra 3:34; T.Abr. 12:4–14; 13:10–11. Further, Volz, *Eschatologie der jüdischen Gemeinde*, 95–96, 293; and Heiligenthal, *Werke als Zeichen*, 247–270.

[141] Travis, *Christ and the Judgment*, 16. T.Abr. 12–14(A) unequivocally portrays a weighing of deeds which are balanced (12:18), and which is to lead to the determination of eternal destiny based on the majority of deeds (see Sanders, *OTP*, I.878.) However, the importance of this exception is diminished due to the probable date of composition (c. 75–125 CE), and to the possibility of late redactional activity.

[142] Only with the paraenesis of the tannaitic rabbis ("who repeatedly emphasize that at the last judgment every individual must appear before God's throne and give account of his or her life," Reiser, *Jesus and Judgment*, 161) was the preparation for a truly "individual" judgment given.

Judgment according to deeds and the soteriological pattern of the OT pseudepigraphical writings

I will seek here simply to draw together a number of threads already noted at various places above. In so doing I am cognizant of the inherent risks involved in speaking of *the soteriological pattern* of this group of writings,[143] and thus can strive at best for an outline of what seems to be more or less common to most of them.

Sanders' depiction of this soteriological pattern as *covenantal nomism* has been confirmed by my studies; namely, the "noble idea of the covenant as offered by God's grace and of obedience as the consequence of that gracious gift," and according to which "obedience maintains one's position in the covenant, but it does not earn God's grace as such."[144] I would modify this only insofar as "evidences" or "manifests" might be a better term than "maintains," since even this obedience is ultimately credited to God's mercy.[145] Earlier interpreters of this literature almost uniformly ignored or downplayed the role of the *covenant* in early Judaism, and thus placed judgment according to deeds within the context of a supposedly mechanical legalism.[146]

In reality, one's *works* are not viewed mechanically or atomistically, but are a unitary whole revealing one's inner character or

---

[143] This is due both to the great variety of eschatological conceptions, and to the unsystematic nature of much Jewish thought and writing.

[144] *PPJ*, 419–420; see 346–430 for the extended treatment of this literature. This same covenantal religion has been found by J. Schüpphaus in the Psalms of Solomon (*Die Psalmen Salomos*, 94–105), a work traditionally thought to exhibit a clear-cut Pharisaic legalism.

[145] Jub. 5:12; 1 En. 92:4–5.

[146] Even Christoph von Münchow's otherwise excellent monograph fails to consider the influence of the covenant idea on Jewish apocalyptic literature (*Ethik und Eschatologie*, esp. 154–161). For Paul, Münchow asserts, behavior is the *consequence* of one's future hope, while for apocalyptic the *condition* (154). This ignores the unity of faith and works common to both the OT and the Pseudepigrapha which makes behavior in apocalyptic writings equally a *consequence* of divine grace rather than its condition. When contrasting Paul with Jewish apocalyptic he says for the latter, "ethical conformity to the will of God is the foundation of the eschatological hope" (156). Yet when Paul lists the works of the flesh in Gal. 5:19–21 and concludes, "those who do such things will not inherit the kingdom of God," is not his eschatological hope likewise ethically founded? Von Münchow must relativize such passages in Paul by appealing to their traditional character (159), and ultimately he must relativize all judgment statements in favor of justification by faith by claiming that for Paul the judgment is no longer essential for God's saving activity (159).

faith.[147] Faith and works are not in competition with one another. Rather they represent two sides of the single coin of human response in the light of God's gracious covenantal arrangement. The "righteous" are not necessarily characterized by a *flawless* obedience, but by the proper attitude of faith and commitment, evidenced by generally consistent outward obedience.[148] Most occasional or unintentional sins would not exclude one from the covenant relationship, but could be dealt with via repentance, atonement and forgiveness. The sufferings of the righteous were sometimes viewed as divine chastisements for these sins, and usually as a stimulus to the required repentance rather than in and of themselves of atoning value.[149] Consistent, flagrant, or intentional sins demonstrated fundamental covenant disloyalty (= unbelief) and brought the threat of God's judgment according to deeds.[150] There is thus in this literature ultimately no tension or conflict between salvation by faith and divine judgment according to deeds.

Likewise grace and works, or salvation by grace and judgment according to deeds, are not felt to be in theological tension. The general avoidance of applying judgment according to deeds explicitly to the righteous can be better explained on historical and rhetorical grounds, and (theologically) because the righteous were already assured of a positive verdict in accordance with their conduct.[151]

In *Divine Sovereignty and Human Responsibility* D. A. Carson argues for a quite different pattern of soteriology in this body of

---

[147] D. Rössler, *Gesetz und Geschichte: Untersuchungen zur Theologie der jüdischen Apokalyptik und der pharisäischen Orthodoxie* (2nd edn.; WMANT 3; Neukirchen: 1962), 87, 100–105; *pace* Volz, *Eschatologie der jüdischen Gemeinde*, 95–96.

[148] I did not consider 4 Ezra since the motif is not found in this work. Sanders contends that 4 Ezra differs from the rest of the pseudepigraphical literature in that it teaches a legalistic perfectionism (*PPJ*, 409–418). On this question, see M. E. Stone, *Fourth Ezra* (Hermeneia; Minneapolis: Fortress Press, 1990), 24, 30–33; Münchow, *Ethik und Eschatologie*, 76–95; Harnisch, *Verhängnis und Verheißung*, 19–60.

[149] Against the idea of a *Leidenstheologie* in this literature (i.e., present suffering of the righteous *atones for* sins), see Mattern, *Das Verständnis des Gerichtes*, 30–31.

[150] See PssSol. 2:16.

[151] Travis attributes inconsistency to these writings in regard to retributive judgment, because (a) they extend mercy instead of strict judgment to the righteous, (b) the allowance of anything less than perfect obedience "undermines the idea of a strictly retributive recompense," and (c) the heavenly records never contain a mixture of good and bad deeds (*Christ and the Judgment*, 15–16). However, such an overly strict and mechanical view of retributive justice is foreign to the writings examined above.

literature, involving the ascendance of "merit theology," a redefinition of election based upon Israel's merit rather than divine grace, and a dilution in the value of grace and mercy so that they become merely "a kind response to merit."[152] His thesis deserves a more thorough response than I am able to provide within the scope of this book. Nevertheless, I suggest that a more rigorous attempt to understand the various texts in their unique historical and rhetorical situations might have produced different results. As one example, take his use of Psalms of Solomon 9:4 (not 9:7), supposed proof of "man's unfettered choice between good and evil ... his unrestricted capacity to obey the law and to transgress it," and thus proof that "the freedom of man is expressed more strongly in apocalyptic than in anything so far mentioned" (57).

> Our works (are) in the choosing and power of our souls,
> to do right and wrong in the works of our hands,
> and in your righteousness you oversee human beings.

I have already mentioned above that this passage is most likely *not* aimed at teaching a doctrine of free-will, but wishes to highlight *individual accountability* in contrast to the tradition that the individual is subject (without personal choice or authority) to the fate of the nation. This interpretation is confirmed by the flow of thought in the psalm: Israel's evildoing justly brought God's judgment of exile (verses 1–3); yet there is hope now if they call upon the Lord and repent, since "[their] works are in the choosing and power of [their] own souls" (verses 4–7); God's gracious covenant gives hope "when [they] turn [their] souls toward [him]," leading to the concluding benediction, "May the mercy of the Lord be upon the house of Israel forevermore" (verses 8–11). There is no stress whatsoever upon one's "unrestricted freedom," but rather upon human failure, divine mercy (offered in the face of human demerit!),[153] and individual accountability. Divine mercy is explicitly grounded in God's initiative and compassion as seen in the covenant, not in some ascending merit theology.[154]

Finally, the reader should note the nuanced way in which this

---

[152] See esp. pp. 55–74.

[153] *Pace* Carson: "it is no longer grace in defiance of demerit and rooted in the sovereign goodness of God. Rather it is a kind response to merit" (69).

[154] Carson admits the weakness of his case. "Few of the above examples in themselves would be conclusive to establish this shift in initiative [i.e., from divine to human initiative in salvation]. Moreover, it would be inaccurate to suggest that human freedom is *completely* unbounded [i.e., in this literature]" (59).

motif is applied to empirical Israel, the visible community of the saved. In the main this literature has addressed situations of collective crisis in which a consolidation or strengthening of group identity was called for.[155] To those whose behavior marked them as disloyal to the covenant relationship, the motif functions as a *warning* of impending judgment. Especially for those who might be wavering and tending toward laxity in observance of God's demands, the motif stresses the certainty, thoroughness and impartiality of this judgment as a prod to repentance. For the faithful, on the other hand, it works to encourage continued faith in God's justice and concomitant obedience to his ways.

[155] D. Kuck, *Judgment and Community Conflict*, 93–94.

3

THE USE OF THE MOTIF IN THE QUMRAN LITERATURE

It is generally agreed that Paul shows the influence of numerous traditions found represented in the Judaism of the scrolls.[1] These include such themes as salvation *sola gratia*, human sinfulness and inability, the contrast of light and darkness, and even justification (by faith).[2] Divine judgment according to deeds is another such theme, and I would suggest that apparent tensions between grace and obedience, salvation and judgment, similar to those so often felt in Paul's letters, are to be found in the Qumran documents, raising at least the possibility that Paul's "resolution" of this tension is prefigured in Judaism.

I will restrict my attention to those principal documents which are considered by most to represent the distinctive views of this community:[3]

> Manual of Discipline (Community Rule) (1QS)
> Thanksgiving Hymns (1QH)
> War Scroll (1QM)
> Damascus (or Zadokite) Document (CD)
> and the Commentaries on Habakkuk (1QpHab.) and Psalm 37 (4QpPs37).[4]

---

[1] See, for instance, H.-W. Kuhn, "The Impact of the Qumran Scrolls on the Understanding of Paul," *The Dead Sea Scrolls: Forty Years of Research* (ed. D. Dimant and U. Rappaport; STDJ 10; Leiden: E. J. Brill, 1992), 327–339.

[2] W. Grundmann, "The Teacher of Righteousness of Qumran and the Question of Justification by Faith in the Theology of the Apostle Paul," *Paul and the Dead Sea Scrolls* (ed. J. Murphy-O'Connor and J. H. Charlesworth; New York: Crossroad, 1990), 85–114 (= *RevQ* 2 [1960], 237–259).

[3] Cf. Hermann Lichtenberger, *Studien zum Menschenbild in Texten der Qumrangemeinde* (SUNT 15; Göttingen: Vandenhoeck & Ruprecht, 1980) 13–45; also M. Hengel, *Judentum und Hellenismus: Studien zu ihrer Begegnung unter besonderer Berücksichtigung Palestinas bis zur Mitte des 2.Jh.s v. Chr.* (WUNT 10; Tübingen: J. C. B. Mohr (Paul Siebeck), 1988), 407–414.

[4] 11QMelch. and the Temple Scroll contain no occurrences of the motif.

For an overview of texts and functions in the Qumran literature, see Appendix III.

My procedure and aim will be like those adopted for the study of the OT Pseudepigrapha. The motif-texts belonging to a particular document will be analyzed together and will be placed within their respective rhetorical and theological contexts through a discussion of the soteriology and doctrine of judgment in that document. We will seek evidence of development or change in the function and formulation of the motif as compared with the OT and OT Pseudepigrapha. Additionally, since we are dealing with a Jewish group that understood itself to be the true "planting" or remnant of Israel, the people of God's New Covenant in contrast to the bulk of Jews, special attention will be given to the way in which this sectarian perspective colors their use of the recompense motif.[5]

The Manual of Discipline (1QS)

The scroll recovered from Cave 1 dates to around 100 BCE with most scholars placing the original composition of 1QS between 200 and 100 BCE.[6] The document resembles later monastic "rules," and is sometimes titled "The Community Rule."

> *1QS II,7–8*
>
> Cursed be thou, without mercy,
> according to the darkness of thy deeds!
> Be thou damned (8) in the night of eternal fire!
> May God not favour thee when thou callest upon Him,
> and may He be without forgiveness to expiate thy sins!

1QS I,18–II,10 recounts the ceremony of blessing/cursing performed by the priests and Levites when someone "passes into the Covenant," i.e., enters the community. First they recount the history of God's gracious dealing with Israel *and* of Israel's constant rebellion and sin "under the dominion of Belial" (I,21–23). Following this, the initiates make their own confession

[5] Unless otherwise noted, English translations are taken from A. Dupont-Sommer, *The Essene Writings from Qumran* (trans. G. Vermes; Cleveland: World, 1962), and the Hebrew text follows that in E. Lohse, *Die Texte aus Qumran* (Darmstadt: Wissenschaftliche Buchgesellschaft, 1964).
[6] G. Vermes, *The Dead Sea Scrolls: Qumran in Perspective* (rev. ed.; Philadelphia: Fortress Press, 1981), 45–46.

of solidarity with the sinfulness (= covenant-breaking) of their forefathers (I,24–II,1; cf. also XI,9–11).[7] Interestingly for our purposes, this confession ends with the juxtaposition of divine justice and mercy: "And just is God who has fulfilled His judgment against us and against our fathers. But He extends His gracious mercy towards us for ever and ever" (II,1). That is, justice is acknowledged in bringing the curses of the broken covenant upon the nation; mercy is praised in offering a (new) covenant of grace via the sect.

The priestly blessing occurs in II,1–4, and applies to "the men of the lot of God who walk perfectly in all His ways." The "lot of God" will be contrasted in the ensuing curse with the "lot of Belial" (II,5) and demonstrates the Two-Way theology fundamental to this work. There are only two classifications of humanity, the righteous and the wicked, the elect and the damned; and two ways, that of God and of Belial (cf. IV,15). A mixture of the two ways, or a third middle group (partly righteous/partly wicked) is not envisioned. The reference to the pious as those who "walk perfectly in all His ways" is a common way of designating the community members in this work,[8] but should not be construed to imply sinlessness.[9] Furthermore, it is now no longer "Israel" who is blessed, but only those in Israel who obey the interpretation of the community. The blessing assumes human need of divine grace or assistance for proper behavior, wisdom and "eternal bliss."

The motif occurs as part of the curses (II,5–10), and thus is used only on the negative side (punishment rather than reward). As was the case with the judgment of the wicked in the OT Pseudepigrapha, the wicked are cursed "without mercy."[10] Rather than "judgment," a divine "curse" is present which takes its inspiration from Deuteronomy 27–30,[11] but has become eschatologically

---

[7] The sect believed that Israel had broken the covenant, necessitating confession by those desiring entry into the community of the new covenant. On this *Bundeserneuerungsformula* [covenant renewal], cf. K. Baltzer, *Das Bundesformular* (2nd edn.; WMANT 4; Neukirchen: Neukirchener, 1964), 58–59.

[8] I,8; II,2; III,3, 9–10; IV,22; VIII,1, 9, 10, 18, 20, 25; IX,5, 6, 8–9, 19; X,21; XI,11, 17.

[9] Community members are not free from sins; see III,21–24; (IV,20–21: fully cleansed only at the Eschaton); VI,24–VII,25; VIII,24–IX,2; X,11–12; XI,9–10, 12, 14.

[10] See also II,8, 15.

[11] See J. A. Loader, "The Model of the Priestly Blessing in 1QS," *JSJ* 14/1 (1983), 11–17.

oriented resulting in eternal damnation.[12] "Eternal" has here,
however, the more Hebraic sense of "long-lasting" rather than that
of an other-worldly eternity, and the Manual's eschatology will
ultimately have to be termed "historical eschatology" in contrast to
more transcendent alternatives.[13] The difficult final phrase in line 8
probably indicates exclusion from forgiveness, pardon and atonement, i.e., from salvation.

As to the intended objects of this curse-threat, reference to the
"lot of Belial" (II,5) seems to direct it at those who stand outside,
who do not pass into the sectarian covenant community. Yet, while
the community did expect the divine judgment to fall upon outsiders, the continuation of the curse in II,11–18 makes clear that it
is really the *hypocritical entrant*[14] who is being threatened.

> (11) And the priests and Levites shall say again: Cursed be
> he when he passes,[15] together with the idols of his heart,
> (12) who enters into this Covenant leaving before him
> whatever causes him to fall into iniquity and to turn away
> (from God)! Behold, (13) as he listens to the words of this
> Covenant, he blesses himself in his heart, saying: May
> peace be with me (14) when I walk in the stubbornness of
> my heart!

One should also note that there is no gradation of obedience or
disobedience, just as there is one blessing or curse which strikes all
equally who belong to the one group or the other. This suggests that
"according to the darkness of thy deeds" has no quantitative
nuance, but assumes the unity of human activity as seen in the OT.[16]

1QS X,11

> (10) When day comes and the night, I will enter the
> Covenant of God,

[12] II,8 (and 15).
[13] See J. Licht, "Time and Eschatology in Apocalyptic Literature and in Qumran," *JJS* 16 (1965), 177–182; and Reiser, *Jesus and Judgment*, 81–82.
[14] On this section see esp. C. Newsom, "Apocalyptic and the Discourse of the Qumran Community," *JNES* 49 (1990), 139–140. She notes "the emphatic position given to the problem of the person who would enter the covenant community hypocritically."
[15] I.e., "passes [צבר] into the covenant"; cf. I,16, 18, 19, 24; II,10.
[16] See H. Lichtenberger, *Studien zum Menschenbild*, 112–113. See also the similar phrase a few lines earlier (II,5b): "Be thou cursed in all the works of thy guilty ungodliness!" See also "the good" (I,2, 5; II,3, 24; X,18).

when night and morning depart, I will recite His precepts,
and for as long as they are, I will establish in them (11) my
   boundary so as not to turn back.[17]
I will show His judgment to be right according to my
   iniquities,[18]
my rebellions shall be before my eyes like the graven
   Decree.
But to God I will say, My righteousness!
(12) (and) to the Most High, Support of my goodness!
Source of Knowledge! Fountain of Holiness!
Infinite Glory and Might of Eternal Majesty!
I will choose whatever (13) He teaches me
and will delight in His judgment of me.

X,1–XI,22 contains a series of psalmic liturgical pieces in the first person singular, within which X,10–13a forms a discrete unit dealing with the daily renewal of one's covenant commitment. It begins (X,10) with the sectary's vow to renew constantly this commitment, to recite God's precepts, and thereby set up a fence to keep oneself within the realm of salvation. X,11 consists of a "doxology of judgment," a vow always to remind oneself that God's (condemning) judgment, even of the community member, is justly deserved, "according to my iniquities."[19] But this focus on one's own unrighteousness gives way (X,11b–12) to praise of God's righteousness ("But to God I will say, My righteousness!") as the source of human goodness, knowledge, etc. Here we see the same juxtaposing of human inability and divine grace which can be witnessed elsewhere in this literature.[20] Finally (X,13) the psalmist learns to "delight in His judgment of me," since, for the elect, even God's punitive judgments lead to their purification.

---

[17] This rendering of the last phrase is preferable to Dupont-Sommer's "establish in them my realm of no return." See P. Wernberg-Møller, *The Manual of Discipline: translated and annotated with an introduction* (STDJ 1; Grand Rapids: Eerdmans, 1957), 37; and E. Lohse, *Die Texte aus Qumran*, 36. Cf. also 1QS X,25 for similar use of גבול [boundary].

[18] Dupont-Sommer translates: "I will *pronounce my judgment* ..." However, יכה is better rendered "to prove" and has מִשְׁפָּטוֹ [his judgments] for its object (cf. E. Qimron, *The Hebrew of the Dead Sea Scrolls* [Harvard Sem. St.; Atlanta: Scholars Press, 1986], 101). The justification of God is a common theme in Jewish literature of this period.

[19] In such "doxologies" sinners confess their guilt and declare God to be righteous (cf. Lev. 26:20; Josh. 7:19; 1 Kgs. 8:33, Ezra 10:11).

[20] Outside Qumran, see Isa. 45:7; Amos 3:6; Wis. 12:12; Rom. 9:14–29. Cf. further, Becker, *Das Heil Gottes*, 115–118.

Thus, the motif functions as part of a confession of human unrighteousness, which, however, is a necessary element of the humble godly attitude toward the divine righteousness and mercy in salvation. The same is found in XI,9–11, and in X,23 ("my tongue shall ever recount the deeds of God, together with the unfaithfulness of men"). There is little "pleading of one's own righteousness" such as was seen in the canonical Psalms.

This text functions clearly as justification of God's righteous judgment, but this time directed against the elect themselves (in the Psalms and elsewhere, it was generally directed against outsiders or apostates). A pronounced sense of unworthiness and human sinfulness seems to lie behind this, and is juxtaposed with the divine righteousness. This is connected with a strong note of dependence on divine enabling and predestination, leading ultimately to the wholly submissive exclamation: "I will choose whatever He teaches me and will delight in His judgment [= guidance] of me" (X,12b–13).

1QS X,17b–18

To no man will I render the reward (18) of evil,

[לוא אשיב לאיש גמול רע]

with goodness will I pursue each one;
for judgment of all the living is with God,
and He it is who will pay to each man his reward.

[והואה ישלם לאיש גמולו]

X,17b–XI,2a deals mainly with proper attitudes toward others, both within and without the community. X,17b–18a opens this section on attitudes toward others with a commitment to do good to the one who has done personal harm, rather than taking personal revenge. Because elsewhere the sectary is exhorted to hate the wicked and the enemies,[21] some commentators have sought to emend the syntax which appears to contradict such an attitude. Thus they connect בטוב[22] [with good] with the first stanza and translate, "I will not repay evil with good, each one will I pursue."[23] Fabry, however, has brought convincing arguments

---

[21] I,3, 10; II,6; IX,21f.; X,19–20. See also Josephus, *The Jewish War*, II, §139: "He (the Essene) swears...to hate the wicked always and to fight together with the good" (quotation taken from Dupont-Sommer, *The Essene Writings*, 73, n. 3).

[22] Or לטוב which is found in the fragment of the Manual from Cave 4.

[23] K. Schubert, "Die jüdischen und judenchristlichen Sekten im Lichte des

against this translation.[24] The avoidance of personal vengeance is not so uncommon in this literature.[25] Further, this usage of divine judgment as a denial of the appropriateness of *human* retribution has been seen earlier in the OT (Prov. 24:29). The perceived tension between this rejection of personal revenge and the hatred toward the wicked found elsewhere is resolved when one recognizes that these verses are directed not at the wicked outside the community, but refer only to other community members who may have caused personal affront or harm. That it is not the wicked outside the community who are in view in lines 17b–18 is confirmed by 19b–20 which begins: "As for the multitude of the men of the Pit ...."; i.e., shifting now to the enemies of the sect. Furthermore, the other extra-canonical references to avoiding taking personal vengeance consistently refer to fellow Israelites or sect-members, not to the wicked in general.[26]

Refraining from human retribution is then grounded in the axiom of divine recompense of deeds: "He it is who will pay to each man his reward." Human (i.e., personal) retribution is improper since it encroaches upon divine prerogatives.[27] This is the one instance I can discover in the Qumran literature suggesting an acceptance of dual recompense. The language mirrors that expression familiar to the reader now from the OT and the Pseudepigrapha, whereby it is axiomatic that God will "repay" [שׁלם] to each (i.e., both good and bad) their "recompense" or "dealing" [גמול].[28] This divine repayment is called "judgment" [מׁשׁפט] in the preceding line, where also its universality is noted ("of all the living"). Since it is clear from X,19b–20 that the writer has the final day of reckoning in view, X,18 will also probably have included eschatological recompense, rather than referring only to recompense in this life.

Handschriftenfundes von En Fešcha," *ZTK* 74 (1952), 1–62, esp. 55; and H. Wildberger, "Die 'Sektenrolle' vom Toten Meer," *EvT* 13 (1953), 25–43, esp. 37.

[24] *Die Wurzel ŠÛB*, 195–196, n. 392: (a) השׁיב is never connected with its direct object by ב or ל; (b) this makes the first stanza too long; and (c) comparison with Ps. 7:5–6 makes it probable that רע was meant to end the first stanza.

[25] Cf. 1QS VII,9; CD IX,2–5; see also 2 En. 50:4; T.Gad 6:1–7; T.Jos. 18:2; T.Benj. 4:2–4; cf. further Hippolytus, *Elenchos*, IX, §23: the Essenes were required "to hate no man, neither the unjust nor the enemy, but to pray for them" (citation in Dupont-Sommer, *The Essene Writings*, 99, n. 2).

[26] See also Lev. 19:18 as the probable source of this prohibition of intra-community vengeance.

[27] Note emphatic והואה: "and *He it is* who ...."

[28] Prov. 19:17; Isa. 59:18; 66:6; PssSol. 2:35.

Having acknowledged the presupposition of a dual recompense here, however, it must be added that as rhetoric the passage is interested in only one side of this dual recompense. The argument runs against human *vengeance*. Although the motif as cited here was admittedly understood broadly in Judaism as a dual recompense, in this context the author will have intended to utilize only the punishment aspect since it is God's prerogative to *punish* the wicked which effectively prohibits human vengeance. That he may also reward the righteous is incidental to the argument.

As the theological basis against human retribution, this usage of the motif represents a new category in the functional typology.[29] Although Proverbs 24:29 likewise restricts personal vengeance and uses recompense terminology, it does not give divine retribution as the grounds for this restriction. Proverbs 20:22 roots a similar restriction in patient waiting for divine *aid*, not in retribution. Of course, the idea that vengeance belongs to God was common enough,[30] but joining it in this way with the prohibition against personal vengeance seems to have occurred first in the intertestamental period.[31] Of interest for Pauline studies, of course, is the correspondence between this passage and Romans 12:17–21.

Rom. 12:17, 19//1QS X,17b–18a   no personal repayment of evil[32]
Rom. 12:20, 21//1QS X,18   render good for evil
Rom. 12:19//1QS X,18   retribution belongs to God[33]

Conclusions

Although the idea that God will recompense according to deeds is clearly present in the passages considered above, the terminology is still variable. Alongside the familiar שלם גמול (X,18), there appears also a divine "curse according to the darkness of thy deeds" (II,7) and an instance of "proving God's judgment right according to deeds" (X,11). The motif can be applied to the punishment of the wicked (II,7) as well as to pedagogical punishments

---

[29] This usage does *motivate* to obedience, but not by a promise of reward or warning of punishment to the doer; nor does it aim primarily at *comforting* the oppressed righteous by promising the punishment of their enemies.

[30] Deut. 32:35; Ps. 94:1–3.

[31] Besides this passage, cf. CD IX,2–5; T.Gad. 6:1–7; 2 En. 50:4; (Ps.Phoc. 77).

[32] Cf. also 1 Thess. 5:15; 1 Pet. 3:9.

[33] On the relationship between Rom. 12:14–21 and this intertestamental tradition, see K. Yinger, "Romans 12:14–21 and Nonretaliation in Second Temple Judaism" (*CBQ* 60/1 [1998], 74–96).

upon the godly (X,11; cf. XI,13). In the case of these latter, the strong sense of human inability and sinfulness which pervades this document means that such chastising punishments are welcome not only because they lead to repentance from occasional sins, but even more because each individual stands fundamentally under divine judgment. Even for the righteous this remains true (X,11), and their constant remembrance of this leads them to an equally constant reliance on divine grace for renewal, obedience and justification (X,11b–13; XI,2b–3a).

We did not wholly clarify in what sense the motif is eschatological in this document, but did note at one point (X,17–18) that the retribution can be placed within the context of the final War between the Sons of Light and Darkness, and is thus more akin to forms of OT historical eschatology than other-worldly conceptions found in apocalyptic writings. Along these lines, the elect can be portrayed as executors of divine judgment according to deeds in their destruction of the wicked at the time of this last battle (VIII,6–7, 10); and the yearly examination to which all community members were subject can be portrayed in terms that suggest a degree of proleptic experience of God's own judgment according to deeds (V,24; IX,14b–16a).

The Thanksgiving Hymns (1QH)

The scroll from cave 1 dates to the first century CE or somewhat earlier, but most would not even attempt to date the *composition* of the hymns themselves. There is still no agreement as to whether these compositions are by a single author – perhaps the Teacher of Righteousness – or should be viewed as community products.[34] There does seem to be agreement, however, that whoever the author(s) were, and however the compilation came about, this document represents the views of the Qumran community. The numerous copies found in caves 1 and 4 witness to its great popularity.

1QH IV,18–19

The content of this psalm (IV,5–V,4) can be summarized as follows: "Praise of God for salvation through the covenant, to

---

[34] E. P. Sanders gives a helpful overview of the debate up to 1977 in *PPJ*, "Appendix I: The Authorship and *Sitz im Leben* of the Hodayot,", 321–323.

which the psalmist will adhere despite the deceitful enemies who entice him away from it. Their temptation will only lead to their own perdition."[35] There is a great deal of emphasis on the enemies, who are described as "interpreters of falsehood and seers of deceit" (IV,9b–10a), "hypocrites" who seek God "with a double heart" (IV,13–14), "they who have fallen away from Thy Covenant" (IV,19), and "who transgress Thy word" (IV,26b–27a). Interpreters are divided as to possible historical allusions contained in these descriptions. In any case, their opposition to the psalmist (and the sect) is traced to their rejection of the revelation that has now been granted Israel through the sect's teaching:

> For [they have] not [heeded] Thy [voice]
> nor lent their ear to Thy word;
> for they have said (18) of the vision of knowledge, It is not true!
> and of the way of Thy heart, That is not it!   (IV,17–18a)

This rejection of the truth results in divine judgment according to works:

> But Thou, O God, wilt answer them,
> judging them (19) in Thy might [according to] their idols
> and according to the multitude of their sins,
> that they who have fallen away from Thy Covenant
> may be taken in their thoughts.
> (20) And at the time of ju[dg]ment Thou wilt cut off all the men of deceit
> and there shall be no more seers of error ... (21) But they that are according to Thy soul shall stand before Thee for ever,
> and they that walk in the way of Thy heart (22) shall stand fast eternally.   (IV,18b–22a)

This judgment results in death ("cut off") which, though certainly physical, is also a soteriological category in contrast to the hope of the righteous who "shall stand before Thee for ever" (IV,21). Although not addressed to the wicked themselves, the motif amounts here to a declaration of God's coming judgment upon them, and thus has some similarity to the prophetic sentence

---

[35] S. Holm-Nielsen, *Hodayot: Psalms from Qumran* (Acta Theologica Danica 2; Aarhus: Universitetsforlaget, 1960), 79.

of judgment. At the same time, the entire psalm is aimed at extolling God, so that even this judgment announcement is an important element that brings praise to God. His judgment demonstrates the triumph of his truth and power.[36]

Here is a very clear instance of the unity of observable deeds and inner disposition. The judgment is explicitly "according to[37] their abominable idols" and "the multitude of their sins," which are themselves the expression of their fundamental rejection of the divine word and knowledge (IV,17–18). This is termed being "estranged from Thy Covenant."[38] Behind their works lies a "double heart," a "stubbornness of heart," because they are not "firm in Thy truth" (IV,14–15).

As for the psalmist, he seeks God whose Law is "graven in [his] heart" (IV,6, 10); and one may assume he counts himself among those "that are according to Thy soul" and "that walk in the way of Thy heart" (IV,21). Yet the emphasis in this psalm is not upon his own obedience, but upon God's mercy and the necessity of human dependence upon divine grace in the light of human frailty and sinfulness (cf. esp. IV,29–33). Righteousness and perfection of way are beyond mere human achievement, attainable only through divine intervention.

> And I, I know that righteousness is not of man,
> nor of the sons of men perfection (31) of way;
> to the Most High God belong all the works of righteousness,
> whereas the way of man is not firm
> unless it be by the Spirit which God has created for him
> (32) to make perfect a way for the sons of men. (IV,30–32)

Unlike any spirit of works-righteousness, he stresses "because I lean on Thee I shall rise and stand," and "I leaned on Thy favours and on the greatness of Thy mercy" (IV,22, 37).

---

[36] IV,13, 20b–21a, 25–27; (V,4).

[37] Though the first prefixed כ [according to] is illegible, experts are unanimous in reading it here in parallelism to the immediately following ... וכרוב.

[38] זור (Niphal) = "be estranged"; cf. Ezek. 14:5; Isa. 1:4. The similarities of thought and expression between this psalm and Ezek. 14:1–5 have been noted by others. In the Ezekiel passage, idolatry and iniquity are combined with an emphasis on the "heart" of the house of Israel which has thus become "estranged" from Yahweh.

1QH V,5–6

In a similar manner this psalm (V,5–19) extols God, who does not forsake the psalmist in the danger caused by his adversaries. Here it is God's *negation* of the principle of judgment according to deeds which prompts the psalmist's praise.[39]

> [For it is not][40] according to my sin that (6) Thou has judged me
>
> [[ולוא] כאשמתי שפטתני]
>
> and Thou hast not abandoned me because of the wickedness of my inclination,[41]
>
> [ולא עזבתני בזמות יצרי]
>
> but hast succoured my life from the Pit.   (V,5–6)

The nature of this sin or guilt of the psalmist is not explored. In fact, it is probable that specific transgressions are not in view at all, but rather the evil imaginations or shameful intrigues [זמות] which spring from one's evil inclination [יצר].[42] If so, this expresses an attitude which finds application at all times for the community member and is seen repeatedly in these psalms: innate sinfulness obviates reliance on one's own righteousness, leading one to cling to divine mercy and pardon which are offered in the Covenant. Or as Kittel phrases it: "The poet's theological statement is one of salvation by grace alone, not due to any righteous works on the part of the poet."[43]

This text raises acutely the question of the relevance of the motif to the elect in the hymns. The writer seems to be asserting that divine judgment according to works *does not apply* in their case. It

[39] A similar usage in Ps. 103:10 was already examined in an earlier chapter. Both praise God because he does *not* judge the righteous strictly according to deeds. The two passages differ in that Ps. 103:10 has occasional sins in view, while 1QH V,5–6 focuses more on sinful desires which characterize all humanity.

[40] With most interpreters I read ולוא at the end of the lacuna immediately preceding כאשמתי [according to my guilt] since this is suggested by the parallelism with the following phrase. See B. Kittel, *The Hymns of Qumran* (SBLDS 50; Chico, CA: Scholars Press, 1981), 87–88.

[41] Or, "Thou hast not left me in the shameful intrigues of my desire" (Holm-Nielsen, *Hodayot*, 90).

[42] Cf. VII,6; XI,20; XVIII,11, 13; also Gen. 6:5. Though G. Jeremias is correct to caution against exact identification with the later rabbinic t.t. (*Der Lehrer der Gerechtigkeit* [SUNT 2; Göttingen: Vandenhoeck & Ruprecht, 1963], 218, n. 6), יצר does refer to human nature as inclined to evil (cf. R. E. Murphy, "Yêṣer in the Qumran Literature," *Bib* 39 [1958], 334–344).

[43] *Hymns of Qumran*, 97.

must be noted that this text has an historical focus, looking *back* to a situation of adversity in which God did not abandon [עזב] but helped or rescued [עזר] the psalmist's life from the grave. Since the psalmist is ever aware of human frailty and sinfulness, "not according to my sin" need indicate no more than a reference to divine benevolence in the treatment of the elect; i.e., God does not treat them as they should deserve in the light of their sin. This historical focus likewise means that the text should not be taken as a categorical denial of the principle of judgment according to deeds with regard to future salvation.

1QH XIV,24[44]

This short piece (XIV,23–[27])[45] praises God, who forgives the penitent, but punishes the ungodly, and has taught the psalmist to do the same.

> Thou who pardonest them that are converted from sin
> and visitest the iniquity of the wicked [upon them][46].
>
> [ופוקד עון רשעים [עליהם
>
> [Thou lovest them that seek Thee] with a generous (25) [heart],
> but Thou hatest perversity for ever.

God is praised both for his forgiveness of the repentant and his just retribution upon the wicked. What apparently distinguishes the one group from the other is the repentance of the former, whereas the wicked continue in their transgression. I noted earlier the negation of the retribution motif for the righteous (V,5–6), but this passage makes clear once again that this differential treatment is based not merely upon election, but upon a fundamental difference in inner disposition between the two groups, the one seeking God with a generous heart (though not entirely free from sins), the other

---

[44] Some translations suggest an additional occurrence of the motif at XIV,11b–12: "For according to the spirits [he divides] them between good and evil," in which case we have a possible reference to God's separation of the wicked from the righteous on the basis of their "spirits". The thought is found elsewhere (cf. VII,12; 1QS IX,14–15). However, the lacunae in the MSS render any reconstruction suspect. See the thorough discussion of the textual problems in Holm-Nielsen, *Hodayot*, 220, nn. 5–6.

[45] The text is missing between XIV,27 and XV,9, so one cannot be certain of the ending of this psalm and the beginning of the next.

[46] Reading על following רשעים; cf. Holm-Nielsen, *Hodayot*, 225, n. 5.

characterized by perversity. A few lines later the psalmist makes
equally clear that this distinction must ultimately be traced to
God's gracious initiative.

> Thou hast favoured me, Thy servant, with the Spirit of
>   Knowledge,
> [to love tr]uth (26) [and righteousness]
> and to loathe all the ways of perversity.
> and I will love Thee generously
> [and seek] Thee with all my heart.
> (27) [...] for it is by Thy hand that this is,
> and without [Thy might has nothi]ng [been made ...].
>
> (XIV,25–27)

Judgment according to works and the soteriological pattern in 1QH

The thanksgiving hymns are not infrequently singled out as
showing remarkable similarity to Paul's theology at a number of
points: emphasis on grace in salvation, utter dependence of sinful
humanity on this grace, the same dependence for the saved who
remain frail and sinful even after conversion (prompting comparison with the idea of *simul iustus et peccator*), a proleptic experience
of salvation "already" by the saved, etc. Since a number of previous
studies have resulted in a generally agreed upon outline of the
soteriology of 1QH,[47] a summary of their results should suffice
here. Since, however, the motif has not played much of a role in
any of these previous studies, it will be my particular contribution
to attempt to place it within that pattern.

Humanity's frailty and sinfulness are "more distinctly expressed
in 1QH than any other doctrine of the Sect. Man is a sinner, utterly
helpless but for the grace of God upon him."[48] We read:

> Yet am I but a creature of clay and a thing kneaded with
>   water,
> a foundation of shame and fount of defilement,

---

[47] M. Mansoor, *The Thanksgiving Hymns* (STDJ 3; Grand Rapids: Eerdmans,
1961), 52–92; J. Licht, "The Doctrine of the Thanksgiving Scroll," *IEJ* 6/1 (1956),
1–13, 89–101; S. Holm-Nielsen, "The Theological Concepts of the Hodayot,"
Hodayot, 273–300; and E. H. Merrill, *Qumran and Predestination: A Theological
Study of the Thanksgiving Hymns* (STDJ 8; Leiden: E. J. Brill, 1975).
[48] Mansoor, *Thanksgiving Hymns*, 59; see 58–62.

a crucible of iniquity and fabric of sin,
a spirit of straying, and perverse,
void of understanding,
whom the judgments of righteousness terrify. . . .
But how can a man count up his sins,
and what can he answer concerning his iniquities?
And how can he, perverse, reply to the judgment of
righteousness?   (I,21–23, 25–26)[49]

Thus it is no surprise that God's *election* and *grace*, not human obedience or righteousness, are the main themes when the hymns reflect on the source or cause of salvation.

And I know that the inclination of every spirit is in Thy
hand
[and that] Thou hast ordained [the way of every man]
[together with his visitation]
before ever creating him.
And how can any man change Thy words?   (XV,13–14)[50]

And I have no fleshly refuge;
[and man has no righteousness o]r virtue
to be delivered from si[n]
[and wi]n forgiveness.
But I, I have leaned on Thy abun[dant mercy]
[and on the greatness of] Thy grace.   (VII,17–18)[51]

As in Paul, this is grace to the *undeserving sinner*:

I give [Thee thanks, O Adonai],
for Thou hast given me understanding of Thy truth
and hast made me know Thy marvellous Mysteries
and Thy favours to [sinful] man
[and] the abundance of Thy mercy toward the perverse
heart!   (VII,26–27)

---

[49] See also IV,29–31, 33–35; VII,16–17, 28; IX,13, 15–17; XII,19, 24–35; XIII,14–16; XVII,18–20. Note the repeated phrase, *creature of clay* (e.g., XI,3; XVIII,31).

[50] See further, on election/predestination: I,7–31; III,19–25; XIV,13; XVI,10; XVII,21. Merrill's study on predestination remains the most comprehensive to date (*Qumran and Predestination*).

[51] See further on grace in salvation: II,23, 25; IV,31–33; VII,6–9, 27, 30–31;IX,7, 29–34; X,5–7, 14–19; XI,7–14; XIII,17–18; XVI,11–12; XVIII,26–29.

Grace is likewise the cause of the continued obedience and perseverance of the saved:

> for Thou hast upheld me by Thy might
> and hast poured out Thy holy Spirit within me
> that I should not stagger! . . .
> Thou hast not permitted me cravenly to desert Thy Cove-
>   nant . . .
> And Thou knowest the inclination of Thy servant,
> that right[eousness] is not [of man].
> [But] I have [le]aned [upon Thee]
> that Thou shouldst lift up [my] hea[rt]
> [and] give (me) strength and vigour.   (VII,6–7, 8, 16)

This last citation also reveals faith, or reliance upon God's grace
and mercy ("I have leaned upon Thee"), as a central element in the
human appropriation of this gracious salvation.[52]

At the same time, the human response is emphasized as a vital
element in the elect's salvation, even though this too is a result of
grace. The elect are those who have been "converted from sin,"
who "know" and "adhere" to the covenant revealed to the
Community.[53] These are granted a spirit which produces obedience
to the commands of God and the precepts of the community.[54]
They walk in God's ways, do not pervert, transgress or depart from
his word and commands, nor sin against him in any way.[55] They
can, hence, be described as perfect of way or heart,[56] though this
cannot be taken in an absolute sense in the light of the frequent
confessions of continuing sinfulness.

Although final salvation is ultimately grounded in Qumran's
emphasis on *sola gratia*, did the community also make it in some
sense conditional upon this grace-induced obedience?[57] Would they
be judged according to their works? In none of the three instances
of the motif adduced above was there a warning or threat addressed

---

[52] See also II,21b–22a, 28b; IV,22, 37; IX,10.
[53] II,9, 21–22, 28; IV,24, 35, 39; VI,6; X,30; XIV,24; XV,15; XVI,7, 17; XVIII,9.
[54] V,19–20; VI,6–7; VII,19–20; XIV,17–18; XV,11–12; XVI,17–18.
[55] IV,21, 24; VI,7; XII,24; XIV,15, 17–18; XV,11–12, 15; XVII,22–23.
[56] I,36; XII,24; XVI,7.
[57] "Salvation includes not only deliverance from persecution but also deliverance
from sin itself. Though man is predestined to belong to the elect *his election is
dependent on his being of a righteous and moral character*. It is one of God's gifts to
him; the ability to live a righteous life" (Mansoor, *Thanksgiving Hymns*, 64; my
emphasis).

to community members, nor did we find elsewhere language of God rewarding or repaying the righteous according to their works. Rather in XIV,24 God pardons the converted in explicit contrast to judgment according to works upon the wicked.[58] God's judgment of the converted is also stated elsewhere to be according to pardon or mercy.

> Thou wilt judge them with abundant mercy and pardon
> because of Thy favours.   (VI,9)

> Thy loving keeping is for the saving of my soul
> and over my steps is abundance of pardon
> and when Thou judgest me, greatness of [mer]cy.
>   (IX,33–34)[59]

Nevertheless several observations support the contention that salvation is dependent upon continuance in obedience in 1QH. In addition to the stress on obedience already noted above in describing the elect, one wonders how else to take such a passage as the following:

> And I knew there was hope for them that are converted
> from rebellion and that abandon sin by [...] and by
> walking in the way of Thy heart without any perversion.
> (VI,6–7)[60]

Future hope is clearly contingent upon obedience, and a fairly radical obedience at that ("without any perversion"). Furthermore, the possibility of apostasy seems to be envisioned in a couple of places in a way that connects loss of salvation with departure from obedience.[61] To all these may be added I,21–23 which testifies to

---

[58] In the OT Pseudepigrapha we observed the same dichotomy (mercy to the righteous, strict judgment without mercy to the wicked), yet without thereby intending to exempt the covenant people from divine judgment according to deeds.

[59] Cf. also I,6.

[60] Cf. also XVI,16–18.

[61] XVI,15; XVII,21–24. It is unclear whether the oft-used phrase "those who have fallen away (are estranged) from Thy Covenant" refers to apostate former community members or non-sectarians (see Sanders, *PPJ*, 256–57, nn. 48–49). Eugene Merrill appears to deny the possibility of apostasy in 1QH due to its radical predestinarianism (*Qumran and Predestination*, 44). He cites 1QH II,35–36 to the effect that God prevents the psalmist from exercising his free choice of abandoning the Covenant. The text reads: "in the midst of their outrages Thou hast not left me without courage to the point of departing from Thy service," or as Merrill translates, "Thou hast not caused me to be dismayed into forsaking Thy service." But is this statement not simply thanksgiving *post facto* rather than a universal dogma? It is one

the psalmist's fear of divine judgment in the light of his own sinfulness:

> Yet I am but a creature of clay ... a crucible of iniquity and fabric of sin ... whom the judgments of righteousness terrify.

Divine pardon does not eliminate the urgency or necessity (with respect to salvation) of moral renewal; rather these are viewed as two sides of the same coin:

> For Thou pardonest iniquity
> and clean[sest m]an of sin by Thy righteousness.   (IV,37)

Thus, inasmuch as the righteous are walking faithfully in the covenant, future divine judgment according to deeds has little practical relevance. They need not fear it and it is seldom utilized in relation to their situation (except as part of their own confessions). On the other hand, inasmuch as a covenant member strays (or in the light of potential straying), divine judgment according to deeds (= punishment) becomes immediately relevant once again as a threat to be taken seriously.

The War Scroll (1QM)

As with many of the Qumran documents any suggestion as to the date of composition of 1QM is tenuous. Suggestions range from the mid-2nd century BCE to the early or even latter first century CE, with the earlier date generally favored.[62] Whatever the exact genre and character of the work, its aim in giving these detailed regulations as to tactics, weaponry, etc. will likely have been to prepare for the imminent eschatological conflict, to encourage the sons of light, and to "inflame their zeal" in the light of the coming holy war. In this light the stress on purity in the document may be explained by

thing to look back on preservation, and thank God and His sovereignty for it; and another to look forward and declare "God will never allow me to ..."

[62] Early dating: D. Dimant, "The War Scroll," *Jewish Writings of the Second Temple Period: Apocrypha, Pseudepigrapha, Qumran Sectarian Writings, Philo, Josephus* (ed. M. E. Stone; Compendium Rerum Iudaicarum ad Novum Testamentum 2/2; Assen/Philadelphia: Van Gorcum/Fortress Press, 1984), 517. Later dating: Y. Yadin, *The Scroll of the War of the Sons of Light against the Sons of Darkness* (trans. B. and C. Rabin; London: Oxford University Press; 1962), ix, cf. also 4–7, 243–246. In favor of the earlier dating, Dimant notes that the MS from Cave 1 probably dates to the 2nd century BCE ("The War Scroll" in Stone, ed., *Jewish Writings*, 515).

the fact that the angels were to be co-warriors, and successful warfare depended on the purity of the human partners.

1QM XVIII,14 [63]

In spite of the badly damaged MS the text can be reconstructed and almost assuredly contained the motif:[64]

> (13b) Thine is the might, and in Thy hand is the battle, and there is no one (14) [to save them   ] Thy times and appointed times according to Thy pleasure, and retribution [of the wicked Thou wilt render unto Thine ene]mies, and Thou wilt cut off from [. . .].

[67 לאויב]יכה ⁶⁶[רשעים תשיב ⁶⁵ל[וגנ]מו[ן

A reference to divine retribution is also supported by the context, since a divine punishment ("Thou wilt cut off . . .") follows immediately afterward.

The fragmentary nature of columns XVIII and XIX make a reconstruction of the literary context somewhat conjectural. Columns XV,1–XVIII,5 describe the ebb and flow of the final battle between the sons of light and the sons of darkness. Sunset is

---

[63] I do not consider the difficult text XIV,11b–12 to be a motif occurrence. The most extensive discussion can be found in Fabry, *Die Wurzel ŠÛB*, 207–211, who does find the motif here and translates "And their nobles you repay according to their contempt" [ולנכבדיהם תשיב לבוז] (210). To my knowledge such a use of the prefix ל to express the *standard* ("according to...,") would be singular in occurrences of the motif (cf. also Yadin, *Scroll of the War*, 328, note). Perhaps השיב + ל should be taken quite naturally in the sense "to cause (someone) to return to (location)" as in Jer. 12:15: "and I will bring them [והשבתים] again to their heritage [לנחלתו] and to their land [לארצו], everyone of them." The translation would then read: And as for their nobles you will return (them) to contempt.

[64] Yadin's reconstruction and translation will be adopted for the most part below, cf. *Scroll of the War*, 346–347. Most other translations have not attempted a reconstruction and contain no reference to the motif.

[65] The initial וג and final ל are visible making the reconstruction of וגמול certain.

[66] שוב (Hiph) is somewhat more speculative, but eminently reasonable as the complement of גמול (cf. 1QM VI,6; XI,13–14; also Ps. 28:4; 94:2; Lam. 3:64; Joel 3[4]:4, 7; Sir. 35:24.). The verb שלם is ruled out, since the ל would have been visible (cf. Yadin, *Scroll of the War*, 347, note). It may also be reasonably conjectured that the space between גמול and תשיב contained the word רשעים [of the wicked], since this space is the right size and the construct "recompense of the wicked" is commonly used in Qumran (cf. 1QM VI,6; XI,13–14; 1QS X,17; CD VII,9; XIX,6; see also Fabry, *Die Wurzel ŠÛB*, 188–213).

[67] The restoration of a concluding לאויביכה [your enemies] is almost certain, some of the letters being partly visible.

approaching (XVIII,5b, 12), threatening to stall the final pursuit and annihilation of the enemy. After blessing God for past miracles of victory and remembering that this is the appointed time "to abolish the dominion of the enemy that it might exist no more" (XVIII,11), the missing ending of the column most likely contained the request, patterned after Joshua 10, that God prolong the day for completion of the pursuit, or that he intervene directly in the battle.[68] If this is correct, then lines 13–14 come just before this request.

These lines both praise and remind God that might in battle belongs to him, that he has set the appointed time for victory (i.e., now), and that retribution and punishment upon the enemies will assuredly come from him. Praise as a motivating reminder to God in preparation for a request is a normal part of Jewish piety.[69] Alongside this primary function of the motif, it will also have had the subsidiary aim of encouraging the zeal of the Israelite warriors who were hearing this prayer.

Here also, the motif deals strictly in terms of divine punishment upon the wicked. Although the language of organic consequences is still employed (שוב גמול), it is difficult to ascertain whether the ancient *synthetische Lebensauffassung* is still understood, or whether the phrase has simply become a periphrasis for divine punishment. Although the sinfulness of the wicked is everywhere assumed, this particular passage does not seem as interested in stressing the *appropriateness* of retribution (i.e., *in accordance with their sins*) as in raising confidence in the *certainty* of coming punishment based upon God's power and character. These enemies who are to experience divine retribution are the forces of Belial, including both foreign nations and apostate Jews (i.e., those who reject the Covenant offered through the community).[70] Their end is to be "cut off" and "destroyed utterly."

---

[68] See Yadin, *Scroll of the War*, 12–13, 222–223; and P. R. Davies, *1QM, The War Scroll from Qumran: its structure and history* (BibOr 32; Rome: Biblical Institute Press, 1977), 73, 82.

[69] See 1 Kgs. 8:22–53; Ezra 9:6–15; Neh. 9:6–37; Jer. 32:17–25.

[70] Cf. I,2 ("and in league with them the offenders against the covenant"); IX,9; XI,9. On the "enemies" in 1QM, see Sanders, *PPJ*, 248–249; and Yadin, *Scroll of the War*, 26. Another occurrence of the motif directed against "all the nations of vanity" can be found in VI,5b–6. See also IV,12, where גמול אל [recompense of God] and שלומי אל [repayment of God] occur alongside "battle," "vengeance," "power," "annihilation," etc. as descriptions of this phase of the final war.

(1QM XI,3–4)

Although the motif does not occur here, the reference to "deliverance because of mercy and not according to our (sinful) works" forms an important corollary and deserves brief mention.

> For Thine is the battle!
> And (3) he [i.e., David] struck [down] the Philistines many times by Thy holy Name.
> And Thou hast also saved us many times by the hand of our kings (4) because of Thy mercy and not according to our works by which we have done evil nor (according to) our sinful deeds.

A three-fold refrain, "Thine is the battle,"[71] stresses the contrast between divine and human ability. David is remembered first, who "set his trust in Thy majestic Name and not in the sword and the spear" (lines 1–2); then God's deliverance of Israel via her kings is cited "because of Thy mercy and not according to our works" (lines 3–4); and finally God's might alone is praised: "From [Thee] comes the power; truly (the battle) is not ours! Nor our might nor the strength of our hands display valour, but it is by Thy might and the strength of Thy tremendous valour" (lines 4–7). That God deals with his covenant people "according to compassion [רחמים]" and "not according to our sinful deeds" was already noted as a central tenet of Israel's faith in the Pseudepigrapha. A clearer statement of reliance upon grace instead of works could hardly be demanded.[72] While the possibility exists that this implies a negation of judgment according to works for covenant members, that is not a necessary logical conclusion.[73]

Conclusions (1QM)

Since this writing is focused on tactics, weapons, etc. connected with the final war, there is less material of a theological nature, and little here that one could call strictly apocalyptic. On the other

---

[71] XI,1, 2b, 4b; cf. also 1 Sam. 17:47: "but the battle is the Lord's."

[72] On the possibility that this text lies in some way behind Titus 3:5, see J. A. De Waard, *A Comparative Study of the Old Testament Text in the DSS and in the NT* (STDJ 4; Leiden: E. J. Brill, 1965), 73–76.

[73] See the discussion on this question in chapters 1–2 above, and below in connection with other theological statements in 1QM.

hand, this is clearly the final war which is expected to usher in the everlasting age of blessing upon the people of the Covenant, and in that sense it is "eschatological."[74] Thus 1QM seems to operate with a "historical eschatology" much as in the OT, in which God's judgment occurs at the end of, but still *within*, human history. Courtroom scenes and terminology are absent,[75] and the execution of judgment occurs via the physical annihilation of the wicked in battle. This eschatological judgment is seen as the necessary prelude to the restoration of God's kingdom on earth and the everlasting blessedness of the righteous.

In the salvation of the sons of light priority is clearly given to God's mercy and might (cf. esp. on XI,3–4 above), and as elsewhere in Judaism God's gracious covenant is the basis of all divine–human interaction.[76] At the same time this deliverance involves a considerable measure of human synergy. The retribution texts fuse divine and human activity in the eschatological recompensing of the wicked. In fact a new twist in the use of the motif to motivate the righteous to obedience is found in these texts. Whereas in the Jewish Scriptures the righteous were thereby encouraged to continued faithfulness to Torah, in 1QM the motif encourages them to valiant action in battle.

In 1QM the motif is taken up only in reference to the destruction of the wicked, and only within a setting of praise and prayer to God. In addition there seems to be a certain hardening of the terminology:[77]

> *God repays/returns* [השיב, שלם]
> *the recompense of the wicked* [גמול רשעים/רעתם]
> *to his enemies* (various formulations).

Certainly with the attached phrase – "of the wicked" – the motif has become simply another way of saying "God will destroy the wicked." There is little evidence that the *synthetische Lebensauffassung* which originally stood behind these words was any longer felt or implied by the speaker.

---

[74] See esp. I,5, 8–9a; also I,9b–12; VII,5; IX,5–7; XI,11–15; XII,10–15; XIV,5; XV,1–2; XVIII,11.

[75] Only the "book of the names" of the elect is mentioned as being beside God in his holy abode (XII,2).

[76] I,2; X,10; XII,3; XIII,7–8; XIV,4, 8; XVII,7, 8; XVIII,7.

[77] But see pp. 132–133 below on Fabry's thesis of "terminologische Verhärtung" [terminological rigidity] and my criticism.

The Damascus Document (CD)

This composite work,[78] consists of two parts; Admonitions (I–VIII) and Ordinances (IX–XVI). The two additional columns (XIX–XX) discovered on a separate fragment appear to be a slightly later recension of the ending of the Admonitions. All occurrences of the motif fall within the Admonitions. Due to serious questions about the relation of this document to the rest of the DSS,[79] I will pay less attention to parallels from other Qumran documents. It seems reasonable to assign a date no later than 100 BCE to the composite work in its present form, though as with all Qumran literature, dates of composition remain highly uncertain.[80]

CD III,4–5

After the exhortation to "choose that which [God] desires and reject that which He hates" (II,15) the compiler recounts Israel's history. He demonstrates how those who "did their own will and did not keep the commandments of their Maker" were cut off in God's anger (II,17–III,1; III,4b–12), whereas Abraham, Isaac and Jacob "kept them and were inscribed as Friends of God and party to the Covenant for ever" (III,2–4a).

> The sons of Jacob strayed because of this
> and were punished <according to>[81] (5) their straying.
>
> [בני יעקב תעו בם וינשו לפני משגותם]

As consistently throughout this salvation-history the *children* of the faithful are portrayed as straying from God's covenant and commandments. They are therefore punished according to their

---

[78] See the series of articles in *RB* by Murphy-O'Connor on the literary structure of CD: "An Essene Missionary Document? CD II,14–VI,1," *RB* 77 (1970), 201–229; "A Literary Analysis of Damascus Document VI,2–VIII,3," *RB* 78 (1971), 210–232; "The Critique of the Princes of Judah (CD VIII,3–19)," *RB* 79 (1972), 200–216; "A Literary Analysis of Damascus Document XIX,33–XX,34," *RB* 79 (1972), 544–564.

[79] Cf. P. R. Davies, *The Damascus Covenant: An Interpretation of the "Damascus Document"* (JSOTSup 25; Sheffield: JSOT, 1982).

[80] See Dimant, "The War Scroll" in Stone, ed., *Jewish Writings*, 487–490. The question of date and composition is tied to the thorny question of the relationship between CD and 1QS. The priority of 1QS seems to be the majority view, but arguments have been advanced as well for the opposite order (cf. O. Eissfeldt, *The Old Testament: An Introduction* [trans. P. R. Ackroyd; New York: Harper and Row, 1965], 652). If correct, Davies' thesis noted above calls for a complete reevaluation of the evidence in this regard.

[81] On this reading, see Lohse, *Die Texte aus Qumran*, 70, n. *a*.

errors. From the context it is clear that divine punishment is meant and is further described with the terms "cut off" (III,1, 7, 9), "perish" (III,9, 10), and "divine Anger kindled against" them (II,21; III,8). What appears to be described as physical destruction has, however, a clear soteriological implication. According to III,10–12 such rebels place themselves outside the Covenant relationship ("abandoned the Covenant") and suffer the punishments of those who are not under God's covenant mercy, including exposure to the "Anger of God." Their fate is contrasted with that of Abraham, Isaac and Jacob who are "inscribed as Friends of God and party to the Covenant for ever" (III,3–4).

The clear soteriological implications in this text should give some insight into the meaning of "destruction" in other texts as well. The author appears to be working with a remnant-theology, in which divine destruction connotes the punishment expected upon those who have abandoned the covenant (i.e., covenant curses) and are treated no longer as Friends and party to the Covenant. In the light of the hortatory introduction to this section (II,14–16) the purpose of this motif usage will be to motivate the righteous to obedience by portraying the punishment according to deeds that befalls those who choose their own desires over God's. The use of עָנַשׁ [punish] and מִשְׁגָּה [error] is unusual for this motif, probably under the influence of the surrounding context,[82] and showing once again that divine recompense according to deeds was a fundamental axiom in Jewish thought which could be expressed with a great variety of terminology.

CD V,15–16

A midrash on Isaiah 24:17 begins at IV,12b, focusing on Israel's transgressions ("snares") in the past (IV,17–V,15a), and finishing with the warning for the current generation: "He who associates with them will not be held innocent; the more he does it the guiltier he is, if he is not compelled" (V,14b–15a).[83]

The motif comes at this point in the argument, as a transitional piece, giving justification for the warning just stated, and leading into the ensuing account of Israel's infidelity (V,17–VI,1).

---

[82] Though they use other Hebrew words, see the references to punishment (II,18; III,1, 7, 9–10) and straying (II,17; III,1, 11–12).

[83] Following P. R. Davies' translation (*Damascus Covenant*, 245).

For formerly <also> God visited (16) their works,
and His anger was kindled against their forfeits ("practices").

כי אם למילפנים פקד את מעשהק]
[ויחר אפו בעלוהיהם

The use of both פקד [visit, punish] and מעשה [works] in the motif is known from the Jewish Scriptures,[84] with פקד both as verb and substantive ("visitation") quite popular in CD and the other Qumran literature. The warning of (current) punishment upon Jews who fall prey to falsehood is grounded in God's punishing visitations upon Israel in the past.[85] The current snares all stem from Israel's rejection of the (community's) true understanding of the law.[86] Thus the warning has all the more force because God's past punishments were likewise directed against "a people without understanding," "a nation void of counsel" (V,16b–17a; cf. Isa. 27:11, Deut. 32:28a) who were "led astray" by those who "preached rebellion against the commandments of God" and "prophesied falsely to turn Israel away from following God" (V,18–VI,1).

Thus the motif refers in this instance to *past retribution* against Israel, not to eschatological recompense. Having said this, however, it is certainly intended (in the light of V,15a) as a pattern for the current judgment warning as well, which does have a future reference, though not necessarily an eschatological one. The motif functions here as part of an admonition to community insiders[87] to avoid associating with or adopting the views and practices of non-community Jews. By means of a warning it seeks to motivate them to the more stringent interpretation of and obedience to Torah required by the sect.

Both in its past point of reference (i.e., Mosaic and exilic periods) and its present application to community members, the motif is applied to those among God's people who allow themselves to be led astray into "rebellion against the commandments of God

[84] They do not, however, occur together in the motif in the OT.
[85] למילפנים: formerly, beforehand, in ancient times. The usage in CD points consistently to Israel's (pre-exilic) history (II,17; III,19; V,17b).
[86] So for instance V,7 ("inasmuch as they do not distinguish in accordance with the Law") and V,12 ("with a blaspheming tongue have opened their mouth against the precepts of the Covenant of God, saying, They are not true!"; i.e., they reject the community's stricter interpretation).
[87] Or "newcomers"; see Davies, *Damascus Covenant*, 108–119.

(revealed) by the hand of Moses" (V,21). The nature of this retribution in Israel's past history involved divine "anger" (V,16) leading to the desolation and ravaging of the land (V,20–21). Its application to the community of the Damascus Document, as suggested above, probably involved community sanctions upon the transgressor and ultimately exclusion, with obvious soteriological implications.

CD VII,9 = XIX,6

And (as for) all who reject – when God shall visit the earth to repay the reward of the wicked upon them, when there shall come to pass the word which is written in the words of Isaiah . . .   (VII,9)

וכל המואסים בפפד אל את הארץ]
להשיב גמול רשעים עליהם
[בבוא הדבר אשר

And (as for) all who reject the commandments and the ordinances, to bring the reward of the wicked upon themselves when God shall visit the earth, when there shall come to pass . . .   (XIX,6)[88]

The syntax of this text has consistently puzzled translators.[89] If Davies is correct that VII,9–10 is part of a larger "covenant formulary" and forms the curse counterpart to the blessing promised in VII,4–6, then perhaps comparison with that text will yield some light.[90]

(Promise) For all who walk in these (precepts) . . . the
    Covenant of God is assurance . . .
[ברית אל נאמנות להם]   [כל המתהלכים באלה]
(Curse) And (as for) all who reject – when God shall visit
    the earth to repay the reward of the wicked upon them . . .
[וכל המואסים   בפקד אל להשיב גמול עליהם]

It would appear that in both cases the addressees are indicated by the first phrase ("All who . . ."). This is apparently a proleptic

---

[88] Following Davies' translation which better reflects the syntactical ambiguities discussed below (ibid., 251, 257).
[89] Overview of the problems in H.-J. Fabry, *Die Wurzel ŠÛB*, 193–194.
[90] *Damascus Covenant*, 143, 148–150. See also J. Murphy-O'Connor, "A Literary Analysis" (1971), 211, 220–228.

casus pendens construction, and may thus be best translated "as for...," to be taken up again by the concluding להם/עליהם in the second phrase.[91] In the promise the relation of the ensuing clause to these addressees is clear enough: [lit.] "for them the covenant of God stands firm." On this pattern the sense of the curse must be "upon them God will repay the recompense of the wicked."[92] Even if the solution to the syntactical problems lies elsewhere, the sense will almost certainly remain as stated above. On this understanding then, VII,9b–10a is, like the promise, directed at would-be entrants into the community, but who, unlike the recipients of the promise, will decide not to accept the community's rigorous standards ("all those who despise").[93]

Retribution upon the wicked takes place "when God visits the earth." The Admonitions use both the verb פקד and the substantive פקד(ו)דה to refer consistently to a divine visitation for punishment, either in Israel's past or in the future.[94] Whether an eschatological future punishment is meant must await the examination of the eschatology of this document, but if I am correct to see it in apposition to the promise of lines 4–6 ("they will live for thousands of generations"), then this punishment will certainly have been understood as having ultimate soteriological implications.[95]

If my understanding of the literary context is correct, this motif-text functions as a warning to those about to enter the covenant community so as to motivate them to accept the sect's interpretation of Torah and the associated behavior. If they do not, they shall suffer the same punishment to be accorded the rest of the wicked.

---

[91] See Fabry, *Die Wurzel ŠÛB*, 193 (n. 388), and 199. He lists III,20; XIV,1–2; XV,5–6 as additional examples of this construction, which he calls "almost typical" for CD.

[92] The parallel text (XIX,6) seems to confirm this by its reversal of the two clauses (להשיב עליהם בפקד אל), thus bringing the recompense statement into closer proximity to the addressees (cf. Fabry, *Die Wurzel ŠÛB*, 202–203).

[93] The addition in XIX,6 of "commandments and ordinances" illumines the intended sense of the compact formulation in the earlier text – "all those who despise." It refers to the rejection of the community's Torah by initiates/members/apostates, a fact made clear from the use of the verb מאס [reject] in the surrounding material (VIII,19 [= XIX,32]; XX,8, 11; also III,17; different II,15).

[94] Past visitation: I,7; V,15; VII,21; XIX,11. Future (or present?) visitation: VIII,2, 3; XIX,10, 14, 15. In the Ordinances one finds only the meanings "muster" and "oversee" (X,2; XIII,11; XIV,3, 6; XV,6, 8). For its use elsewhere in the Qumran literature for divine retribution, see 1QS II,6; 1QH XIV,24.

[95] This soteriological implication is even clearer in the B recension of this passage.

(CD XX,24)

Though not an instance of *divine* recompense according to deeds, I mention this text briefly in order to demonstrate how the motif was applied in an analogous way to human or community judgment. Though the deterioration of the MS demands some conjectural restoration, the judgment motif is clearly recognizable.

> B[ut] in the holy Council the people will be judged with few
> words,
> each one of them according to his spirit.

Or perhaps:

> but (they) returned again [to the wa]y of the people in a few
> respec[ts. Ea]ch of them is to be judged individually, ac-
> cording to his spirit in the holy council.[96]

[בדברים מעטןים כון]לם איש לפי רוחו ישפטו בעצת הקדש]

This section deals with a group called "the house of Peleg" (XX,22b) who were either apostates from the community (XX,25ff.), or a group of non-community members in sympathy with the covenanters, but who differed in some matters of interpretation.[97] Whichever the case, the stress on individuality of judgment (איש) calls for an individual examination of "each ... according to his spirit" rather than according to one's group affiliation. The phrase "according to one's spirit," though unique here to CD, means in 1QS according to whether one follows the spirit of God or of Belial.[98] Elsewhere in the Damascus Document community judgment is to be conducted on the basis of the community's legal standards (XIX,31–32; XII,3). In all these cases, observable behavior does not "earn" one's status in the community, but "reveals" the spirit according to which one lives. Even though this is a human judgment, it has a clear connection with divine judgment. "The pericope embodies a certain duality; there is, on the one hand, the judgement pronounced by the community, and on the other, the punishment executed by God (XX,24 and 26). One reflects the other in a way that very

---

[96] Davies, *Damascus Covenant*, 265; textual problems are discussed on pp. 191–193.
[97] Cf. Ibid., 191–194.
[98] 1QS II,20; IV,26.

effectively emphasizes the importance of the present for the future."[99]

Conclusions (CD)

It should not surprise us to find in these Admonitions to (prospective) community members the motif used exclusively to motivate the righteous to obedience. Yet in spite of this singularity of purpose considerable variety in formulation has been discovered. One instance, where language heretofore unknown in the motif is clearly prompted by the context, suggested a deep-rooted axiom of Jewish thought which can be formulated with great freedom according to the need of the moment.

In attempting to fit the motif into the larger pattern of religion in CD, I would note first that this document appears to represent an exilic theology. Accordingly Israel's consistent rebellion against God's covenant and Law, especially that leading up to the destruction of Jerusalem in 721 BCE and the deportation, is seen to result in the continuation of the genuine covenant relationship through a remnant only, not the whole nation. God at that time made for himself a remnant, called in IV,2 the "converts of Israel," who were converted "from the sin of Jacob" (XX,17) and began to heed the voice of the Teacher, fearing God once again and walking according to his commandments. The CD community considers itself to be the bearers of this remnant line in Israel. From those days until now are the "times of ungodliness" (VI,10) and "Israel's blindness" (XVI,2) when the Angel of Hostility is with(in) the Jew who has not yet converted (XVI,5).[100]

The key to salvation lies in "entering the covenant" (VI,11; XX,25) and then "clinging to it" (III,20; XX,27) or "walking in perfection" (II,15–16; VII,5; XX,2, 6–7; [XIII,6]), i.e., rigorous obedience to the Torah as interpreted in the community (XX,29, 32; II,18, 21; III,2, 6, 15–16). That a thorough conversion of the heart or inner person is meant, and not simply outward conformity, is clear from comments regarding the need to "choose God's will" rather than "one's own will" (III,3, 7, 11; VIII,7–8) and the

---

[99] J. Murphy-O'Connor, "A Literary Analysis" (1972), 558.

[100] On this exilic theology in CD, see especially Davies, *Damascus Covenant*, 61–72, 76–104. For a helpful summary of exilic theology as contemporaneous with Paul, see Frank Thielman, *Paul and the Law: A Contextual Approach* (Downers Grove, IL: IVP, 1994), 48–68, and the works cited by him (p. 254, n. 2).

warnings against superficial conversion (XIX,14, 16–17, 33–35; XX,3, 25; XV,13).

However, although this is occasionally termed a "new covenant" (VI,19; VIII,21) it is in actuality nothing other than the "covenant appointed for Israel forever" (XV,5), the covenant given to the patriarchs (VI,2; VIII,14–18; XII,11) and through Moses (XV,8–9, 12). Unlike 1QS, in CD one hears little of the "spirit of holiness" as constituting that which is "new"; rather it is the revelation of the previously hidden (true) understanding of the Law through the sect that constitutes the major difference. Thus the acceptance of that knowledge constitutes salvation; this is entering the covenant.[101]

Yet all this legal focus should not cover up the fact that the religious framework, the soteriology, of this group is little different from that seen in the OT, namely covenantal nomism.[102] Election (double-predestination), grace and mercy remain fundamental (II,7–8; IV,3; XIX,1; XX,21, 34). In spite of an emphasis on rigorous obedience, divine forgiveness remains fundamental (II,5; III,18; IV,6, 10; XX,34), and it is clear that "perfection of way" refers to the whole of one's behavior pattern, not to an atomistic legalism or perfectionism.[103] It is even stated explicitly that one's standing before God must stem ultimately from God's love, not from one's own righteousness (VIII,14–18). One "gets in" by covenantal grace, involving of course a personal choice for God's truth, and "stays in" this merciful arrangement by not abandoning the covenant and its required obedience (III,11, 20; XIX,14; XX,17; *et al.*). The entrance was apparently connected as well with a thoroughgoing recognition and confession of one's wickedness (I,8–9; XX,28–30). One never "earns" salvation, but is "given" it, along with the concomitant obligations of that covenant relationship.

What of judgment and retribution? God tries and judges all who "scorn" him (I,2). Scorning God, or "despising His commandments and statutes" (XIX,6), means following one's own way, being led astray by Belial. In the Ordinances it leads to disciplinary measures

[101] For "covenant" in CD, see R. F. Collins, "The Berith-Notion of the Cairo Damascus Covenant and its Comparison with the NT," *ETL* 39 (1963), 556–582.

[102] Against J. A. Huntjens who attempts to portray the "legalistic" and "covenantal" patterns as "contrasting notions of covenant and law" in CD ("Contrasting Notions of Covenant and Law in the Texts from Qumran," *RevQ* 8 [1974], 361–380, esp. 362–370).

[103] See XII,4–5 where one's "perfection of way" can be restored after committing sin(s).

or exclusion (or even death). Where a fundamental apostasy is indicated in the Admonitions (e.g., XIX,14, 16–17, 33–35; XX,3, 25), the punishment is variously described as covenant curses (I,17), covenant avenging (I,17–18; XIX,13), flames of fire (II,5), being cut off (III,1, 7, 9; XX,26), being delivered to the sword (VII,13; VIII,1; XIX,10, 13), divine anger (VIII,3, 13, 18; XIX,16), and having no share in the house of the Law (XX,13).

None of the above designations need necessarily lead in the direction of an eschatological or apocalyptic judgment, and we nowhere have a depiction of a universal divine forensic judgment.[104] While it is possible that "flames of fire" and references to "that day" (Day of Yahweh?; cf. VIII,2; XX,15) could be given an apocalyptic twist, all could equally well be understood as referring to punishments within history (e.g., "cut off" = removed from the covenant and community by death) or to the final divine battle at the End. Certain phrases suggest a perspective of historical eschatology[105] and the expectation of a future blessed existence on earth of unending duration,[106] none of which take us much beyond what one can already find in the OT. It is clear, however, from the analysis of III,4–5 and VII,9 that historical divine judgments were understood in CD to have ultimate soteriological meaning. To be "cut off" and "delivered to the sword" meant to suffer the fate of those outside the covenant relationship.

The axiom of divine punishment according to deeds is meant to motivate current and prospective members of the community to accept the sect's doctrine, to confess their own wickedness, and to submit in obedience to God's grace and the interpretation of the divine will revealed through the community. The warning is meant with utmost seriousness, and apostasy is repeatedly referred to as a possibility which will lead to nothing less than exclusion from the salvation-blessings promised in the new covenant.

---

[104] See H. W. Huppenbauer, "Zur Eschatologie der Damaskusschrift," *RevQ* 4 (1963/1964), 567–573. Against L. Ginzberg (*An Unknown Jewish Sect* [New York: Jewish Theological Seminary of America, 1970], 160) "angels of destruction" in II,2ff. do not point to a post-mortem judgment, but are simply present at the final eschatological battle.

[105] Cf. "end of days" (IV,4; VI,11); "consummation of time" (IV,8–9); "last generation" (I,12). See further M. Reiser, *Jesus and Judgment*, 78–79.

[106] "for a thousand generations" (VII,6; XIX,1).

Additional texts

1QpHab. XII,2–3[107]

Following the citation of Habakkuk 2:17 we read:

> The explanation of this word concerns the Wicked Priest inasmuch as he will be paid (3) his reward for what he has done to the Poor.

The Habakkuk text spoke of "violence done to Lebanon" and "cruelty used against the beasts" (XI,17). These are now interpreted as referring to the evil actions undertaken by the Wicked Priest against members of the sect (XII,4–5), including plans to "destroy" them (XII,6) and "steal their goods" (XII,10). For this he shall be "repaid his recompense" by God, the recompense being analogous to the very actions he himself did against the poor. The underlying *talio* conception is made clear in lines 5–6 where it is stated that God will determine to "destroy" the Wicked Priest just as he planned to "destroy" the poor.

Although at first glance this text would seem to be a sentence pronounced against the Wicked Priest, the fact that the document was addressed to the sectarians means looking deeper for its ultimate purpose. Brownlee lists six aims of these midrash pesharim, two of which are "to strengthen the faith and endurance of the Teacher's adherents" and "to warn the wavering of the dangers of apostasy."[108] This would best fit the category "to motivate the righteous to obedience." The context itself offers little in the way of rhetorical clues.

In spite of its brevity, 1QpHab. places divine judgment (on the wicked) according to deeds clearly within a framework of historical eschatology familiar from the OT.[109] There is a universal final judgment.[110] The readers are given to understand that they are

---

[107] The pesher commentary on Hab. 1–2 (1QpHab.) is probably to be dated in the second half of the first century BCE (K. Elliger, *Studien zum Habakuk-Kommentar vom Toten Meer* [BHT 15; Tübingen: J. C. B. Mohr (Paul Siebeck), 1953], 226–274, esp. 270–274).

[108] *The Midrash Pesher of Habakkuk* (SBLMS 24; Missoula, MT: Scholars Press, 1979), 35–36.

[109] See especially the comments of K. Elliger (*Studien zum Habakuk-Kommentar*, 278–284) and W. H. Brownlee (*Midrash Pesher*, 214–218), to whom I am indebted in what follows.

[110] V,4; VIII,2; X,3–4; XII,14; XIII,1–4.

living in the "last generation" at the "consummation of time."[111] Although the righteous must still suffer for a time, soon God (through his elect, V,4), will without mercy (VII,16–17) eradicate all the wicked from the earth (XIII,4), including the "wicked of His people" (V,5), that is, Jews who reject the Teacher's message. Alongside battle imagery for this final destruction, there also occur forensic notions and destructive judgment by "fire."[112] "Fire" could be taken as a reference to an apocalyptic world conflagration, but, since the earth clearly remains intact (XIII,2–4), Elliger is surely correct to perceive in this judgment by fire the same "destruction of the wicked by fire" as that found in the OT.[113] The righteous need not ultimately fear this judgment, for "God will deliver them from the House of Judgment because of their affliction and their faith in the Teacher of Righteousness" (VIII,2–3). The scroll ends[114] with the climactic announcement:

> But on the Day of Judgment God will destroy all those who serve idols, together with the wicked, from the earth.
>
> (XIII,2–4)

4QpPs37 IV,9

> And God will not let [the Wicked Priest go] un[punished for the blood which] he has shed, but [God will] pay him his [re]ward by delivering him into the hands of the violent of the nations to execute [vengeance] upon him.

This badly damaged line consists of a midrash pesher on Psalm 37:32–33 applying these words to the Wicked Priest. The OT text is one of comfort to the afflicted righteous that Yahweh "will not abandon them into the hand of the wicked." Actually judgment is not mentioned in the Psalm text until the next verse (verse 34) which is cited and commented on in IV,10–12 ("the wicked are cut off"). Nevertheless, the interpreter includes the motif of divine recompense upon the wicked already, apparently viewing it as an important element explicating God's comfort for the righteous.

The divine recompense consists in "delivering him [i.e., the Wicked Priest] into the hands of the violent of the nations to

---

[111] VII,2, 7, 12; IX,5.
[112] IV,12–13; IX,6–7, 9–12; X,5 ("declare guilty"), 13.
[113] *Studien zum Habakuk-Kommentar*, 280–281; cf. Isa. 66:24; Mal. 3:19.
[114] The ending is uncertain; see Brownlee, *Midrash Pesher*, 218–219.

execute [vengeance] upon him." In the following midrash (IV,11) it
appears that the righteous are permitted to look on at the judgment
of the wicked. This is an historical judgment, which, however, may
well have been part of an historical eschatology.

Summary

Wording and functions

Motif-terminology in this literature has yielded few surprises. The
writers utilized the same verbal elements as the OT and the
Pseudepigrapha, namely שוב (Hiph), שלם (Piel), פקד and שפט.
New is the usage of ארור [curse] and ענש [punish], which arose
naturally within their respective literary contexts, demonstrating
that the formulation of this Jewish axiom has not become merely a
rigid formulaic expression, but is a living belief seeking appropriate
expression in varying historical situations.

I thus differ from H.-J. Fabry in one of the few studies devoted
to the retribution formula in the Qumran literature.[115] His conclusions may be summarized briefly in the following four points: (1)
The Qumran documents evince "a marked narrowing of terminology" as over against the OT. The retribution formula occurs
only in the form גמול + השיב/שלם, whereas the OT can use a
variety of object-nouns, and God alone is the agent of retribution.
There is, in fact, a definitive consolidation of the formula with the
construct expression גמול רשעים. (2) This "terminological rigidity"
has a theological explanation. There is, namely, "a theologically
rigid dogmatism at work"; i.e., a restriction to the meaning
"punishment upon the enemies".[116] (3) This hardening of the
formula can, in fact, be dated to around 100 BCE by an examination
of early (1QS), middle (CD), and later (1QM) documents. (4) This
hardening was probably prompted by a military defeat prior to the
writing of CD, because of which the community recognized that
God alone would bring the retribution, excluding all human
instrumentality.

While correct that השיב and שלם are followed only by the noun
גמול in retribution formulae, Fabry failed to note the *other* forms
of the motif which employ alternative verbal elements (שפט, פקד,

---

[115] *Die Wurzel ŠŪB*, 185–213.
[116] Agreeing with K. Seybold, "Zwei Bemerkungen zu גמול/עמל," *VT* 22 (1972), 117.

עונש) and a wide variety of object-nouns or expressions of standard. This alone should warn against overemphasizing a supposed formulaic hardening which then requires historical and theological explanation. His text-basis for such assertions is simply too small. The key expression (גמול רשעים) is found in only four texts (!) in all the literature (and he ignores the simple שלם גמול [without רשעים] in 1QpHab. and 4QpPs37). Is it not more likely that the Qumran writings simply reproduce some of the variety in the motif known from OT and intertestamental writings, with the emphasis on the negative retribution already prepared for in the Jewish apocalyptic writings? Neither he nor Seybold give any evidence to support the assertion of "theologically hardened dogmatism." The restriction of the motif to punishment may, instead, admit of a rhetorical explanation, while the avoidance of a positive recompense (reward) could have roots in the sect's stress on human inability. Any theory of chronological development must remain highly suspect in light of the difficulties attached to dating the composition of any of these documents, even relative to one another. Point 4 is pure speculation. It could be just as easily argued that a crucial military defeat and subsequent sense of powerlessness might lead to even greater visions of future (apocalyptic) instrumentality in retribution.

Returning to my conclusions, unlike the Pseudepigrapha the motif is *not* expressed with a *standard* ("according to...") in the majority of cases. Instead, seven of the fourteen instances used גמול + השיב/שלם, making this clearly the predominant formulation in the Qumran literature. Evidence is lacking that a *synthetic view of life* is any longer a major conceptual element behind this formula, while the *talio* concept appears still to play an active role. Explicit *judgment* terminology is not quite as prevalent in Qumran as compared with the Pseudepigrapha, though it should be noted that most of the motif occurrences do come in a larger context of divine judgment. The same interchange between singular and plural (deed/deeds) can be observed in this literature, suggesting once again that one's "works" (pl.) constitute one's "work" (sg.) viewed as a unity.

The motif still functions in a broad array of purposes as in the OT and the Pseudepigrapha, including as a *sentence* pronounced against the wicked both within and without Israel. The fact that a few categories did not turn up in the texts considered may be simply coincidental, due either to the limited quantity of material studied, or to the particular genre of literature involved.[117] On the other hand the lack of any texts used as an *appeal* to God to intervene on behalf of the righteous, or as a *benediction*, may well have a theological explanation. The *appeal*-texts in the OT often involved the *assertion of one's own righteousness* to appeal for a *positive recompense* from God. As seen repeatedly in the Qumran literature, the sectarians tended to stress human inability and sinfulness very strongly and to attribute all blessings to God's gracious initiative. Add to this the fact that the motif is never used to inculcate the idea of God's positive reward of the righteous,[118] and it is not surprising that this category seems to have disappeared. One point of particular interest for Pauline studies was the appearance of a new category of usage in 1QS X,17–18, namely as a theological argument against inter-personal retribution (cf. Rom. 12:17–20).

Judgment according to deeds = punishment of the wicked

Not wishing to reiterate all that has been said about the doctrine of divine retribution in the foregoing exegetical sections, I will merely highlight two salient points in that regard. First, in Qumran God's judgment according to deeds meant almost exclusively *the punishment of the wicked*. Even the two texts which apply the motif to the righteous do so in the sense of "there but for the grace of God go I."[119] There is no evidence of the motif being used to inculcate a dual retribution, i.e., reward for the righteous *and* punishment for the unrighteous. In fact, there is not a single example of the motif being used to refer to the positive rewarding of the righteous.[120] The sectaries, of course, believed that the righteous would receive the covenantal blessings; they refrained, however, from using reward terminology in such instances. Whereas the OT had relatively little hesitation in speaking of the "reward of the righteous"

[117] For example we examined no texts that might be called a "prophetic summons to repentance" and thus the category connected with that genre in the OT was likewise missing.

[118] While 1QS X,18 does seem to presuppose a belief in dual recompense, I have argued that the belief in God's rewarding of the righteous is incidental to the purpose (cf. p. 106 above).

[119] 1QS X,11 and 1QH V,5–6.

[120] Although Dupont-Sommer translates 1QS IV,16, 25 and 1QH XIV,12 with "reward," suggesting a positive or dual reward, the Hebrew word common to all three passages should more likely be translated "doing, work" [פעולה].

and even appealed to one's own righteousness to call upon God's reward or judgment (= vindication), this has apparently all but vanished in the second temple period.[121] An explanation of this development in Qumran has been suggested in the preceding paragraph.

Especially in contexts related to the final War the "wicked" are understood universally, i.e., as including heathen nations.[122] Otherwise the emphasis falls upon (potential) apostates, hypocrites within or Jews outside the sect's membership. These are judged "without mercy" (just as in the Pseudepigrapha), whereas the judgment of the righteous is according to mercy and pardon.[123]

Judgment in the context of historical eschatology

The second point I wish to highlight concerns the eschatological conceptions surrounding judgment in the Qumran literature. Although not all the documents give an equally clear answer,[124] there is no evidence of the sort of transcendent eschatology normally associated with apocalyptic literature.[125] The stark contrasts between this age and the age to come in terms of *earthly* versus *heavenly* are missing in Qumran. There is no mention of a post-mortem resurrection of either the righteous or the wicked to judgment, and no "tours of hell" to depict what awaits sinners in the afterlife. No mention of any intermediate state can be found, and we are, in fact, left in the dark as to the post-mortem fate of either group.[126]

On the other hand a considerable body of evidence points to

[121] For the same phenomenon in the OT Pseudepigrapha and its explanation, see pp. 89–90 above.

[122] Cf. 1QS X,16–18; 1QM VI,5–6; XI,13; XVIII,14.

[123] 1QH I,6; VI,9; IX,33–34.

[124] See J. Pryke, "Eschatology in the Dead Sea Scrolls," *The Scrolls and Christianity* (ed. M. Black; Theological Collections II; London: SPCK, 1969), 45–57, esp. 48.

[125] See Licht, "Time and Eschatology," 177–182. On the use of the term "apocalyptic" for Qumran's eschatological thought, see the series of articles in *JNES* 49/2 (1990): R. L. Webb, "'Apocalyptic': Observations on a Slippery Term," 115–126; P. R. Davies, "Qumran and Apocalyptic or *OBSCURUM PER OB-SCURIUS*," 127–134; and C. A. Newsom, "Apocalyptic and the Discourse of the Qumran Community," 135–144.

[126] Pryke, "Eschatology" in Black, ed., *The Scrolls and Christianity*, 55. According to Lichtenberger the graves at Qumran testify to a belief in an afterlife (*Studien zum Menschenbild*, 229). For a different view, cf. Nickelsburg, *Resurrection, Immortality, and Eternal Life*, 144–169.

historical eschatology similar in many respects to the perspective of the Jewish Scriptures.[127] Judgment upon the wicked is generally seen as occurring during the final eschatological War between the Sons of Light and of Darkness. The result of this judgment is consistently depicted as the physical destruction of the wicked under the anger and fury of God. References to being "damned in the night of eternal fire" (e.g., 1QS II,7–8) are not inconsistent with this finding. "Fire" certainly need not refer exclusively to hell-fire, but can just as easily be used as the means of God's destruction of the wicked on earth at the end of this age of evil, as is clear both from the OT and Qumran; and "eternal" is more likely used in the sense of "long-lasting, unending" than of a transcendental eternity. While God is ultimately seen as the Judge and Executor of judgment, in some cases the angels play an instrumental role, and in others the elect can witness or carry out God's judgment.[128] That a historical eschatology of judgment is intended in these documents is further confirmed by the way in which the future blessedness of the righteous is portrayed. Rather than angelic or heavenly images, the saints enjoy unending bliss ("for a thousand generations") on a renewed and fruitful earth purged of all evil. Here at last the triumph of the divine righteousness is experienced and God's promises to His people fulfilled. The eradication of the wicked as well as the purging of all sinfulness (including that *within* the elect) is a necessary eschatological prelude to this final revelation of God's victory.

Judgment and soteriology in Qumran

Finally, the place of judgment according to deeds within the soteriology of the Qumran sect should be commented upon, noting particularly the sectarian slant given to the interaction between judgment and salvation.[129] The sectaries appear to have viewed themselves as living in the final period of history, just prior to the

---

[127] See E. F. Sutcliffe, *The Monks of Qumran: As Depicted in the Dead Sea Scrolls* (Westminster, MD: Newman, 1960), 88–90.

[128] 1QS VIII,6–10; 1QM VI,5–6.

[129] On Qumran soteriology see esp. D. Flusser, "The Dead Sea Sect and pre-pauline Christianity," in *Aspects of the Dead Sea Scrolls*, eds. C. Rabin and Y. Yadin (ScrHier 4; Jerusalem: 1965), 215–266; P. Garnet, *Salvation and Atonement in the Qumran Scrolls* (WUNT 2nd ser., vol. III; Tübingen: J. C. B. Mohr (Paul Siebeck), 1977); J. G. Harris, "The Covenant Concept among the Qumran Sectaries," *EQ* 39 (1967), 86–92; and Sanders, *PPJ*, 233–328.

eschatological War in which all wickedness would be destroyed and God's triumphant rule on earth would be established. With a distinctly sectarian narrowing of the people of God, it is now through the sect alone that God's saving (new) covenantal relationship is available.[130] They appear to have subscribed to an "exilic soteriology"; i.e., all (physical) Israelites are defiled and blind, belonging to the "Lot of Belial," and subject to God's (punishing) judgment.[131] Entry into the realm of salvation is identical with entry into the sect, the "Sons of Light," the "Lot of God." This is first and foremost an act of God's grace in election, and on the level of observable behavior occurs via acceptance of the sect's teaching and wholehearted submission to the sect's rigorous ordinances and interpretation of Torah.[132] Only belonging to this remnant or "planting" assures salvation from the coming judgment. Clearly, the covenant blessings are not earned by obedience, nor could they ever be merited by such inherently blind and sinful creatures;[133] rather they are given out of God's love and mercy in remembrance of his gracious covenant with the patriarchs.

These blessings of divine mercy could, on the other hand, be *kept* only by those who were "perfect," upholding the covenant obligations of belief and obedience in all respects. Such "perfection" coexisted paradoxically with the recurring confession of one's own wickedness and inability combined with praise to God alone and his enabling unto righteousness.[134] Remaining in the salvific

---

[130] "[M]erely being born a Jew no longer constituted membership in the people of God. Israel as a whole had rejected and disobeyed God, and thus it was that the sectarians felt called through repentance and dedication to the Law to enter into a new covenant with God, the new covenant foretold by Jeremiah (Jer. 31.31–34, cf. CD viii.21, xx.12). They formed the new Israel, existing at the present time in the "dominion of Belial" but soon to enjoy all the blessings promised to God's people in the new age" (C. H. H. Scobie, "John the Baptist," *The Scrolls and Christianity* [ed. M. Black; Theological Collections II; London: SPCK, 1969], 65).

[131] I.e., "that Israel was still in exile as regards the fulfilment of God's purposes, so that she needed to pursue the kind of behaviour, including Law observance, which would bring the promised national restoration" (P. Garnet, "Qumran Light on Pauline Soteriology," *Pauline Studies: Essays Presented to Professor F.F. Bruce on his 70th Birthday* [Exeter: Paternoster, 1980], 23).

[132] "Thus, conversion signifies a heightened obedience to the Torah" (H. Braun, "'Umkehr' in spätjüdisch-häretischer und in frühchristlicher Sicht," *ZTK* 50/3 [1953], 248).

[133] Against H. Braun: "Qumran combines faith and works, Paul deals with them antithetically. In Qumran the means of salvation are meritorious works, in Paul faith" (*Qumran und das Neue Testament* [2 vols.; Tübingen: J. C. B. Mohr (Paul Siebeck), 1966] II.170; see also 229–235).

[134] See especially 1QH IV,30–32. It is too facile to equate "perfectionism" and

relationship with Israel's God was indeed conditional upon maintenance of one's initial faith-commitment which was evidenced by obedience.

Divine judgment according to deeds did not amount to a future (and currently unknowable) determination as to whether one had measured up. It was rather the inevitable sentence upon those who had disdained God and his ways as revealed in the sect, behavior which would be more or less manifest to all the initiated. For this reason as well, within the community members were regularly judged according to their deeds or spirit to weed out hypocrites and hidden apostates, or, in cases of lesser offence, to give opportunity to be restored to perfection. Thus for believers there would, in one sense, be no eschatological judgment (= punishment) according to deeds, at least as long as they remained faithfully within the sect and its way of life. On the other hand, as a number of texts addressed to newcomers, hypocritical sect members, or potential apostates make clear, *if* they fail to keep the covenant, they will assuredly share in the punishment of the wicked, for now their works are evil just as the rest. Thus the righteous are both subject to and exempted from the future judgment according to deeds. It is not contradictory for the righteous to be terrified when contemplating the righteous judgments of God (1QH I,21–23) as well as to be assured of deliverance from judgment through faith (1QpHab. VIII,2–3). This tension, if one wishes to call it that, is partly explainable as differing rhetorical strategies, and partly eschatologically. Salvation, while *already* assured to the sectary on the basis of grace and the covenant, had *not yet* arrived in its eschatological fulfillment, and thus would only be experienced in that Eschaton *if* one remained in that grace and covenantal relationship. Whether this is brought into proximity to either *synergism* or *Paulinism* will depend, in large part, on how one defines those terms.[135]

"legalism" with the rigorous obedience demanded by the sect as M. Black does (*The Scrolls and Christian Origins: Studies in the Jewish Background of the New Testament* [Brown Judaic Studies 48; Chico, CA: Scholars Press, 1983], 18–24). For this reason, when admitting the "evangelical religion" of the Hodayot, he must appeal to variety of belief at this most fundamental level of how one's religion "works" as it were (125). On this coexistence of "perfection" and "confession of sinfulness," see E. P. Sanders, *Judaism: Practice and Belief, 63 BCE-66 CE* (London/Philadelphia: SCM/ Trinity, 1992), 367–379, esp. 375–376.

[135] For example, J. Becker acknowledges the *sola gratia* of 1QH X, but then distinguishes it from Paul's by arguing that in the former salvation is still *conditional* (*Das Heil Gottes*, 125; cf. also 238–279). But does Paul really place no *conditions* upon believers vis-à-vis behavior?

Excursus: post-mortem judgment in Greco-Roman literature

Since the primarily Jewish roots of Paul's judgment conception are widely accepted, I will content myself with a brief summary of Greco-Roman perspectives for comparison.[136] On the one hand "the language and conceptions of postmortem judgment were widely known and used on both the philosophical and popular levels."[137] Two different images dominated, the mythology of the underworld (Hades), and the transmigration of souls.

> The εἴδωλον or shadowy relic of the individual person apparently continued to exist for ever, without change, in Hades. Under Pythagorean and Orphic influence, this conception was transformed, so that the destiny of the uninitiated soul conformed to a cyclic pattern in time. Metempsychosis meant an endless process of birth and death, interspersed with periods of reward or punishment. Initiated souls learned how to break out of this ever recurring cycle of existence in time, and return to a state of eternal bliss. The temporal process was, accordingly, conceived as unceasing, and thus differed radically from the conceptions current in the Judaeo-Christian religions, in Islam and Zoroastrianism; for these faiths envisaged a definitive end to the temporal process, and this end would be coincident with a Final Judgment, conducted by God or his representative.[138]

A number of forms and functions can be identified.[139] There is a stress on the therapeutic value of the process of (repeated) purgation and rebirth as the soul wanders toward its final rest. The terminology of *praise*, one of the highest goals in Greco-Roman society, is often found in such judgment contexts. A favorable post-mortem judgment is often seen as an extension of the sort of honors desired from the civic or athletic realm – a "prize," a "victor's

---

[136] The following is in large part a summary of D. W. Kuck, *Judgment and Community Conflict*, 96–149. See also S. G. F. Brandon, *The Judgment of the Dead: The Idea of Life After Death in the Major Religions* (NY: Scribner, 1969), 76–97. H. Braun concludes that the "Pauline dilemma" of grace versus works could never have arisen on Greek soil. "Their optimistic self-assessment was not shaken even by an imminent judgment" (*Gerichtsgedanke und Rechtfertigungslehre*, 3, see also 2–5).

[137] Kuck, *Judgment and Community Conflict*, 97.

[138] Brandon, *Judgment of the Dead*, 96.

[139] Kuck, *Judgment and Community Conflict*, 142–143.

crown," being called a "hero," a place on thrones beside the gods. A favorable verdict could be termed a "wage" [μισθός], viewing post-mortem judgment as the pay-off for individual exertion in life.

The vast majority of moral philosophers appear not to have used post-mortem judgment in their writings; temporal reward and punishment were the primary motivators of behavior. Nevertheless, "there is no doubt that an inhabitant of Corinth in the mid-first century CE would have at least been familiar with some conception, whether Homeric or Platonic, of a judgment for individuals after death."[140] Its main functions appear to have been in moral exhortation, or in consolation regarding death.

Thus, Greco-Roman judgment language dealt generally with the everyday concerns of individuals – death and morality – not with situations of group conflict or historical crisis.[141] Post-mortem judgment was not a final apocalyptic act of God; in fact, it was generally the other semi-divine figures, or even other very righteous persons, who passed judgment.

[140] Ibid., 120.
[141] Ibid., 149.

PART TWO

Judgment according to deeds in Paul's letters

4

JUDGMENT ACCORDING TO DEEDS IN
PAUL'S LETTER TO THE ROMANS

The simple verb κρίνειν [to judge] is found in Romans eighteen times[1] with noticeably heavy concentrations in chapters 2 (7x) and 14 (8x). The noun κρίμα [judgment] is found six times,[2] while the derivatives κατακρίνειν [to condemn] and κατάκριμα [condemnation] are found four and three times respectively.[3] Δικαιοκρισία [just judgment] is found only at 2:5 in the NT.

The heavy concentration of judgment terminology in chapter 2 is understandable since Paul is seeking to demonstrate that Jewish covenant privilege does not mean "escaping the judgment of God" (verse 3). In chapter 14 the problem of intra-community judgment leads to the high incidence of κρίνειν and derivatives. The four occurrences in chapter 3 (verses 4, 6, 7, 8) testify to Paul's belief in a universal divine judgment of humanity, but add little to our understanding of his expectation for Christians in judgment. Similarly the praise of God's unfathomable κρίματα need not detain us here.

Since the only occurrence of the recompense motif is in chapter 2, that will be the focus of this chapter. In what ways does Paul's use of the motif coincide with, or differ from, its use in Judaism? What role does the motif play in Paul's argument? How does the motif relate theologically to the theme of justification by faith for Jew and Gentile alike? This will be followed by looking at the other judgment texts in Romans and at two texts which use recompense terminology (μισθός/ὀψώνιον – 4:4; 6:23) in order to confirm or supplement the findings.

Without falling prey to the older view of Romans as a systematic theological treatise, it may still be granted that this letter is Paul's most thorough extant treatment of his gospel of God's saving righteousness in Christ. Particularly in chapters 1–8, with their

---

[1] 2:1(3x), 3, 12, 16, 27; 3:4, 6, 7; 14:3, 4, 5(2x), 10, 13(2x), 22.
[2] 2:2, 3; 3:8; 5:16; 11:33; 13:7.
[3] (Verb): 2:1; 8:3, 34; 14:23. (Noun): 5:16, 18; 8:1.

explication of righteousness by faith apart from works, we may hope to discover increased clarity regarding the relationship of justification to judgment and recompense.

The exact occasion and purpose of Romans is considerably more complex than in some of the other letters.[4] The immediate situation is stated clearly enough by Paul: he plans to visit the believers in Rome and preach the gospel there (1:10–15); and he hopes to be helped by them on his mission to Spain (15:23–24, 28–29). Yet this hardly explains the unusually thorough presentation of his gospel. Hence, scholars have rightly perceived his upcoming visit to Jerusalem to deliver the collection to be in the back of Paul's mind (15:25–32).[5] Particularly his request for intercessory support reveals the depth of this concern ("that I may be rescued from the unbelievers in Judea, and that my ministry to Jerusalem may be acceptable to the saints," verse 31); and Acts confirms Paul's fears ("[The Jewish believers] have been told about you that you teach all the Jews living among the Gentiles to forsake Moses," 21:21). The struggle for his law-free gospel in Galatia is still a fresh memory, and he is rightly concerned that his apostolic message and strategy be acceptable to the church in Jerusalem. To have not only the prayer support, but also the *endorsement* of his gospel by the mixed congregation in Rome would greatly aid his case in Jerusalem.[6]

Furthermore, there is certainly a need to win the Roman church itself to his way of thinking. Chapters 14–15 reveal Jew–Gentile tensions,[7] tensions which would certainly not be unknown to Paul if one accepts chapter 16 as part of the original letter.[8] The

[4] On the continuing debate over the occasion and purpose of Romans, see K. P. Donfried (ed.), *The Romans Debate: Revised and Expanded Edition* (Edinburgh: T. & T. Clark, 1991); and N. Elliott, *The Rhetoric of Romans: Argumentative Constraint and Strategy and Paul's Dialogue with Judaism* (JSNTSup 45; Sheffield: 1990), esp. 9–94. For the view taken here of multiple purposes, see J. D. G. Dunn, *Romans 1–8* (WBC 38a; Waco: Word, 1988), liv-lvii; and J. C. Beker, *Paul the Apostle: The Triumph of God in Life and Thought* (Edinburgh: T. & T. Clark, 1980) esp. 71–74.

[5] For this view see esp. J. Jervell, "The Letter to Jerusalem" in Donfried, ed., *The Romans Debate*, 61–74.

[6] A. J. M. Wedderburn, "Purpose and Occasion of Romans Again" in ibid., 195–202.

[7] On the nature of the Roman congregation, see P. Lampe, *Die stadtrömischen Christen in den ersten beiden Jahrhunderten: Untersuchungen zur Sozialgeschichte* (Tübingen: Mohr, 1987); and W. Wiefel, "The Jewish Community in Ancient Rome and the Origins of Roman Christianity" in Donfried, ed., *The Romans Debate*, 100–119.

[8] For a defense of Romans 16 as an original part of Paul's letter, see P. Lampe, "Zur Textgeschichte des Römerbriefs," *NovT* 27 (1985), 273–277.

"strong" (mostly Gentiles) are judging the "weak" (mostly Jews),[9] while the Jewish-Christian minority still considers itself to be at a spiritual advantage over against Gentile Christians (14:3b). Such behavior threatens not only Paul's plans for making Rome a mission base to the west, but even worse, weakens the credibility of the collection he is presenting at Jerusalem since their conflict speaks against his approach to uniting Jew and Gentile in the one body of Christ. Thus Paul writes "rather boldly by way of reminder" (15:15), so as to assure their adherence to his gospel and persuade them to behave accordingly (chapters 12–15).

Chapters 1–4 have traditionally been interpreted against the backdrop of the individual conscience, now convicted of sinfulness and needing to be shown the way to peace with God. Instead the hermeneutical key lies in the social relation of Jew and Gentile in the church as outlined above.[10] It is against this backdrop that Paul's focus on justification by faith coupled with the unusual emphasis on divine impartiality in this letter is best understood.[11] For if neither Jew nor Gentile can claim an advantage over the other before God, but both must be accepted on the same basis, by grace through faith, then a proper understanding and appropriation of this doctrine should provide a foundation for overcoming potentially destructive social tensions in the church at Rome or at Jerusalem.[12]

Thus, the motives for this correspondence are complex, and no single one seems able alone to explain the epistle, which also makes understandable the difficulty in defining a single addressee. At times Paul seems to be addressing Jewish tendencies, while elsewhere Gentile concerns are voiced. It lies beyond the scope of this chapter to attempt a solution to the still-debated issues of exact audience and theological intention in Romans. My working hypothesis will treat the letter as being addressed to both Gentile and Jewish elements of varied Roman house churches, with the emphasis shifting according to the need of the argument.

---

[9] 11:18 – "do not boast over the branches"; cf. further 14:1, 13; 15:1.

[10] See H. Moxnes, "Honour and Righteousness in Romans," *JSNT* 32 (1988), 61–77; and K. Stendahl's now-classic essay, "The Apostle Paul and the Introspective Conscience of the West," *HTR* 56 (1963), 199–215 [reprinted in K. Stendahl, *Paul Among Jews and Gentiles* (Philadelphia: Fortress Press, 1976), 78–96].

[11] See Bassler, *Divine Impartiality*, 166–170.

[12] This corresponds to K. Haacker's description of the letter as "a plea for peace in various dimensions and historical contexts" ("Der Römerbrief als Friedensmemorandum," *NTS* 36 [1990], 29).

Rhetorical analysis now generally views Romans as an epideictic argument designed to "increase the intensity of adherence to certain values ... which (Paul) wants to reinforce until the desired action is actually performed."[13] Thus, in spite of the "summary" or "treatise-like" nature of chapters 1–11, I interpret them, along with the remainder of the letter, as addressed to specific house churches in Rome in order to intensify adherence to the Pauline gospel and ultimately to lead them to "Welcome one another" (15:7; also 14:1).

Romans 2:6–11

(6) For he will repay according to each one's deeds: (7) to those who by patiently doing good seek for glory and honor and immortality, he will give eternal life; (8) while for those who are self-seeking and who obey not the truth but wickedness, there will be wrath and fury. (9) There will be anguish and distress for everyone who does evil, the Jew first and also the Greek, (10) but glory and honor and peace for everyone who does good, the Jew first and also the Greek. (11) For God shows no partiality.

How can the preacher of justification by faith alone apart from works of the Law here promise eternal life to "those who by patiently doing good seek for glory and honor and immortality?" If "there is no one who is righteous, not even one" (3:10), how serious can Paul be in referring to "everyone who does good," or a few verses later claiming that "the doers of the law will be justified" (verse 13)?

These difficulties have called forth numerous interpretations, all wrestling to fit this troublesome passage into the larger thought-world of Romans and of Paul.[14] The problem, of course, lies less with the negative side of Romans 2 than with the positive. That Paul counted evildoers as worthy of destruction is seldom disputed. Hence, taking statements about "faith apart from works" and "no

---

[13] W. Wuellner, "Paul's Rhetoric of Argumentation in Romans," *CBQ* 38 (1976), 343.

[14] C. E. B. Cranfield lists ten different approaches (*The Epistle to the Romans* [2 vols.; ICC; Edinburgh: T. & T. Clark, 1979], I.151), D. J. Moo seven (*The Epistle to the Romans* [NICNT; Grand Rapids, MI: Eerdmans, 1996], 140–141), and T. Schreiner five (*The Law and Its Fulfillment: A Pauline Theology of Law* [Grand Rapids: Baker, 1993], 180–189).

one who does good" as foundational, one group concludes that a judgment according to deeds resulting in eternal life cannot be intended as a real possibility. Perhaps Paul was speaking only hypothetically, or meant the positive side (life according to deeds) as no more than a foil for the real point: everyone will incur wrath since their deeds are evil. This is not to say that such a positive outcome could not be theoretically possible, but since in reality no one is perfect or righteous according to deeds, the practical result is that no one will experience the positive side of this particular judgment.

Another group of exegetes, however, finds that there have been, or will be, individuals who experience even the positive side of this judgment according to deeds. These might be faithful Jews, or anyone who lives up to the light given him or her. Or perhaps the reference is to Christians whose deeds are nothing other than the Spirit-inspired fruit of faith. Within this group of interpreters a further divide occurs between those who see "deeds" as human "works," and those who take it here as simply another way of saying "faith." That is, "patiently doing good" is not a human work, but is actually Christian belief, so that it is "according to faith" that they are judged (and vindicated).

Finally, there are not a few who find Paul quite simply inconsistent in what he asserts in this chapter over against Romans chapter 3. And there are others who downplay the theological aspect of the assertions in favor of their rhetorical or sociological import. Paul's point, for instance, was not to teach about judgment, but to convince Gentile believers that those following Paul's gospel were at no disadvantage to Jews and the synagogue, and thus should go their separate ways.[15]

[15] Significant recent treatments of Rom. 2 include: J. M. Bassler, *Divine Impartiality* (1982), 121–170, 201–202; E. P. Sanders, *Paul, the Law and the Jewish People* (Philadelphia: Fortress Press, 1983; hereafter *PLJP*), 123–135; K. Snodgrass, "Justification by Grace – to the Doers: an Analysis of the Place of Romans 2 in the Theology of Paul," *NTS* 32 (1986), 72–93; F. Watson, *Paul, Judaism and the Gentiles* (Cambridge: Cambridge University Press, 1986), 106–122; J. D. G. Dunn, *Romans 1–8* (1988), 76–128; G. N. Davies, *Faith and Obedience in Romans: a study in Romans 1–4* (JSOTSupp 39; Sheffield: Sheffield Academic Press, 1990), 47–71; N. Elliott, *The Rhetoric of Romans* (1990), 119–131, 167–204; D. B. Garlington, "The Obedience of Faith in the Letter to the Romans: Part II, The Obedience of Faith and Judgment by Works," *WTJ* 53 (1991), 47–72; G. P. Carras, "Romans 2, 1–29: A Dialogue on Jewish Ideals," *Bib* 73 (1992), 183–207; J. A. Fitzmyer, *Romans* (AB 33; New York: Doubleday, 1993), 296–305; T. R. Schreiner, *The Law and Its Fulfillment* (1993), 179–204; D. J. Moo, *The Epistle to the Romans* (1996), 125–157.

The flow of Paul's argument in Romans 1–4

"There is no reason here to depart from the usual recognition that 1:16–17 are the climax of the introduction and theme for what follows."[16] Paul announces that he has no grounds for shame with regard to his gospel of faith-righteousness for Jew and Gentile alike, a sentiment very understandable in the light of approaching events in Jerusalem, and especially Jewish(-Christian) objections to his law-free gospel to Gentiles.

In 1:18–32 Paul has taken up standard elements of Hellenistic Jewish condemnation of the heathen world to stress the rightful judgment of God upon sinful humanity as a whole.[17] In good rhetorical fashion Paul begins his argument with a reminder of shared convictions before approaching possibly controversial matters. The divine righteousness always manifests itself as "wrath ... against all the ungodliness and wickedness of those who by their wickedness suppress the truth." J. Bassler has noted that already in this section Paul is preparing the way for his discussion of impartial judgment in chapter 2. Following E. Klostermann's division of the periods (verses 22–24, 25–27, 28–31), there is "a consistent pattern of sin followed by retribution and in each case the retribution follows the law of talio and corresponds exactly to the previously named theological perversion."[18]

Chapter 2:1–11 brings a sequel to this denunciation of heathen idolatry by now speaking in diatribal style[19] with those who sin and yet would exclude themselves from this strict judgment (2:3) because of "the riches of [God's] kindness and forbearance and patience" (2:4). While phrased generally enough to be applicable to hypocrites of any race,[20] the very similar language in Wisdom

---

[16] Dunn, *Romans 1–8*, 38.

[17] The parallels with The Wisdom of Solomon 13–14 and its scathing denunciation of Gentile idolatry and immorality have been sufficiently noted by other commentators. See, for example, J. Ziesler, *Paul's Letter to the Romans* (Trinity Press International NT Commentary; London: SCM, 1989), 74–79.

[18] "Divine Impartiality in Paul's letter to the Romans," *NovT* 26/1 (1984), 47–48. Reference is to E. Klostermann, "Die adäquate Vergeltung in Rm. 1:22–31," *ZNW* 32 (1933), 1–6; see also Bassler, *Divine Impartiality*, "Appendix E: Objections to Klostermann's Analysis of 1:22–31", 201–202.

[19] On the use of diatribe in this passage see S. Stowers, *The Diatribe and Paul's Letter to the Romans* (SBLDS 57; Chico, CA: Scholars Press, 1981), 110–117. The introduction of diatribe at 2:1 is only a change of rhetorical style, not of audience (112).

[20] F. F. Bruce cites Seneca for similar "excuses" among cultured Greeks (*The Epistle of Paul to the Romans* [TynNTC; Grand Rapids: Eerdmans, 1963], 86–87).

13–15, as well as the subsequent development of the argument (see below), suggest that Paul already has a *Jewish* presumption in mind here.[21] Again, his point to the one who would presume on God's kindness for some advantage at judgment is: "do you imagine you will escape the judgment of God?" (verse 3). I will return shortly to verses 6–11 in greater detail, but it should be noted here that impartial divine judgment according to works constitutes the capstone of Paul's attack on any sense of distinction or advantage in judgment. Rather than attacking supposed Jewish legalism, Paul is here found criticizing an over-reliance on grace which makes forgiveness too easy to obtain due to the supposed soteriological advantages of the Jew.

Since "audience" and "addressee" are sometimes confused in discussions of this passage, a brief clarification is in order. Paul's *audience* in this argument with Judaism is the mixed congregation of Jews and (mostly) Gentiles in Rome.[22] His *target* (or *imaginary debate partner*) in this diatribe is a "Jew."[23] His primary *addressee* in these verses – the group he is particularly concerned to persuade among his audience by these arguments – is the Jewish-Christian minority.[24]

Having introduced "the Jew" by name in verse 9, Paul continues his argument against Jewish presumption in 2:12–29, now naming the supposed protective privileges – the law and circumcision – and arguing that such badges of membership are no substitute for heartfelt obedience (verses 25–27). In fact, the uncircumcised Gentile is at no disadvantage to the Jew, and this because of Paul's radical adherence to "doing" as the criterion of eschatological judgment (2:12–16).

This debate is concluded with responses to various Jewish

On the condemnation of hypocrisy as typical of diatribe, see Stowers, *The Diatribe*, 100–118.

[21] See Carras, "Romans 2, 1–29," 183–207. For caution, however, against over-dependence on Wis. 13–15, see Elliott, *The Rhetoric of Romans*, 174–182, and H. Räisänen, *Paul and the Law* (2nd edn.; WUNT 29; Tübingen: Mohr, 1987), 94–109.

[22] This "double character" of Romans (i.e., an argument with Judaism sent to a mostly Gentile audience) is conveniently summarized by W. G. Kümmel, *Einleitung in das Neue Testament* (18th edn.; Heidelberg: Quelle & Meyer, 1973), 270–271.

[23] This is made explicit in 3:17, and strongly suggested by the Jewishness of the presumptions in 2:1–5 (see above). At this level, the argument has more the character of an inner-Jewish debate (i.e., Paul *the Jew* opposing a different *Jewish* position; cf. Carras, "Romans 2, 1–29,") and explains why some scholars see here little more than a modified synagogue sermon devoid of Christian perspective.

[24] A. Lincoln, "From Wrath to Justification," SBLSPS 1993 (Atlanta: 1993), 196–200.

objections (3:1–8) and a catena of scriptural testimonies (3:9–20) designed to demonstrate once and for all the equality of Jew and Gentile in judgment.[25] All alike are subject to the reign of sin [ὑφ᾽ ἁμαρτίαν, 3:9], and equally accountable [ὑπόδικος, 3:19]. Having thus demonstrated that being Jewish – possessing Torah and circumcision – provides no decisive advantage in eschatological judgment, Paul will proceed in the remainder of chapters 3–4 to argue for the same impartiality and equality in justification.

What has been said above highlights an important fact for this study of 2:6–11, namely that impartial divine judgment strictly according to works functions as the main theological foundation to Paul's argument for Jew–Gentile equality in judgment. The literary structure of the larger passage confirms this pivotal position of 2:6–11, since these verses sum up the argument for impartial judgment in the face of gross sin and hypocrisy (1:18–2:5), and introduce the discussion of impartiality in the light of Jew–Gentile distinctions such as the Torah and circumcision (2:12–3:20).[26]

Universal sinfulness or Jewish advantage? An unnecessary antithesis

Traditionally Romans 1:18–3:20 has been understood to demonstrate (or illustrate) the universal sinfulness of all human beings (3:9, 20), so as to lay the groundwork for Paul's solution: righteousness by faith in Christ.[27] This long-standing consensus has been challenged vigorously, mainly on the grounds that 1:18–3:8 do not, in fact, prove that every individual without exception is a sinner.[28] The charge of universal sinfulness would seem to be ameliorated by the admission that there are some who live righteously (2:7, 10, 13–14, 26). Furthermore the arguments against hypocrisy in 2:1–4 and 17–24 would have force only for those who "practice the same things" (2:1, referring to the idolatry and immorality of 1:18–32) or are hypocritical "thieves," "adulterers,"

---

[25] Note the repetition of the programmatic phrase "the Jew first and also the Greek" at critical junctures: 1:16; 2:9, 10; 3:9.

[26] J. Bassler, "Divine Impartiality," 43–58.

[27] "Paul's aim is to show that the whole of humanity is morally bankrupt" (Bruce, *Romans*, 81). This is "the testimony to a universal accusation against all men without exception" (Cranfield, *The Epistle to the Romans*, I.104, n. 1).

[28] See, for instance, Räisänen, *Paul and the Law* 97–109; C. Cosgrove, "What if some have not believed? The occasion and thrust of Romans 3.1–8," *ZNW* 78 (1987), 90–105; and Elliott, *The Rhetoric of Romans*, 191–198.

or "temple robbers." As Sanders remarks, "Did they all (viz. Jews) rob temples?"[29] According to these scholars Paul is not so much seeking to prove every individual a sinner, but is primarily arguing against some form of Jewish soteriological advantage.

Perhaps in this case we can have our cake and eat it too if we distinguish between *what* Paul says, and *why* he says it. Paul states that "all, both Jews and Greeks, are under the power of sin" (3:9), then cites numerous Scripture texts to the effect that "there is no one who is righteous, not even one" (3:10–18), and concludes on the note of universal accountability (3:19b). Whatever else it is, this is certainly an assertion that every human being without exception both sins and is subject to sin just as the traditional interpretation claims.

On the other hand it is undeniable that the apostle returns again and again to the issue of advantage in judgment.

> Do you imagine . . . you will escape the judgment of God?
> (2:3)

> God shows no partiality. (2:11)

> But if you call yourself a Jew and rely on the law and boast of your relation to God and know his will and determine what is best because you are instructed in the law.
> (2:17–18)

> Then what advantage has the Jew? (3:1)

> What then? Are we [Jews] any better off? (3:9)

> For there is no distinction, since all have sinned and . . . are now justified by his grace as a gift. (3:22–24)

> Then what becomes of boasting? (3:27)

> Not only to the adherents of the law but also to those who share the faith of Abraham. (4:16)

The question either interpretation must answer is – *Why* does Paul argue against certain Jewish soteriological advantages and for universal sinfulness? The traditional interpretation answers: because universal unrighteousness is the logical prerequisite of Paul's gospel of righteousness to all through faith alone apart from works. That is, Paul must convince the hearers of the gospel that

[29] *PLJP*, 125.

they need this faith-righteousness, that they have sinned and fallen short of the glory of God (3:23). However, while it may be agreed that universal sinfulness is logically necesary to Paul's gospel, one may still be allowed to ask, "Who would need convincing of this?" The idea that every person, including Jews, commits sins was a shared conviction between Paul and his Jewish debater.[30] Thus Paul affirms this shared conviction. *But 'why' and 'for whom?'* He does so *in order to convince Jewish Christians that Jewishness will not prevent Jews from being judged as "sinners" equally with Gentiles.* Thus he indeed asserts universal subjection to sin (3:9b), but makes the point of this assertion and of the scriptural catena[31] clear (verse 19) by arguing that these accusations must be allowed their full force equally upon "those who are under the law" (= Jews) *for the purpose* [ἵνα] of eliminating any and all excuses ("that every mouth may be silenced") and making all *accountable to God* [ὑπόδικος τῷ θεῷ]. This is also the point of the thematic phrase "both Jews and Greeks" (1:16; 2:9–10).

Thus Paul's purpose in Romans 1–4 is to destroy any sense of distinction, privilege, or advantage before the divine tribunal based on racial or religious differences.[32] These chapters constitute Paul's initial defense of this equal treatment of both Jew and Gentile, focusing first on equal treatment in judgment due to God's impartial judgment of a universally sinful world (1:18–3:20), then on equal treatment in salvation (3:21–4:25). It is not against a world claiming "we have not sinned" that he is arguing, but against

---

[30] See Eccles. 7:20; 1 Kgs. 8:46; Ps. 51:5; 1QH IV,29–30; VII,17–18; IX,14–15; PssSol. 9:6–7. See also G. F. Moore, *Judaism in the First Centuries of the Christian Era, The Age of the Tannaim* (3 vols.; Cambridge: Harvard University Press, 1954 [orig. 1927]), I.468, 479–489; and F. Thielman, *From Plight to Solution, A Jewish Framework for Understanding Paul's View of the Law in Galatians and Romans* (NovTSup 61; Leiden: E. J. Brill, 1989), 28–45.

[31] It is quite possible that Paul here draws on preformed material used by faithful Jews in the condemnation of Gentiles and apostates. See CD V,13–17; 4 Ezra 7:22–24; and L. E. Keck, "The Function of Romans 3:10–18 – Observations and Suggestions," *God's Christ and His People, FS N. A. Dahl* (ed. J. Jervell and W. A. Meeks; Oslo-Bergen Tromsö: Universitetsforlaget, 1977),141–157.

[32] In his thorough rhetorical analysis of Romans, N. Elliott comes to a similar conclusion: "The offense at the center of Paul's apostrophic indictment is nothing other than considering oneself "excused" from God's righteous demand" (*The Rhetoric of Romans*, 123, 126). Elliott, however, views this as directed at Gentile Christian smugness. Against this, Dunn concludes with most others, "the principal focus of critique is Jewish self-assurance that the typically Jewish indictment of Gentile sin (1:18–32) is not applicable to the covenant people themselves" (*Romans 1–8*, 51; cf. pp. 51–88). Similarly G. P. Carras, "Romans 2, – 29," 183–207.

Jews or Jewish-Christians claiming that they will not be treated the
same as the "sinners" in the judgment of God. "Do you imagine . . .
you will escape the judgment of God?" (2:3).

The chiastic structure and the content of Romans 2:6–11

Verses 6–11 detail the eschatological basis for this divine impartiality in judgment; namely, it will be strictly ἑκάστῳ κατὰ τὰ ἔργα
αὐτοῦ [to each according to works]. Paul structures this
chiastically:[33]

A   v. 6   divine judgment is according to deeds
B   v. 7   do good/seek glory, etc. – eternal life
C   v. 8   obey unrighteousness – wrath and fury
C'   v. 9   do evil – anguish and distress
B'   v. 10   do good – glory, honor, and peace
A'   v. 11   no partiality with God

A number of observations regarding Paul's intent can be made
from this structure. Verses 7–10 elucidate Paul's understanding of
the motif of divine recompense according to deeds (verse 6). It is a
dual recompense in that it encompasses both reward for good
(verses 7, 10) and punishment for evil (verses 8–9). Its *universality* is
made explicit by the addition of "the Jew first and also the Greek"
(verses 9–10) and its *individuality* by the use of ἕκαστος [each,
verse 6]. The use of ζωή αἰώνιος[34] [eternal life, verse 7] in opposition to ὀργὴ καὶ θυμός [wrath and fury, verse 8] makes of it an
eschatological recompense issuing in one's ultimate *soteriological*
fate. Thus this repayment [ἀποδώσει] is none other than the last
judgment which takes place on the apocalyptic "day of wrath"[35]
(verse 5). Then sinners will "perish" [ἀπολοῦνται, verse 12] while
the righteous will be "justified," "on the day when, according to my
gospel, God, through Jesus Christ, will judge the secret thoughts of
all" (verse 16). Excepting the christological comment of verse 16,

---

[33] See esp. K. Grobel, "A Chiastic Retribution-Formula in Romans 2," *Zeit und
Geschichte: Dankesgabe an Rudolf Bultmann zum 80. Geburtstag* (ed. E. Dinkler;
Tübingen: J. C. B. Mohr, 1964), 255–261. However, Grobel's assertion that this is a
pre-Pauline chiasm with several (Pauline?) insertions seems difficult of demonstration.
[34] "Eternal life," while comparatively rare in Paul, is attested: Rom. 5:21; 6:22, 23;
Gal. 6:8. See Ziesler, *Paul's Letter to the Romans,* 171.
[35] On "the day (of wrath)" in Paul, cf. G. Delling, *TDNT,*II.952.

all of the above characteristics of Paul's use of the motif have manifold parallels in the materials studied in chapters 1–3 above.

There is also a crucial rhetorical move to be noted. Verses 7–8 unfold the principle of recompense using language unmistakably reminiscent of the Jewish denunciations of pagan wickedness in chapter 1. If the wicked there are those who exchange the glory [δόξαν] of the immortal [ἀφθάρτος] God and are recompensed with dishonor [ἀτιμάζεσθαι, verses 23–24], then the righteous, in precise contrast, are those who seek δόξαν and τιμήν and ἀφθαρσίαν (2:7). Likewise the description of the wicked – those who obey not τῇ ἀληθείᾳ but τῇ ἀδικίᾳ (2:8) – parallels the ἀδικία and suppression of τὴν ἀλήθειαν among the heathen (1:18). In both places the evildoers are consigned to divine wrath [ὀργή, 1:18; 2:8], now contrasted with the eschatological reward of eternal life to the righteous (2:7). To Jewish ears this would all sound quite unexceptional: salvation for Israel in covenant obedience; eschatological punishment for the nations or the apostates in their wickedness.

However, while repeating the foregoing in reverse order and with synonymous terminology, verses 9–10 contain one crucial addition – the two-fold reference to "the Jew first and also the Greek." This harks back to the thematic introduction of the whole section (1:16), and with it Paul springs his trap on the diatribal target, hoping thereby to persuade his Jewish-Christian addressees of the wrong-headedness of the thinking outlined in 2:1–5. He interprets and radicalizes the recompense concept of verses 6–8 in a way that strips the Jew of any eschatological advantage. The divine wrath, now termed "anguish and distress," cannot be restricted to the Gentiles alone, but must apply to "everyone [ἐπὶ πᾶσαν ψυχὴν ἀνθρώπου] who does evil." Thus the Jews' priority is turned against them, making them equally first in judgment. Correspondingly, the eschatological reward cannot be limited to the Jews alone, but is for the Gentiles on the same basis.

> The underlying thrust of 2:1–11 now becomes explicit: the target is Jewish presumption of priority of privilege, which however soundly rooted in God's election of Israel – a fact which Paul does not dispute (1:16) and to which he will return (3:1–4; chapters 9–11) – has led Paul's kinsfolk to the effective conclusion that God's judgment of Israel will be on different terms from his judgment of the nations as a whole ... In reformulating verses 7–8 Paul insists that both

verses apply equally to both Jew and Gentile. Paul's whole point here is that the terms of judgment are precisely the same for everyone.[36]

Whether this "Jewish presumption" was thought by Paul to be characteristic of the Judaism he knew, or was simply a position he attributed to his diatribal target, will be discussed below. It was not, however, a characteristic of the motif use in second temple Jewish texts. Both in the OT Pseudepigrapha and the Qumran literature, admonitions were regularly addressed to members of the covenant communities, and to Jews at large, using this recompense motif, warning them of the loss of covenant status and blessings if they walked in wickedness.[37] We did trace a developing dichotomy between God's treatment of the righteous and the wicked in judgment. However, the division between the righteous and the wicked in these texts did not correspond generally to the division between Jews and non-Jews. Instead, the division was between the righteous and the wicked *within* Israel according to their deeds. The motif was seen to have been used especially in contexts of community conflict in order to identify true Jews within Israel. In a few instances the motif even asserted the equality of Jews and Gentiles in this judgment,[38] and in 2 Baruch "it is neither election nor external participation in the chosen nation which guarantees salvation, but 'the doers of the law will be justified'."[39]

This understanding of the rhetorical target also explains why punishment stands at the center of the chiasm (verses 8–9). Against the Jewish presumption so described it is the point of *judgment to the Jew first* which Paul must make. Whether this means that the positive statements (verses 7, 10) are merely a foil, a Jewish assumption which the apostle will later subvert, will be taken up at a later point in our discussion.

This equality in judgment (and destruction of Jewish presumption), finally, is rooted in the very character of God himself, namely his impartiality [προσωπολημψία, verse 11].[40] The combination of

---

[36] Dunn, *Romans 1–8*, 88. Likewise Carras, "Romans 2, 1–29," 206.

[37] See pp. 87–91, 136–138.

[38] See Jub. 5:12–16; and p. 93 above.

[39] P. 86. The same removal of soteriological distinction between Jewish and non-Jewish sinners was found in the PssSol. (see p. 74).

[40] Rooted in the OT (2 Chron. 19:7; Deut. 10:17; Job 34:19), divine impartiality became axiomatic during the intertestamental period (Bassler, *Divine Impartiality*, 7–44).

these two motifs – impartiality and judgment according to deeds – had already become traditional by Paul's time.[41] This is one more indication that Paul is reliant on Jewish tradition for his argument here. However, his particular use of the doctrine of divine impartiality in this text, namely to relativize Jewish covenant advantage before God, may have been surprising to first-century Jews. Note Peter's surprise in Acts 10:34–35: "I truly understand that God shows no partiality [προσωπολήμπτης], but in every nation anyone who fears him and does what is right is acceptable to him."[42] Bassler's study likewise concludes that this surprise attack on Jewish privilege via the axiom of impartiality, while not entirely novel, still represents an element of Pauline (or early Christian) originality.[43]

With verse 12 Paul begins a new section (2:12–29) focusing on the obvious advantage of the Jew in the possession of the Torah.[44] However, even though lacking the Jewish Torah, the Gentile is at no disadvantage, because judgment according to deeds (here "doing" versus "hearing" [= possessing]) allows for differing standards of "law" against which one will be judged (verses 12–16).[45] Likewise (verses 17–29) the Jew who sins will find possession of the Torah and circumcision to be of no advantage in God's impartial judgment according to works.

Quotation or allusion

Our attention now turns to the motif statement in verse 6, in particular to Paul's handling of the motif tradition, and to points of continuity or discontinuity with that same tradition. Commentators remain uncertain in identifying the precise source of this supposed quotation or allusion.[46] Reference is usually made to one or both of the following OT texts:

---

[41] Cf. Sir. 35:12–19, 24; Jub. 5:15–16; T.Job 4:7; PssSol. 2:16, 18. On their continued combination in rabbinic literature, see Bassler, *Divine Impartiality*, 17–76.

[42] A somewhat different attack on Jewish covenant presumption can been seen in Matt. 3:9 (= Luke 3:8).

[43] *Divine Impartiality*, 44, 65, 76, 119.

[44] Not mentioned previously in the letter, νόμος and its cognate ἀνόμως are used twenty-one times in 2:12–29!

[45] It has only rarely been noted by NT scholars that Paul's idea of "differing standards" in judgment was not unknown in Judaism: cf. Jub. 5:12–19 (see on this text above, pp. 66–67); Wis. 6:6–8. See also H. Schlier, *Der Römerbrief* (HTK 6; Freiburg/Basel/Vienna: Herder, 1977), 75, n. 22.

[46] Dunn favors a "direct citation" (*Romans 1–8*, 85) and Hays a "virtual citation" (Hays, *Echoes of Scripture*, 42–43), while Ellis lists the text under "allusions" to the

Ps. 62:13[47] ὅτι σὺ ἀποδώσεις ἑκάστῳ κατὰ τὰ ἔργα αὐτοῦ,
Prov. 24:12 ὃς ἀποδίδωσιν ἑκάστῳ κατὰ τὰ ἔργα αὐτοῦ,
Rom. 2:6 ὃς ἀποδώσει ἑκάστῳ κατὰ τὰ ἔργα αὐτοῦ.

Paul's wording is not an exact quotation of either of these passages in their LXX form; nor is he reflecting their MT form.[48] It is doubtful, in fact, that Paul intends to quote or allude to any specific passage of the OT, or of any other Jewish literature for that matter. There is no introductory formula or other contextual clue that would alert one to the presence of a scripture citation. Interestingly, throughout the considerable usage of the motif in the Jewish literature traced in the previous chapters not a single instance was found of a writer citing the motif as a quotation of scripture. Instead, its use was so deep-rooted and widespread in second temple Judaism that Paul, like others before him, simply draws the motif from this storehouse of Jewish tradition in which it was everywhere recognized as a fundamental religious axiom rooted firmly in the OT.[49]

Lexical considerations

Paul's wording of the motif likewise reflects traditional usage without necessitating citation of a particular text. His choice of ἀποδίδωμι reflects the preference, seen already in the LXX, for forms of δίδωμι in motif occurrences,[50] while the future tense mirrors the increasing tendency in second temple Judaism to place this recompense in the realm of eschatological fulfillment.[51] The employment of κατά + ἔργα (pl.) appears to be a preferred mode of expression among Hellenistic Jewish writers,[52] and the individuation of judgment [ἑκάστῳ] was likewise common throughout the literature surveyed earlier. The purpose of this individualizing, however, both in that earlier literature and here in Romans 2:6, is not so much to stress the *individuality* (i.e., judgment person by person) but the *inescapability* of judgment for every single person,

OT (E. E. Ellis, *Paul's Use of the Old Testament* [London: Oliver and Boyd, 1957], 153).
[47] LXX = 61:13.
[48] In both cases the MT reads a *singular* ("according to his *work*").
[49] Heiligenthal, *Werke als Zeichen*, 174.
[50] See pp. 22–23 above.
[51] See pp. 89, 135–136 above.
[52] Cf. pp. 23, 87.

and in Romans 2:6 specifically for the Jew. This thought of "no escape" or "no excuse" has been highlighted already in verses 1 and 3. "To each according to deeds" in verse 6 is then explained to mean *for both good and evil to the Jew first and also the Greek without impartiality* (verses 7–11).

"Work" versus "works"

As noted earlier the use of the plural [ἔργα] is what one would expect following the preposition κατά in the motif. However, attempts have been made to avoid the close juxtaposition of good works and justification/judgment by positing a technical distinction in Pauline literature between ἔργα (pl.) and ἔργον (sg.).[53] Allegedly the plural, with or without the addition of (τοῦ) νόμου, always has a negative connotation, referring to meritorious human achievement and self-righteousness. The singular, on the other hand, is supposedly reserved in Paul for Christians, whose entire life is but a single, indivisible participation in Christ's own work. Thus, it is not the "work," as such, which results in salvation or condemnation, but the faith or unbelief which comes to expression in the same. Mattern can go so far as to declare, "A Christian has no *works*."[54] This, then, enables her to interpret ἔργον ἀγαθόν (Rom. 2:7) as "faith" rather than as actual "good works," so that technically the judgment of believers is not according to "works" but according to "faith."[55]

The fact is, as Mattern herself admits, Romans 2:6–11 does not follow this supposedly technical usage, since the *plural* (ἔργα) in verse 6 entails both good and bad deeds, followed immediately by the usage of the *singular* in verses 7 and 10 with no demonstrable difference in meaning. This is especially the case since verses 7–10 with their singular nouns are intended as an expansion upon the meaning of verse 6 with its plural ἔργα. While one can acknowledge a general pattern in Paul's usage of "work/works" along the lines of Mattern's analysis, this cannot be pressed so as to remove the "works" themselves as the basis of the eschatological judgment.

---

[53] See for instance Mattern, *Das Verständnis des Gerichtes*, 141–151; also Beker, *Paul the Apostle*, 247–248; and (apparently) Dunn, *Romans 1–8*, 85.

[54] *Das Verständnis des Gerichtes*, 151.

[55] "Judgment is not passed upon the good or evil achievements [*Leistung*] of the individual... but upon a Christian's varying participation in God's work" (ibid., 151).

2 Corinthians 5:10, like Romans 2:6, clearly refers to concrete deeds (pl.), both good and evil, as the basis of judgment.[56] Similarly, passages such as 1 Corinthians 7:19 ("obeying the commandments of God") and 2 Corinthians 9:8 ("you may share abundantly in every good work" – implying multiplicity; cf. also Colossians 1:10) speak against a rigid view of "works" in Paul as negative.[57] The switch from plural to singular in Romans 2:6–7 is better explained as due to the Jewish background of his thought here, than to a supposed aversion to "work<u>s</u>." The easy interchange between singular and plural "work(s)" in motif contexts was found to be characteristic of Jewish literature.[58] This linguistic phenomenon is grounded in the view of human works not so much as individual achievements or merits, but as together giving unified and visible expression to the unseen character of the person. The good person does good works, the evil person evil works. Non-Jewish readers of Romans would have understood this point equally well, since Hellenistic literature testifies to the same view among pagan Greeks; namely, ἔργα are the visible revelation of the true essence or character of an individual.[59] Rather than being some coded reference to (Christian) faith, the patient doing of "the good" [τὸ ἀγαθόν; verses 7, 10][60] is language that would appeal broadly to both Jews and Greeks, referring simply to behavior which is recognized to be excellent, and which brings honor rather than shame.[61] This "doing (the) good" is contrasted stereotypically with the actions of the wicked (verses 8–9) along the lines of Two-Way traditions in Judaism, according to which the righteous inherit life, while the wicked are visited with destruction.

[56] See chapter 6 below on this passage and on 2 Cor. 11:15.
[57] This is even clearer in the disputed letters: Eph. 2:10; 1 Tim. 2:10; 5:10, 25; 6:18; 2 Tim. 1:9; Titus 2:7, 14; 3:8, 14.
[58] See pp. 24–26, 87, 133 above.
[59] R. Heiligenthal, *Werke*, 1–25, 195.
[60] On the genitive construction in verse 7, cf. *BDF*, 163.
[61] On "the good" in Greek philosophy, Hellenism and Judaism, see W. Grundmann, *TDNT*, art. ἀγαθός, 1.10–15. The correspondence of "the good" to the ἔργα of verse 6, and the contrast with the way of the wicked (verse 8) indicate that for Paul "doing (the) good" here is simply an alternative way of describing those whose goal [ζητοῦσιν] remains unswervingly obedience to God (cf. Rom. 12:2 – the will of God = τὸ ἀγαθόν). This usage of ἀγαθός/τὸ ἀγαθόν for the will of God which the pious are expected to fulfill is not otherwise foreign to Paul; cf. Rom. 13:3; 2 Cor. 9:8; Gal. 6:9; Col. 1:10; 2 Thess. 2:17; also 1 Tim. 5:10; 2 Tim. 2:21; 3:17.

Excursus: "Works" as *manifestation* rather than as merit

The above perspective on ἔργον/ἔργα goes against the grain of a long-standing tendency in Protestant scholarship to suspect all "works" of being the result of fleshly effort and achievement They are thought to be tainted by the motivation to acquire thereby one's own status or merit before God, and thus always akin to the alleged "works-righteousness" of Pharisaic Judaism. A classic example is Rudolf Bultmann, for whom not merely ἔργα νόμου, but equally human ἔργα *per se*, must be interpreted as the epitome of human achievement or performance, and thus always in opposition to grace and leading to fleshly boasting [καύχημα] before God. Ἔργα (νόμου) speak of that proud human attitude which wants to stand before God in its own power.[62]

My understanding draws upon the work of Roman Heiligenthal, *Werke als Zeichen: Untersuchungen zur Bedeutung der menschlichen Taten im Frühjudentum, neuen Testament und Frühchristentum* (WUNT 2/9; Tübingen: J. C. B. Mohr (Paul Siebeck), 1983; originally Diss.: Heidelberg, 1981), whose "analysis is built upon the thesis that *works* in the New Testament possess above all the character of a sign; that is, they reveal the inner reality of the person to others and to God. Functioning thus, they are assessed more positively in the New Testament than the traditional Protestant rejection of 'works righteousness' would lead one to assume" (Preface).

This revelatory or sign-character of works is shown to be fundamental to the Hellenistic understanding of ἔργον/ἔργα (1–25). Whether it is a matter of human or divine evaluation, "in both cases it is the value of deeds as manifesting something [*der Erkenntniswert der Taten*] which stands in the foreground, rather than being a matter of performance [*Leistungscharakter*]. Works are not understood primarily as a proof of performance [*Leistungsausweis*] but as a means of knowing and assessing [*ein Erkenntnis- und Beurteilungsmittel*]" (25). He finds the same understanding in second temple Judaism (cf. 72–84, 143–164, 234–263, 290–296, 314).

In the judgment according to deeds in Romans 2:6–11 "the concern is not to reject achievement [*Leistungen*], but to stress the

---

[62] *Theologie des Neuen Testaments*, 284; cf. also 280–285. Heiligenthal shows clearly how this understanding of "works" (= meritorious achievements) has guided Protestant interpretations of Rom. 2 (*Werke als Zeichen*, 167–170).

relevance of good and evil deeds in the judgment as the means of recognizing the inner character of the person [*als Erkenntnisprinzip des inneren Seins des Menschen*]" (171, n. 69; cf. also 165–197). The definition of Christians' behavior as "fruit of the Spirit" in Galatians 5:19–26 shows once again that their actions are not being viewed as meritorious human "achievements," but are the product of the new Spirit-worked inner reality of believers in Christ (201–207).

Lest the above be misunderstood as demanding a strict either/or, Heiligenthal is not intent on denying all possibility of ἔργα = "achievement,"[63] but merely on demonstrating that this was not the normal or primary understanding for Jews and Greeks.

This thesis can be strengthened by two additional observations. Both the OT and second temple Jewish texts testify to a unitary versus atomistic view of human deeds, as has been demonstrated in the earlier chapters. Thus the multiplicity of one's deeds constitutes one's "way" or "work" (sg.), the visible manifestation of one's wickedness or uprightness of heart. Deeds are not merits which gain entry into a particular status with God; rather they reveal the status which one has already gained via election and covenant. Second, since the work of E. P. Sanders and others, first-century Judaism can no longer properly be characterized as a legalistic religion of works-righteousness. Thus, the foil commonly used to interpret Paul's contrast between grace and works (i.e., works = Jewish merit theology) is no longer valid.

Function: summons to repentance

The fact that the motif occurs in this instance as one element within a larger diatribal unit (2:1–11) means that we must distinguish at least three levels of its function: (a) its role within the unfolding diatribal argument; (b) its intended effect, as part of the diatribe, upon the diatribal critic; and (c) its intended rhetorical force upon

---

[63] For instance, Eph. 2:8–9 contrasts salvation by grace through faith with salvation ἐξ ὑμῶν, thus focusing on the origin or authorship of salvation. "Not from yourselves" is then expanded in terms of οὐκ ἐξ ἔργων [not of works], so that human activity or achievement is contrasted with God's gift [δῶρον], and self-praise [καυχήσεται] is excluded. However, even here human ἔργα are rejected not because they lay claim to *legalistically earning* salvation, but because they are the *wrong source*. This same contrast between grace and works in order to emphasize the divine origin of salvation can be found in Hellenistic Judaism of the period (Heiligenthal, *Werke als Zeichen*, 290–291).

the addressee. Verses 1–5 are addressed in the form of a diatribe to
an imaginary dialogue partner, in this case a Jew who condemns
sinful Gentiles but presumes upon God's covenant mercy to Israel
for his/her own deliverance in spite of committing the same sins as
the Gentiles. The pointed charges and rhetorical questions in verses
1–4 culminate in the judgment-sentence of verse 5. The motif in
verse 6 supplies the theological basis for this sentence. The central
position of punishment for evil (verses 8–9) in the chiasm of verses
6–11, along with the appearance in verse 9 of the thematic "to the
Jew first," support this contention that the purpose of the motif
within this diatribal setting is to press home the propriety of God's
judgment-sentence upon disobedient and impenitent Jews. Thus on
the level of the logic within the diatribe itself (level *a* above), the
motif functions simply as an explanation or a theological warrant
for the charge made in verse 5.

As for the intended effect upon the imaginary critic (level *b*), the
diatribe reads like a *sentence* or *summons to repentance*,[64] or more
generally as a *warning*. The critic should recognize his/her presumptuous reasoning and hypocritical behavior (cf. verses 1–3),
and allow God's kindness to produce repentance (verse 4); otherwise wrathful judgment is threatened (verse 5). As in numerous
Jewish texts already studied, the motif is brought in as a conclusion to such a warning, providing theological warrant and stressing
the certainty and inescapability of the coming judgment if the
warning is not heeded.[65] This characterization as a summons to
repentance in the face of Jewish presumption finds support in
those studies which see in this section an inner-Jewish debate.
According to G. P. Carras Paul takes the side of a Jew who finds
fault with an opposing position within Judaism because the latter
"violated central tenets of his own religion by claiming a criterion
of judgement for himself different from all others."[66] Specifically,
the opponent claimed preferential treatment due to a supposed
moral superiority (2:1–11), possession of the Torah (2:12–16),
national privilege (2:17–24, = "Jewishness"), and circumcision

[64] This is a *conditional* form of the prophetic sentence upon Israel (cf. pp. 56–60).
See also Heiligenthal, *Werke als Zeichen*, 167, 184 (Rom. 2:1–11 = *Bekehrungspre-
digt* [a sermon on repentance]).
[65] See esp. Ezek. 18:1–30; 33:10–20. See also the use of the motif as a concluding
rhetorical device in Judg. 1:7; Ps. 94:23; Zech. 1:6; 1 Macc. 7:42; Ju.b 5:11; 2 Bar. 54:
16, 21; 1QM VI,6.
[66] "Romans 2,1–29," 206.

(2:25–29).[67] In a fashion possibly reminiscent of Jewish synagogue sermons,[68] those who hold such a position are called to repentance (2:4), since their thought and behavior contradict belief in God's impartial judgment according to deeds.

As for Paul's Jewish-Christian addressees in Rome (level *c*) the diatribal form is meant to challenge them in an indirect way to correct possibly faulty attitudes. Paul is not accusing them of impenitent sinning or apostasy; rather he is concerned lest their thinking mirror that of the diatribe partner, believing that Jewish covenant privileges will make a decisive difference for the Jew in judgment. As I have argued, it is this issue of Jewish advantage over Gentiles that is at the center of the theological argument of chapters 1–11 and of the social conflict reflected in chapters 12–15. Understood as a call to abandon wrong attitudes, the motif and the diatribe function to summon the addressees to repentance.

Dual retribution

As a *warning* or *summons to repentance* Romans 2:6 continues the tradition which began in the OT of using the motif to threaten punishment upon the consistently rebellious or potentially apostate in Israel, or upon Jewish opponents in later contexts of sectarian Judaism.[69] This fits in quite well with the exigencies of Romans since Paul's diatribe in 2:1–11 can be viewed in the context of inner-Jewish conflict. Why, then, does Paul deviate from this traditional use (for punishment only) and explicate the motif in terms of an eschatological-soteriological duality (i.e., salvation to the good, wrath to the wicked)? Although the use of the motif for a positive reward for the righteous was not uncommon in the OT, it had all but disappeared during the two centuries preceding the common era.[70] Recompense according to deeds nearly always

---

[67] I would fault Carras only for failing to appreciate adequately the radicalization of Paul's side of the debate, in that Paul goes beyond the point that even most Jews of his persuasion were prepared to go. That is, Paul relativizes the Jews' covenantal salvation privileges vis-à-vis the Gentiles. Jews and Gentiles have *equal access* to God's grace and salvation without regard to Jewishness. Carras also fails to explain why such an inner-Jewish debate was necessary in a letter to Roman Christians.

[68] See Sanders, *PLJP*, Appendix: "Romans 2," 123–135. Until more examples of such Hellenistic-Jewish sermons turn up, this must remain only a plausible hypothesis.

[69] See pp. 50–60, 70–73 (cf. 1 En. 95:5; 100:7), 100–102, (cf. 1QS II,7–8).

[70] Only a few texts in the Pseudepigrapha and the Qumran literature testify to a belief in a positive retribution according to deeds (cf. pp. 89, 105–106, 134–135).

meant punishment. Mention of a dual retribution can be found a handful of times in the OT use of the motif,[71] and such a comprehensive statement of its duality was found (only) in Sirach 16:12–14:

> Great as his mercy, so also is his chastisement;
> he judges a person according to one's deeds.
> The sinner will not escape with plunder,
> and the patience of the godly will not be frustrated.
> He makes room for every act of mercy;
> everyone receives in accordance with one's deeds.

Interestingly, this passage shows several parallels with Romans 2.[72] Its aim is ultimately to motivate the wise member of the covenant to choose obedience and fidelity to God's will. It is likewise a warning directed against the presumption that sinful Jews can "escape" [ἐκφεύξεται] God's judgment according to deeds, as well as a comfort to the "patience of the godly" [ὑπομονὴ εὐσεβοῦς] whose obedience will be rewarded.[73]

While this singular text illustrates that Paul's expression of dual retribution was not un-Jewish, it nevertheless remains true that the emphasis on only one aspect of the recompense (reward *or* punishment) was by far the more common. The choice appears to have been largely dictated by the purpose and context of the saying. What was it in the rhetorical exigency of writing to the Romans that called forth this comprehensive expression of dual retribution, in particular the positive aspect of reward? As the examination of the structure and occasion of these early chapters in Romans suggested, Paul's purpose is to demonstrate the equality of Jew and Gentile, in terms of both divine wrath and justification, with 2:6–11 occupying a central role in the theological foundation of this argument. With few exceptions, Gentiles as Gentiles (non-proselytes, outside the covenant) were assumed by most Jews to be among the wicked. Paul's use of the motif puts them on an equal footing with Jews, since all is "according to works" without respect

---

This is not to deny their belief in the reward of the righteous, only that such was not commonly expressed in the terminology of the motif.

[71] Job 34:11, Eccles. 12:14, Ezek. 33:20, and in the explication of divine judgment found in 1 Kgs. 8:32 (= 2 Chr. 6:23).

[72] See my discussion on pp. 41–42 above.

[73] Note the verbal parallels to Rom. 2:3 ("Do you imagine . . . you will escape [ἐκφεύξῃ] the judgment of God?") and 2:7 ("by patiently doing good" [καθ' ὑπομονὴν ἔργου ἀγαθοῦ]).

to Jewishness. Beginning with the OT prophets, various streams within Judaism likewise challenged the presumption that Jewishness alone (i.e., without the accompanying wholehearted devotion and obedience) was a sufficient protection against divine judgment; but this challenge did not generally include the further conclusion that Gentiles were thereby put on the same footing *in regard to salvation*. That was still a matter exclusively of God's covenant *with Israel*. Because Paul *is* taking that next step, he feels the necessity to stress as well the positive side of the recompense duality. In order to prepare the way for the equality of Jew and Gentile in justification (not just in condemnation), he uses the motif to urge that *both* (justification and condemnation) are impartially according to deeds. Granted, he follows up this point by stressing the punishment aspect in verse 12 (and that is certainly the primary issue in the argument with Judaism), but if the point had been only that "Jews shall be *condemned* on the same basis as Gentiles," verses 13–16 would seem to pose an unnecessary risk by their assertion that equally "the (Gentile) doers of the law will be justified." Similarly in verse 29 the point is not simply to disqualify faithless Jews from bearing that name, but to redefine "Jew" so as to include both Jews and Gentiles in Israel's inheritance ("Such a person receives praise ... from God").

Thus, in 2:6–11 divine impartiality and the associated principle of judgment according to works are radicalized[74] by Paul to mean that Jewish sin will be treated no differently than Gentile sin, *and* that Gentile obedience must carry the same reward as Jewish (= eternal life). To restate my position, this last positive conclusion ("glory, honor and peace for everyone who does good") represents Paul's mature Christian thought as equally as the negative, and cannot be explained as hypothetical, a mere foil, an unreflected survival from Paul's Jewish background. For Paul the eschatological judgment, whether resulting in destruction or rewards will be "according to works" for all without distinction. Thus, not only in

---

[74] The idea that Paul has "radicalized" Jewish views of judgment was central to Braun's study (*Gerichtsgedanke und Rechtfertigungslehre*, esp. 59). He posited three areas in which Paul had radicalized Jewish views: (1) strict carrying out of impartiality, (2) demand of perfection, and (3) nature of the "reward" (= eternal life). It is my view that points (2) and (3) are no radicalization, being based on Braun's misreading of both Paul's and Judaism's position at these points. It is point (1), the strict adherence to impartiality in judgment, thus stripping the Jews of salvific advantage, which constitutes Paul's radical stance vis-à-vis Judaism.

the form and function of the motif, but also in its soteriological implications, Paul is arguing in a manner consistent with his Jewish background as viewed through the motif usage studied in chapters 1–3.

Objections: (1) Is perfection required?

But does this not involve us at once in a blatant contradiction with Romans 3:20 ("For by law-works no flesh shall be justified in his sight" [διότι ἐξ ἔργων νόμου οὐ δικαιωθήσεται πᾶσα σὰρξ ἐνώπιον αὐτοῦ]) and Paul's alleged insistence elsewhere that "perfection" is required if one is to come to God by "doing"? Taking the second objection first, nothing in Romans 2 indicates that Paul is envisioning perfect (= flawless) obedience. As noted above (p. 159), "patiently doing good" is the language of broad appeal to both Jews and Greeks and shows affinities to the Two-Way tradition in Judaism. In none of these contexts would it typically be understood in a perfectionistic sense. As discovered repeatedly in the previous chapters, such behavior of the righteous in Judaism does not imply flawless obedience or sinlessness on their part. Paul's language is a typically Jewish way of describing those who live with consistency and integrity according to God's ways. Neither do the various formulations which follow for "keeping the law" refer to anything more than godly obedience.[75] Here Paul reflects his Jewish background, properly understood, which did not require a legalistic perfection (otherwise repentance would not have been so important in Judaism!), but submission to God's commandments and the intention to obey them.[76]

Typically Galatians 3:10 and 5:3 are cited as proof that Paul understood *perfect keeping of the law* to be necessary if one would seek to be justified by works.[77] Yet, as even the proponents admit,

---

[75] Verses 13 ("doers of the law" [οἱ ποιηταὶ νόμου]), 25 ("if you do the law" [νόμον πράσσῃς]), 26 ("if you keep the righteous requirement of the law" [τὰ δικαιώματα τοῦ νόμου φυλάσσῃ]), and 27 ("keeping the law" [τὸν νόμον τελοῦσα]). Cf. Cranfield, *The Epistle to the Romans*, I.155, 171 (n. 3), 173–174; Don B. Garlington, *Faith, Obedience and Perseverance: Aspects of Paul's Letter to the Romans* (WUNT 79; Tübingen: J. C. B. Mohr (Paul Siebeck), 1994), 44–71. The same language can be used for the obedience expected of Christians toward Jesus' teaching (John 12:47) as well as apostolic injunctions (Acts 16:4; Snodgrass, "Justification by Grace," 83–84). Cf. also Acts 21:24.

[76] E. P. Sanders, *PPJ*, 75, 94–101, 137–147, 175–176, 419–428 (an exception being possibly IV Ezra, cf. 416–417). Cf. also G. F. Moore, *Judaism*, I.494–495.

[77] H. Hübner, "Gal. 3:10–12 und die Herkunft des Paulus," *KuD* 19 (1973),

this involves a syllogism whose crucial middle step is more assumed than stated by Paul.

(1) All who do not keep the law [perfectly] are cursed (Deut. 27:26, cited in Gal. 3:10b).
(2) No one can keep the law [perfectly] (implied premise).
(3) Therefore, all who rely on the works of the law are under a curse (Gal. 3:10a).[78]

This study has repeatedly emphasized that such a form of "perfect law-keeping" was hardly typical of Judaism in Paul's time.[79] "True enough," say the proponents, "but this is Paul's insight into the true nature of Jewish religion, which the Jews themselves failed to see or accept." Even if this were correct, it is almost certain that his Jewish listeners would not have accepted that Deuteronomy 27:26 necessitates "perfect law-keeping," and it must be doubted whether Paul intended such an idea.

Why then does he stress the necessity (under the law) of "abiding by all things ... in the law" (3:10)? Paul's concern in the section (3:6–14) is to demonstrate to the Galatians from Scripture that righteousness and the blessing of Abraham for the Gentiles have always been intended to come through faith, not (work of) Torah (cf. esp. verses 6–9, 14). Thus Paul's argument in this section consists of a string of assertions all connected with the above thesis, and each with an accompanying Scripture proof. Hermeneutically, this means that our attention should focus first on Paul's assertions in order to ascertain the thrust of that point in the argument, not on the Scripture proof, since the latter (in typical rabbinic fashion) is closer to what one might call "proof-texting." This is crucial for understanding 3:10.

Focusing on Paul's assertions, the argument in verses 6–14 runs as follows:

> Verses 6–7: "Believing" is connected with being "descendants of Abraham."

215–231; *idem.*, "Pauli Theologiae Proprium," *NTS* 26 (1980), 445–473; T. R. Schreiner, "Is Perfect Obedience to the Law Possible? A Re-Examination of Galatians 3:10," *JETS* 27/2 (1984), 151–160; F. Mussner, *Der Galaterbrief* (5th edn.; HTKNT 9; Freiburg/Basel/Vienna: Herder, 1988), 223–226, 347–348.

[78] Schreiner, "Perfect Obedience," 160.

[79] See also G. Howard, *Paul: Crisis in Galatia* (Cambridge: Cambridge University Press, 1979) 49–54: the Jerusalem temple was a visible monument to all that Judaism believed not in perfect law-keeping, but in God's forgiveness for sins.

Scripture proof: Abraham's righteousness is connected with believing.

Verse 8: The gospel-inclusion of Gentiles in Abraham's blessing by faith was declared beforehand in Scripture.

Scripture proof: The Gentiles are blessed in Abraham. (That this is by faith can now be assumed from verses 6–7 and will be stated again verse 9.)

Verse 9: Restatement [ὥστε] of the thesis of a connection between believing and Abrahamic blessing. [No scripture proof]

(Verses 10–13 bring subsidiary arguments that further demonstrate the thesis of verses 6–9:)

Verse 10: Works of law are connected with a curse.

Scripture proof: "Curse" is connected with the law [νόμος].

Verse 11: Justification is not by law.

Scripture proof: Righteousness comes by faith.

Verse 12: The law is not from faith [ἐκ πίστεως].

Scripture proof: Law is connected with "doing."

Verse 13: The curse of the law (verse 10) was removed by Christ.

Scripture proof: Crucifixion = being accursed.

Verse 14: Abraham's blessing (and reception of the Spirit, cf. 3:1–5) comes "in Christ Jesus" to the Gentiles through faith.

Following this, 3:15–18 brings another argument for this same thesis – the Torah covenant (Sinai) cannot supersede the promise (i.e., Christ) given beforehand to Abraham.

Thus, Paul's point in verse 10 is not to explain *why* the Law and the curse must be connected, but simply to assert their connection in parallel with the connection between "from faith" [ἐκ πίστεως] and "blessing" (=righteousness/justification, verses 6–7, 9), and to prove this via the citation of an authoritative Scripture text. His choice of Deuteronomy 27:26 is an obvious one, since this is the only text in the LXX connecting νόμος with a curse. Besides the syllogistic explanation noted above, two additional suggestions have been made to explain *why* a curse would be connected with the law. E. P. Sanders considers all this to be strictly terminological: as "blessing" was connected with "faith," so now "curse" with "law."[80] J. Scott, on the other hand, sees Jewish traditions behind

---

[80] *PLJP*, 20–23. Critical: H. Räisänen, *Paul and the Law*, 95, n. 13.

Paul's reasoning, traditions which asserted that disobedient Israel was under the divine curse of Deuteronomy 27:26 until a future time when God would redeem her from this curse. Thus, becoming part of national Israel (i.e., accepting circumcision and the works of the law) means coming under the divine curse now in effect upon her.[81]

The similar-sounding statement in chapter 5 (verse 3) makes no reference to a "curse," emphasizing instead the "obligation [ὀφει-λέτης ἐστὶν] to do the whole law [ὅλον τὸν νόμον ποιῆσαι]" falling upon anyone who accepts circumcision (i.e., comes under the yoke of the Jewish law). In line with Jewish tradition about proselytes, Paul here is reminding the Galatians of something the Judaizers failed to tell them; namely, that entry into Judaism entails not merely a few ceremonial or ritual observances, but commitment to observe all the law.[82] Again, the point of the language about "the whole law" is not flawless obedience, but wholehearted and thoroughgoing (versus selective) obedience.

Objections: (2) ἔργα νόμου

The other objection to my interpretation revolves around the meaning of *works of (the) law* [ἔργα νόμου]. What is the relationship between Paul's fundamental statements on justification in chapter 3 ("not by works of law" [ἐξ ἔργων νόμου] verse 20, "apart from works of law" [χωρὶς ἔργων νόμου] verse 28), and those in chapter 2 that eschatological glory and wrath will be given "according to works" [κατὰ τὰ ἔργα, verse 6] and justification will be to "the doers of the law" [οἱ ποιηηταὶ νόμου, verse 13]?

This phrase, which Paul apparently felt able to employ without further definition, has been the subject of considerable debate.[83]

---

[81] " 'FOR AS MANY AS ARE OF WORKS OF THE LAW ARE UNDER A CURSE' (Galatians 3.10)," *Paul and the Scriptures of Israel* (ed. C. A. Evans and J. A. Sanders; JSNTSup 83; Sheffield: JSOT, 1993), 194–221.

[82] "A proselyte who accepts all commandments of the Tora except for one is not accepted" (cited in P. J. Tomson, *Paul and the Jewish Law* [Assen/Maastricht: Van Gorcum, 1990], 88–89). Perhaps the Judaizers were like many of the Jewish missionaries of the day, who advised introducing Gentile proselytes only gradually to "the whole law"; cf. Sanders, *PLJP*, 29, and 56, n. 58 (thus reversing his position in *PPJ*).

[83] Helpful overviews are found in the articles by D. Moo ("Paul and the Law in the Last Ten Years," *SJT* 40/2 [1987], 292–298), T. R. Schreiner ("'Works of Law' in Paul," *NovT* 33/3 [1991], 218–225), and Scott ("FOR AS MANY," 188–194).

Interestingly, the two dominant options are tending toward agreement on at least two points: (1) ἔργα νόμου refers to all that the
Torah requires in terms of obedience,[84] and (2) it is a Jewish code-
phrase (not a Pauline creation) defining the conditions to be met
for entry into, or maintenance of, the status of justification.[85] They
radically disagree, however, over the nature of these conditions.
The **traditional interpretation**, sometimes called the "Quantitative"
or "Legalistic" view, places the emphasis on "works" understood
as meritorious obedience.[86] Thus the phrase serves in Paul as a
generic rebuttal of all human attempts to attain righteousness *by
doing*. For this reason, no significant difference is posited between
this phrase and Paul's use of "works" alone. They all refer to
"justification before God on the ground of one's obedience to the
law."[87] Paul rejects "works of the law" because they ignore human
inability under sin. Since everyone sins (Rom. 1:18–3:20), and since
it is *perfect* keeping of all the Law's demands which is required
(Gal. 3:10; 5:3), no one can be justified by this means. Such a way is
also excluded because it would lead to *boasting* in meritorious
human achievement (Rom. 3:27; 4:1–5). However, alongside the
problem of attributing to Paul the demand for "perfect law-
keeping" (see above), this interpretation sets him historically adrift.
Who were these Jewish(-Christian) opponents who taught such a
form of legalism?[88]

The so-called "new perspective" on Paul generally holds to what

[84] See esp. Gal. 3:10–12. On this agreement, see J. D. G. Dunn, "Yet Once More
– 'The Works of the Law': A Response," *JSNT* 46 (1992), 100–102.

[85] Moo, for instance, accepts the verbal parallels in the Qumran literature as the
background of Paul's usage ("'Law,' 'Works of the Law,' and Legalism in Paul,"
WTJ 45 [1983], 92, 94).

[86] See H. Hübner, "Was heißt 'Werke des Gesetzes'?" in *Glaube und Eschatologie:
FS für Werner Georg Kümmel* (eds. E. Gräßer and O. Merk; Tübingen: J. C. B.
Mohr, 1973), 123–134; D. J. Moo, "'Law,' ... and Legalism," 73–100; C. E. B.
Cranfield, "'The works of the Law' in the Epistle to the Romans," *JSNT* 43 (1991),
89–101; Schreiner, "'Works of Law'," 217–244. Additional proponents are listed in
Schreiner, "'Works of Law'," 218, n. 6 and 220, nn. 10–11.

[87] Cranfield, "'The Works of the Law'," 95, also 93–95, 98.

[88] For attempts to answer this challenge to the traditional interpretation, see
Moo, "Paul and the Law," 298 (Judaism was more diverse than Sanders allows), and
Schreiner, "'Works of Law'," 241–244 (although Judaism thought it had properly
balanced grace and works, Paul's new perspective led him to see it as legalism).
Schreiner, in particular, seems to have missed the force of Sanders' work. He can still
describe Jewish self-understanding (i.e., not just Paul's new perspective) in terms of
"the delusion of those who think they can earn merit before God by their obedience
to the law, even though they fail to obey it" (244).

may be termed a **nationalistic interpretation**.[89] Works of the law
refer indeed to the obedience demanded by the Torah; not,
however, in terms of *earning righteousness*, but (in line with
covenantal nomism) as the God-given means of determining (or
maintaining) membership in God's people (= the righteous, the
justified). What Paul rejects as law-works is not some form of merit
theology but Judaism's own understanding of the identity of God's
people and the conditions for belonging. Though the meaning of
ἔργα νόμου is broader than a few selected identity markers, the
focus of Paul's usage is on circumcision and food laws because it
was precisely this subset of religious activity which both Jews and
non-Jews recognized as *the distinguishing identifiers* of Jewishness
and which Paul understood to be relativized through faith in
Christ.

Since a thorough examination of all the texts and arguments
pertaining to this disputed phrase is impossible within the limits of
this chapter, I will simply outline here four arguments which tip the
scales in favor of this nationalistic or social interpretation. (1) The
few Pauline occurrences of ἔργα νόμου[90] all evince the same limited
literary context, viz., To what extent can Torah-observance (in
particular, circumcision and regulations for table fellowship) still be
considered a necessary condition for God's vindication of his
people? Must Gentiles live like Jews in order to be assured of God's
grace? This is, perhaps, most clear in Galatians 2:16, where the
preceding verses (11–15) formulate the issue as "compel[ling] the
Gentiles to live like Jews" [τὰ ἔθνη ἀναγκάζεις ἰουδαΐζειν, verse
14b]. This argument continues in 3:1–5 where Paul cites their own
experience of God's favor visibly evidenced in the reception of the
Spirit and miracles (3:1–5). This should prove to the Galatians that
their own status in the grace of God came when they believed [ἐξ

---

[89] See esp. Dunn, "The New Perspective on Paul," 95–122; *idem.*, *Romans 1–8*,
I.153–155; *idem.*, "Yet Once More," 99–117; also R. Heiligenthal, "Soziologische
Implikationen der paulinischen Rechtfertigungslehre im Galaterbrief am Beispiel der
'Werke des Gesetzes.' Beobachtungen zur Identitätsfindung einer frühchristlichen
Gemeinde," *Kairos* 26 (1984), 38–53; *idem.*, *Werke als Zeichen*, 127–134; R. G.
Hamerton-Kelly, "Sacred Violence and 'Works of Law': 'Is Christ then an Agent of
Sin?' (Galatians 2:17)," *CBQ* 52 (1990), 55–75.
[90] Only eight times in the NT, all in Paul, and concentrated in three chapters of
his letters (Rom. 3:20, 28; Gal. 2:16 [3x]; 3:2, 5, 10). The use of the *singular* in Rom.
2:15 [τὸ ἔργον τοῦ νόμου], combined with the fact that it is used in a clearly *positive*
sense (the Gentiles "do instinctively [φύσει] what the law requires [τὰ τοῦ νόμου]"
and thereby demonstrate that it is "written on their hearts," 2:14–15), warns against
trying to equate this phrase with the ἔργα νόμου of 3:20.

ἀκοῆς πίστεως], and was not based on identifying with Judaism (justification cannot be διὰ νόμου, 2:21). Similarly in Galatians 3:6–18 the larger context focuses on the role of Torah vis-à-vis status as heirs of Abraham ("if the inheritance comes from the law," verse 18). The options are "faith in Christ" or "law-works," and again the argument revolves around whether Gentiles must adopt Judaism (at least circumcision and food laws) in order to be among the righteous, or whether faith in Christ is sufficient. Although the historical exigency behind Romans 1–3 is different from that behind Galatians, the value of Jewishness is still the focal point (2:17; 3:1). Jewish confidence in the law (2:12–24) and circumcision (2:25–29) are insufficient guarantors of God's favor. Finally, that Jew–Gentile distinctions are at the heart of Paul's use of ἐξ/χωρὶς ἔργων νόμου is made certain by Romans 3:28–29. Having stated his thesis once again (verse 28), he poses a rhetorical question in verse 29 based on the supposition that justification were, in fact, based on works of the law. If this were the case, then God would be "the God of the Jews only." Justification by works of the law would mean, and does mean for Paul, a restriction of God's saving activity to Jews only. Such a *national restriction* is the root of the problem.

(2) The second argument turns to the **social context** of Paul's debate with Jews and Jewish Christians over works of the law.[91] There are sufficient indications in the texts that behind the literary-contextual issues noted above lies the broader issue of the social function of the law in Judaism. Paul's use of the disparaging term "Gentile sinners" (Gal. 2:15) reflects the typical Jewish insistence on observing the law, an attitude "which regarded Gentiles ipso facto as 'sinners', that is, ignorant of and outside the law, and therefore outside the realm of righteousness."[92] The Maccabean crisis had impressed on Jews loyalty to the Torah (specifically circumcision and the food laws) as a life and death issue (see 1 Macc. 1:60–63). Maintaining Israel's distinctive identity over against apostates and "Gentile sinners" became crucial to the social fabric of Judaism; hence the reaction in Antioch on the part of "certain people from James" to the Jewish-Christians' ignoring of

---

[91] See esp. J. D. G. Dunn, "Works of the Law and the Curse of the Law (Galatians 3.10–14)," *NTS* 31 (1985), 524–532; and R. Heiligenthal, "Soziologische Implikationen," 38–53.

[92] Dunn, "Yet Once More," 102.

the food laws (Gal. 2:11–13).[93] Participation in God's covenant, and thus in God's righteousness, was inextricably tied to the loyal observance of these works of the law (especially those works which Jews were tempted to abandon), not as meritorious human achievements, but as the obligatory conditions laid upon those whom God had graciously favored with salvation. Thus Paul and his opponents have a common understanding of "works of the law." They are Israel's covenant obligations – in short, *Jewish covenantal nomism*. When Paul rejects works of the law, it is not a legalistic caricature of Judaism he is castigating, but the very obligations which Jews and some Jewish-Christians considered essential to covenant righteousness.

(3) Third, Paul's stress lies not on the character of ἔργα νόμου as "works," but on their **relation to the *law***. In Romans 3:20 it is the relationship of justification to Torah that is center stage, not its relationship to human effort. Thus Paul follows 3:20a not with a statement about human inability to perform the requisite "works," but with a statement about the true function of the Law, "for through the law comes the knowledge of sin." Furthermore, Paul repeats the theme of 3:20a in verse 21 and this time uses the simple χωρὶς νόμου in place of "works of the law," showing once again that the issue is the relationship of justification to the Law, not so much its relation to human achievement. Likewise in Romans 3:28, after discussing the exclusion of Jewish "boasting" and works of the law, verse 30 shows that the central issue in all this is the place of the Torah in determining who is "righteous before God" ("Do we then overthrow *the law* by this faith?"). The same focus on the Torah-related aspect of these works is found in the occurrences in Galatians.[94] Against this emphasis on "*Law*-works," proponents of the traditional interpretation usually point to the instances where Paul appears to use "works" alone as a shorthand for "works of the law."[95] The strongest arguments in this regard stem from

[93] Circumcision was accorded the same critical significance as a boundary marker, a fact made clear by Paul's description of the Jews as "the circumcision" and Gentiles as "the uncircumcision" (Rom. 2:26; 3:30; 4:9; Gal. 2:7–9)

[94] Gal. 2:21b; 3:11, 18. Three times Paul substitutes "by [διά/ἐν/ἐκ] (the) law" for the fuller "by works of the law." See J. B. Tyson, " 'Works of Law' in Galatians," *JBL* 92 (1973), 429–430.

[95] Rom. 4:1–6; 9:11–12, 32; 11:6. See, for example, Schreiner, " 'Works of Law'," 232–238. In addition, reference is usually made to the manifold occurrence of "doing"-language in Rom. 2 (verses 6–10, 13–14, 25–27), assuming such to be equivalent to "works of the law.".

Romans 4:1–5, where it seems that Abraham might boast in works which earn a reward. The reader may refer to the discussion of this passage below for my view, but note in passing that in 4:9–16 Paul seems to abandon any supposed interest in "works" per se, and returns clearly to the place of circumcision and Torah in Abraham's righteousness.

(4) Finally, attention should be paid to the **linguistic parallels** in the Qumran literature since these testify to an understanding of the phrase in Judaism similar to that which I have posited for Paul.[96] In these texts "works of the law" refers to a sectarian understanding of what was required to maintain proper status within the true people of God. The Manual of Discipline, for instance, gives detailed instructions for the examination of a novice before full entry into the covenant community (V,1–24). Specifically, it is one's readiness to obey the particular interpretations of the commandments given by the community that is under examination, thus proving one's preparedness to separate from the abominable ways of outsiders (i.e., Jews outside the sect, V,10) and their "works of vanity" [מעשי הבל] (V,18–19). Therefore, it is one's "understanding and *deeds in Torah*" [מעשיו בתורה] (V,21) which must be confirmed, i.e., to what degree one understands and lives according to the sect's distinctive interpretation and requirements.[97]

Given this understanding of "works of the law" there is then no contradiction with Paul's more positive statements about "works" in chapter 2. These latter refer not to disputed conditions for entry into or identification with the people of God ("works of the law"), but to that godly obedience which Paul everywhere expects as the response to grace, and elsewhere terms "the obedience of faith."[98] The statement that only the doers of the law will be justified (2:13)

---

[96] 1QS V,21, 23; VI,18; 4QMMT; also 2 Bar. 57:2. Dunn's inclusion of 4QFlor. 1:7 as another occurrence of the phrase should probably be rejected, since the badly damaged text most likely reads מעשי תודה ["works of *thanksgiving*"] rather than תורה ["of *Torah*"]. See H.-W. Kuhn, "Die Bedeutung der Qumrantexte für das Verständnis des Galaterbriefes," in *New Qumran Texts and Studies: Proceedings of the First Meeting of the International Organization for Qumran Studies, Paris 1992* (ed. G. J. Brooke; Leiden/New York/Cologne: E. J. Brill, 1994), 173–175; and G. J. Brooke, *Exegesis at Qumran: 4QFlorilegium in its Jewish Context* (JSOTSup 29; Sheffield: JSOT, 1985), 108.

[97] See also CD VI,18. In 4QMMT the phrase clearly has reference to the distinguishing halakhic regulations of the sect. See L. H. Schiffman, "MIQSAT MA'ASEH HA-TORAH and the Temple Scroll," *RevQ* 14 (1990), 435–457; and J. D. G. Dunn, "Echoes of Intra-Jewish Polemic in Paul's Letter to the Galatians," *JBL* 112/3 (1993), 459–477.

[98] See, A. B. Du Toit, "Faith and Obedience in Paul," *Neot* 25/1 (1991), 65–74;

is, after all, simply the flip side of Paul's repeated insistence that those who do unrighteousness will not inherit the kingdom of God.[99]

C. H. Cosgrove suggests one additional linguistic clue that Paul intends the statements in Romans 2 to be understood differently than the "works of the law" in chapter 3. Both Hellenistic Greek and Paul's usage are fairly consistent in employing certain prepositions to express the *evidential basis* of judgment and others to express *instrumentality*.[100] Thus, it must be seen as significant when Paul so consistently uses prepositions of instrumentality in disjoining "works of the law" from (and joining faith to) justification, while avoiding these same constructions in favor of those which express the evidential basis or norm of judgment when speaking of "works" in Romans 2.

Thus, there is no reason to avoid the clear implication of this text – the eschatological judgment of Jews and Gentiles, both for salvation and for damnation, will be on the basis of works. This is not a justification ἐκ τῶν ἔργων and thus contradictory to the justification ἐκ πίστεως and χωρὶς ἔργων νόμου. Paul is concerned here with the necessary *congruence* [κατά] of deeds and judgment in the context of an argument with Jewish presumption of advantage via election. Neither one's deeds nor "works of the law" will be the cause or instrument for the attaining of righteousness, but this verdict will be *congruent* with one's deeds, i.e., will be pronounced on the basis of a norm or standard of behavior.[101]

Hypothetical argument?

If no contradiction between 2:6 and 3:19–20, 28 is present, then the chief reason for terming Paul's statements here *hypothetical* is likewise removed. However, because this interpretation is particularly influential and comes in several varieties, it is worthwhile

D. B. Garlington, "The Obedience of Faith in the Letter to the Romans. Part I: The meaning of ΥΠΑΚΟΗ ΠΙΣΤΕΩΣ (Rom. 1:5; 16:26)," *WTJ* 52 (1990), 201–224.

[99] E.g., 1 Cor. 6:9–10; Gal. 5:19–21; Rom. 1:29–32.

[100] "Justification in Paul: A Linguistic and Theological Reflection," *JBL* 106 (1987), 653–670, esp. 656–661. Evidential basis: ἐπί + dat., κατά + accus., διά + accus.; Instrumentality: ἀπό + gen., ἐν + dat., διά + gen., simple dat., ἐκ + gen.

[101] See also D. B. Garlington, "The Obedience of Faith in the Letter to the Romans: Part II, The Obedience of Faith and Judgment by Works," *WTJ* 53 (1991), 47–72.

examining it in greater detail. Hans Lietzmann is generally cited as the major early proponent of this view:

> In verses 5–12 Paul expresses the principle of the final judgment from a hypothetical perspective; that is, how the judgment would work itself out (1) if the gospel were not present, and (2) if it were possible to fulfill the law. The leading thought is as follows, "Assuming everything were to come to pass just as the Jews justifiably expect on the basis of the Old Testament, even so you would have no occasion to consider yourselves better than the pagans. For upon you, and you first of all, God's wrath would be poured out, since in such a case all would depend solely upon what one has done; and you do not keep the law."[102]

Lietzmann's second argument (legal righteousness would be impossible to obtain since it demands perfection) has been dealt with above. Besides, to argue that Paul pressed the motif in such a perfectionistic or legalistic direction (i.e., if you were to be judged according to your deeds you would all fail because you have not kept the law perfectly) not only places his use in radical discontinuity with that in second temple Judaism as seen in chapters 1–3, but must also explain why his use of the motif elsewhere assumes the typical holistic understanding, rather than a hypothetical one. In 2 Corinthians 5:9–10, for instance, he assumes that the norm of God's final judgment – specifically whether one has "done" good or evil while in the body – will be met by Christians. In Romans 2 as well, Paul's use of judgment according to deeds can be understood perfectly well in continuity with Jewish tradition.[103]

The first argument (Romans 2:5–12 is written from a viewpoint without the gospel) can appeal to the fact that, apart from verse 16 ("according to my gospel, God, through Jesus Christ, will judge the secret thoughts of all"), there is nothing specifically Christian about any of 2:1–16. But what about verse 16? Lietzmann admits that it cannot be fitted properly into the flow of a hypothetical argument and suggests either, (1) this is a later interpolation, (2) in a brief mental lapse, Paul steps out of the hypothetical rhetoric to exclaim "at the last judgment you will know that I speak the truth!" or (3)

---

[102] *Die Briefe des Apostels Paulus I: Die vier Hauptbriefe* (HNT 3; Tübingen: J. C. B. Mohr, 1910), 13.

[103] See P. Stuhlmacher, "Exkurs V: Das Endgericht nach den Werken," *Der Brief an die Römer* (NTD 6; Göttingen: Vandenhoeck & Ruprecht, 1989), 44–46.

verse 16 refers back to verses 12–13 (verses 14–15 forming a parenthesis).[104] Lietzmann himself rejects option (3), since it still has Paul admitting to justification for the doer of the law. But, likewise, option (1) must be judged a counsel of despair, since there is no MS evidence in this direction. Against (2) the syntax of verse 16 marks it as a continuation of the previous argument, not a disconnected exclamation.

Thus, with verse 16 the gospel is indeed present in Paul's thought, weakening the argument that the eschatological statements here are in some way hypothetical. Likewise, a review of the other references to eschatological judgment as well as of the terminology for the eschatological punishment/reward in 2:1–16 gives no support to the idea that we have here a viewpoint somehow removed from Paul's own gospel-informed expectation.[105] Apart from the concern over contradiction, nothing would incline us normally to view these statements as hypothetical or in any way unpauline.[106]

A variation of the hypothetical interpretation is E. Synofzik's attempt to view the positive recompense statements as a "foil" for the negative.

> Although Paul applies retribution both positively and negatively in verses 7–10, his real interest rests only on the negative recompense. The statements about a positive outcome of judgment in 2:7, 10, 14, and 26–27 are only a foil for his accusation against the Jews ... The dual scheme of good and evil, reward and punishment, serves only to illustrate that God's judging activity is carried out "in accordance with the truth" (2:2).[107]

Synofzik is certainly correct in noting that the negative side of the judgment is Paul's rhetorical focus in this passage. However,

---

[104] *Die Briefe*, 15.

[105] The use of δικαιωθήσονται (verse 13) is a particularly risky choice of words for Paul if he is intending in some sense *ante Christum.*

[106] This is not, of course, to deny the possibility of "hypothetical arguments" in the Pauline correspondence or ancient writers in general (cf. F. Thielman, *From Plight to Solution*, 86, n. 36). However, even in Thielman's examples from both Hellenistic and rabbinic sources, the hypothetical nature of the argument is clearly signalled. "To argue that the text is hypothetical is rather difficult when there is nothing (such an an ἀνθρώπινον λέγω) in this extended section to suggest this option. Rather, the passage is assertive in character and has every indication of being meant seriously" (Snodgrass, "Justification by Grace," 74).

[107] *Die Gerichts- und Vergeltungsaussagen*, 159.

apart from this appeal to "focus" he can give no justification for declaring the positive side "only a foil," that is, not to be taken as expressing Paul's own viewpoint. This fits in with Synofzik's attempt generally to play down the theological weight of the judgment and recompense statements as merely *Argumentationsmittel*. However, Paul will repeat the idea of a positive outcome in judgment in a non-hypothetical fashion:

> The doers of the law ... will be justified.   (2:13b)

> Their conflicting thoughts will ... perhaps excuse them.
> (2:15b)

Furthermore, Paul is, in fact, convinced that believers by the Spirit will fulfill the Law's requirement (8:4, ἵνα τὸ δικαίωμα τοῦ νόμου πληρωθῇ ἐν ἡμῖν).[108] Finally, as I have argued above, this view does not do justice to the rhetorical function of the positive side of the dual recompense statement in verse 6.

Hence, in favor of my interpretation and against the "hypothetical" interpretation may be brought at least five arguments: (1) the text itself gives no indication that it contains a hypothetical case; (2) the eschatological referents are otherwise perfectly at home within a Christian perspective; (3) the thought of judgment according to works (both good and evil) is not at all unpauline;[109] (4) the rhetorical argument makes good sense without resort to this theory; (5) as Snodgrass notes, it is difficult to understand how Paul could expect his argument to have any force with those of Jewish background when he ultimately rejects or subverts such a fundamental Jewish tenet as judgment according to works.[110]

Jewish presumption as Paul's foil

Finally, an assumption of the above exegesis is the existence of a "Jewish presumption" vis-à-vis eschatological judgment, against which Paul is arguing. The apostle attributes to his diatribal critic a

---

[108] See also 13:8, 10. On 8:4, see below.

[109] Cf. Rom. 14:10–12; 1 Cor. 3:8, 13–15; 2 Cor. 5:10*; (9:6); (11:15); Gal. 6:7–8*; Col. 3:24–25*; Eph. 6:8*; 1 Tim. 5:24–25*; 2 Tim. 4:14. These passages expect a judgment according to works for believers in Christ; an asterisk marks a usage that includes *positive* retribution.

[110] "Justification by Grace," 79. Further on rejection of the "hypothetical" interpretation, see Travis, *Christ and the Judgment*, 58–59; Schreiner, *The Law and Its Fulfillment*, 183–185.

specifically Jewish reliance on divine mercy (2:4 τοῦ πλούτου τῆς χρηστότητος ... καταφρονεῖς) which granted forbearance to Jewish sins, while maintaining a strictness of judgment upon the same sins among Gentiles (1:18–2:5). Such reliance was not predicated on any supposed works-righteousness or self-righteous boasting,[111] but on the covenant privileges of the elect, on grace. Thus Paul argues against Torah (2:12–24) and circumcision (2:25–29) as providing any protection against judgment upon Jewish sin, all of which is ultimately rooted in the question of Israel's advantage as God's elect (Romans 9–11).

That Israel's knowledge of election and covenant privilege *could* lead to such a presumption of "divine partiality" to the Jew in judgment in spite of sinful ways, should be clear enough from the warnings against the same in Jewish writings.[112] However, such a hypocritical abuse of covenant privileges was by no means typical of second temple Judaism,[113] and Part One has shown that Jewish writers themselves used the motif of judgment according to deeds against such presumption. Unless one is prepared to assert that Paul has misunderstood or misrepresented Judaism, or was convinced that his former faith leads by some inherent logical necessity to such presumption, we will need to seek the actual source of this presumptuous thinking elsewhere.

Paul is engaged here in a diatribe, and the presumptuous attitude is attributed to the critic. The apostle's aim throughout is to lead Jewish-Christians to acknowledge that membership in the eschatological people of God no longer has anything to do with Jewishness (Torah, circumcision, law-works), but is by faith in Christ. He does this by putting the opposite assumption – being Jewish *does* constitute a soteriological advantage – in the mouth of the diatribal critic, and then proceeding to demolish this assumption; hopefully

---

[111] On my view, the "boasting" in Rom. 2:17, 23; 3:27; and 4:2 refers not to legalism, but to confidence in Israel's covenant privileges (see esp. 2:17 [boasting ἐν θεῷ] and 23 [boasting ἐν νόμῳ]) versus confidence in Christ (cf. 5:11; 15:17).

[112] See, for instance, Sir. 5:4–7. Further H. D. Betz, "Christianity as Religion: Paul's Attempt at Definition in Romans," *JR* 71/3 (1991), 315–344.

[113] The standard proof that such presumption was, indeed, typical is normally found in Wis. 15:2 – "For even if we sin we are yours." However, this is an affirmation of divine mercy to Israel (verse 1) in spite of occasional sins. That no such presumption is in mind is clear from verses 2b–6 ("but we will not sin"; see E. G. Clarke, *The Wisdom of Solomon* [CBC; Cambridge: Cambridge University Press, 1973], 98–99). For opposing views on the question of Jewish over-confidence in election, see Sanders, *PPJ*, 147–182; Dunn, *Romans 1–8*, 91; and Räisänen, *Paul and the Law*, 168, n. 39.

in a way his reading audience will accept. This strikes at the roots of Jewish covenantal nomism[114] and goes to the heart of the debate between Paul's gospel and some forms of Jewish-Christianity. Is "Jewishness" ultimately an advantage?[115] Thus, the form which this presumption takes is, to some extent, a fiction, a foil to advance Paul's argumentative strategy. The potential for such a presumption was certainly recognized within Judaism itself, but such a presumption, even if occasionally met with, was not characteristic of the second temple period.

In spite of the exaggerated portrayal, this issue of the advantage of being Jewish would be of great relevance in the Roman congregation, not in the form of a "judaizing threat" as in Galatians, but inasmuch as Jewishness was threatening to undo the unity of the mixed congregation over the question of table fellowship (chapters 14–15). Although the paraenesis of these latter chapters appears to be addressed primarily to the Gentile majority, Paul's attempt at conflict-resolution must encompass the whole congregation. His resolution, however, is so non-Jewish[116] that he cannot hope to gain the full adherence of the Jewish minority without first neutralizing this Jewish-Christian sense of advantage.

Beyond the specifically Roman concern looms Jerusalem and the debate over the proper mode of integrating Jew and Gentile in the one people of God. That there were Jewish-Christians who saw Jewishness as a decisive advantage before God (and a necessity for Gentile proselytes as well) seems clear enough from the NT and post-apostolic developments. More to the point for Romans is the existence of a Jewish-Christianity which, without requiring proselytism of Gentiles, still regarded its own Jewish status as conferring advantage or at least demanding adherence by Gentiles to Jewish

---

[114] On the whole question of Christian rejection of Israel's election and subsequent Jewish reaction, see B. W. Helfgott, *The Doctrine of Election in Tannaitic Literature* (New York: King's Crown, 1954). Helfgott sees many instances in Tannaitic literature of rabbinic reaction to a Christian rejection of Jewish election privileges.

[115] Paul, of course, affirms Judaism's clear advantages of knowledge and priority (3:1–2). What he denies is an intrinsic *salvific* advantage. Texts such as 1 Cor. 10:1–13 ("Nevertheless [i.e., in spite of the covenant privileges listed in verses 1–4], God was not pleased with most of them") and Matt. 3:9 ("Do not presume to say to yourselves, 'We have Abraham as our ancestor'" [= Luke 3:8]) testify to the consistent Christian challenge to this fundamental Jewish tenet.

[116] Cf. "nothing is unclean in itself" (14:14); "the kingdom of God is not food and drink" (14:17); "(t)he one who thus [i.e., not according to Torah prescriptions but according to love] serves Christ is acceptable to God" (14:18).

standards in mixed situations. Paul's contribution to this debate in Romans 2 is to deny any such privilege thus understood, and this by appeal to the Jewish axiom of impartial judgment according to works, and to the righteousness of God through faith for both Jew and Greek alike.

Summary of Romans 2:6–11: no tension

Although it is common to perceive an inherent *tension* between this text and the apostle's subsequent statements on justification, chapters 1–3 of the letter give no evidence of such in Paul's own mind. He uses the judgment motif, both for eternal punishment and reward, without apology and with no seeming fear of misunderstanding. For my explanation as to why and how Paul felt no tension on this matter the reader may turn to the final chapter.

In Romans 2, Paul's use of the recompense motif evinces near-complete continuity with its use in second temple Judaism. The wording, its function within the argument, the eschatological framework, and the association with divine impartiality all point to Paul's adoption of this motif from the broad stream of traditional Jewish use of this axiom. It is the standard Jewish expectation that one's outward behavior (one's *works* or *way*) will correspond to, and be a visible manifestation of, inward reality. Thus, neither in Judaism nor here in Paul does one obey *in order to become* righteous. Nor is such obedience understood as sinless perfection, but as a consistent and wholehearted conformity to God's will. At two points a modification (or radicalization) by Paul of this Jewish motif was noted: (i) the comprehensive duality of recompense, and (ii) its employment in order to establish the soteriological equality of Gentiles with Jews. However, both these modifications relate directly to Paul's rhetorical purpose in the letter, and need not be construed as a rejection of the traditional Jewish concept of recompense according to deeds.

Is Paul, then, teaching that believers' eschatological destiny will be dependent upon the outcome of this judgment according to deeds? Looking at the rhetoric of the text the answer will be "no," since the aim is not to instruct regarding believers' eschatological future, but to challenge faulty thinking about presumed Jewish soteriological advantages. Nevertheless a "yes" is surely implied. Whether Jew or Gentile, Christian or not, at this final judgment God's apportioning of glory or wrath will be in accord with conduct, whether one's life-pattern was to practice good, or to do evil. Divine judgment according to deeds is no less a fundamental axiom for Paul the apostle of Christ than it was for Saul the Pharisee.

Romans 4:4–5

Now to one who works, wages are not reckoned as a gift but as something due. But to one who without works trusts him who justifies the ungodly, such faith is reckoned as righteousness.

Although this text does not make reference to judgment according to works and is not generally considered to be of major significance for understanding Paul's concept of judgment and recompense, it does appear to bring recompense terminology [μισθός] into direct connection with the concepts of justification, works, grace, faith, and merit or earning [κατὰ ὀφείλημα, verse 4]. For many, these verses are conclusive evidence that Paul's argument in Romans stands primarily in opposition to Jewish legalism, to a reliance on human works *qua* achievement which thinks it can earn righteousness and which leads to fleshly boasting in merit.[117] For these scholars Romans 4:1–5 constitutes important proof that ἔργα νόμου implies Jewish merit theology. Further, this text is sometimes cited as evidence of a fundamental Pauline opposition to the (Jewish legalistic) idea of recompense based on merit or deeds, suggesting instead a "reward of grace," a *Gnadenlohn*.[118]

While acknowledging that Romans 4 has been a battleground over important questions regarding salvation history and genre, this study will focus on a few issues related specifically to my thesis. First, the crucial terms must be interpreted within the context of this argument: justification ἐξ ἔργων, boasting, reward (or "pay"), and grace versus debt. In tandem with the terminological investigation we will need to determine to what degree legalism and Jewish

---

[117] For example, H. W. Heidland, art. λογίζομαι, *TDNT* IV.290–292; Bultmann, *Theologie des Neuen Testaments*, 242, 264–265, 281; and Cranfield, *The Epistle to the Romans* I.224–229.

[118] This concept is particularly prominent among Roman Catholic theologians as a solution to the tension between salvation by grace and judgment according to works. "Rather 'works' are 'the fruit of the Spirit,' and the reward is a reward of grace [*Gnadenlohn*]" (R. Schnackenburg, *Die sittliche Botschaft des Neuen Testaments* [Munich: Max Hueber Verlag 1954], 198, cf. also 104ff.).

covenantal presumption play a role in this argument. Then, the significance of these findings for an understanding of judgment according to works in Romans 2 must be explored.

Literary and traditio-historical context

In 3:21 Paul returns explicitly to his thesis regarding the divine righteousness (cf. 1:17), giving it now its full expression in verse 28: "For we hold that a person is justified by faith apart from works prescribed by the law." This is a direct challenge to Jewish particularism since both the circumcised and uncircumcised come to God on the same basis of faith ("Or is God the God of Jews only?"). This, in turn, raises the question of the relevance and authority of the Torah (verse 31: "Do we then overthrow the law by this faith?"). Such an inclusion of Gentiles in the eschatological people of God, without respect to Israel's election and the sign of circumcision, would seem to be a direct abrogation of the Torah. Is this faith-righteousness without regard to "law-works" indeed testified to by the law and the prophets as Paul has claimed (3:21; cf. 1:17)? As a demonstration in the affirmative, Paul turns to Abraham (4:1–25).

His choice of Abraham and of Genesis 15:6 was almost a necessity at this stage in the light of Jewish tradition.[119] As father of the nation, Abraham was regularly presented as a model of the devout Jew, one who exercised faith (= faithful obedience) under pressure. Scholars remain divided as to the precise significance of this faith of Abraham in Jewish tradition. Was it *ein verdienstliches Tun*, simply one among many other meritorious works;[120] or was Abraham's faith primarily viewed by those under the pressure of Hellenization during Maccabean times as a model of loyalty to Israel's particular customs (esp. circumcision, Sabbath, idolatry and unclean foods)?[121] Both find in Romans 4 Paul's reaction to a

---

[119] For details, including relevant passages, see F. Hahn, "Genesis 15:6 im Neuen Testament," *Probleme biblischer Theologie: FS G. von Rad* (ed. H. W. Wolff; Munich: Kaiser, 1971), 94–97; and A. T. Hanson, *Studies in Paul's Technique and Theology* (Grand Rapids: Eerdmans, 1974), 60–62.

[120] See, for example, U. Luz, *Das Geschichtsverständnis des Paulus* [Munich: Kaiser, 1968], 177–180; Cranfield, *The Epistle to the Romans*, I.224, 226–227, 229; and E. Käsemann, *An die Römer* (HNT 8A; Tübingen: J. C. B. Mohr, 1973), 99.

[121] See Watson, *Paul, Judaism and the Gentiles*, 136–138; and Dunn, *Romans 1–8*, 196–201.

Jewish interpretation of Abraham's faith, but in one instance he is opposing legalism, and in the other Jewish particularism.

Paul opens his own midrash on Genesis 15:6 with an exegetical question: *So then, what shall we say that Abraham, our forefather according to the flesh, has found* [i.e., found to be the case regarding justification by faith or by works of the law]? (my translation)[122] The issue remains precisely that raised in his previous discussion (3:27–31) as demonstrated by the reoccurrence in 4:2 of the key terms of that discussion: *For if Abraham was justified* [ἐδικαιώθη] *by works* [ἐξ ἔργων = ἐξ ἔργων νόμου], *he has something to boast about* [καύχημα]. In my discussion of the phrase "law-works" I argued that this refers to Jewish confidence in covenantal privileges accruing only to those who identify with the nation, most notably by submission to circumcision and the food laws. Paul counters this Jewish particularistic understanding of law-works and of Abraham's faithfulness by appeal to Genesis 15:6: *Abraham believed God, and it was reckoned to him as righteousness* (verse 3). His aim in this citation will become explicit in verse 5b: Abraham's *faith* [ἡ πίστις αὐτοῦ], not any "doing," is reckoned as righteousness.

Exegesis: verses 4–5

The mere citation of this passage, of course, does not prove his point, since Jews used the same text in support of the necessity of faithfulness to the covenant demands. Thus verses 4–5 are crucial to Paul's argument, for in them he will argue that *"doing" and "believing" are mutually exclusive as the basis for reckoning*. This exclusivity is set up nicely by the verbal contrast between "one who works" [τῷ δὲ ἐργαζομένῳ] and "one who does not work but trusts" [τῷ δὲ μὴ ἐργαζομένῳ, πιστεύοντι δὲ]. Paul's *proof* of their mutual exclusivity is, however, not entirely clear in its logic, owing

[122] This verse is fraught with difficulties of text, translation and context (my conclusions differ from his own, but see esp. R. B. Hays, "'Have we found Abraham to be our forefather according to the flesh'? A reconsideration of Rom. 4:1," *NovT* 27/1 [1985], 76–98). In my translation εὑρηκέναι echoes the specialized usage of the verb "to find" [מצא] known from rabbinic exegesis in the idiom "What do we find (in Scripture) concerning ... ?" (suggested and rejected in Hays, "Have we found Abraham," 82; but see M. Jastrow, *A Dictionary of the Targumim, the Talmud Babli and Yerushalmi, and the Midrashic Literature* [Brooklyn: Traditional Press, 1903], 825). More often an allusion to Gen. 18:3 (LXX) is suggested ("If I have *found favor* [εὗρον χάριν] before you"), thus setting the stage for a contrast between grace and works. This is unlikely since Paul gives so little attention to *grace* in the ensuing argument (only verses 4[?], 16).

in part to the confusing mixture of secular analogy (verse 4) and theological assertion (verse 5).

The commercial analogy in verse 4 can be read straightforwardly without resort to a theologizing of the language. Ὁ ἐργαζόμενος is any common worker, and λογίζεσθαι a technical term for the reckoning of one's wage [μισθός] according to the work done.[123] Similarly κατὰ χάριν and κατὰ ὀφείλημα simply state that such a wage arrangement is a matter of "what is owed" rather than "as a favor."[124] Now in which of these elements (or combination of them) does Paul find a contrast with "the one who does not work but believes," so that their mutual exclusivity is proven? One common interpretation can be formulated in the following syllogism:

> (major premise): Based on an everyday analogy justification ἐξ ἔργων must be associated with ideas of earning and quid pro quo recompense – all clearly antithetical to grace.
>
> (minor premise): But we know justification to be κατὰ χάριν.
>
> (conclusion): Thus (Abraham's) justification by faith could not have been in any sense ἐξ ἔργων.

If this was Paul's point, it must be admitted that he has left the crucial minor premise implicit, or assumes the reader will supply δικαιούμενοι τῇ χάριτι from 3:24. The "justification of the ungodly" and the "reckoning of faith for righteousness" in verse 5 must in that case be *assumed to imply* "by grace."

I would suggest instead that Paul's contrast lies on the surface, in the presence or absence of *work*. First, this opposing of *the one who works* to *the one who does not work* remains the fundamental and explicit verbal contrast in verses 4–5 as noted earlier. Second, the rather shocking language of belief in "the one who justifies the ungodly" was not meant by Paul to overturn a fundamental biblical axiom,[125] but to hint at Abraham's lack of crucial law-works at the time of his believing in Genesis 15:6. Jewish tradition itself could

---

[123] H. W. Heidland, art. λογίζομαι, *TDNT*, IV.284; H. Preisker, art. μισθός, *TDNT*, IV.695–698. Paul uses ἐργάζεσθαι for manual labor in 1 Thess. 4:11 and 2 Thess. 3:10–12 (see also Eph. 4:28).

[124] See Hauck, *TDNT*, V.565.

[125] The biblical axiom can be found in Exod. 23:7; Prov. 17:15; 24:24; Isa. 5:23; Sir. 42:2; CD I,19.

speak of Abraham as the prototypical proselyte, the stranger who is converted from idolatry to the one true God (Joshua 24:2).[126] Calling Abraham one of the "ungodly" looks ahead, therefore, to Paul's discussion of Abraham's uncircumcised condition at the point of his faith and initial justification (verses 9–12). At this stage in the argument it simply marks him as one who lacked the works crucial to Jewish identity, a fact of great importance in the light of the Jew–Gentile tensions central to the contingent concern of this letter. Third, though it may seem quite a leap in logic to the modern reader, the bald fact that *only* Abraham's *faith* is mentioned in Genesis 15:6 as the basis of the reckoning of righteousness means that works were not present.[127] Finally, it is the reckoning of righteousness *without works* [χωρὶς ἔργων] that is highlighted by Paul in the supporting witness from the Psalms (verses 6–8).

Thus, in summary, verses 4–5 are not about grace versus works-righteousness, but are about the conditions required for membership in the new people of God – faith in Christ or law-works. Abraham is a fitting case study since he was regularly used in Judaism as a model of loyalty to Israel's particular customs. Paul will argue instead that Abraham's justification, his inclusion among the recipients of the covenant blessings, came by faith (alone) apart from and prior to any works (of the law). The point of verses 4–8 is simply that the faith-reckoning of Genesis 15:6 excludes any consideration of doing on Abraham's part, this point of its being χωρὶς ἔργων finding confirmation in the Psalm quotation (verses 7–8).

Second, the alleged use of recompense language in Romans 4:4 [μισθός] arises in a commercial analogy and not in polemic with a supposed Jewish theology of merit. Though from a later period, the rabbis were themselves adamant in rejecting the idea that God "owes" a person any reward as a sort of "obligation," the fulfillment of which claim a person could press upon God.[128] Romans 4:4 does not constitute Paul's rejection of a "Jewish theology of recompense." Neither does he replace μισθὸς κατὰ ὀφείλημα with μισθὸς κατὰ χάριν, a "reward of grace."[129] Within

---

[126] Cf. A. T. Hanson, *Studies in Paul's Technique*, 60–62.

[127] "*quod non in thora, non in mundo*," Str-B III.694. Cf. Heb. 7:3 – Melchizedek had no father, mother, genealogy, birth or death (because they are not mentioned in the Genesis account).

[128] Cf. Moore, *Judaism*, II.89–111, esp. 90. Note Paul's same hesitance to speak of eternal life as the wages of sanctification (Rom. 6:23b).

[129] See above n. 118.

the commercial analogy of verse 4 a wage [μισθός], by its very definition, cannot be κατὰ χάριν but only κατὰ ὀφείλημα. It should not be deduced from this text that Paul is fundamentally opposed to the idea of a reward related to achievement or obedience. When speaking of the rewards of the righteous Paul can use recompense terminology without embarrassment, and speak explicitly of rewards κατὰ ἔργα.[130]

Third, the above should alert us to how carefully nuanced Paul's thought is. In Romans 4 he can speak of "the one who justifies the ungodly," meaning the uncircumcised, or Gentile "sinners," i.e., those who can bring no prior (covenant) claim to bear before God for their justification. In these cases "ungodly" is a *status* term. Yet in other contexts, speaking of the *character* of those whom God justifies (by faith), Paul will unequivocally side with the OT and Judaism which affirmed that God "will not acquit the guilty" (Exod. 23:7). Humanity's ungodliness brings divine wrath, while only those who "do good," who are "doers of the law," will enjoy eternal life.[131] This should at least caution the interpreter against too quickly ascertaining inherent contradiction in Paul's statements about justification and judgment according to works. Distinguishing between texts which speak of the character of the righteous and those which deal with the cause of justification just might reflect such nuanced distinctions in Paul's own mind.

Romans 6:23

For the wages of sin is death, but the free gift of God is eternal life in Christ Jesus our Lord.

Here I will limit myself to answering two questions relative to Romans 6 and judgment in Paul. To what extent is ethical righteousness here made necessary to ultimate salvation? Does Paul's avoidance of wage-terminology in relation to eternal life (verse 23) contradict the interpretation of 2:6–11 in which eternal life is explicitly a recompense to those who do good?

In chapters 6–11 the apostle takes up a series of objections to, or

---

[130] Rom. 2:6; 1 Cor. 3:8, 14; cf. also 2 Cor. 5:10; Col. 3:24.
[131] Rom. 2:5–11, 13; cf. also Gal. 6:7–8; 1 Cor. 6:9, which affirm that only the righteous, those who "sow to the Spirit" and "do good" as opposed to "unrighteousness," will enter the kingdom.

false conclusions from, his gospel of faith-righteousness.[132] The concluding assertion of chapter 5 leads to the possible misunderstanding, "What then are we to say? Should we continue in sin in order that grace may abound?" (6:1). Similarly, "you are not under law, but under grace" (6:14) brings forth the false inference, "What then? Should we sin because we are not under law but under grace?" (6:15). A careless reading of the apostle's position thus far could have led to antinomian license: grace makes conduct irrelevant. If justification is by faith apart from Torah, then perhaps one's subsequent behavior can neither supplement nor endanger this justification (also 3:8).

To this false inference of antinomianism Paul gives two answers in Romans 6. First, in Christ the believer has died to the ruling power of the old master, Sin, making renewed service to Sin unthinkable (verses 1–14). And second, this freedom from Sin leads not to human autonomy but to a change of masters (verses 15–23; esp. verse 22, "you have been freed from sin and enslaved to God"). Fundamental to the entire chapter is what Tannehill terms "two dominions":

> Paul sees man's situation as characterized by two sets of powers which "reign" or "have dominion over" men ... The two dominions are different because they are ruled by different powers. It is the powers operative in the dominion which determine its nature, which mark it off from another dominion where other powers are operative ... Since Paul sees human existence as being determined by such powers, this existence can be characterized by speaking of it as "in sin," "in law," "in flesh," or "in Spirit."[133]

Romans 6:15–23 constitutes a running comparison and contrast between these two dominions. Servitude to the one or the other is inescapable and it is one's conduct which manifests to which dominion one belongs: "you are slaves of the one whom you obey, either of sin, which leads to death, or of obedience [= God], which leads to righteousness" (verse 16). Dale Martin has demonstrated that the point of this extended comparison is missed if limited to

---

[132] These false inferences are clearly marked by rhetorical questions (6:1, 15; 7:7, 13; 9:14, 19; 11:1, 11).

[133] *Dying and Rising with Christ: A Study in Pauline Theology* (Berlin: Alfred Topelmann, 1967), 15, 19. See also K. Snodgrass, "Spheres of Influence, A Possible Solution to the Problem of Paul and the Law," *JSNT* 32 (1988), 93–113.

the moral-ethical function. Paul is not simply exhorting the readers to obedience because they are *obligated* as slaves to do so. Rather against an antinomian charge he is seeking to portray the way of gracious faith-righteousness as a new slavery, whose "end" [τέλος] and "advantage" [καρπός] are inestimably better than under the old slavery to Sin. It is not so much the *obligation* as the *attractiveness* of the new servitude that is front and center.[134] Transfer from the old dominion to the new occurs for the individual definitively at conversion-initiation,[135] which can thus be described equally as faith or as wholehearted obedience to the teaching (verse 17).[136]

As the last in this series of comparisons, verse 23 functions to summarize and clarify the argument of what precedes, contrasting once again the two spheres of servitude and their respective results. Verse 23a reiterates the thoughts already present in verses 16b ("slaves ... of sin, which leads to death") and 21b ("The end of those things is death"). Sin, the old master, pays its appropriate "wage" [τὰ ὀψώνια] to its subjects.[137] Originally the technical term for a soldier's subsistence pay or ration money, by NT times ὀψώνιον had broadened to encompass "salary, wages, allowance" in general, including the allowance or pocket-money (lat. *peculium*) which a slave received, a usage strongly favored by the present context.[138] The wage which Sin pays is death. This is set in opposition to righteousness (verse 16b) and eternal life (verses 21–22, 23), and denotes "death as God's final eschatological judgment of condemnation."[139] In 2:6–10 God rather than Sin is the paymaster, but the idea is the same. Evildoers will be paid [ἀποδίδωμι] with the opposite of eternal life, namely eschatological wrath and fury.

Also summarizing the previous argument, verse 23b now contrasts

---

[134] *Slavery as Salvation: the metaphor of slavery in pauline Christianity* (New Haven and London: Yale University Press, 1990), 61–62.

[135] See esp. the baptismal reference (verses 3–5) and the then/now scheme (verses 21–22).

[136] Thus "the obedience of faith" (1:5; cf. 15:18).

[137] In parallel with the free gift of God [χάρισμα τοῦ θεοῦ], τὰ ὀψώνια τῆς ἁμαρτίας should be read as a subjective genitive (the wages which Sin pays; so nearly all commentators) and not "wages for sin."

[138] Ὀψώνιον is used elsewhere non-metaphorically in Paul (1 Cor. 9:7; 2 Cor. 11:8; cf. also Luke 3:14). See further H. W. Heidland, *TDNT* V.591–592. C. C. Caragounis proposes "provisions, viands" instead of "wages," but fails to explain why Paul would have shifted to χάρισμα in verse 23b on this basis ("ΟΨΩΝΙΟΝ: A Reconsideration of its Meaning," *NovT* 16 [1974], 35–57).

[139] Cranfield, *The Epistle to the Romans*, I.322, n. 3.

the new dominion, slavery to God, and its incomparably greater benefit, eternal life. The careful listener might have expected the counterpart to "death" as "Sin's wages" to have been "eternal life" as "God's wages." Instead Paul substitutes "gift" [χάρισμα] for "wage" on the divine side of the contrast. Thus not only is the result of the two dominions in starkest contrast (eternal life versus death), but the method of reckoning as well (wage versus gift). The gift of eternal life is freely bestowed as an unearned favor in contrast to a wage.

However, it is not entirely correct for Cranfield to assert broadly, "God does not pay wages, since no man can put Him in his debt."[140] The apostle can, indeed, speak of a Christian's wage [μισθός] according to works.[141] True, the benevolent gift of God is contrasted with the meager rations doled out by Sin, but throughout chapter 6 Paul has been at pains to demonstrate that this gift applies exclusively to the slaves of God. The free gift of salvation is to the obedient. The concluding "in Christ Jesus our Lord" is not merely a formulaic ending, but reiterates the thesis fundamental to 5:12–6:23, that all the benefits of the new righteousness are available only "in Christ," and thus only to those who by faith are in Him.

Is a return to Sin's servitude (and thus to death) considered possible by Paul in this passage for believers? On the one hand "in Christ" believers have already been set free from Sin's dominion and have already become servants of righteousness (6:1–11, 18). From this perspective it must be termed an "impossibility" for a Christian to live in the service of Sin: "How can we who died to sin go on living in it?" (verse 2). This impossibility constitutes Paul's first answer to the charge that faith-righteousness might open the door to libertinism (verses 1–11). On the other hand, believers do not yet fully partake of this new existence ("we will certainly be united with him in a resurrection like his," verse 5b). Their mortal bodies have not yet entered the new aeon where they, too, will reflect the glory of Christ's resurrection (verses 12–13). Those who are already freed from Sin's dominion have not yet been removed bodily from the sphere of its power; hence the exhortations to avoid Sin's reign in verses 11–13, 19.

What then is the soteriological implication of this "impossible

---

[140] Ibid., I.330. Braun calls Romans 6 a complete "revocation of the doctrine of merit" (*Gerichtsgedanke und Rechtfertigungslehre*, 67).

[141] 1 Cor. 3:8, 14; 2 Cor. 5:10; Col. 3:23–25; further 1 Cor. 9:24–27; (2 Tim. 2:5).

possibility,"[142] of a potential return to the "old slavery" (cf. Galatians 5:1, "do not submit again to a yoke of slavery")? To attempt an answer would take us well beyond the bounds of Romans 6. In such an eventuality (not excluded, but certainly not expected by Paul in Romans 6) Paul's summation would presumably apply: "the wages of sin is death." Thus, the possibility of a return to the old slavery to Sin is implied in Romans 6:15–23. If this threat of death to the subjects of Sin is not (at least theoretically) applicable to believers, then the second half of Paul's argument in Romans 6 (verses 15–23) against grace as license is robbed of a good deal of its motivating power ("Do you not know that [slavery to sin] leads to death?" verse 16). That Paul did have concerns about such an eventuality is amply demonstrated in his letters.[143]

Summarizing the findings, justification by faith may not be taken as making the believer's obedience or sanctification somehow irrelevant, secondary, or optional in relation to the eschatological enjoyment of salvation.[144] It is probably just such a misinterpretation in the direction of libertinism or antinomianism which Paul is concerned to combat in chapter 6, a misinterpretation which would lead to grave conflict in a congregation composed of both Jews and Gentiles. The concluding "in Christ Jesus our Lord" is no mere formality, but highlights once again that God's gracious gift of future life is only to be found within the sphere of Christ's dominion.

Second, the imperatives in Romans 6 do not become a new ground or cause for the indicative ("you will be in Christ if you are

---

[142] The phrase is found in Beker, *Paul the Apostle*, 219.

[143] Rom. 13:11–14; 1 Cor. 5:6–7; 6:12–20; 10:1–22; 2 Cor. 12:20–13:10; Gal. 4:8–11; 5:16–21; 6:7–8; 1 Thess.3:1–5, 8.

[144] "For Paul the principle that eternal life is bestowed upon the basis of righteousness [= ethical righteousness as in Judaism] remains central, and the passages from here down to 8:13 are concerned with the possibility and necessity of living out that required righteousness. Paul's grace-vision is not to injure one bit the ethical seriousness of the Jewish tradition presupposed in Romans" (B. Byrne, "Living out the Righteousness of God," *CBQ* 43 [1981], 562–563). Byrne's article is an excellent attempt from a Roman Catholic perspective to relate grace, obedience, and salvation against the background of Romans 5–8. I would only question whether he has sufficiently acknowledged the forensic finality of Paul's use of the verb δικαιοῦν (for instance, δικαιωθέντες οὖν ἐκ πίστεως, 5:1). When he formulates, "The union with the risen Lord … is the means whereby God creates a new moral possibility in Christians (cf. 7:4–6), a new righteousness and, on the basis of this righteousness, a destiny to resurrection life" (570), the "already" of justification by faith would seem to be lost.

obedient") replacing grace (6:23); nor is the indicative "realized" or "actualized" in the imperative ("what we are or have in principle in Christ only becomes ours in reality or experience via obedience"). Rather obedience can better be described as the necessary *manifestation* of the indicative.

Paul is careful throughout that obedience does not replace grace as the cause of, and faith as the instrument of, salvation. Yet it is clear that for him this gracious salvation is wholly unthinkable apart from the ensuing obedience of the redeemed (6:16, 22). Thus, just as Paul could speak of God giving eternal life "to those who by patiently doing good seek for glory and honor and immortality" (2:7), so now slavery to obedience (= God) is εἰς δικαιοσύνην (= resulting in the final verdict of life-giving righteousness versus εἰς θάνατον, 6:16b), and eternal life is viewed as the result [τέλος] of a life of enslavement to God which produces holiness (6:22).

Romans 8:1–4

(1) There is therefore now no condemnation for those who are in Christ Jesus. (2) For the law of the Spirit of life in Christ Jesus has set you free from the law of sin and of death. (3) For God has done what the law, weakened by the flesh, could not do: by sending his own Son in the likeness of sinful flesh, and to deal with sin, he condemned sin in the flesh, (4) so that the just requirement of the law might be fulfilled in us, who walk not according to the flesh but according to the Spirit.

At first glance, verse 1 would seem to remove all concern for believers vis-à-vis a future judgment to (eternal) life or death. For the Christian condemnation at the judgment must be an impossibility – οὐδὲν ἄρα νῦν κατάκριμα.[145] I will attempt to examine briefly the correctness of such an implication from this text. In

---

[145] For this common interpretation, see L. Mattern, *Das Verständnis des Gerichtes*, 92, 110; and J. M. Gundry-Volf, *Paul and Perseverance* (WUNT 2.37; Tübingen: J. C. B. Mohr (Paul Siebeck), 1990), 68, 157, 285. Interestingly, medieval exegetes went in the opposite direction, making the indicative of verse 1 dependent on the condition implied in verse 4b – "*if* someone does not walk according to the flesh but the Spirit" (K. Fröhlich, "Romans 8:1–11: Pauline Theology in Medieval Interpretation," *Faith and History: Essays in Honor of Paul W. Meyer* [ed. J. T. Carroll, *et al.*; Atlanta: Scholars Press, 1990], 245).

addition, we must note whether, according to verse 4, Paul does indeed expect that believers will fulfill the law.

The exclusion of condemnation harks back to Paul's only previous use of this noun (5:16, 18; cf. 2:1 [verbal form]). There he described all humanity in Adam as being under the sentence of condemnation through Adam's one trespass. Now, however, this situation has been reversed for those in Christ Jesus. As F. Büchsel has shown, the noun κατάκριμα can convey the notion of both a *sentence* of condemnation as well as its *execution*.[146] In this latter sense it could be better translated "damning situation" or "doom." In 8:1 κατάκριμα has reference primarily to the execution of the sentence, now being played out in the doomed situation of Adamic humanity (cf. 5:12–21; 7:7–25). Paul is not merely saying Christians need not fear a sentence of condemnation at the future judgment, but even more to the point in this context, they are now released from the wretched "penal servitude" (Bruce's translation) to which they were doomed in Adam.

The correctness of this view is confirmed by Paul's explanation of freedom from condemnation in verses 2–3 which is intimately connected to the work of the Holy Spirit in believers' lives and conduct.[147] It is the Spirit who liberates the believer from the "law of sin and death," viz. from the damning condition of chapter 7. This liberation by the Spirit is in turn grounded in God's condemnation [κατέκρινεν] of sin in Christ's flesh (i.e., in his death). This latter use of condemnation means not so much that the sentence of destruction has been pronounced against sin (for in this the law was surely not ἀδύνατον, verse 3a), but first of all that the sentence has been *executed* upon the twin powers of Sin and Death.[148] It is this destruction of the *power*, not just the guilt, of Sin which was indeed τὸ ἀδύνατον τοῦ νόμου according to chapter 7, and which has now been applied by the Spirit to believers, thus freeing them from this damning situation and enabling the fulfillment of "the just requirement (sg.) of the law," here understood in the broadest sense as

---

[146] Art. κατακρίνω, *TDNT*, III.951–952.

[147] With most commentators I take τοῦ πνεύματος here as a reference to God's Spirit rather than the human spirit, as generally throughout the chapter (verse 16 is the only clear exception; cf. 2 Cor. 3:6). The precise meaning of νόμος here ("principle" or "Torah"?) need not detain us, since the stress on the liberating role of the Spirit remains unchanged in either case.

[148] J. Murray, *The Epistle to the Romans* (NICNT; Grand Rapids: Eerdmans, 1968), I.277–279, (though on p. 282 he reverts to "the strictly forensic import of condemnation").

conformity to the divine will.[149] For Paul this freedom from condemnation under Sin's power occurs for "those who live according to the Spirit," i.e., who have "set their minds on the things of the Spirit" (verses 5–6), who are indwelt by the Spirit (verse 9), and are led by the same Spirit (verse 14).

Thus freedom from condemnation is nothing other than victory over the power of Sin and Death, accomplished already in the death of Christ, appropriated by faith, and now made an ethical reality for those in Christ by the operation of the Holy Spirit. For "those who are in Christ Jesus," who walk κατὰ πνεῦμα and thereby fulfill the law's requirement, there is indeed "no condemnation" to be feared in the future (verse 34). They are free from its curse now and need not fear it in the future judgment. This positive assurance of deliverance is the burden of chapter 8, and to this extent condemnation is an impossibility for those in Christ, just as judgment (= punishment) according to deeds was not a threat for the faithful in the Jewish literature surveyed in the earlier chapters. But precisely the "in Christ" language with its nuance of eschatological tension should warn against pressing this assurance to mean a security with no relation to the believer's pilgrimage [περιπατεῖν, verse 4] between Christ's resurrection and parousia. Should they return to living κατὰ σάρκα and under the dominion of Sin and Death, then they do not belong to Christ (verse 9) and will find themselves back under the same condemnation to death (verse 13).[150] Thus, while Romans 8:1 may rightly be celebrated as Paul's great shout of victory and assurance for believers vis-à-vis condemnation, this may not be taken as an unqualified denial of all relevance of present and future condemnation for Christians, nor as contradicting Paul's expectation of judgment according to works in 2:6. If anything, his connection between freedom from condemnation and the fulfillment of the law points in the same direction. The forensic and the ethical dimensions of righteousness may not be so easily separated in Paul's thinking.[151]

---

[149] The closest parallel to this phrase is 2:26 where τὰ δικαιώματα (pl.) τοῦ νόμου refers to that which the Torah justly requires (so also 1:32). It is thus equivalent to τὸ ἔργον τοῦ νόμου (2:15), and will not be much different than what Paul intends in 8:29 with "conformity to the image of His Son." See also Dunn, *Romans 1–8*, 423–424.

[150] The conditional sentences in verse 13 (εἰ + indicative) emphasize "the reality of the assumption," "the condition is considered 'a real case'" (BDF, §371(1); cf. also 372(2a)).

[151] Brendan Byrne has attempted to apply modern insights on justification

Romans 14:10–12

(10) Why do you pass judgment on your brother or sister? Or you, why do you despise your brother or sister? For we will all stand before the judgment seat of God. (11) For it is written,

"As I live, says the Lord, every knee shall bow to me, and every tongue shall give praise to God."

(12) So then, each of us will be accountable to God.[152]

Although exhortation has not been entirely lacking from the earlier chapters,[153] 12:1–15:13 constitute the apostolic paraenesis proper, the rhetorical *exhortatio* which "sets forth the ethical implications of the main thesis."[154]

(Käsemann, Stuhlmacher, Ziesler, *et. al.*) to the interpretation of Rom. 8 ("Living out the Righteousness of God," 557–581). Much of his study will be found reflected in my interpretation. I part company only over the relation of the forensic (or participationist) and ethical categories, since Byrne seems to want to subordinate the former almost totally to the latter. "The nub of Paul's distinctiveness lies in the way participationist categories are placed at the service of righteousness, i.e., are presented as *the way in which the required righteousness is produced*" (571, emphasis mine). Although Byrne acknowledges the forensic categories, and repeatedly stresses that justifying righteousness is nothing other than Christ's righteousness, nevertheless the language of "producing," of "a new righteousness created" via "fulfillment of the moral demand" (569), leaves one wondering if a verse such as Rom. 5:1 (δικαιωθέντες, aor. pass.) has been fully appreciated. I have already suggested that the language of "manifestation" more appropriately expresses the relationship between the ethical and forensic aspects of justification.

Luise Mattern represents the opposite tendency, namely to subordinate the ethical to the forensic, the pneumatological to the christological (*Das Verständnis des Gerichtes*, 91–94). She views verse 1 ("a cry of victory?") as a slight interruption between the question in 7:24 and its answer in 8:2ff. This freedom from the law of sin, and hence from condemnation, has its basis (verse 3) in the divine execution of judgment on Sin at the cross. The result of Christ's saving act is past and future freedom from the "law of sin and death" and fulfillment (as a "reality" which "is fulfilled," not a "possibility" which "can be fulfilled") of the law's just requirement. She concludes: "The reason that ἐν χριστῷ no κατάκριμα is any longer possible is God's work in Christ, and that alone." This exegesis skips over the central pneumatological basis of freedom from condemnation given in verse 2. Granted, Paul ultimately bases all of Christian existence, and especially life in the Spirit, upon Christ's work; nevertheless the burden of Rom. 8 is to demonstrate how believers are delivered *by the Spirit* from the *damning condition* under Sin. Their deliverance from Sin's power *in Christ* was sufficiently dealt with in Rom. 6.

[152] On reading τῷ θεῷ, see B. Metzger (ed.), *A Textual Commentary on the Greek New Testament* (London/New York: UBS, 1971), 531–532.

[153] 6:12–14, 19b; 11:17–24.

[154] R. Jewett, "Following the Argument of Romans" in Donfried, ed., *The Romans Debate*, 272.

With 14:1 begins a lengthy unit focused on two groups, "the weak" and "the strong" (to which latter group Paul reckons himself, 15:1), which is most likely addressed to a concrete situation in Rome, about which Paul is somehow informed.[155] At issue between the two groups is whether a fellow Christian should eat meat.[156] For Paul the more fundamental issue lies in the threat thus posed to the maintenance of love[157] and to the peace or unity of the one church in Rome.[158] Members of the two groups are failing to "accept one another" (14:1, 3; 15:7), instead despising, judging or even condemning. Schneider has pointed out that all this probably takes place in the context of the Christian communal meal in Rome.[159] Chapter 14:1–12 constitutes a sustained argument against such mutual judgment around the Christian table:

> Who are you to pass judgment on servants of another?
> (verse 4a)

> Why do you pass judgment on your brother or sister?
> (verse 10a)

> Let us therefore no longer pass judgment on one another.
> (verse 13a)

The validity of the argument rests, in turn, upon the principle taken from the then-current practice of slavery stated in verse 4 – a servant's judgment is the exclusive prerogative of the master.[160] Neither the strong nor the weak may judge the other, for Christ has become the master of both. Each with their own conviction is

---

[155] See above on "Occasion" (144–145); also J. Mosier, "Rethinking Romans 12–15," *NTS* 36 (1990), 571–582.

[156] 14:2, 5–6, 14, 20–23. These mention, in addition to "meat," "observing sacred days" and "abstaining from wine." The exact views of the "strong" and the "weak" are not relevant to this chapter. For various reconstructions see Cranfield, *The Epistle to the Romans* II.690–697. According to N. Schneider (*Die "Schwachen" in der christlichen Gemeinde Roms: Eine historisch-exegetische Untersuchung zu Röm 14,1–15,13* [Dissertation, Wuppertal, 1989], 3, 62–155) the current majority opinion favors a Jewish background.

[157] 14:15; also 15:1–3. Thus, 14:1ff. is a specific application of the previous general exhortation to love (12:9–21; 13:8–10).

[158] 14:17–18, 19–20a; 15:5–6.

[159] *Die "Schwachen,"* 139–150.

[160] "Paul pictures this in terms of ancient slave-law according to which the slave is subjected to the jurisdiction of the master... No other slave is permitted to infringe upon this jurisdiction" (O. Michel, *Der Brief an die Römer* [5th edn.;MeyerK 4; Göttingen: Vandenhoeck & Ruprecht, 1978], 424).

serving this master, whether by eating or by abstaining, as evidenced in either case by "giving thanks to God" (verses 5–8).

This line of argument is then capped by the reference in verses 10–12 to divine judgment, which, following the two rhetorical questions of verse 10a, functions as a theological reason [γάρ] for rejecting such intra-community judgment.[161] In other texts this judgment motif can serve as a warning to motivate correct ethical behavior (2 Cor. 5:10; 1 Cor. 3:16–17; Gal. 6:7–8), along the lines of Matthew 7:1, "Do not judge, so that you may not be judged." Here, however, those guilty of judging another are not threatened with an equivalent divine judgment upon themselves for doing so. Not the effect upon those judging, but the right of the Judge is preeminent in this passage. In correspondence with the preceding social metaphor of slave–master relations, judgment is reserved for God alone as a means of eliminating human judgment upon one another. This purpose of the judgment motif is made explicit in verse 13a, "Let us therefore no longer pass judgment on one another." A similar use of divine judgment to invalidate intra-community judgment can also be found in Romans 12:19; 1 Corinthians 3:5–9a; 4:1–5; Galatians 6:1–5.[162]

As usual, details of judgment scenery are sparse, making dogmatism difficult regarding Paul's larger conception of this judgment. As in 2 Corinthians 5:10 the imagery for the locale of this judgment is borrowed from Paul's cultural environment. The judgment seat [τὸ βῆμα] was an elevated platform common in cities of the Roman empire for speeches in the public assembly,[163] and before which litigants *appeared*.[164] Its usage for the divine judgment seat (or "throne") is also attested in Judaism.[165] Unlike the text in 2

---

[161] Of course, in matters of overt sinning Paul applies a completely different principle: "I have already pronounced judgment ... on the man... Is it not those who are inside that you are to judge?" (1 Cor. 5:3–4, 12b).

[162] Wayne Meeks suggests that such use of divine judgment to restrain judgmental and divisive tendencies may have been a Jewish theologoumenon. Pseudo-Phocylides 10–11 reads, "Cast the poor not down unjustly, judge not partially. If you judge evilly, God will judge you thereafter" ("Judgment and the Brother: Romans 14,1–15,13," *Tradition and Interpretation in the New Testament: Essays in Honor of E. Earle Ellis* [ed. G. Hawthorne; Grand Rapids: Eerdmans, 1987], 294; cf. also Jas. 4:12). See also K. Yinger, "Romans 12:14–21 and Nonretaliation in Second Temple Judaism" (*CBQ* 60/1, [1998], 74–96).

[163] So Matt. 27:19; John 19:13; Acts 18:12. Further BAGD, 140. Partial remains of such a seat can still be seen in Corinth.

[164] Παραστησόμεθα can refer to a required court appearance to present a legal case (BAGD, 628); cf. Acts 23:33; 27:24 (different 2 Cor. 5:10, φανερωθῆναι). However, there appears to be in this text a mixing of legal and slavery metaphors,

Corinthians ("the judgment seat *of Christ*") here it is *God*[166] who presides. In line with the OT, Paul and the rest of the NT can speak of God as the final Judge of the world.[167] Yet, probably following the lead of apocalyptic Judaism which can substitute the Son of Man or Messiah for God on the judgment throne,[168] they can equally name Christ as the Judge.[169] 1 Corinthians 4:4–5 and Romans 8:33–34 seem to retain both figures. A theological explanation in terms of delegated authority is found in Acts 10:42, "he is the one whom God appointed as judge of the living and the dead" (also John 5:22, 27).

There will be an individual accounting given to God about oneself [περὶ ἑαυτοῦ]. The nature of this accounting takes its cue from the slave–master analogy begun in verse 4 and is well illustrated by the parable in Luke 16:

> There was a rich man who had a manager, and charges were brought to him that this man was squandering his property. So he summoned him and said to him, "What is this that I hear about you? Give me an accounting of your management, because you cannot be my manager any longer."   (verses 1–2)

In each case it is faithfulness in service which is under examination (cf. 1 Cor. 4:2), i.e., whether one has served in a manner consistent with the master's will. In regard to such issues as eating meat and observing holy days, the criterion of judgment is not some new halakhic ruling for the churches, but behavior consistent with one's own conviction or conscience [ἕκαστος ἐν τῷ ἰδίῳ νοϊ πληροφορ-είσθω, verse 5b], which in its turn is not autonomous but must reflect life τῷ κυρίῳ. Though Paul does not use the specific motif of judgment according to works here, the scene is one and the same. In the place of the motif language we have each rendering a

---

and in 2 Tim. 2:15 παραστῆσαι can be used for a "workman" [ἐργάτης] *presenting* himself for the employer's approval.

[165] See 1 En. 62:3, 5; also *Str-B*, 1.1031–1032.

[166] Following a textual tradition as early as Marcion and Polycarp, the KJV reads "the judgment seat of Christ" at Rom. 14:10. This reading must be regarded as secondary, arising through assimilation to the immediate context (verse 9) and possibly to 2 Cor. 5:10. External attestation clearly favors the reading τοῦ θεοῦ here.

[167] Rom. 2:2–3, 5–6, 16; 3:5–6; 14:10; 1 Thess. 3:13; 2 Thess. 1:5–6; Heb. 10:30; 12:23; Jas. 4:12; 5:9; 1 Pet. 1:17; 2 Pet. 2:4–6; Rev. 14:7; 18:20; 20:11–15.

[168] See Dan. 7; further references in Volz, *Eschatologie der jüdischen Gemeinde*, 274–275.

[169] 2 Cor. 5:10; 2 Thess. 1:8; 2 Tim. 4:1, 8; Matt. 25:31–46; Rev. 22:12.

personal account of service to God. The standard of judgment has nothing to do with a legalistic balancing of good and evil works, but the making public ("we must all appear ... to give account") of whether one has lived consistently τῷ κυρίῳ.

Apart from its futurity Paul is not particularly concerned to define more precisely the "when" of this judgment.[170] L. Mattern appeals to the stress on individuality of judgment in this text [ἕκαστος ἡμῶν περὶ ἑαυτοῦ] as favoring a judgment (immediately) following the death of the individual rather than a general last judgment.[171] This conclusion seems, however, to owe more to her desire to keep the believer's judgment according to work separate from the final judgment determining salvation/damnation, rather than to clear exegetical considerations. As Mattern herself admits, what hints there are in the text point to a universal final judgment. Paul's citation of Isaiah 45:23, originally referring to the future homage of all nations before Yahweh (see esp. verse 22), is also used in the hymn quoted in Philippians 2:6–11 as a reference to the universal acknowledgment of Christ's Lordship,[172] an expectation associated in Paul's mind with the end [τέλος] and the parousia of Christ (cf. 1 Cor. 15:24–28).

Ernst Synofzik, on the other hand, wishes to deny that a passage such as this one reveals anything of Paul's eschatological convictions, a denial which is central to his thesis. He compares Romans 14 with 1 Corinthians 8–10, following Conzelmann in terming the former a "revision and extension" of the latter, and noting about the Corinthian passage, "In contrast to Romans 14:1–12, Paul does not require mention of the eschatological judgment in order to stress the Christian's individual accountability before God" (*Die Gerichts- und Vergeltungsaussagen bei Paulus*, 82). Thus he can conclude that the judgment motif for Paul is "but one among many, and in 1 Corinthians 8–10 nonessential. By contrast, the ecclesiological and christological rationale is more important" (84; also 80, 213). This lesser importance of the judgment motif is, then, one more reason for viewing it as only an *Argumentationsmittel* (209). A correction must be made in the evaluation of the evidence

---

[170] Note the future verbs in this passage: παραστησόμεθα, κάμψει, ἐξομολογή-σεται, δώσει (v.l. ἀποδώσει).

[171] *Das Verständnis des Gerichtes*, 161, 211–215.

[172] "Even denizens of the underworld as well as inhabitants of heaven are included along with dwellers upon earth. That is, the entire cosmos is brought under the lordship of Christ, as in a vision the poet sees the fulfillment of God's purpose in the endtime" (R. Martin, *Philippians* [NCB; Grand Rapids: Eerdmans, 1980], 101).

he advances for this "lesser importance" of the motif. Its absence in
the 1 Corinthians passage is due not to its lesser importance but to
the difference in occasion. Intra-community judgment plays almost
no role in 1 Corinthians 8–10. Thus Paul had no need to point out
to the Corinthians at this stage the answerability of each to God
alone (and not to each other) in the judgment. On the other hand
judgment as a warning against improper behavior is quite in
evidence elsewhere in 1 Corinthians (8:11–13; 9:24–27; 10:5–12,
22); and where the problem of judging one another does arise
(4:1–5) the importance of judgment as a response is quite in
evidence.

A particular emphasis in this passage lies on the inclusive nature
of this judgment: πάντες, (verse 10); πᾶς γόνυ ... πᾶσα γλῶσσα,
(verse 11); ἕκαστος ἡμῶν, (verse 12). Rather than "each of us"
(verse 12) limiting the "all" of verses 10–11 to believers only, I
understand verses 10–11 to be referring to the appearing of all
humanity before the eschatological judgment seat (clearly the case
in Isaiah 45), with verse 12 providing Paul's application [ἄρα οὖν]
to his audience. Thus, since every individual servant of God/Christ
(along with all humanity) must give account of their service at this
divine judgment, it is in every case a usurping of God's role for one
to sit in judgment on another.

While it is certainly the divine prerogative and not the outcome
of such judgment that is at issue in verses 10–12, nevertheless there
are hints as to its outcome for believers in the larger context. "Who
are you to pass judgment on servants of another? It is before their
own lord that they stand or fall. And they will be upheld, for the
Lord is able to make them stand" (14:4). Paul's concern here is to
overcome the mutual disdain and judgment occurring in the house
churches in Rome (verses 1–3). In verse 4a he compares their
situation to that of a slave-owner and a family servant, with the
point being that anyone other than the slave's owner has no
business judging such service. It is only in reference to their own
master that they will "stand" or "fall." In this context the metaphor
of "standing" and "falling" will refer to the master's acceptance or
rejection of service, in line with Paul's desire for mutual acceptance
(verse 1) patterned after God's acceptance of each (verse 3). Paul's
total confidence in God's approval (verse 4b) is directed in this case
against the mutual judgment occurring in the Roman church. That
this was not an unconditional confidence on Paul's part is,
however, made clear by his demand that each one act in full accord

with personal conviction (verse 5b) and the condition that one's behavior be "to the Lord" (verses 6–8).

If the "standing" in verses 1–12 refers primarily to divine approval or censure regarding such matters as eating meat, the ensuing section (verses 13–23) drives home to the strong the ultimate effect on the weaker believer who is led to act contrary to conscience, causing him to "stumble" or be "destroyed." The image of stumbling has a rich OT background reminiscent especially of Israel's idolatry (Exod. 23:33; 34:12), or other occasions for disobedience leading to destruction (Ps. 9:4; Prov. 4:19; Isa. 8:14).[173] In the Synoptics destruction awaits anyone who would lead another believer into sin (Mark 9:42–47, par.). "At issue in the question of *proskomma* are ultimate decisions, conscience and faith, sin and perdition."[174] This stumbling represents nothing other than a denial of Christ's lordship.

The language of destruction serves to reinforce the ultimate seriousness of what is at stake. Ἀπόλλυμι is regularly employed by the apostle to signify eschatological destruction,[175] and κατακρίνειν likewise for ultimate condemnation.[176] Thus Paul urges the strong in faith to limit their own exercise of freedom in regard to eating meat, lest the weak be thereby led to stumble (i.e., to sin by eating meat against their conscience) and fall into eternal destruction. At first glance the threat of damnation for such *adiaphora* as eating or not eating meat may seem much overdrawn. It is not the eating per se, however, which brings condemnation ("all food is clean," verse 20), but an eating which is not ἐκ πίστεως[177] and hence is ἁμαρτία (verse 23). The gravity and sin of being led to act against one's own conviction consists in rebellion against what, to one's own mind, is God's will and thus in no longer living τῷ κυρίῳ. Such faithfulness to the will of one's lord has already been demonstrated as the criterion of the coming judgment (verses 4, 10–12). As in chapter 6 the possibility is once again contemplated

[173] G. Stählin, *TDNT*, VI.748–751; VII.340–344.

[174] Ibid., VI.753. Cf. 1 Cor. 8:9–13; 10:32; and esp. Rom. 9:32–33 in reference to Israel's unbelief. A somewhat weakened sense is found in 2 Cor. 6:3, where it denotes "cause offense at Paul's ministry."

[175] Rom. 2:2; 1 Cor. 1:18; 8:11; 15:18; 2 Cor. 2:15; 4:3; 2 Thess. 2:10.

[176] Rom. 8:34; 1 Cor. 11:32. See esp. L. Mattern, *Das Verständnis des Gerichtes*, 116–117, who notes that this destruction is contrasted explicitly with the salvific intent of Christ's death (verse 15). See also 1 Cor. 8:11–12 for a similar argument.

[177] On this difficult phrase, see Cranfield, *The Epistle to the Romans*, II.727–29.

that a believer might yield anew to the rule of sin resulting in eschatological condemnation and destruction.[178]

Summary

The examination of relevant judgment/recompense texts in Romans has confirmed my interpretation of the motif in 2:6–11. Paul did expect believers (along with all humanity) to face the final judgment according to works resulting in eternal life or divine wrath. In 14:10–12 a scene similar to 2:6–11 is painted, stressing not perfect law-keeping or merit, but consistent living τῷ κυρίῳ. Nor does Romans 8:1 contradict this expectation since freedom from the condemning slavery to Sin is made dependent upon walking according to the Spirit.

When Paul speaks of being judged *according to works*, this does not have a legalistic connotation (weighing good deeds against bad deeds), but operates within the framework of what has been termed covenantal nomism. Although Romans 4:4–5 is not infrequently taken to mean that Paul's message of faith-righteousness must be interpreted against a backdrop of Jewish legalism, he was found to be operating with the same dichotomy as in chapters 1–3 – faith in Christ versus law-works (Jewish boundary markers). In continuity with his covenantal-nomistic background, Paul expected those incorporated into the people of God by grace to continue in obedience to God rather than to Sin (6:15–23), to fulfill the just requirement of the law (8:4), and to live to the Lord according to their conscience (14:1–23). Consistent failure (not temporary backsliding or occasional failure), obeying unrighteousness instead of righteousness, will bring eternal death (6:23) and ruin (14:15, 20–23). Obedience cannot *earn* life or salvation, but it remains nevertheless the evidential basis or norm for the final verdict.

At the same time, we have discovered significant points of *discontinuity* between Paul and Judaism. Most obviously, faith in Christ replaces submission to the Torah (law-works) as *the definitive identifier* of who does, or does not, belong to the people of God. This does not in any way diminish for Paul the importance of *works*, understood as obedience to God's will, within the process of salvation. At this point, in fact, Paul radicalized the motif of

---

[178] Likewise Phil. 3:12–14, 18–19; 1 Cor. 8:11; 9:24–27. See Mattern, *Das Verständnis des Gerichtes*, 112–120.

judgment according to works beyond what Judaism was typically prepared to do – namely, to apply this standard of judgment with complete impartiality to both Jew and Gentile, thus exposing Jewish boasting as presumption upon God's kindness. Paul also places ethical righteousness much more clearly within the context of his pneumatology than was the case in Judaism, since for Paul it is precisely the Spirit which does what the Torah could not do, namely liberate from Sin's condemning slavery and produce the fulfillment of the law (8:1–4). Because of Paul's confidence in the Spirit's ability and readiness to bear fruit in the believers' lives, he could look with confidence toward the final judgment according to works; for such works, such "patient doing of the good," were but the visible manifestation ("fruit") of that righteous status granted and maintained through faith in Christ. Thus, for Paul, there was no sense of tension or antinomy between justification by faith apart from law-works, and judgment according to deeds.

5

JUDGMENT ACCORDING TO DEEDS IN 1 CORINTHIANS

The motif occurs in this letter explicitly only in 3:8b. However the judgment statements in 3:14–15, 16–17, and 4:5 must be considered as well, both because the terminology evidences their close relation to the motif in 3:8b (the repetition of "receive reward" [μισθὸν λήμψεται] in 3:14–15 for instance), and because they shed crucial additional light on Paul's understanding of judgment as it relates to members of the Christian community. My aim will be to examine the wording, function, and contextual meaning of the motif and related judgment sayings, noting along the way points of continuity or discontinuity with the same features in second temple Judaism. Of particular interest theologically will be 3:14–15, since this text has become a standard proof for many that no amount of disobedience on the part of one who has been justified by faith can ever endanger that one's ultimate salvation. Such a one shall "suffer loss" but still "be saved." Does Paul, after all, give a nod toward the typically Protestant tension felt to exist between judgment according to works and justification by grace through faith?

1 Corinthians 3:5–9a

Nearly all commentators agree that the initial larger unit in the letter runs from 1:10–4:21. The opening subsection (1:10–17) names "divisions" and "quarrels" as the problem at hand, whereby the Corinthians are boasting in some leaders to the denigration of others. There appears to be a developing conflict between Paul himself and the church at Corinth, relating both to his apostolic authority and his kerygma.[1] Some of the Corinthians view themselves as *spiritual ones* [πνευματικός],[2] but are not so sure about

---

[1] 2:1–5; 4:1–5, 8–21; 9:1–23.
[2] 2:6–16; 3:1; 14:37.

Paul, who has not exhibited the power, prerogatives or wisdom of a truly spiritual leader-teacher.[3]

After an initial appeal to the church to cease their disagreements and quarrels regarding the merits of various leaders, Paul turns immediately to the underlying error in their thinking – an exaltation of "eloquent [human] wisdom" which empties his message of its power (1:17). The message of the cross of Christ is opposed to the wisdom of this world (1:18–25), something evidenced both by God's choice of the Corinthians who were weak and foolish in the world's eyes (1:26–31), as well as by Paul's original preaching which was without persuasive words of wisdom, yet with divine power and results (2:1–5). Ultimately, of course, God's wisdom is indeed wise not foolish, but this is discerned only through the Spirit by those who are spiritual (2:6–16). Here Paul wrests the label πνευματικός away from those who would tie it to a form of worldly wisdom, binding it instead to "the mind of Christ" (2:16).

Chapter 3:1–4 is a transitional paragraph connecting the fore-going discussion of wisdom to the problem of boasting in various leaders. Far from being wise, the Corinthians reveal themselves by their boasting to be immature and fleshly. Then over against their notion of attachment to a particular wise leader, Paul unfolds his view of Christian teachers/leaders (3:5–23), emphasizing that they are servants of God, and to be valued equally (in spite of diversity), though the servants themselves must be careful to build in accor-dance with the one gospel foundation (= Christ). Thus neither worldly wisdom (3:19–20) nor boasting in persons (3:21) have any place, but only Christ (3:21b–23).

Then in chapter 4 Paul turns to the issue which has been beneath the surface all along, his own apostolic relationship to the church at Corinth. As God's servant, a judgment upon his service lies in God's hands, not theirs (4:1–5). With biting sarcasm he contrasts their expectation of worldly wisdom and power in the present ("Already you have all you want!" verse 8) with his apostolic weakness and suffering which identify him with Christ (4:6–13). He concludes with the reminder that he alone is their "father through

---

[3] On the occasion of the letter, see J. C. Hurd; *The Origin of I Corinthians* (2nd edn.; Macon, GA: Mercer University Press, 1983), esp. 97–105; S. M. Pogoloff, *Logos and Sophia: The Rhetorical Situation of 1 Corinthians* (SBLDS 134; Atlanta, GA: Scholars Press, 1992), 99–104. Still valuable is J. Munck's study, *Paul and the Salvation of Mankind* (London: SCM, 1959), esp. chap. 5 ("The Church Without Factions: Studies in I Corinthians 1–4").

the gospel" (4:15) and a warning against arrogance in the light of his planned coming (4:18–21).

Having exposed their false view of who is really wise and scolded their fleshly attachment to supposedly wise teachers, Paul sets forth in chapter 3 his view of Christian leadership in a series of three metaphors (verses 5–9a, 9b–15, 16–17), with the goal of his argumentation made clear again in verse 21, "So let no one boast about human leaders" (cf. also 3:3). He begins by singling out Apollos and himself as a case study "so that none of you will be puffed up in favor of one [Apollos] against another [Paul]" (4:6).[4] The opening question raises the issue of comparative status – "What, then, is Apollos? What is Paul?" (3:5). That is, "as what (or "with what sort of status") should one regard them?"[5] In contrast to the Corinthians' proclivity to evaluate them as competing itinerant philosophers, Paul calls them servants [διάκονοι, verse 5] and co-workers [συνεργοί, verse 9] in God's field, the church.[6] Thus, he can answer the question as to comparative status – "So neither the one who plants [Paul] nor the one who waters [Apollos] is anything, but only God who gives growth" (verse 7). In comparison to the true source of growth, the servants cannot lay claim to great status. How foolish for the Corinthians to be quarreling about whether one belongs to Paul or to Apollos. The conclusion (verse 9a) captures the heart of the entire argument,[7] Paul and

[4] This holds true regardless of how one chooses to translate the notoriously difficult phrase in 4:6b – τὸ μὴ ὑπὲρ ἃ γέγραπται ["Nothing beyond what is written," NRSV]. In any case the second ἵνα-clause expresses the purpose of the previous metaphors (G. D. Fee, *The First Epistle to the Corinthians* [NICNT; Grand Rapids: Eerdmans, 1987], 166, n. 6).

[5] The answer to this question (οὔτε... ἐστίν τι, verse 7) is decisive for reading Τί... ἐστιν [what is] rather than Τίς [who] in verse 5. See G. Zuntz, *The Text of the Epistles* (London: Oxford University Press, 1953), 131–132. On the use of ἐστίν τι as a term of status used especially in comparing one person to another as more important or superior, see Gal. 2:6; 6:3; Acts 5:36.

[6] The widespread popularity of agricultural metaphors in both Hellenistic and Jewish circles cautions against seeking the background of the field-metaphor [γεώργιον] in the OT imagery of Israel as vineyard. See E. M. Embry, *NIDNTT*, III.865–867.

[7] Some interpreters take verse 9a as explanatory [γάρ] of either (i) verse 8a (apostles are "one" because co-workers with/for God), or (ii) verse 8b (as God's co-workers they may expect to be rewarded for their labor). My arguments in favor of (ii) can be found below. Nevertheless, the fact that συνεργοί and γεώργιον explicitly reiterate the metaphor of verses 5–8, and the possibility that the emphatic θεοῦ is intended as a direct counter to the Corinthian slogans, allow verse 9a to function as both the logical explanation of verse 8b and an encapsulation of the point of verses 5–8.

Apollos are laborers together[8] (not in competition) in God's field, the church; and most importantly, as such they are *God's* workers in *God's* field.

The relative insignificance of the human workers certainly does not, however, make them altogether worthless. It was, after all, "through [them] you came to believe" (verse 5). Their respective status, like their differing tasks and abilities, can be determined not by comparing them with one another – as co-workers in a common task they are "one" (NRSV: "they have a common purpose," verse 8)[9] – but only in relation to their Master. It is "as the Lord assigned to each" (verse 5b).[10] Paul is perfectly ready to acknowledge individually differing achievements (verse 8b), but this gives no occasion for exalting one servant over another (verse 9a).

How then does the recompense statement of verse 8b function within this argument?

> and each will receive wages according to the labor of each.
> (NRSV)
> [ἕκαστος δὲ τὸν ἴδιον μισθὸν λήμψεται κατὰ τὸν ἴδιον κόπον]

Many commentators have found this phrase disturbing to the flow of the argument, contending that it can be no more than a parenthetical thought, with the emphasis on unity before God (verses 6–8a) carried on smoothly in verse 9a: "for we are God's servants, workers together."[11] Others find it at best surprising or

---

[8] Although "we are laborers together with God" (KJV) is a possible translation of θεοῦ ἐσμεν συνεργοί, the immediately following θεοῦ γεώργιον, θεοῦ οἰκοδομή clearly favors taking the genitive as a possessive – "co-laborers in God's service" (cf. 4:1, ὑπηέτας Χριστου). This creates a stark contrast with the Corinthian slogans, and corresponds to Paul's general usage of συνεργός as a designation for his pupils and companions (cf. Bertram, *TDNT*, VII.874; and M. M. Mitchell, *Paul and the Rhetoric of Reconciliation: An Exegetical Investigation of the Language and Composition of 1 Corinthians* [HUT 28; Tübingen: J. C. B. Mohr (Paul Siebeck), 1991], 98–99), and thus corresponds also to διάκονοι (verse 5).

[9] The phrase (ἕν εἰσιν) speaks of the "unity of the church's task" (H. Conzelmann, *1 Corinthians* [Philadelphia: Fortress Press, 1975], 74, n. 49). This is preferable to seeing a reference to "equality" (RSV) or "inseparability" (Lietzmann).

[10] That this phrase has reference to the differing tasks given to each by the Lord, rather than to the faith given to each believer (KJV), is confirmed by the immediately following reference to those differing assignments – "I planted. Apollos watered" (verse 6a).

[11] So, for example, J. Moffatt, *The First Epistle of Paul to the Corinthians* (MNTC; London: Hodder and Stoughton Ltd., 1938), 39.

obscure in its relation to the context.[12] However, these views miss the dynamic at work in Paul's argument, which must stress not only the leaders' relative *unimportance* and *equality* before God (against the divisive Corinthian boasting), but likewise their individual *accountability* to God alone for the legitimate *diversity* of task.[13] This individuality and diversity of the workers, which forms the basis of the Corinthians' quarrels, must be somehow sustained by the apostle if he is to defend his unique position as founder (3:6–7) and father (4:14–17) of the church, yet without allowing it to remain a basis for human comparison and division.

Perhaps the place of verse 8b in the argument can be better seen if the verses are arranged chiastically.[14] Verses 5a and 9a are not part of this structure, but function as an opening and conclusion to the subsection:

(Opening question) What then is Apollos? What is Paul? (verse 5a)

A   Servants through whom you came to believe, as the Lord assigned to *each*. (verse 5b)

B   I *planted*, Apollos *watered*, but *God* gave the *growth*. (verse 6)

B'   So neither the one who *plants* nor the one who *waters* is anything, but only *God* who gives the *growth*. (verse 7)

A'   The one who plants and the one who waters have a common purpose, and *each* will receive wages according to the labor of each. (verse 8)

(Conclusion) For we are God's servants, working together; you are God's field. (verse 9a)

The clearly-paralleled central lines (B–B') express the main point of

---

[12] E.g., W. Schrage, *Der erste Brief an die Korinther* (EKKNT 7/1; Zürich: Benziger, 1991), 292, n. 88.

[13] So Kuck, "the individual differences will be confirmed by God's future judgment" (*Judgment and Community Conflict*, 164). Kuck's analysis supports mine in seeing a two-fold thrust in verses 5–9a (*unity* and *uniqueness*, 164–167). This stress on individual accountability is further confirmed by the five occurrences of ἕκαστος (3:5, 8, 13 [2x]; 4:5).

[14] Whether one wishes to classify verses 5b-8 as a literary chiasm is unimportant to the point I am making, which is concerned primarily with the thematic echo of verse 5b found in verse 8 (see below). On NT chiastic structures in general, see N. W. Lund, *Chiasmus in the New Testament* (Chapel Hill: University of North Carolina Press, 1942); and on 1 Cor. 3:5–17, *idem.*, "The Significance of Chiasmus for Interpretation," *Crozer Quarterly* 20 (1943), 113–114 [quite different from my reconstruction, however].

Paul's argument; diverse gifts among the laborers are no cause for division or boasting since all that really counts comes ultimately from God alone. The lines A–A′ do not exhibit the same degree of terminological linkage (only "each"–"each"), but one can discern a thematic echo. In both verses 5b and 8, the first line recognizes their sharing in a common task, while the second line stresses their individual accountability for the diverse tasks assigned to them:

Verse 5b	Verse 8
Servants	The one who plants and the one who waters
through whom you came to believe	have a common purpose,
to each	and each
as the Lord assigned	will receive wages according to the labor of each.

Thus, while Paul's primary concern in this passage is to eliminate diverse abilities as a grounds for fleshly comparison and boasting (B–B′), he cannot eliminate such recognizable diversity altogether. Instead he must set it within the context of accountability to the Lord (A–A′), and thereby take it out of the realm of fleshly comparisons. Viewed in this manner, the motif of recompense according to labor is not an interruption, but is the structurally expected thematic echo of verse 5b.[15]

Furthermore, this connection with verse 5b helps clarify the *function* of the motif in this passage. Just as the diverse assignments of Paul and Apollos are traced to the prerogative of the κύριος in verse 5b, thereby providing a bulwark against fleshly assessments; so likewise in verse 8b their diverse wages will have to await the future pay-day according to individual labor, the payment of which belongs to the same Lord. Although the master's prerogative to determine and distribute appropriate wages is only implicit in the motif itself, this point is made explicit in verse 9a ("For we are *God's* servants, working together"). θεοῦ is in the leading, emphatic position, laying stress on the fact that the servants *belong to God*; i.e., he alone can determine and distribute individually appropriate wages.[16]

---

[15] L. Mattern's view is similar, *Das Verständnis des Gerichtes*, 169–170.
[16] E. Fascher, *Der erste Brief des Paulus an die Korinther* [3rd edn.; THKNT 7/1; Berlin: Evangelische Verlagsanstalt, 1984], 133. See also the discussion of this same prerogative in Rom. 14:10–12 (chap. 4 above).

This also explains the unusual two-fold use of ἴδιος ("one's own"), something the NRSV translation obscures. Literally one would have to render the motif here: each will receive *his/her own* wage according to *his/her own* labor. Rather than an equal or common [κοινός] wage, each receives τὸν ἴδιον μισθόν, meaning a wage peculiar to that individual or according to his/her particular effort.[17] This two-fold ἴδιος appears to be Paul's own addition to the motif tradition and indicates his particular concern at this point – the determination of the recompense (or status in the Corinthian situation) appropriate to the diverse assignments and labors of leaders like Paul and Apollos must be reserved for God. Thus, the motif serves to restrain intra-community judgment, a function found elsewhere in Paul and in second temple Judaism.[18]

Up to this point I have assumed that verse 8b contains the motif of divine recompense according to deeds in spite of the fact that "God" is not named as subject, and the typical words for "recompense" (or "judge") and "works" are absent. Paul is not citing or alluding to any known formulation of the motif. Nevertheless, I am suggesting that Paul here takes up that same motif tradition,[19] formulating it in an unusual but not wholly unprecedented manner, and demonstrating theological tendencies which one sees mostly in later rabbinic literature.

The lack of explicit reference to God as the subject of the recompensing activity is not crucial in this instance. As suggested above, the future "will receive reward" implies the distribution of wages by the servant's master. Just as the "Lord" assigns a differing task to each (verse 5b), so he will grant to each the appropriate pay (verse 8b), for God is the master of each partner (verse 9a). The same terminology [μισθὸν λήμψεται] recurs in verse 14b, clearly in the context of God's fiery judgment day (see below). In addition, reference may be made to 4:5b where this future reception of

---

[17] In Koine Greek ἴδιος was generally little more than a simple possessive pronoun or reflexive adjective (= ἑαυτοῦ/αὐτοῦ). However, the classical meaning – "peculiar, private" (opposite κοινός) – can still be found in the NT (Acts 4:32; 1 Cor. 3:8; 7:7; 12:11; 15:38; Titus 1:12; Heb. 7:27), and is favored by grammarians for this text; see BDF, §286(1), and N. Turner, *Syntax*, Vol. III in *A Grammar of New Testament Greek* by J. H. Moulton (4 vols.; Edinburgh: T. & T. Clark, 1963), 191–192.

[18] Rom. 12:19; 14:10–12; 1 Cor. 4:4b; CD IX,2–5; 1QS X,17b-18; 2 En. 50:3–4; T.Gad 6–7; Ps.Phoc. 76–78; Jos.Asen. 28:10, 14.

[19] The linguistic criteria identifying motif occurrences are given on pp. 20–21 above.

reward is expressed in different terminology ("Then each one will receive commendation" [ὁ ἔπαινος γενήσεται ἐκάστῳ]), but in this case explicitly "from God" [ἀπὸ τοῦ θεοῦ].

This precise expression of the verbal component in terms of "to *receive* reward" [μισθὸν λήμψεσθαι] appears to be unique to 1 Corinthians 3:8b and 14b among motif occurrences.[20] Of course, apart from the motif, and without a standard ("according to..."), the phrase "to receive/have a wage" carried a straightforward economic meaning,[21] which could then be applied figuratively to the religious sphere:

> Whoever welcomes a prophet in the name of a prophet will receive a prophet's reward [μισθὸν προφήτου λήμψεται]; and whoever welcomes a righteous person in the name of a righteous person will receive the reward of the righteous [μισθὸν δικαίου λήμψεται] (Matt. 10:41).[22]

Of particular interest in this regard is 2 John 8, which, much like 1 Corinthians 3:8b, combines this figurative use of the phrase with human works. "Be on your guard, so that you do not lose what we (v.l. you) have worked for, but may receive a full reward." Thus Paul's terminology here might be easily explained as the combining of this commercial phraseology with the ideas of equivalent recompense.

Paul, however, was not the originator of such a combination. A similar expression can be found in Sirach 16:14b.[23]

> (12)As great as his mercy, so also is his reproof;
> he will judge a person according to their deeds.
> (13)The sinner will not escape with plunder,
> and the patience of the godly will not be frustrated.
> (14)He will make room for every act of mercy;
> each will receive [lit. "find"] in accordance with their deeds.
> [ἔκαστος κατὰ τὰ ἔργα αὐτοῦ εὑρήσει]

Like Paul, Sirach uses this formulation to speak of God's *positive*

---

[20] See Prov. 11:21 (LXX): "The one who sows righteousness shall receive a faithful reward" [λήμψεται μισθὸν πιστόν]; and the very similar ἀπολήμψεσθε τὴν ἀνταπόδοσιν in Col. 3:24.

[21] See for instance John 4:36 (though used figuratively); Eccles. 4:9; 9:5. This was also true in classical Greek (LSJ, 1137).

[22] Cf. also μισθὸν ἔχειν or ἀπέχειν (Matt. 5:46; 6:1, 2, 5, 16). Its opposite is "to lose one's reward" (Matt. 10:42; Mark 9:41).

[23] See above pp. 41–42 on this text.

benefits which await the righteous in the future. One other text which speaks of future divine recompense (punishment) according to deeds in terms of "receiving" is 1 Enoch 100:7,[24]

> because you shall receive according to your deeds.
> [ὅτι κομιεῖσθε κατὰ τὰ ἔργα ὑμῶν][25]

Thus, although unusual, it does appear that the righteous "receiving [reward] according to their deeds" could substitute for the more typical "God will recompense them according to deeds." It may also be the case that the increasing use of passive constructions in second temple Judaism ("shall be recompensed/judged") shaded over eventually into "shall receive."[26]

Paul's use of the term "reward/wage" [μισθός] deserves special attention at this juncture, since it testifies to his belief in a *positive* reward to the righteous according to their deeds, and may hint at a belief in *varying* rewards. As suggested earlier, it is all too common in NT scholarship to pass over the common everyday meanings of Greek words in favor of more religious meanings. In this instance, μισθός [wage] will have come to Paul's mind via the metaphor of agricultural workers (verses 5–8), and should not immediately be understood with reference to some sort of heavenly rewards. Nevertheless, the obvious interplay and alternation in the text between this metaphor and the reality in Corinth suggest that Paul may indeed be willing to carry wages into the theological realm.[27] The OT was certainly not averse to speaking of Yahweh's wage for those who serve him.[28] Ruth 2:12, examined above, equates the divine recompense according to deeds with receiving "a full reward [μισθός; שכר] from the Lord." However, while the belief in Israel's reward continued unabated in the second temple period,[29] we have traced a firm resistance to speaking of this positive reward with the terminology of the motif, i.e., as being given "according to

---

[24] See on this text pp. 70–73 above. Cf. also 1 En. 102:8b, "What will they receive?"

[25] This text is of particular interest because Paul will elsewhere use κομιοῦσθαι [receive (pay, wages)] in the motif (2 Cor. 5:10; Col. 3:25; [Eph. 6:8]).

[26] See p. 87 above; also 1 En. 95:5; 100:7 (Heb.); PssSol. 17:8; Obad. 15: Prov. 19:17 (LXX, v.l.).

[27] Cf. "I planted, Apollos watered"; "through whom you came to believe"; and the repeated reference to "God."

[28] Gen. 15:1; 30:18; Num. 18:31; Isa. 40:10; 62:11; Jer. 31:16 (LXX, 38:16). See Fuller, *A Pauline Understanding of Rewards*, 16–107.

[29] Tobit 4:5–11, 14; 4 Ezra 7:83; 8:33, 39; 13:56; 2 Bar. 52:7; 54:16; 59:2; Josephus *Antiquities*, 1.183; 18.309; Philo *Leg.All.* 1.80; *Som.* 2.34, 38. See above, 89, n. 120.

deeds."[30] One explanation, suggested especially by the Qumran literature, lies in the heightened sense of unworthiness among the righteous produced by the situation of exile and oppression, yet without lessening the sense that such rewards, though originating in God's grace, will ultimately be given only to those who deserve them by faithful obedience. By the time represented in the rabbinic literature, however, this hesitation has been overcome, and the rabbis once again speak of the rewards of obedience corresponding to deeds, or in terms of "measure for measure," yet without falling prey to mechanical or mercenary excesses. "The reward is measured according to the labor."[31] Paul's readiness to speak of believers' *reward(s)* according to their deeds may be taken as evidence that this rabbinic tendency was present already in the first century.

But what of the idea that rewards are seen here to vary as appropriate to the varied work of each?[32] I have argued above that Paul's two-fold addition of ἴδιος is testimony to his concern to stress the diversity of tasks and of appropriate rewards. The reward of each is individually appropriate to one's labor [κατὰ τὸν ἴδιον κόπον]. Paul's argument at this stage hinges upon the belief that the meting out of appropriate, individually diverse, wages lies within the prerogative of God alone. The situation in Judaism with respect to *varied rewards* corresponds to what was discovered above regarding rewards according to deeds. The OT Pseudepigrapha and the Qumran literature give no evidence of a belief in differing rewards, in most cases reward being another way of describing salvation, or life's blessings in the age to come. Rabbinic Judaism, on the other hand, spoke of great rewards for great obedience and small rewards for lesser obedience, and of particular rewards being

[30] See 163, n. 70 (with references to earlier chapters).

[31] Aboth 5:23 (Str-B III.333). See A. Melinek, "The Doctrine of Reward and Punishment in Biblical and Early Rabbinic Writings," *Essays Presented to Chief Rabbi Israel Brodie* (ed. H. J. Zimmels; London: Soncino Press,1967), 275–290, esp. 285–287; and M. Brocke, "Tun und Lohn im nachbiblischen Judentum: Ein Diskussionsbeitrag," *BibLeb* 8 (1967), 167–168. Brocke suggests that this renaissance of "rewards according to deeds" is a reaction to Epicurean and Sadducean teachings about divine indifference to human activity (168).

[32] *Favoring graded rewards*: Fuller, *A Pauline Understanding of Rewards*, 221–229; W. Pesch, "Der Sonderlohn für die Verkündiger des Evangeliums," *Festschrift für J. Schmid: Neutestamentliche Aufsätze* (eds. J. Blinzler and O. Kuss; Regensburg: Friedrich Pustet, 1963), 199–206; H.-D. Wendland, *Die Briefe an die Korinther* (4th edn.; NTD 7; Göttingen: Vandenhoeck & Ruprecht, 1946), 23. *Against*: Mattern, *Das Verständnis des Gerichtes*, 178. *No decision possible*: Fee, *First Epistle to the Corinthians*, 143; Schrage, *Der erste Brief*, 293, n. 90; Synofzik, *Die Gerichts- und Vergeltungsaussagen*, 41.

connected with particular commandments (though these were not
made explicit in the Torah in order to avoid encouraging obedience
to some commandments over others).[33] In this respect as well Paul
shows his affinity with tendencies that will flower in rabbinic
Judaism in the use of the motif.[34] Kuck has demonstrated, furthermore, how the thought of variegated post-mortem rewards would
have gained ready acceptance in a Greco-Roman environment.[35]
However, apart from the bare *fact* of differing rewards κατὰ τὸν
ἴδιον κόπον, we learn little here as to their precise nature.

Paul's choice of κόπος [labor] rather than the more usual ἔργον
should likewise occasion no surprise, since it was an appropriate
term in connection with the agricultural metaphor,[36] and was also a
favored term of his to refer to specifically apostolic labors.[37] In
spite of the fact that κόπος, unlike the broader term ἔργον, usually
refers to heavy, laborious work, there is no indication that the
effort or *toil* involved in such work is central to the usage here.[38]
Pesch argues for a distinct apostolic reward on the basis of this text,
an "aureola doctorum" which elsewhere consists of the "corona
discipulorum."[39] However, the return to ἔργον (verses 13–15) and
the expansion beyond strictly apostolic labors (verses 9b–17) argue
against this interpretation.[40]

While it is likely that Paul envisioned this varied recompense as
being granted at the eschatological judgment, this notion remains

[33] Melinek, "Reward and Punishment," 285–287.

[34] Attempts to tease out fundamental differences between Paul and rabbinic
Judaism at this point are not convincing. L. Mattern's interpretation of 1 Cor. 3:8b
relies on her portrayal of rabbinic faith as a synergistic "Leistungsreligion" in which
"die Leistung wird *entlohnt*" [effort receives its wage]. Paul, by contrast, allegedly
speaks of both work and wage in terms of a passive "receiving" (= grace) in which
"der Gehorsam wird *belohnt*" [obedience receives its reward] (*Das Verständnis des
Gerichtes*, 170–173; original emphasis). In German, "entlohnen" carries a stronger
contractual-commercial connotation than "belohnen," the latter being motivated by
thankfulness rather than contractual obligation. Mattern's portrayal both misrepre-
sents rabbinic religion in order to make Paul look superior, and ignores Paul's own
language and metaphor of a pay-day.

[35] *Judgment and Community Conflict*, 143–144; 233–234.

[36] The verb [κοπιάω] is used this way in 2 Tim. 2:6. See further, F. Hauck, *TDNT*
III.827–830.

[37] A. von Harnack, "Κόπος (Κοπιᾶν, Οἱ Κοπιῶντες) im frühchristlichen Sprach-
gebrauch," *ZNW* 27 (1928), 1–10.

[38] Ἔργον replaces κόπος in verses 13–15.

[39] "Sonderlohn," 199–206.

[40] A parallel to Paul's usage is found in Wis. 10:17 – "She [Wisdom] gave to holy
people the reward of their labors" [μισθὸν κόπων αὐτῶν].

entirely in the background in this particular text.[41] Paul's sole concern here is to stress the divine prerogative in determining and distributing varied wages to his servants, and thereby to deny to the Corinthians this right.

1 Corinthians 3:9b–15

This text has played a central role in a number of different Christian debates over issues of soteriology. In certain traditions of popular piety it is the key passage demonstrating that "how I build my own Christian life on Christ" cannot affect ultimate salvation (only the degree of reward). Closely related are Calvinist-Arminian debates over eternal security. Finally, Roman Catholics have in the past found proof of purgatory here.

The change from an agricultural to an architectural metaphor is syntactically abrupt, but such a linking of the two metaphors was fairly common in antiquity and would probably not have occasioned much surprise among the Corinthian hearers.[42] This new subsection is a continuation of Paul's attempt to stop their boasting in human leaders begun in verse 5. However between verses 5–9a and 9b–15 a slight shift in tone and focus is noticeable. Whereas the previous verses were more instructive and only gently admonitory, verses 9b–15 carry a much sharper tone of warning – "let each beware how he/she builds" (verse 10c, my translation).[43] Likewise verses 13–15 mention not only the promise of reward (as in verse 8b) but threaten with loss as well. Further, while the text certainly carries implications for the whole congregation's view of their leaders, Paul is now addressing a warning more specifically to the

---

[41] While an eschatological recompense is explicit at 3:14 and 4:5, it is not really part of Paul's purpose in 3:8b to argue that such recompense will have to *wait* until the final judgment (*pace* D. Kuck, *Judgment and Community Conflict*, 170, 186). Paul's rhetorical goal revolves around the divine prerogative to recompense, and holds true regardless of the timing of this recompense. Rather than postponing judgment, Paul is urging the Corinthian teachers to apply now the right criterion – Christ versus human wisdom – to make certain in the present that they are building upon the foundation properly.

[42] W. Schrage, *Der erste Brief*, 294–295, nn. 102–103. On the metaphorical use of οἰκοδομή/οἰκοδομεῖν, see P. Vielhauer, *Oikodome: Das Bild vom Bau in der christlichen Literatur vom Neuen Testament bis Clemens Alexandrinus* (Karlsruhe-Durlach: Tron, 1939), esp. 74–81; and Mitchell, *Paul*, 99–105.

[43] The NRSV ("Each builder must choose with care how to build on it") loses this sharp tone of Paul's "Let each beware" [ἕκαστος δὲ βλεπέτω] (cf. 1 Cor. 8:9; 10:12; 16:10; Gal. 5:15; Phil. 3:2; Col. 2:8; also Eph. 5:15).

Corinthian leaders and wisdom teachers.[44] The rather detailed judgment imagery of verses 12–15 lends weight to Paul's warning, stressing that "how" one builds the church carries with it eschatological reward or loss. Although the architectural metaphor is, to a certain extent, carried forward in verses 16–17, the introduction of "temple" terminology, as well as the heightened sharpness of the warning ("God will destroy that person"), signal some degree of disjunction with what follows (see below).

Our attention will focus on verses 12–15 where Paul expands upon his warning (verse 10c) by describing in terms of eschatological judgment the consequences for those who are building upon his foundation in Corinth.

> (12) Now if anyone builds on the foundation with gold, silver, precious stones, wood, hay, straw – (13) the work of each builder will become visible, for the Day will disclose it, because it will be revealed with fire, and the fire will test what sort of work each has done. (14) If what has been built on the foundation survives, the builder will receive a reward. (15) If the work is burned up, the builder will suffer loss; the builder will be saved, but only as through fire.

Six different building materials are listed whose only significance as the metaphor progresses will be their resistance to fire (verses 14–15).[45] "Take care how one builds" now means "Take care that one is building with imperishable materials," i.e., that one's work will survive at the judgment.

What then is the criterion by which their work of edifying the church will be deemed perishable or imperishable? The answer, according to verse 11, is consistency with the sole possible foundation of the church, Jesus Christ. Paul's message of Christ crucified operates as a yardstick for all further builders (and by implication

---

[44] Whereas verses 9 and 16 explicitly address the whole congregation, verses 9b–15 clearly address those in the congregation (ἄλλος, ἕκαστος [3x], τίς [3x]) engaged in "building upon" Paul's foundation of Christ crucified. See F. L. Godet, *Commentary on St. Paul's First Epistle to the Corinthians* (trans. A. Cusin; Edinburgh: T. & T. Clarke, 1886 [reprinted: Grand Rapids: Kregel, 1977]), 180.

[45] Although a "descending scale of values" is, perhaps, evident in Paul's list, he makes nothing of the element of costliness in the unfolding metaphor, referring only to their susceptibility to being "burned up." See H. W. Hollander, "The Testing by Fire of the Builders' Works: 1 Corinthians 3.10–15," *NTS* 40 (1994), 93–95, esp. nn. 19–20; otherwise Fascher, *Der erste Brief*, 135.

for the congregation's evaluation of its leaders). This all harks back to Paul's earlier discussion pitting God's wisdom in the message of Christ crucified over against all forms of human wisdom. That such was in his mind is confirmed by his reference to himself as a "wise master builder" [σοφὸς ἀρχιτέκτων], that is, as the one who had begun the work in accordance with the wisdom [σοφία] of God.[46]

In verse 13, through a series of phrases, Paul stresses that each builder's choice of materials will be revealed at the eschatological judgment day [ἡ ἡμέρα]. Thus each builder's work will become known,[47] being tested by the fire that accompanies the day of judgment in order to determine "what sort of work" [τὸ ἔργον ὁποῖόν] one has done.[48] As consistently throughout the metaphor this "work" [ἔργον, sg.] refers to both the *process* of building (i.e., their choice of perishable or imperishable building materials)[49] and the *product* resulting from this activity.[50] This strongly revelatory function of the judgment day is brought out by the verbs "disclose" [δηλώσει] and "reveal" [ἀποκαλύπτεται].[51] Both judgment *qua* disclosure and the unitary understanding of one's work (sg.) are central features of judgment in second temple Judaism,[52] and point

---

[46] Although σοφός may be translated "skilled" (NRSV) or "expert" (NIV), this fails to alert the English reader to the renewed presence of the wisdom theme here (C. K. Barrett, *The First Epistle to the Corinthians* [HNTC; New York: Harper & Row, 1968] 86). On this relation of 3:5–17 to the earlier wisdom discussion in chapters 1–2, see J. A. Davis, *Wisdom and Spirit: an investigation of 1 Corinthians 1:18–3:20 against the background of Jewish sapiential traditions in the Greco-roman period* (Lanham/New York/London: University Press of America, 1984), 131–136.

[47] Φανερὸν γενήσεται = become visible, open, manifest.

[48] Generally "testing" [δοκιμάζειν] can refer to either "purifying" or "testing" (i.e., determination of quality); cf. 1 Pet. 1:7; Prov. 17:3; Wis. 3:6. Here the substances are not "purified" or "refined" but are judged as to their imperishability. On "fire" as an element in eschatological judgment, see F. Lang, *TDNT*, VI.928–952.

[49] Πῶς ἐποικοδομεῖ (verse 10b).

[50] Τὸ ἔργον ὃ ἐποικοδόμησεν (verse 14). A few commentators favor viewing ἔργον as the persons converted or influenced by the Corinthian teachers, but it is difficult to imagine that Paul wished to say such teachers could lead others into destruction and themselves be saved.

[51] The same note of revealing and disclosure (of secrets) at the judgment day can be found in Rom. 2:16. See also 2 Cor. 5:10 [φανερωθῆναι]. Although "work" might conceivably be the subject of the compact ὅτι ἐν πυρὶ ἀποκαλύπτεται, "the day" lies closer at hand, which also avoids any redundancy with verse 13d (see Barrett, *First Epistle to the Corinthians*, 88; for the opposite view, H. W. Hollander, "Testing by Fire," 97, n. 31). Thus "fire" is both the accompanying phenomenon and the instrument of judgment.

[52] See 4 Ezra 7:35; 1 En. 45:3; 100:10; 2 En. 44:5; 2 Bar. 83:2–3; also 2 Clem. 16:3; Hermas Sim. 4:3.

up once again that Paul is not thinking of a weighing of individual deeds.[53]

Verses 14–15 detail the consequences for those who built well or poorly. At this fiery judgment their work will either remain (μενεῖ = survive the fire)[54] or will be burned up. Those who have taught and ministered in a manner compatible with the Pauline kerygma, and thus whose "gold, silver, and precious stones" survive the test by fire, "will receive a reward" [μισθὸν λήμψεται]. This echoes what was already said at 3:8 about recompense for faithful service, but here without the stress on differentiation. The nature of this promised eschatological wage is left unspecified (though on its relation to "salvation," see below). Attempts have been made to fill out the meaning of this reward by importing ideas found elsewhere in Paul. These include *praise, union with converts at the parousia, superior privileges,* and *the fact that the work abides.*[55] However, beyond establishing the eschatological nature of the reward in this text, any attempt to specify what the apostle leaves vague will have to remain uncertain. In line with the character of a *warning*, it is not the promise, much less the nature, of the reward, but the consequences of failure that are uppermost in Paul's interest here.

The consequence for those whose work is consumed (verse 15), who taught and ministered on a basis of human wisdom rather than Christ, is termed ζημιωθήσεται ["will suffer loss," NRSV]. This word carries the sense of "suffering damage, injury or loss" and has led to two differing translations:

(a) "the builder will suffer damage," i.e., punishment,[56]
(b) "the builder will suffer loss," i.e., of reward.[57]

---

[53] Heiligenthal, *Werke als Zeichen*, 212. C. W. Fishburne's thesis of literary dependence on T.Abr. 13 has found few proponents in spite of the striking similarities of the two texts ("1 Cor. iii.10–15 and the Testament of Abraham," *NTS* 17 [1970], 109–115; critical: Kuck, *Judgment and Community Conflict*, 89–92, 184; Hollander, "Testing by Fire," 90–102).

[54] Herm. Vis. 4.3.4; Did. 16:5.

[55] For this last option, cf. Travis, *Christ and the Judgment*, 115. Such is, however, unlikely since μισθὸν λήμψεται is seen as the *consequence* not the equivalent of τὸ ἔργον μενεῖ. Travis' interpretation is dominated throughout by the avoidance of anything smacking of retribution.

[56] "Surely what is meant is that he will be saved after some punishment [ζημιωθήσεται = ὡς διὰ πυρός]: similarly 5,5; 11,32" (Lietzmann, *Die Briefe*, 93). This rendering was also favored, naturally, by proponents of the doctrine of purgatory. (See the critique of this view by J. Gnilka, *Ist 1 Kor.3.10–15 ein Schriftzeugnis für das Fegfeuer? Eine exegetisch-historische Untersuchung* [Düsseldorf: Triltsch, 1955].)

[57] So, for instance, Gundry-Volf, *Paul and Perseverance*, 242, 261; and Schrage, *Der erste Brief*, 303.

Option (a) assumes some sort of post-mortem chastisement for believers, an idea not found elsewhere in Paul.[58] The other NT occurrences of ζημιόω favor (b) "suffer loss."[59] Further, the antithetical parallelism with "receive reward" (verse 14) expects the loss of reward as its counterpart in verse 15.

The final phrase of verse 15 has long played a critical role in the attempt to understand Paul's perspective on the judgment of believers – αὐτὸς δὲ σωθήσεται, οὕτως δὲ ὡς διὰ πυρός. For many interpreters this is an afterthought, a correction added by the apostle to guard against equating, or in any way connecting, one's reward with one's salvation. In this case, the text "stresses that the salvation of the Christian preacher is not affected in spite of the destructive judgment upon his labor. Thus, the concluding prover-bial utterance is a qualification or correction of the preceding idea of judgment which brought only reward or punishment (i.e., loss) into its purview."[60] This would testify to a sense of theological tension in Paul. These same commentators, however, consistently fail to see that immediately following this Paul explicitly connects the Corinthian teachers' activity with their salvation (see below on verses 16–17).[61] If Paul had meant to say "take care how you build, for it will affect your eschatological reward, though, of course, not your eternal salvation," he would hardly have followed it with verse 16 and its threat of eternal destruction.

I would suggest that verse 15b is not a correction or afterthought,

---

[58] Reference is sometimes made to 1 Cor. 5:5 and 11:32, but see below on these texts.

[59] Phil. 3:8; 2 Cor. 7:9(?); Matt. 16:26; Mark 8:36; Luke 9:25. The sense of this text is well illustrated by 2 John 8 – "Be on your guard [βλέπετε ἑαυτούς], so that you do not lose [ἀπολέσητε] what we have worked for, but may receive a full reward [μισθὸν πλήρη ἀπολάβητε]" (see Kuck, *Judgment and Community Conflict*, 182–183). J. Shanor suggests "to be fined" based on ancient construction contracts ("Paul as master builder: construction terms in First Corinthians," *NTS* 34 [1988], 462, 468–470). While this would provide a nice contrast with "receive wage" (verse 14), "suffer loss (of the wage)" makes better sense within the whole argument. Translating "to be fined" would seem to necessitate viewing "as through fire" as some form of punishment, and leads Shanor to interpret verses 16–17 not as a threat of destruction but of God levying "damage" in some way against the careless builder (see below on φθείρειν).

[60] Synofzik, *Die Gerichts- und Vergeltungsaussagen*, 66.

[61] L. Mattern ends her lengthy treatment of 1 Cor. 3:5ff. with verse 15 (*Das Verständnis des Gerichtes*, 168–179). Verses 16–17 are treated only superficially in a footnote (169, n. 528), where she acknowledges that (i) either φθείρειν [destroy] refers to something entirely distinct from the ἐποικοδομεῖν [build (poorly)] of verses 10–15, or else (ii) these verses constitute a direct contradiction to her interpretation of the preceding section.

not some form of reassurance to the erring Corinthian leaders that they will be saved in spite of their erroneous teaching, but instead intensifies the warning of verse 15a.[62] Thus the emphasis lies on the final "as through fire" which is in some measure a modification of the Corinthians' expectations that "the builder will be saved." "As through fire" was an idiomatic way of saying "just barely," "by the skin of one's teeth."[63] Paul is not reassuring the one who built poorly (i.e., though you lose your reward you will still be saved) but warning – though you may attain salvation, it will be by the skin of your teeth as it were.[64] The point here is to stress the risk being entertained by those who may be building in a manner incompatible with the teaching of Christ. That risk will be amplified in verses 16–17 where Paul warns that improper building can, in fact, edge over into actual destruction of the church, resulting in the eternal destruction of the builder. To teach human wisdom instead of Christ carries with it the gravest of risks; at best the loss of any recompense for all one's labor, at worst the loss of eschatological life itself. The dividing line between poor building and destruction is not clearly marked out, making Paul's initial warning to "beware how you are building" all the more potent.[65]

---

[62] "Paul did not write this passage to reassure those who feared their salvation was in jeopardy, but he wrote to unnerve those who believed their salvation was assured" (Roetzel, *Judgement in the Community*, 169).

[63] Favored by most commentators, this sense can be found in the OT (Amos 4:11; Zech. 3:2; *et al.*) and in Greek antiquity (references in Conzelmann, *1 Corinthians*, 77, n. 85). J. T. Townsend argues that this phrase reflects instead a Shammaite doctrine that those who were neither wholly good nor wholly bad would be saved, but only after passing through the fires of Gehinnom ("1 Corinthians 3:15 and the school of Shammai," *HTR* 61 [1968], 500–504). However apart from a general similarity, the parallels are hardly convincing (see the differences Townsend himself notes, 501).

[64] See J. Moffatt's translation:
   if a man's work is burnt up,
   he will be a loser –
   and though he will be saved himself,
   he will be snatched from the very flames.

(*First Epistle*, 39, emphasis added)

[65] A similar phenomenon, suggested in a letter by Prof. A. Lincoln, may be observed in Rom. 14:13–23, where "to put a stumbling block or hindrance in the way of another" (verse 13; = to injure, verse 15) may "cause the ruin of one for whom Christ died" (verse 15). Paul does not say that they have already caused the ruin of others, but that their current injurious behavior can easily (and perhaps imperceptibly) shade into the more lethal. One might perhaps say that it is characteristic of the NT writers in general, when speaking of spiritually lethal behavior, to assert its reality without quantifying the precise dividing line between occasional sins and a life in subjection to sin. See also, for example, Heb. 6:1–12

Nevertheless, in verses 9b–15 "reward" is clearly distinct from "salvation." Paul does seem to assume here that it was possible to enjoy salvation plus reward (verse 14) or salvation stripped of reward (verse 15). "It is only when graded positions in the Kingdom are accepted as Paul's meaning that justice is done to the basic idea of judgment and to Paul's words about receiving a reward for good done."[66] Mattern denies this conclusion, but only by isolating Paul completely from his Pharisaic background and by contending that salvation and reward/punishment must always be viewed as strictly independent of one another (two-judgment theory). In her view this rewarding judgment is nothing more than Paul's attempt to "interpret the relationship between master and servant," a sort of metaphor meaning "God takes the servant and his service seriously."[67] However, such a demythologizing of Paul fails to do justice to the rising strength of a doctrine of varied rewards which flowers later in rabbinic Judaism and which has exercised clear influence on early Christian thought and terminology.[68]

Most exegetes of a Reformed or Lutheran persuasion find in this passage a first line of defense against allowing the works of believers any *salvific* significance.

> Obviously the idea has to be understood in the wider context of the doctrine of justification. The loss of faith means the loss of salvation. On the other hand, unsatisfactory works performed by the Christian as a Christian do not cause his damnation. This is the reverse side of the fact that works do not bring about salvation. But we remain responsible for our works before God ...; for the life of believers is service.[69]

Besides the fact that this text is not about Christians' works in general, but about the specific work of teaching/leading, my

where this situation is described metaphorically as being "on the verge of being cursed" [κατάρας ἐγγύς] (verse 8).

[66] Filson, *St. Paul's Conception of Recompense*, 115 (based on 1 Cor. 3:8–15; 2 Cor. 5:10; Eph. 6:8 and 2 Cor. 4:17).

[67] *Das Verständnis des Gerichtes*, 177–178.

[68] See above on 3:8b. The synoptics give clear evidence in this direction; see O. Michel, "Der Lohngedanke in der Verkündigung Jesu," *ZST* 9 (1932), 47–54. Cf. also Eph. 6:8; Matt. 5:12, 19; 10:41–42; Heb. 10:35.

[69] Conzelmann, *1 Corinthians*, 77. Interestingly, John Calvin was not nearly so squeamish regarding the conditional relationship between salvation and obedience in this passage (*The First Epistle of Paul the Apostle to the Corinthians* [trans. J. W. Fraser; Calvin's Commentaries 9; Grand Rapids, MI: Eerdmans, 1960], 77–78).

interpretation turns this interpretation on its head. Rather than assurance that their poor work will not affect their salvation, one finds in fact a warning that they are putting that very salvation at risk. Thus, having admonished the Corinthians against judging one leader at the expense of another in verses 5–9, Paul switches metaphors and tone in verses 10–15 and warns the leaders themselves (and implicitly the congregation) that the preceding does not render the "how" of their effort superfluous. The fact is, only those who build in line with the message of Christ rather than human wisdom will receive the reward mentioned in verse 8. Those who disregard this warning risk finding all their labor eternally worthless; and, in fact, could be endangering their salvation. In order to drive home this ultimate danger, Paul now turns in verses 16–17 to a new metaphor, that of the temple.

1 Corinthians 3:16–17

As noted above, the relation of these verses to the preceding is crucial to a proper understanding of judgment in Paul.[70] The introduction ("Do you not know?"), the shift in metaphor (from architecture in general to "temple" specifically) and the heightened form of warning (*lex talionis*) suggest that verses 16–17 constitute to some degree a new thought. This has led a large body of interpreters to stress a logical disjunction between verses 15 and 16.[71] While generally acknowledging a certain logical progression through the three metaphors (promise of reward to leaders – warning of loss of reward to poor leaders – threat of destruction to destroyers of the church), such interpreters stress the discontinuity rather than the continuity with the foregoing. Its "character" is entirely different (Conzelmann), the action of "destroying" is something quite different from the careless building in verses 10–15 (Mattern, Hollander), or the "destroyers" of verse 17 are actually "enemies of the gospel" in distinction from the poor but still saved builders (Synofzik).[72] Stressing the disjunction leads, then, to a crucial theological observation. The judgment on believing leaders

---

[70] Failure to consider the implications of 1 Cor. 3:16–17 weakens the work of L. Mattern (*Das Verständnis des Gerichtes*) and J. M. Gundry-Volf (*Paul and Perseverance*).

[71] E.g., Barrett, *First Epistle to the Corinthians*, 90–91.

[72] However as to "careless" versus "destructive" leaders, Barrett admits, "Probably Paul himself found it hard, in the situations with which he had in practice to deal, to distinguish between the two possibilities" (ibid., 91).

resulting in (loss of) reward (verses 10–15) has little to do with a judgment as to their salvation (verses 16–17).[73] The intent here is usually to safeguard the doctrine of justification by faith lest works somehow sneak in to play a determinative role. Without this disjunction, not only reward but equally salvation itself seems to become dependent on "how one builds."

The a priori assumption behind this approach (i.e., unsatisfactory works cannot be a cause or condition of a Christian's salvation/damnation) will be examined later. Here I wish to concentrate on the exegetical evidence for a relationship of *continuity* rather than discontinuity flowing from verse 15 to verses 16–17.

The abrupt οὐκ οἴδατε which opens verse 16 is a rhetorical device used heavily in this letter, perhaps meant ironically in the light of the Corinthians' boast in knowledge.[74] Rather than signalling a logical disjunction, it always introduces a further argument on a subject already opened in the material immediately preceding its appearance. In some of these cases it introduces a strong warning which serves to intensify the risk involved in the wrong behavior Paul wishes to restrain. Thus in speaking against intra-community lawsuits we read,

> Why not rather be wronged? Why not rather be defrauded? But you yourselves wrong and defraud – and believers at that. *Do you not know* that wrongdoers will not inherit the kingdom of God?   (1 Cor. 6:7–9)

And against sexual immorality,

> Should I therefore take the members of Christ and make them members of a prostitute? Never! *Do you not know* that whoever is united to a prostitute becomes one body with her?   (1 Cor. 6:15–16)

The use of οὐκ οἴδατε in 3:16 follows this same pattern. Following the warning (not reassurance! see above) of verses 10–15, verses 16–17 serve to intensify the risk involved in building upon human wisdom rather than Christ.

---

[73] See above, 219–220.

[74] 3:16; 5:6; 6:2, 3, 9, 15, 16, 19; 9:13, 24. Cf. also Rom. 6:16 (the only other occurrence in Paul outside 1 Cor.), John 19:10, Jas. 3:3. On "do you not know" as irony, see Fee, *First Epistle to the Corinthians*, 146, n. 3. Others suggest it is simply a reminder of previous teaching (B. Gärtner, *The Temple and the Community in Qumran and the New Testament* [SNTSMS 1; Cambridge: Cambridge University Press, 1965], 57).

As throughout 3:5–17, these verses are directed both at the whole congregation and to its teachers and leaders.[75] Those who "destroy God's temple" are not a different group (e.g., enemies of the gospel; nonbelievers) from those in view in verses 14–15. Rather this new description highlights the risk entertained by any teacher who builds with human wisdom. Harming the church shades imperceptibly into destroying the church, magnifying the risk for any who dare build with "wood, hay and stubble." These same hearers are in view in Paul's continued admonition in verses 18–20 addressed to those in the church who consider themselves to be "wise in this age."

In verse 16 Paul reminds the congregation of who they are, and hence of the seriousness of building poorly or even destroying the church. They are collectively[76] God's sanctuary, the dwelling place of God's Spirit, making them holy. This sacrosanct character of the divine sanctuary is the reason [γάρ] that destruction of the same is such a heinous act and will be repaid in kind by destruction at the hands of God himself.

In a striking chiastic formulation of the OT *lex talionis* Paul threatens future divine destruction upon any potential destroyer of the congregation:

A   εἴ τις
B   τὸν ναὸν τοῦ θεοῦ
C   φθείρει
C'   φθερεῖ[77]
B'   τοῦτον
A'   ὁ θεός

The exact meaning of φθείρειν in this particular context is disputed. J. Shanor has argued, for instance, for the meaning "damage" rather than "destroy," based on a technical usage in Greco-Roman construction contracts.[78] Others have pointed out

---

[75] On this dual audience in 1 Cor. 1–4, see Kuck, *Judgment and Community Conflict*, 187. The second person plural verbs and pronouns in verses 9 and 16 clearly have the whole community in view, while the indefinite singular pronouns used in the warnings (τίς, ἕκαστος; verses 8b, 10b, 12, 13, 14–15, 17) target the teachers and leaders.

[76] See further on this community focus, Roetzel, *Judgement in the Community*, 163–170.

[77] A few, mostly Western, MSS read the present [φθείρει] under the influence of the preceding verb form.

[78] "Paul as master builder," 470–471.

the sense of "injure" or "corrupt" elsewhere, thus reducing Paul's threat to something less than eschatological destruction.[79] The verb, however, was most commonly used to indicate the ruin or destruction of things, structures, animals or persons.[80] When used of the latter it could even mean "to kill," or could be used as a curse – φθείρεσθε [May you perish! Ruin take you!].[81] In 1 Corinthians 3:16–17 the threat is related directly to the church's nature as the divine temple in which God's Spirit dwells, thus making it sacrosanct.[82] The violation of holy objects and places was widely held to be a capital offense in ancient society, with the sentence often executed by the deity directly.[83] The presence of the *lex talionis* ("ruin for ruin") likewise points to divine judgment. Thus it matters little whether we take the protasis to refer to profanation, damage, the actual demolition of a building, or as a known Greek rhetorical *topos* for the destruction of group unity through factionalism. Regardless of the exact manner, the ruining of God's holy temple will inevitably bring ruin at God's own hand in return, a sentiment not unlike the inscription found in Herod's temple prohibiting Gentiles in the forecourt: "Whoever is caught [in the sacred precincts] is alone responsible for the death[-penalty] which follows."[84]

Thus Paul is continuing the warning of verse 15. Those who lead and minister in the congregation on the basis of human wisdom rather than Christ crucified imperil their own salvation. The sanctity of the congregation in Corinth spells ruin for anyone who would dare to ruin the church by replacing the cross with human wisdom and banishing the Spirit through boasting and division. Paul's switch to the future tense in the apodosis ("God *will destroy* that person") suggests that *eschatological* destruction is in view. As an intensification of the warning about imperiling one's *salvation*

[79] See 2 Cor. 7:2; Rev. 19:2.
[80] Rev. 8:9 (destruction of ships); Jude 10 (destruction of individuals; cf. 2 Pet. 2:12b[?]); and Luke 12:33 (destruction of clothes by moths).
[81] LSJ, art. φθείρω, 1928 (II.1). See also G. Harder, *TDNT* IX.93–106.
[82] See Gärtner, *The Temple and the Community*, 56–60.
[83] Cf. 1 Sam. 6:19–20; 2 Sam. 6:6–7 (= 1 Chr 13:9–10); Num. 4:15, 19–20; Josh. 7:15; Acts 21:28 (also 19:37). On this ancient concept of "holiness," see B. S. Rosner, "Temple and Holiness in 1 Corinthians 5," *TynBul* 42/1 (1991), 137–145.
[84] Cited in E. Käsemann, "Sätze Heiligen Rechtes im Neuen Testament," *NTS* 1 (1954/55), 248–260. Reprinted in *Exegetische Versuche und Besinnungen* (2 vols.; Göttingen: Vandenhoeck & Ruprecht, 1964), II.69–82; ET: *New Testament Questions of Today* (Philadelphia: Fortress Press, 1969), 66–81; the sentence quoted is on p. 67 of the English edition.

(verse 15), this is nothing less than the final destruction of those excluded from such salvation.[85]

Excursus: "sentences of holy law"

If accepted, E. Käsemann's thesis regarding *Sätze heiligen Rechtes* (sentences of holy law) would further strengthen the argument for a reference to eschatological judgment in this text. His article "Sätze Heiligen Rechtes im Neuen Testament" first appeared in 1955 as an attempt to get at the relation of Spirit (*Geist*) and Law (*Recht*) in earliest Christianity.[86] Three formal elements identified such a "sentence": (a) at root was the *lex talionis* of the OT ("an eye for an eye"), (b) now given chiastic form (εἴ τις φθείρει ... φθερεῖ ὁ θεός), and (c) clothed as a casuistical legal saying (εἴ τις, ἐάν τις, ὅς δ᾽ ἄν = rabbinic "should someone ..., then ..."). 1 Corinthians 3:17 constituted his clearest example of such a "sentence," with modified forms found in 1 Corinthians 14:38; 16:22; Galatians 1:6; 1 Corinthians 5:3–5; 2 Corinthians 9:6 and Romans 2:12. Käsemann posited the origin of such Christian "sentences" in Palestinian churches led by prophets who, imitating OT prophets, led the people of God by proclaiming God's eschatological judgments upon sinning members (74–80). For Käsemann the adoption and modification of these "sentences" for purposes of later Christian paraenesis shows that grace does not eliminate the need for divine *Recht*. Christ's purpose, in fact, is to establish God's *Recht* on earth, finding its correlate in Christian obedience. Far from excluding a judgment according to works, such an understanding of "law," "grace" and "spirit" grounds and enables this judgment for Christians (75).

Subsequent analysis, however, has called this thesis into question. Klaus Berger criticized Käsemann's reliance on Bultmann's form-criticism, which did not properly distinguish form, content and *Sitz*. Berger argued instead for a stricter definition of "form" (grammatically and syntactically defined sentence structures must form the start of all form analysis), and concluded, such sentences

---

[85] So most commentators. See also J. A. Draper, "The Tip of an Iceberg: The Temple of the Holy Spirit," *Journal of Theology for Southern Africa* 59 (1987), 57–65. Rev. 11:18 employs a similar chiastic judgment threat to announce divine eschatological destruction upon those who destroy the earth (using the compound form διαφθείρειν).

[86] See note 84 above.

of holy law cannot be demonstrated in the NT on a form-critical basis.[87] Berger saw in them instead a development of Israel's wisdom tradition. David Aune, while not denying the possibility of such *Sätze*, likewise felt "such pronouncements are found in such a wide variety of contexts (sapiential exhortation, eschatological parenesis, prophetic proclamation) that they cannot be tied exclusively to the setting of prophetic speech."[88] These arguments should cause us to hesitate in using Käsemann's "sentence" thesis as further evidence of an eschatological judgment in 1 Corinthians 3:17.

So understood 1 Cor 3:16–17 constitutes one of Paul's most straightforward statements that one's "work" (here specifically the "work" of edifying [οἰκοδομεῖν] the church) is directly related not only to one's level of reward (as distinct from salvation), but also to "being saved" [σωθήσεται]. Those who build so poorly that the church herself is destroyed are threatened themselves with sure and eternal destruction at God's judgment. Attempts to circumvent this exegetical conclusion by defining those in view as nonbelievers or enemies of the gospel are implausible. It is likewise futile to assert that the judgment here is actually pronounced on the basis of whether one had "faith" or not, and not directly on the basis of "work." As certainly as the wage in verses 14–15 is granted or withheld on the basis of one's work of building, equally so is the threatened destruction meted out because one has destroyed the church. This is not to deny that, as always in Paul, there is a most intimate and indissoluble connection between faith and works, but in this context Paul seems to have no qualms about warning even members of the congregation of a potential eternal judgment according to what they have done. Whether this implies that such persons have lost, or perhaps never had, true faith is a larger question of Pauline theology, a question over which Paul shows little concern at this point.[89]

Does this interpretation, then, make salvation dependent on works rather than on grace? As a reminder, this text is not addressing the issue of whether Christians in general can be saved

---

[87] "Zu den sogenannten Sätzen Heiligen Rechtes," *NTS* 17 (1970), 10–40.

[88] *Prophecy in Early Christianity and the Ancient Mediterranean World* (Grand Rapids: Eerdmans, 1983), 240; cf. 166–167, 237–240.

[89] See Fee, *First Epistle to the Corinthians*, 148–149, n. 19.

in spite of sinning (as much popular application asserts). Nor are the problems of immorality which crop up later already in view. Yet in spite of the text's limitation to the "work" of teachers and leaders in the congregation, it confirms what the chapter on Romans discovered. To summarize, the future enjoyment of that salvation, of which even now the believer partakes by faith (1 Cor. 1:2–9; 1:18–2:5), will indeed be conditioned upon one's labor. This work is not, however, a competing criterion alongside grace, but is itself wholly a product of grace (1:2, 4–8, 30–31), being the outworking of the divine righteousness which is the believer's from the beginning by faith alone. Nor am I saying that one "enters" by grace through faith but "stays in" by obedience, or that the verdict of righteousness issued upon entry by faith into the people of God cannot be considered assured until the final judgment when it is certified by works. The righteousness upon which salvation depends is by grace through faith from start to finish, and receives its *necessary confirmation* in the outworking of obedience to be judged at the end. Such a condition adds no uncertainty within the parameters of Paul's normal expectation, that is, for believers who are walking in obedience to the Spirit by faith. For the persistently unfaithful, however, the coming judgment according to works will reveal that they are no partakers of the righteousness of faith, that they are not of the Spirit or of Christ. Thus understood salvation is, in one well-defined sense, dependent upon works; but not in a way inconsistent with Paul's teaching on justification by grace through faith. The above sketch demonstrates Paul's thought to be in considerable continuity with that found in most quarters of second temple Judaism.

1 Corinthians 4:1–5

Chapter 4 should be read as a continuation of Paul's argument with the boastful and divisive Corinthians regarding how they are to view their leaders.[90] It constitutes, however, more of a personal defense than has been evident before.[91] The initial section of this apology

---

[90] Note especially how "servants" [ὑπηρέτας] picks up the servant imagery from 3:5–9 (using the equivalent διάκονοι), and the judgment and reward themes from 3:5–17 are echoed in 4:5.

[91] This is seen in the personal apology of 4:3–4, the appeal to Paul's unique "fatherhood" in the gospel (4:14–17), and the final warning of his personal coming to them (4:18–21). The apologetic function of this section is acknowledged by a

(verses 1–5) revolves around the issue of properly evaluating or judging apostolic leaders.[92] Such judgment can be based upon only one criterion, being found faithful to the task entrusted them as stewards of the mysteries of God (= the gospel of Christ crucified, verses 1–2). Thus the Corinthian standards of human wisdom and rhetoric are abolished. In fact, true judgment is left not even in the hands of individuals in regard to themselves (verses 3–4), but with the Lord alone, who at the parousia will bring even that to light which is hidden in the heart from human view (verse 5). Thus the central point of the section is summed up in verse 5a: "Therefore do not pronounce judgment before the time, before the Lord comes."

For my purposes attention may focus primarily on verse 5 with its reference to divine judgment issuing in *praise* [ὁ ἔπαινος]. It is true that Paul's purpose in this section is not, strictly speaking, to give a depiction of eschatological judgment, but rather to deflect human judgment by appeal to divine judgment. His judgment statements are here *Argumentationsmittel* (Synofzik). Nevertheless it may be properly assumed that Paul's motivational paraenesis employs material and beliefs mutually acceptable to both the apostle and his audience. In spite of their instrumental nature, these judgment statements may be taken as representing the apostle's own convictions regarding such eschatological matters.

That an *eschatological* judgment scene is in view may be substantiated by two observations. First, Paul ties this judgment explicitly to Christ's parousia. The Corinthians are admonished not to judge "ahead of time, prematurely" [πρὸ καιροῦ].[93] Although not necessarily a technical term for Paul, καιρός can be used by him eschatologically,[94] as it is here, since the time before which judgment should not take place is specified as the time of the Lord's coming. This language of Christ's coming [ἕως ἂν ἔλθῃ ὁ κύριος] is not Paul's typical way of referring to the parousia, but one which he can adopt as needed from other traditions in the early church.[95]

majority of commentators (e.g., Schrage, *Der erste Brief*, 318–319; otherwise Mitchell, *Paul*, 54–55).

[92] Note the preponderance of evaluative-judicial terminology: λογίζεσθαι (verse 1), ἀνακρίνειν (verses 3ab, 4b), κρίνειν (verse 5), δεδικαίωμαι (verse 4, see below).

[93] See also Matt. 8:29: πρὸ καιροῦ = the time appointed for torment. Further Fee, *First Epistle to the Corinthians*, 163, nn. 30–31.

[94] Cf. 1 Cor. 7:29; Gal. 6:9; 2 Thess. 2:6.

[95] This phraseology occurs three other times, all in statements stemming from previous tradition: 1 Cor. 11:26 (the Lord's supper); 16:22 (Aramaic); 2 Thess. 1:10 (OT citation).

The picture of a master coming to evaluate the servant's faithfulness flows nicely from the imagery taken up in verses 1–2, but has now been applied by Paul eschatologically.

This eschatological referent is further confirmed by Paul's apparent utilization of a preexisting judgment tradition about this coming Lord "who will bring to light the things now hidden in darkness and will disclose the purposes of the heart."[96] It was axiomatic in Jewish and early Christian literature that God was able to see human thoughts and plans, even prior to their observable expression in words or acts.[97] Likewise "Greco-Roman tradition used the idea of divine omniscience to sanction moral recompense in the present time."[98] The combination of eschatological judgment as *disclosure* with the motif of divine omniscience was already known in second temple Judaism,[99] and is well attested in the NT.[100] In fact, judgment as the *revelation* or *disclosure* of one's (un)righteous character and status, rather than as obtaining or earning such, has been seen to be central to both Paul and second temple Judaism.[101] Thus Paul's phrase is best taken as indicating a universal judgment at Christ's parousia at which the divine omniscience discloses even the inner thoughts and intentions of the individual, and upon which basis each is judged, i.e., their character as righteous or unrighteous is disclosed.

Let us turn now to the conceptual details of this eschatological judgment according to 1 Corinthians 4:5, and especially to any relevance for the issue of judgment according to works in relation

[96] Paul's use of a preexisting tradition is indicated by the introductory ὅς καὶ, *parallelismus membrorum*, and numerous expressions rarely found in Paul – φωτίζειν, τὰ κρυπτὰ τοῦ σκότους, τὰς βουλὰς (Synofzik, *Die Gerichts- und Vergeltungsaussagen*, 71–72).

[97] See for instance God's knowing and judging "the heart" (1 Kgs. 8:39; 2 Chr. 6:30; 1 Chr. 29:17; Prov. 17:3; Jer. 11:20; 17:10; 1QH XVIII,24; also Luke 16:15; Rev. 2:23) as well as what is "hidden" (Eccles. 12:14).

[98] Kuck, *Judgment and Community Conflict*, 206; see further 38–149 on Jewish and Greco-Roman conceptions.

[99] Against D. W. Kuck who claims there are no close parallels in either the OT or pre-Pauline Jewish literature, and suggests that Paul was the first writer in the Jewish-Christian tradition to combine them (ibid., 205–206). Cf. Prov. 24:12; Eccles. 12:14; Jer. 16:16–18; Sir. 11:24–27; 15:19b (with 16:12–14); 17:15, 19–20, 24–27; 1 En. 97:6–7; 98:6–8; 4 Ezra 14:35; T.Abr. 13:9; 2 Bar. 83:1–3. See also Heiligenthal, *Werke als Zeichen*, 156–157, 234–264.

[100] Heb. 4:12–13; Rev. 2:23; Matt. 6:4, 6, 18; Luke 8:17; 12:2–3. For the same in post-apostolic writings, see Heiligenthal, *Werke als Zeichen*, 194, n. 124.

[101] In Paul, Rom. 2:16; 8:19 (= "the revealing of the children of God"); 1 Cor. 3:13; 4:5; 2 Cor. 5:10; 2 Thess. 2:3, 6, 8. In Judaism, see the analysis in the earlier chapters of the texts mentioned in n. 99 above, and pp. 93–94.

to Christian believers. Paul has been at pains in verses 1–4 to thwart all *human* investigation of himself and other ministers.[102] This he does now in verse 5 by portraying final judgment as an examination of service to disclose faithfulness, resulting in praise.

The criterion of this judgment was introduced in verse 2 (ἵνα πιστός τις εὑρεθῇ). This was "a truism in Greco-Roman society – one looks for a steward who will prove to be faithful in carrying out his assigned duties."[103] For Paul this was preeminently the faithful carrying out of his commission to take to the Gentiles this gospel-mystery entrusted to him. Such judgment is not based upon the criterion of faith [πίστις] *qua* belief, but faithful service, the proper management [οἰκονόμος/-ία] of an entrusted task. We would seem to be operating here in the realm of what Paul elsewhere expresses via the motif of judgment according to works,[104] in this case echoing the note of God's prerogative to recompense his servants (3:8–9).

In this instance, however, the criterion of faithful service probes even deeper than the observable works which are visible signs of inner reality. Here even "the things now hidden in darkness," the "purposes of the heart," are examined and judged. It is difficult to ascertain whether τὰ κρυπτὰ τοῦ σκότους include a reference to hidden *faults* in line with the often negative moral connotation of "darkness,"[105] or are to be taken as morally neutral, emphasizing more their *obscurity from view* than any evil character, and thus synonymous with "the counsels of the hearts" which follows.[106] It is also possible that the Corinthians have impugned Paul's motives, thus prompting this reference to one's hidden thoughts and intentions.[107] Whichever the case, Paul is interested here only in such thoughts and motives as may result in a positive outcome ("praise").

The precise nature of this eschatological praise is likewise difficult

---

[102] Note especially his use now of ἄνθρωπος (verse 1) and ἀνθρωπίνης (verse 3) stressing *human* evaluation rather than the indefinite τις as in chapter 3.

[103] Kuck, *Judgment and Community Conflict*, 198.

[104] Cf. Rom. 14:4–5, 10–12; Col. 3:22–24.

[105] So Prov. 4:19 ("the way of the wicked is like deep darkness"); 2:13; 1QM I,10; III,6; T.Reub. 3:8; Philo *Leg.All.* 1:46; John 3:19–21; Rom. 13:2; 2 Cor. 6:14; 1 Thess. 5:4–5; Eph. 5:8, 11; 6:12; Col. 1:13. See further H. Conzelmann, art. σκότος, *TDNT* VII.442. Κρυπτός alone can likewise refer to that which is morally repugnant (2 Cor. 4:2; Eph. 5:12), but would seem to include both good and evil in the similar usage at Rom. 2:16.

[106] Cf. Dan. 2:22 and Matt. 10:27 (= Luke 12:3).

[107] G. Theissen, "Legitimation," *NTS* 21 (1975), 192–221.

to pinpoint. Not a few commentators identify it with the μισθός mentioned earlier, and thus as something distinct from salvation.[108] Others note that justification appears to be in view in 4:4 [δεδικαίωμαι][109] and that Paul can elsewhere use ἔπαινος as an equivalent for salvation (Rom. 2:29) and thus prefer an equation with the salvation in 3:15.[110] Luke 16:8–9 and 1 Peter 1:7 may be taken as witnesses of such an early Christian understanding of eschatological praise as the fundamental approval of a servant's faithfulness to his/her calling, allowing entry into the master's glory and honor at Christ's coming.[111]

It may well be, however, that Paul's choice here of this praise terminology was influenced less by such theological considerations and more by his Hellenistic audience. It is striking that "praise" is quite rare in Jewish and Christian tradition as a term describing the result of God's judgment. On the other hand, Kuck has demonstrated that such language of praise would have struck a very responsive chord among Hellenistic listeners.[112] Attaining the praise of others and of the gods was a "characteristic goal in antiquity."[113] The Corinthians' desire to be recognized as wise and strong, to boast of their attachment to particular leaders, and to take pride in one over against another, all suggest that they continued to seek the praise which had formerly been so important to their pagan social environment.[114] What they are seeking now from one another will, however, according to Paul be awarded at

---

[108] Cf. 3:8, 14. Mattern, *Das Verständnis des Gerichtes*, 183–184; Fee, *First Epistle to the Corinthians*, 143, n. 42; 163, n. 32.

[109] While δικαιοῦσθαι may occasionally carry a non-soteriological meaning in Paul (Rom. 6:7), 1 Cor. 4:4c-5 points unmistakably to a divine verdict in the context of eschatological judgment (against L. Mattern who disputes this connection by appeal to the supposed "parenthetical nature" of 4:4a,b [*Das Verständnis des Gerichtes*, 184]). If this soteriological interpretation is correct, then this is an instance of Paul's combination of judgment and justification language, as well as an instance where δικαιοῦσθαι refers to a still outstanding (future) verdict. See Cosgrove, "Justification in Paul," 663.

[110] Synofzik, *Die Gerichts- und Vergeltungsaussagen*, 72.

[111] See H. Preisker, art. ἔπαινος, *TDNT* II.586–588.

[112] *Judgment and Community Conflict*, 141–143, 208–209. On the rarity of "praise" in such contexts, see esp. 209, n. 309.

[113] Preisker, *TDNT* II.586.

[114] See esp. G. Theissen, "Social Stratification in the Corinthian Community: A Contribution to the Sociology of Early Hellenistic Christianity," chap. 2 (pp. 69–119) in *The Social Setting of Pauline Christianity* (ed. and trans. J. H. Schutz; Philadelphia: Fortress Press, 1982 [originally: "Soziale Schichtung in der korinthischen Gemeinde: Ein Beitrag zur Soziologie des hellenistischen Urchristentums," *ZNW* 65 (1974), 232–272]).

the final judgment by God, and will not be based on human wisdom or rhetorical skill but on trustworthy stewardship of the gospel. "Paul in effect anticipates a postmortem eulogy from God for individual Christians."[115]

Summary of 1 Corinthians 3–4

Paul's use of the motif of divine recompense according to deeds in 1 Corinthians 3:8b suggests that it is a theological axiom central to his religious tradition, whose terminological expression can be adapted according to the need of the argument. Although the expression "receive reward" [μισθὸν λήμψεται] is not a common way of putting the motif, it has been shown to have a place within that tradition. The two-fold use of ἴδιος and the substitution of κόπος for the normal ἔργον/α are easily attributed to Paul's rhetorical purpose. In addition, the explicit use of the talionic formula in 3:17a has a direct relationship to Paul's use of the recompense motif in 3:5–15, as well as being related to the development of the motif in its earliest stages in Israel. The pertinent phrases in 3:14–15 and 4:5 are not themselves occurrences of the motif in Paul, but are clearly related to the same, with 3:14–15 taking up key words of the motif from 3:8b.

The motif functions in 1 Corinthians 3–4 with some of the same variety witnessed in Romans and in second temple Jewish literature. In 3:8b it serves as the theological basis for precluding intra-community judgment (also 4:5). We have already seen this in Romans 14:10–12 (also Romans 12:19). Although this particular function only developed in the second century BCE and later, it has already become important among the uses of the motif in Judaism. Interestingly, Paul's use in 1 Corinthians 3–4 testifies to continued development in the motif's functions, since second temple Judaism generally employed it only in its negative sense (i.e., do not *condemn*, because condemnation belongs to God). Paul now includes the positive side as well: do not be elevating one servant over another, since such rewarding is both premature (esp. 4:5) and belongs to God alone (3:8b–9a). As will be noted shortly, this development in function parallels certain theological developments in contemporary Judaism.

In addition, Paul uses the motif in 3:14–15 simultaneously to call

---

[115] Kuck, *Judgment and Community Conflict*, 209.

leaders of the Christian community to proper service and to warn them against disobedience in this regard. Employing the *lex talionis* in 3:17a he can intensify this to a threat of eschatological destruction against the persistently misdirected. As was typical of similar intra-community warnings and summonses to repentance in the Jewish literature surveyed, Paul does not pronounce sentence here upon named individuals, but allows the conditional form of the threat to motivate the errant by alerting them to the very real danger of falling under divine judgment *if* they fail to heed the warning.

This passage also serves to illuminate Paul's theological understanding of recompense according to works. It is particularly clear from 3:13–15, 17a, and 4:5 that an *eschatological* divine judgment/recompense according to deeds was expected for believers as part of an apocalyptic day of judgment. Paul also witnesses to a strong *individualizing* of future judgment, whereby not only participation in the group of the "saved" is in view, but each individual [ἕκαστος] receives his/her own [ἴδιος] recompense in accordance with his/her own [ἴδιος] labor. Of course, as the earlier chapters of this book have demonstrated, this individualization is not new with Paul. Furthermore, this passage witnesses to the centrality of *disclosure*, rather than weighing, counting or the like, in Paul's conception of this judgment according to labor. One does not first attain to divine approbation via this judgment, rather one's already existing character or status as a faithful servant of God is hereby revealed publicly.

Paul also evidences the influence of developing (rabbinic) Judaism in his belief in positive *reward(s)* according to deeds. As noted earlier in this chapter, such belief, though present in the OT, faded from view during the intertestamental period, but begins to make its reappearance in those traditions which will later be codified in rabbinic writings. The precise nature of such reward is left unspecified in these texts ("praise" in 4:5 is not necessarily an expansion upon the μισθός of 3:8b, 14–15), since such was not Paul's interest here. Nevertheless, it is clear from 3:8b and 14–15 that this μισθός was distinct from "being saved." These verses are, in fact, the clearest evidence of Paul's belief in *varied rewards*, though it is not within his interest to speculate or expand upon what they might actually be.

This distinction between an individually varied μισθός and Christian salvation [σωθήσεται] does not, however, suggest that

Paul draws a strict line of theological separation between an eschatological judgment issuing in μισθός and the final judgment issuing in salvation/damnation. He does not, for example, consistently make the distinction found in this particular text. Romans 2:5–6 can speak of one's behavior storing up a "treasure" resulting in "repayment" of either eternal life or divine wrath. In several places Paul employs an athletic metaphor to picture Christian existence as persistent striving after the "prize" [βραβεῖον], which I will argue is not a reward distinct from eternal life or salvation. Colossians 3:24 uses the motif of divine recompense according to deeds which issues in the "reward [ἀνταπόδοσις] of (i.e., consisting of) the inheritance," again suggesting all that is promised believers through faith. Furthermore, as my exegesis has sought to demonstrate, 1 Corinthians 3:14–15 is too often wrongly interpreted as reassurance to the errant that their inadequate behavior cannot, after all, impinge upon their being saved. Far from reassurance, this text warns such people of the terrible risk they run; namely, although they may be saved, it will be "by the skin of their teeth." This is then heightened in verses 16–17 to form a definite threat of divine destruction upon any in the community who would persist in destroying the church. This is directed to those whom Paul has thus far considered members in good standing of the elect community, and threatens not on the basis of abandoning faith, but of behavior: "If anyone destroys God's temple."

Thus in Paul's wording of the motif and in its rhetorical function, as well as in his theological use of the same, the apostle demonstrates substantial continuity with the Jewish tradition of divine recompense according to deeds. He can put statements about salvation, justification, and eschatological commendation in close proximity with those about eschatological judgment according to deeds, giving no evidence of any theological tension or paradox. Theological continuity with the Jewish covenantal perspective outlined above suggests why that is so for Paul. Faithfulness to God (here in the specific context of ministry rather than in the context of Christian sanctification) is the required outworking of God's justifying work in Christ through faith. This faithfulness will be disclosed at the eschatological judgment, being the criterion according to which one is approved and rewarded, or is destroyed. Paul implicitly acknowledges degrees of faithfulness/unfaithfulness in 3:9b-15, but his point throughout is the *risk* of unfaithfulness. This risk is particularly acute because the point at which one's behavior marks one out as fundamentally unfaithful is left to God's wisdom. Even for Paul, 3:16–17 is a warning, not an irrevocable sentence. As we will observe in 1 Corinthians 5, even in extreme cases, Paul retains the hope of repentance and restoration.

* * *

In addition to those passages discussed above, there are some additional judgment-related texts in 1 Corinthians.

1 Corinthians 5:5

Although the motif does not occur in this text, it cannot be ignored in a study of Paul's understanding of judgment according to works. He is found passing judgment on a member of the congregation [κέκρικα, verse 3] and urging the church to join him in thus judging "those who are inside" (verse 12). Furthermore, this apostolic judgment does seem to have some relation to the individual's ultimate salvation [ἵνα τὸ πνεῦμα σωθῇ ἐν τῇ ἡμέρᾳ τοῦ κυρίου, verse 5], and is clearly prompted by the man's deeds [τὸν οὕτως τοῦτο κατεργασάμενον, verse 3]. Karl Donfried calls this "the single most important passage" among those which "state that God can and will reject disobedient Christians," and, at the same time, "the one most frequently used as a support for the argument that the baptized Christian is guaranteed salvation."[116]

The significance of this passage for our subject is made even clearer by looking at the various conclusions which interpreters have reached in the course of their exegesis. "The most common interpretation is that Satan was expected to cause the man's sudden death or a slower one by illness, that his death would expiate for his sin, and thus his immortal soul or his inner, true self would be saved."[117] For some, this verges on a "guarantee," a sort of *character indelebilis* for the baptized. "Paul's certainty that, at the very least, the spirit will be saved rests upon the belief that this *spirit*, through baptism and contact with the divine Spirit, has been

---

[116] "Justification and Last Judgment," 149–150. He also cites 1 Cor. 10; 11:27–34; Gal. 6:7; (and with less certainty 1 Cor. 6:9 and Gal. 5:21b) as pointing to the same divine rejection of disobedient Christians.

[117] A. Y. Collins, "The function of 'excommunication' in Paul," *HTR* 73 (1980), 257 (not her own position).

consecrated in a manner which makes it impervious to Satan's attacks."[118]

At rather the opposite end of the spectrum are those exegetes who translate "in order that the [*Holy*] Spirit may be preserved," rather than as a reference to the salvation of the offender's spirit. Understood this way, grave moral failure did indeed bring eternal destruction even for the one who had been counted among the justified. The "handing over to Satan" has no remedial purpose for the offender, but is strictly and irreversibly punitive.[119]

A third group of scholars sees the offender's salvation as a distinct possibility, but one which is conditioned upon repentance. There remains an implicit threat of condemnation if the offender does not repent as a result of the discipline. Future judgment can result in damnation, even for one previously counted among the justified, if flagrant and ongoing evildoing is not discontinued.[120] And even within any one of the above interpretive groupings there remains considerable disagreement as to individual details.

If we are to gain any insight as to Paul and judgment from this text, the following questions will have to be addressed and answered with as much certainty as the evidence allows.

(1) What precisely is the congregational action which Paul enjoins? Does "to hand over to Satan" speak of exclusion from the community, some form of solemn curse upon the offender, or perhaps a combination of both?

(2) What is the expected result of this action [εἰς ὄλεθρον τῆς σαρκός]? Is death or physical suffering envisioned? Is it viewed as punishment or as remedial discipline, and are any conditions implied if this result is to be obtained?

---

[118] J. Weiß, *Der erste Korintherbrief* (10th edn.; MeyerK; Göttingen: Vandenhoeck & Ruprecht, 1925) 131. Of much the same opinion is A. Strobel – "an unconditional promise" (*Der erste Brief an die Korinther* [Zürcher Bibelkommtare NT 6/1; Zürich: Theologischer Verlag, 1989], 99).

[119] For example, Collins, "The function of 'excommunication'," 259–260.

[120] See, for instance, G. W. H. Lampe, "Church discipline and the Interpretation of the Epistles to the Corinthians," *Christian History and Interpretation: Studies Presented to John Knox* (ed. W. R. Farmer, C. F. D. Moule and R. R. Niebuhr; Cambridge: Cambridge University Press, 1967), 342–355; V. C. Pfitzner, "PURIFIED COMMUNITY – PURIFIED SINNER: Expulsion from the Community according to Matthew 18:15–18 and 1 Corinthians 5:1–5," *AusBR* 30 (1982), 46–47; and Fee, *First Epistle to the Corinthians*, 208–213 ("this was the standard view in the early church, being found explicitly in Origen, Chrysostom, and Theodore of Mopsuestia" [212, n. 82]).

(3) How do we best understand the expressed purpose of this action [ἵνα τὸ πνεῦμα σωθῇ]? What is this "spirit" which is to be "saved"? Is this purpose ensured by the action itself or is the offender's response implied as a co-condition? Is the loss of salvation implied if the action is not carried out, or if the offender does not respond properly?

(4) Does 2 Corinthians 2:5–11 (also 7:8–13) confirm that repentance was hoped for and not sudden death? Is this passage even speaking of the same situation?

The asyndeton at 5:1 and clear reference to the new topic of sexual immorality [πορνεία] mark out 5:1–6:20 as a new section focusing on problems related to immorality in the community, and especially to questions of community judgment on such behavior. The surface issue is a case of immorality, here specified as a believer living in an ongoing sexual relationship with his step-mother.[121] While Greco-Roman society was much more tolerant on sexual matters than Jewish culture, this particular case of cohabitation between step-son and step-mother was equally abhorrent to both Jews and Greeks.

It is difficult, however, to explain Paul's vehement reaction ("Drive out the wicked person from among you," verse 13) as due to this offense alone.[122] And, in fact, he gives relatively little attention to the offender, focusing instead on the church's response to such sin in their midst.[123] They are arrogant instead of grieving and mourning. They are boasting (5:6) in their tolerance or even support of such behavior. Such behavior, if tolerated, is a dangerous leaven that could threaten to corrupt the entire church (5:6–8). It is even possible that immorality has become a broader problem than this one instance, and that various forms are being practised by segments of the congregation.[124] Thus in examining verse 5 we will have to keep in mind that this brief reference to the sinner's fate is secondary to the main intent of the passage, which is

---

[121] On the nature of the relationship (was a marriage involved? status of the offender's father?), see Barrett, *First Epistle to the Corinthians*, 122.

[122] Serious offenses did not always result immediately in expulsion, cf. e.g., Gal. 5:21; 6:1; 1 Cor. 6:1–11; 11:17–34.

[123] "In chapter 5, one verse deals with the incestuous persons and twelve verses deal with the culpability of the congregation, with its power to rid itself of the 'old yeast'" (P. S. Minear, "Christ and the Congregations: 1Corinthians 5–6," *RevEx* 80 [1983], 343).

[124] Cf. 5:9; 6:12–20; 7:2; 10:8.

to bring congregational attitudes and behavior back into line with Paul's apostolic gospel.

His main interest lies not in the effects of judgment upon this offending believer, but with the purity of the community. Four times he reiterates the charge *to the community* to remove the man (5:2b, 5, 7, 13). In explicit contrast to the congregation's puffed-up permissiveness Paul judges[125] the offender and directs the church to take action which reflects such judgment. The action against the offender is "shrouded in mystery" (Fee) and "permits only hunches as to the interpretation" (Synofzik). Thus while I will lay out the various interpretive options and argue for a particular understanding of verse 5, it would be unwise to allow this verse to carry too much weight in the overall determination of Paul's view of judgment upon believers.

The unusual phrase – "to hand this man over to Satan" [παραδοῦναι τὸν τοιοῦτον τῷ σατανᾷ] – is almost certainly either a curse, a reference to exclusion from the community, or a combination of the two.[126] Nestled as it is within repeated calls for the expulsion of the sinner from the congregation, it seems unlikely that Paul would now, at the point of formal instruction for community action, introduce a new and obscure curse-formula. This contextual factor tips the balance in my view in favor of taking "delivery to Satan" as an alternative formulation for expulsion.[127] The lack of formal parallels to Paul's phraseology may be explained either as an accident of the extant materials, or because its use only occurred

---

[125] Although some translate ἤδη κέκρικα (verse 3) in the milder sense of "already resolved" or "decided" (e.g., Conzelmann, *1 Corinthians*, 94, n. 9), "I have already judged" seems to make better sense of the difficult syntax (see BDF, §389; J. Murphy-O'Connor, "1 Corinthians V, 3–5," *RB* 84 (1977), 239–245, esp. 242–243).

[126] Since the ground has been covered thoroughly by others, I will simply refer here to representatives of the various persuasions; (curse) F. F. Bruce, *1 and 2 Corinthians* (NCB; Grand Rapids: Eerdmans, 1971), 55; (expulsion) Fee, *First Epistle to the Corinthians*, 208–209; (combination) Synofzik, *Die Gerichts- und Vergeltungsaussagen*, 55. For other alternatives, see W. F. Orr and J. A. Walther, *I Corinthians* (AB 32; New York: Doubleday & Co., 1976), 186.

[127] For examples of extra-biblical religious exclusion, see G. J. Blidstein, "Atimia: A Greek Parallel to Ezra X.8 and to Post-Biblical Exclusion from the Community," *VT* 24 (1985), 357–360; and S. C. Barton and G. H. R. Horsley, "A Hellenistic Cult Group and the New Testament Churches," *Jahrbuch für Antike und Christentum* 24 (1981), 7–41. The connections between Paul's use and Jewish sources have been explored by Rosner, "Temple and Holiness," 137–145; and G. Forkman, *The Limits of the Religious Community: expulsion from the religious community within the Qumran sect, within rabbinic Judaism, and within primitive Christianity* (trans. P. Sjölander; ConB 5; Lund: CWK Gleerup, 1972).

within a very limited circle of the early church.[128] While the use here as an execration formula cannot be entirely ruled out, the salvific purpose assigned by Paul to this action places his usage in opposition to all the parallels for such formulae thus far gathered.

The result of this expulsion is termed "the destruction of the flesh" [εἰς ὄλεθρον τῆς σαρκός]. Three main options have generally been considered in the interpretation of this phrase, none of which is without problems. It may possibly refer to physical death, in which case the σάρξ/πνεῦμα contrast in verse 5bc is usually interpreted as something like "body/soul" or "material/immaterial."[129] Others would emphasize physical affliction (sometimes seen as leading eventually to death). Reference is made to Satan's role in Job's afflictions and to Paul's "thorn in the flesh." On this view, it is assumed that such affliction will bring the sinner to his senses, leading to repentance and reinstatement, thus preserving his salvation.[130] In the third place, interpreters have opted for taking σάρξ in the sense of "sinful nature," allowing "destruction of the flesh" as a reference to its mortification along the lines of Romans 6:6.[131] In addition to these positions, some commentators support a combination of the above interpretations.

The interpretive crux lies clearly in Paul's use of σάρξ in this context (opp. πνεῦμα). His normal range of usage is broad, including the concrete material corporeality of an individual; then humanity in its weakness, dependence on God, and perishableness; and extending on to that special sense characteristic of Paul in which it signifies humanity in its sin and depravity and "the sphere of that which is sinful, which does not mean simply the earthly and temporal over against the eternal God, but which also stands opposed to him, as Rom. 8:7 states: τὸ φρόνημα τῆς σαρκὸς ἔχθρα εἰς θεόν."[132]

A. C. Thiselton argues against specifying flesh here as either the

---

[128] 1 Tim. 1:20 testifies to the usage of this phrase in some disciplinary sense in Pauline circles. However its identification with the usage in 1 Cor. 5 is made difficult due to the former's apparent lack of congregational involvement ("whom *I* have turned over to Satan"), and to the difference in purpose ("so that they may learn not to blaspheme").

[129] Reference is often made to 1 Cor. 11:30 and Acts 5:1–11.

[130] This was generally the view of the early church fathers; see K. Staab, *Pauluskommentare aus der griechischen Kirche* (Münster: Aschendorff, 1933), 178, 243–244.

[131] N. G. Joy, "Is the body really to be destroyed?" *Bible Translator* 39 (1988), 429–436.

[132] Bultmann, *Theologie des Neuen Testaments*[8], 237, see also 232–239. On σάρξ

"physical side of a person" (= death or physical suffering) or "lower nature," contending instead for an *evaluative use* of the term derived primarily from the rhetorical context of 1 Corinthians.

> Both the context of situation and the broader linguistic context of the earlier chapters suggest that "flesh" and "fleshly", together with "spirit" and "spiritual" had already acquired a highly evaluative and even emotive significance ... In the overwhelming majority of instances in which σάρξ and πνεῦμα oppose each other, they set up a polarity between what accords with the working of the Spirit of God and human characteristics which, to all intents and purposes, have been arrived at independently.[133]

Paul is not using the terms in a technical sense from his own perspective, but is entering into a "language game" with the Corinthians.[134] Whereas they thought such a demonstration of freedom showed freedom from the flesh in a truly spiritual existence, Paul counters that the flesh is very much alive amongst them and must still be destroyed if the "spirit" (*i.e., that which truly belongs to the realm of the "spiritual"*) is to be saved. By excluding the offender from the community of the wise and spiritual, his boastful fleshly attitude as well as (by implication) that of portions of the congregation will be dealt a mortal blow ("destroyed"). That the removal of such an *attitude* was uppermost in Paul's mind is confirmed by what immediately follows, "your boasting is not a good thing" (verse 6). On this interpretation "destruction" receives a natural rendering, being a severe term, ready to hand in the Hellenistic world, for the destruction or ruin of something. It

in Paul, see esp. R. Jewett, *Paul's Anthropological Terms: A Study of their Use in Conflict Settings* (AGJU 10; Leiden: E. J. Brill, 1971), 49–166, esp. 115.

[133] "The Meaning of SARX in 1Corinthians 5:5: A Fresh Approach in the Light of Logical and Semantic Factors," *SJT* 26 (1973), 204–228, here 215; on the "evaluative use of language," see esp. 205–209.

[134] The concept of "language game" derives from Wittgenstein (whose views are expounded conveniently in A. C. Thiselton, *The Two Horizons: New Testament Hermeneutics and Philosophical Description* [Grand Rapids: Eerdmans, 1980], 407–415). In a similar vein, see J. Benedict, "The Corinthian Problem of 1 Corinthians 5:1–8," *Brethren Life* 32 (1987), 70–73: "Their fleshly attitudes would naturally be cut to the quick when the man, as a symbol of their supposed maturity and knowledge, was delivered to Satan (i.e., expelled)" (72). Benedict, however, restricts the meaning here to a corporate application, rather than allowing that what is said applies equally to the offender.

should not be weakened to mean "affliction,"[135] nor made to correspond to Paul's more normal terminology for "mortification of the flesh."

If asked *how* expulsion results in destruction of the flesh, the interpreter is left to guesswork, since this is not explained by the apostle. If correct that Paul is directing the church to exclude the offender resulting in the destruction of both the individual's and the congregation's fleshly attitudes, then it may well be that the mere fact of such a one being thrust out of the community of the "spiritual" was considered enough to puncture this puffed-up boasting.

Finally, what exactly is one to understand by the salvific final clause: ἵνα τὸ πνεῦμα σωθῇ ἐν τῇ ἡμέρᾳ τοῦ κυρίου? Again, I will here only briefly review the main interpretive options.

(1) Πνεῦμα refers to a constituent "part" of the human being which will be saved. This view has been generally abandoned as reflecting a too Hellenistic, non-Pauline anthropology.[136]

(2) Πνεῦμα refers to the *Holy* Spirit (i.e., in the community), which will be "preserved" by ridding the community of the unholy person.[137]

(3) "The *pneuma* of the sinner which is to be delivered is the I given to him by God, a portion of God's Spirit, though the whole of the new man of the believer is represented therein. But this is not an indelible character, for Paul reckons with the possibility of perdition if judgment is not exercised on the *sarx* (sickness, death? 11:30; cf. Acts 5:1–11). It is the new I of man which perishes if he ceases altogether to be a Christian."[138]

---

[135] Used elsewhere in the Pauline corpus with reference to eternal "destruction" at the parousia (1 Thess. 5:3; 2 Thess. 1:9 [ὄλεθρος αἰώνιος]; cf. also 1 Cor. 10:10 [ὁ ὀλοθρεύτης = OT angel of destruction]; and 1 Tim. 6:9 [par. ἀπωλεία]).

[136] See A. Sand, *Der Begriff "Fleisch" in den Paulinischen Hauptbriefen* (Biblische Untersuchungen 2; Regensburg: F. Pustet, 1967), 143–145; and Jewett, *Paul's Anthropological Terms*, 167–200, esp. 194–198.

[137] Above all, the eschatological referent ("saved in the day of the Lord") renders this interpretation unlikely, since in reference to the Holy Spirit in the community it would have to be the present, not future, "preservation" that is prominent. Cf. E. Schweizer, art. πνεῦμα, *TDNT* VI.435, n. 691, who refers also to 1 Pet. 4:6 against this interpretation.

[138] Ibid., 435.

(4) Like "flesh," "spirit" reflects Paul's evaluative use of language as seen in 1 Corinthians 1–4, rather than any particular technical usage derived from other letters or contexts. It constitutes a "language game." Whereas the Corinthians prided themselves in already being πνευματικοί, and that in the face of flagrant immorality in their midst(!), Paul counters that eschatological salvation of that/those which truly belong/s to the realm of "spirit" will only be achieved by driving out the evil from amongst them.

I have previously noted my preference for this last-mentioned interpretation, in which case Paul's intention can be understood at two levels, the individual and the corporate. Assuming that this individual (along with segments of the congregation) saw himself as already wholly spiritual and freed from the limitations of the flesh, Paul counters with a directive that marks the offender as in fact too much associated with the very realm from which he imagines himself to be free. That which is fleshly must be destroyed by exclusion from the community, in order that that which is genuinely spirit(ual) may be saved. For the individual this most likely involves repentance from the specific form of fleshly behavior he has been practicing (see further on "repentance" below). For the community this means ridding themselves of their blind and boastful attitudes characteristic of the flesh in order that they might be genuinely πνεῦμα (= πνευματικοί, those who participate in the realm of πνεῦμα) and thus be saved. In either case, salvation is assured only to those who belong to the realm of πνεῦμα, or as Paul states in Romans 8, who have τὸ φρόνημα τοῦ πνεύματος (verse 6) and live κατὰ πνεῦμα (verse 4). The ἵνα-clause (1 Cor. 5:5c) should be understood in a strictly final sense, indicating "that the salvation of the πνεῦμα on the Day of the Lord is dependent upon the current carrying out of judgment upon the *sarx*."[139] Salvation is here made conditional upon living in the Spirit, seen as the desired result of this act of exclusion.

It might be urged against this interpretation that it assumes something not explicit in the text itself – repentance.[140] However,

---

[139] Mattern, *Das Verständnis des Gerichtes*, 107, n. 268.

[140] *Against* the assumption of potential repentance, see for instance, G. Harris, "The Beginnings of Church Discipline: 1 Corinthians 5," *NTS* 37 (1991), 18. *Accepting* a hope of repentance, L. Brun, *Segen und Fluch im Urchristentum* (Oslo: I Kommisjon Hos Jacob Dybwad, 1932), 107; and most of the church fathers.

absence of its mention in regard to the individual is easily understandable, since Paul's focus here is not on the offender and his fate, but on changing the congregation's attitude toward this situation. Corporately, Paul most certainly has repentance in view. Πενθέω (verse 2) was used especially for sorrow over sins committed[141] and may be drawn from OT forerunners in which Israel was called to mourn over a sinner in her midst because she shared corporately in the sinner's guilt.[142] This sense of "repent over shared responsibility" corresponds with Paul's only other use of the verb (2 Cor. 12:21), and in 2 Corinthians 7:10 Paul says "godly sorrow produces repentance." The Passover-Leaven motif (verses 7–8) was likewise connected with repentance.

In addition, 2 Corinthians 2:5–11 and 7:12 have been traditionally interpreted (following most church fathers except Tertullian) as referring to this same incident. "This punishment by the majority is enough for such a person; so now instead you should forgive and console him, so that he may not be overwhelmed by excessive sorrow."[143] If correct, this would indicate that not death but repentance had been envisioned for the offender all along by the apostle. This traditional identification, however, is most likely incorrect.[144] Despite this, it may still reasonably be assumed that repentance and restoration were the apostle's (unexpressed) desire. This would be in line with his treatment elsewhere of offenders who had suffered some form of punishment.[145]

1 Corinthians 6:9–11

This sharp warning in the form of a traditional vice-list is closely connected with 6:1–8.[146] One brother has defrauded another, and

---

[141] BAGD, 642; cf. 1 Esdr. 8:69; 9:2; 2 Esdr. 10:6; T.Reub. 1:10.

[142] E.g., Exod. 16:27–28; Num.16:24, 27; Deut. 19:13; Josh. 22:16, 18; 1 Sam. 14:37–38. See also B. S. Rosner, "OYXI MAΛΛON EΠENΘHΣATE: Corporate Responsibility in 1 Corinthians 5," *NTS* 38 (1992), 470–473.

[143] F. C. Baur, *Paulus, der Apostel Jesu Christi. Sein Leben und Wirken, seine Briefe und seine Lehre* (2nd edn.; Leipzig: n.p., 1866), 234–235.

[144] See esp. V. Furnish, *II Corinthians* (AB 32A; Garden City, NY: Doubleday, 1987), 159–166.

[145] See Gal. 6:1; 2 Thess. 3:14–15; 2 Cor. 2:5–11; 1 Cor. 11:27–32. While in itself shocking, it can hardly be said that the individual's sin in 1 Cor. 5 is more serious than in these other passages. Paul's severity here is, in any case, not prompted so much by this sin as by the congregation's response (see above).

[146] For various attempts to reconstruct the exact dispute in these verses, see P. Richardson, "Judgment in Sexual Matters in 1 Corinthians 6:1–11," *NovT* 25/1 (1983), 37–58.

rather than resolving the dispute within the community they have gone to civil court, something which sickens Paul for a number of reasons, not the least because of the shame this brings upon the community (verse 5). After employing several different rhetorical tools to dissuade the Corinthians from this behavior, Paul turns in verses 8–10 to charge and threat,[147] followed immediately, however, by a word of assurance (verse 11), which serves not to dull the threat, but to encourage repentance.

Paul's basic threat was a truism throughout Judaism and early Christianity, "wrongdoers will not inherit the kingdom of God" [ἄδικοι θεοῦ βασιλείαν οὐ κληρονομήσουσιν]. The Jewish Psalter opens with the reminder that "the wicked will not stand in the judgment" and "the way of the wicked will perish" (Ps. 1:5, 6). It recurs in Paul in Galatians 5:21 as an explicit element in his foundational initial teaching of new converts – "those who do such things [i.e., work of the flesh] will not inherit the kingdom of God." Romans 1:18 makes clear that God's wrath rests upon all human ἀδικία, and Paul speaks a few verses later of "God's decree, that those who practice such things deserve to die" (1:32). This is echoed in 2:8–9 ("for those ... who obey ... wickedness [ἀδικία], there will be wrath and fury"), part of an expansion upon the divine recompense according to deeds (2:6). In Colossians 3:25 the recompense of wrongdoing is set in contrast to the Christian inheritance.

While it may be granted that such statements, especially as part of a vice-list, were typically understood to apply to the wicked outside the believing community, this cannot be pressed so as to exclude their usage as a threat to the obstinately disobedient within – certainly not in 1 Corinthians 6:9–11 and Galatians 5:21 where the believing community is explicitly addressed. Such obstinate disobedience raises a fundamental question as to whether the individual actually belongs to the group of the "wicked" or the "righteous," since one's deeds are the visible manifestation of the unseen realities of the heart.[148] In line with the understanding of divine recompense according to works discovered in Judaism and thus far in Paul's letters, so here those whose behavior identifies them consistently as wicked will be excluded from the future

---

[147] On the use of οὐκ οἴδατε (verse 9a) to introduce an intensified warning, see above, p. 223.

[148] They are "in danger of lapsing back into their pre-conversion condition and of forfeiting their entry into the Kingdom of God at the End" (R. H. Fuller, "First Corinthians 6:1–11, An Exegetical Paper," *Ex Auditu* 2 [1986], 102).

inheritance of the elect. Even more significant, perhaps, is the close linkage in this passage of (past) justification "in the name of the Lord Jesus Christ" with the threat of disinheritance based upon behavior. This phenomenon testifies once again to the lack of theological tension felt by Paul in affirming simultaneously justification by grace and judgment according to works, while at the same time heightening the existential tension ("are you what you claim to be?") as a tool against wicked behavior or complacency. The same phenomenon characterized Jewish covenantalism, wherein the faithful drew comfort and assurance from the divine election and covenant mercies, and at the same time lived under God's rule who would bring destruction upon all who chose the path of wickedness.

Those concerned with a more thoroughgoing systematization of Paul's thought on this point not infrequently appeal to the idea of "false profession." That is, those who would actually experience the consequences of this threat are counterfeit believers, not the genuinely converted who thereafter fall into grievous and ongoing sin. "Paul argues ardently against immoral behavior on the part of believers, yet is not saying that such behavior leads to loss of salvation."[149] Instead, ethical failure indicates the prior inauthenticity of Christian profession, divine chastisement, or regression in sanctification. On this view 1 Corinthians 6:9–10 is perhaps a paraenetic device (i.e., hypothetical warning), and at most hints at a minority in the Corinthian congregation who were not genuine believers. However, while such an after-the-fact determination of unauthentic faith may be suggested by texts such as 1 Corinthians 5:11 (*"so-called* brother") and 1 John 2:19, it is excluded for 1 Corinthians 6:9 by Paul's explicit identification of his hearers as those who were washed, sanctified and justified "in the name of the Lord Jesus Christ and in the Spirit of our God" (verse 11). Even those engaged in wrongdoing he still calls ἀδελφοί (verses 5–6).[150] Paul is most assuredly not yet prepared to place the wrongdoers in Corinth with "the wicked" (cf. verse 11a). On the other hand, he

---

[149] Gundry-Volf, *Paul and Perseverance*, 155, 157; cf. also 132–141, 221–225.

[150] Ultimately there may be something to the idea that professing Christians who fall and suffer destruction in judgment are thereby revealed to be wicked and unbelieving (cf. 2 Tim. 2:16–19; 1 Tim. 1:19–20; 1 John 2:19); but such ideas as "counterfeit disciples" or "veiled unbelief" are foreign to this particular text and can only be found by importing them from outside. What Paul says here is – you *are* brothers and have been justified, etc., but *if* you persist in wicked behavior you will suffer eschatological condemnation as an unrighteous person.

describes their current behavior as cut from the same cloth as that of the unrighteous [ἀλλὰ ὑμεῖς ἀδικεῖτε, verse 8]. His threat, if it is to retain any force at all, must imply the possibility that the currently righteous may yet fall under the condemnation reserved for the wicked *if* they persist unrepentantly in their wickedness. This is certainly the pattern discovered in second temple Judaism, and is the force of Pauline statements such as 1 Corinthians 10:12: "So if you think you are standing, watch out that you do not fall."

1 Corinthians 9:24–27

My aim in this section can be phrased as follows: To what extent does Paul envision reception of the imperishable wreath, or on the other hand disqualification from the metaphorical race, to be dependent on his performance in this race? As part of the answer I will need to clarify the meaning of this race metaphor as well as the nature of the prize or wreath.

In the midst of his extended discussion of "food offered to idols" [εἰδωλόθυτος, 8:1–11:1], in which he is particularly urging the strong to limit their freedom in the interests of the weak (8:13; 10:31–11:1), the apostle pauses to offer a defense of his apostolic practice on two fronts: (a) his right to financial support which he has *not* exercised (9:4–18), and (b) his seemingly vacillating behavior when in the company of Jews or Greeks (9:19–23). In both instances the self-imposed limitations on his own behavior have apparently been viewed by some Corinthians as signs of weakness and a lack of spiritual authority (otherwise he would accept monetary support and eat meat without restrictions).[151] Paul caps this defense in 9:23: "I do it all [i.e., restricting voluntarily my own freedom and rights] for the sake of the gospel, so that I may share in its blessings."[152]

Now in verses 24–27 the apostle follows this defense of his self-

[151] On the nature of chapter 9 as defense, or perhaps better "example," see H. P. Nasuti, "The Woes of the Prophets and the Rights of the Apostle: The Internal Dynamics of 1 Corinthians 9," *CBQ* 50 (1988), 246–264; W. Willis, "An Apostolic Apologia? The Form and Function of 1 Corinthians 9," *JSNT* 24 (1985), 33–48.

[152] Lit. "that I may be a fellow participant in it" [ἵνα συγκοινωνὸς αὐτοῦ γένωμαι]. I.e., already Paul ties his own enjoyment of the blessings promised in the gospel to the behavior he has just defended in verses 4–22. For this meaning of συγκοινωνός (= one who shares in the benefits of something), cf. Rom. 11:17 and Phil. 1:7. For the opposite view (= partner *with* the gospel), see Gundry-Volf, *Paul and Perseverance*, 247–254.

restricting behavior with an exhortation that they behave likewise –
"Run in such a way that you may win it [the prize]. Athletes
exercise self-control in all things; they do it to receive a perishable
wreath, but we an imperishable one" (verses 24b–25). Perhaps with
the nearby Isthmian games in mind, and certainly drawing on the
broad Hellenistic tradition of athletic metaphors, Paul frames this
exhortation in terms of two such metaphors.[153] First he points to
the foot-races, and highlights the fact that "only one receives the
prize," namely, the one who "exercise[s] self-control in all things,"
and they do this for a "perishable wreath." We must fill in the
syntactical blanks somewhat to understand properly Paul's application to the readers, which in Greek consists of only three words:
ἡμεῖς δὲ ἄφθαρτον = "but we *exercise self-control in all things in
order that we might receive* an imperishable *wreath*." Just as Paul
controls his liberty in order to share in the blessings of the gospel
(verse 23), so he now exhorts the Corinthians to do the same in
regard to the conflict over idol-meat, in order that they might gain
the imperishable reward. This "imperishable wreath" [στέφανος]
or "prize" [βραβεῖον] (verse 24a) is a metaphorical way of depicting
the gospel-blessings in which Paul also hopes to share (verse 23).[154]

Excursus: the use of "crown" imagery in the NT[155]

The NT exhibits a remarkable unanimity regarding the significance
of crown (or "wreath") imagery.

(1) Jesus is the Christian's example, who through faithful
     perseverance unto death was "crowned with glory and
     honor" (Heb. 2:9; cf. Ps. 8:4–6). This use of the verb
     [στεφανόω] indicates that the *awarding of glory and honor*
     is the central point of the imagery.

(2) In nearly every relevant passage, the awarding of a crown
     as the symbol of one's victory, glory and honor is inti-

---

[153] See V. C. Pfitzner, *Paul and the Agon Motif* (NovTSup 16; Leiden: E. J. Brill,
1967), esp. 187–191.

[154] Although Pfitzner wishes to deny any "independent [metaphorical] weight" to
the victor's prize and crown (ibid., 85–86, 89–90), by his own admission "στέφανος
(like βραβεῖον in Phil. 3:14) is definitely metaphorical," and the prize/crown images
played a more important role in the athletic motif in Hellenistic Judaism than in
purely Hellenistic usage (89, n. 4; cf. also 193: "the heavenly prize and crown" = "the
reward of faithfulness").

[155] On the whole subject see esp. K. Baus, *Der Kranz in Antike und Christentum*
(Bonn: Peter Hanstein, 1940).

mately tied in the immediate context to perseverance, endurance or faithfulness to one's calling. In many of these passages this is connected explicitly with the athletic metaphor noted already in 1 Corinthians 9:24–27 which likewise stresses the strict training and sacrifice necessary for those who would receive this honor.[156]

(3) This crown itself is reflected upon from many angles, which are all simply varied ways of referring to that eschatological life, righteousness and glory which is every faithful believer's inheritance. It is often rewarded explicitly at the parousia, with Christ playing the role of judge, just as the judge in the games awarded the crown to the victor.[157]

(4) There is no evidence that such crowns were understood as varied rewards distinguishable from salvation itself.[158]

Such a use of crown imagery to depict salvation blessings lay ready to hand in the Jewish and Hellenistic environment of the NT authors. The OT used this imagery repeatedly as a way to symbolize the honor, joy, glory and victory promised to the faithful, and thus as a way of speaking of the promised blessed "life" and that which invests life with worth. "Gray hair is a *crown of glory* [στέφανος καυχήσεως]; it is gained in a righteous life" (Prov. 16:31). "The *crown* [στέφανος] of the wise is their wisdom" (Prov. 14:24). "A good wife is the *crown* [στέφανος] of her husband, but she who brings shame is like rottenness in his bones" (Prov. 12:4). "He has stripped my *glory* [τὴν δόξαν] from me, and taken the

---

[156] Cf. 2 Tim. 2:5; 4:8; 1 Cor. 9:25; Rev. 2:10; 3:11; Jas. 1:12; 1 Pet. 5:4.

[157] The varied nouns which follow as genitives after "crown" are to be taken as appositives (cf.BDF, §167). Thus a crown "of righteousness" (2 Tim. 4:8), "of life" (Rev. 2:10; Jas. 1:12), "of glory" (1 Pet. 5:4), "of victory" (Rev. 14:14), and "of boasting" (1 Thess. 2:19) are not various "crowns," but various ways of referring to that righteousness, life, glory, etc., which will be awarded those who have proven victorious in the race of Christian existence. Compare esp. the "crown of righteousness" (2 Tim. 4:8) which is "reserved" [ἀπόκειται] for "all who have longed for his appearing," with the "hope (= salvation) laid up [ἀποκειμένην] for you in heaven" (Col. 1:5).

[158] Those who wish to see in the NT crowns such varied rewards nearly always cite 1 Cor. 3:8–15 as proof (e.g., J. Héring, *The First Epistle of Saint Paul to the Corinthians* [ET; London: Epworth Press, 1962], 80). However, as was discussed earlier, that passage does not speak of the crown or prize awarded to the one who successfully runs the Christian race, but of the wage [μισθός] paid to God's laborers. Furthermore the thrust of 1 Cor. 3:9b–15 is not to reassure the Corinthians of salvation minus rewards, but to warn them of the *risk to salvation* they are entertaining by their behavior.

crown [στέφανον] from my head" (Job 19:9). "In that day the Lord of hosts will be a *garland of hope* [στέφανος τῆς ἐλπίδος], and a *diadem of beauty* [πλακεὶς τῆς δόξης], to the remnant of his people" (LXX, Isa. 28:5).[159]

The intertestamental literature of Judaism continued this usage, and apocalyptic literature transformed it into eschatological blessings.[160] Sometime during the first century BCE tangible varying rewards (crowns, diadems) begin to appear, and the Tannaim testify to both this later conception and the more traditional (= life/salvation and its associated blessings).[161] Likewise in Greco-Roman society a wide variety of prize-imagery was employed "to refer to a favorable postmortem judgment," such prizes being "seen as extensions of the sorts of honors an individual would seek within the city in this life."[162] In general one may conclude from these Jewish and Hellenistic parallels that such crown imagery functioned not to depict literal degrees of reward, but to motivate proper behavior by portraying the blessedness of the future life or salvation in terms of those blessings one most desired even now.

Thus, in opposition to the Corinthians' unrestricted exercise of freedom, Paul's metaphor urges the exercise of self-control [ἐγκρατεύεσθαι] as the only way to successfully pursue Christian existence.[163] Maintaining the metaphor, but now putting himself forth as a model of such behavior (ἐγὼ τοίνυν οὕτως τρέχω, verse 26a), Paul compares such self-control to his own goal-oriented running which is certainly not "aimless" [οὐκ ἀδήλως]; i.e., freedom does not mean "anything goes," but is instead a disciplined pursuit of the goal.

Switching metaphors, Paul now compares his self-limiting behavior to that of a boxer who does not "beat the air" (verse 26b). This is intended to make the same point as the "aimless running" of

---

[159] Cf. also Prov. 4:9; 17:6; Lam. 5:15–16; Isa. 62:3; Ezek. 16:12; Wis. 5:15–16. The same is true of the verb "to crown" which means "to bestow (glory, honor, etc.);" cf. Pss. 8:5; 65:11; 103:4. See further Fuller, *A Pauline Understanding of Rewards*, 16–107.

[160] Fuller, *A Pauline Understanding of Rewards*, 108–211. J. G. Griffiths suggests that images such as a "crown of righteousness" came to Judaism from Egyptian sources where they were widespread (*The Divine Verdict*, 254–255). For usage in the DSS, cf. 1QH IX,25 and 1QS IV,7 (both "crown of glory").

[161] Volz, *Eschatologie der jüdischen Gemeinde*, 404–406.

[162] Kuck, *Judgment and Community Conflict*, 143.

[163] "The central point of the image must lie in πάντα ἐγκρατεύεται in v.25" (Pfitzner, *Paul and the Agon Motif*, 85).

verse 26a, and is contrasted immediately (ἀλλά) with a boxer who would "lay [the opponent] flat with the right blow in the right place."[164] This meaning is obscured by most translations, which render ὑπωπιάζω with "punish" (NRSV), "beat" (NIV) or "buffet" (NASB).[165] However, the literal use of the term – "to strike someone on the face (under the eyes) in such a way that he gets a 'black eye' "[166] – fits Paul's boxing metaphor admirably. Rather than aimlessly beating the air, Paul seeks to land a knock-out punch.

Paul's mixture of metaphor and application at this point has created a great deal of confusion among interpreters, and has provided a mainstay of ascetic theology. The opponent is Paul's own body [μου τὸ σῶμα]! One might conceivably take this as,

(a) the physical body (thus encouraging the bodily austerities of the ascetic tradition),
(b) the body of flesh (equivalent to σάρξ; cf. Romans 8:13, "put to death of the deeds of the body"),
(c) Paul's own physical body.

These all fail to see, however, that Paul uses τὸ σῶμα here only because is the obvious object of one's blows *in the metaphor*.[167] The application of the metaphor is not achieved by an extension of the "body," but by Paul's insertion of *himself* ("*my* body") into the picture. Applied to Paul, his purposeful blows, like his goal-oriented running, are aimed not so much at his "body" as at himself. The point is made clear by the immediately following verb taken from yet another metaphor – "I enslave (it = myself) [δουλαγωγῶ, or "bring into subjection"]." The thrust of Paul's exhortation remains the same throughout verses 23–27a: he subjects himself to voluntary limitations of his spiritual freedom, and so must the Corinthians.

Verse 27b gives a final reason or motivation for Paul's (and the Corinthians') self-controlled actions, putting this in terms of the avoidance of consequences which would result from failure to

---

[164] R. C. H. Lenski, *The Interpretation of St. Paul's First and Second Epistle to the Corinthians* (Columbus, OH: Wartburg Press, 1937) 385.
[165] See also BAGD, art. ὑπωπιάζω (2), "symbolically ... treat roughly, torment, maltreat."
[166] K. Weiss, *TDNT* VIII.590.
[167] Fee, *First Epistle to the Corinthians*, 439, esp. n. 31.

behave in this way[168] – "so that after proclaiming to others I myself should not be disqualified" [ἀδόκιμος γένωμαι]. Regardless of whether the "proclamation" [κηρύξας] is part of the metaphor (i.e., the herald [κῆρυξ] at the games) or (more likely) Paul's own preaching of the gospel, the "disqualification" will almost certainly stem from the sports metaphor, and will have been so understood by the Corinthians. "'Αδόκιμος can be a technical term for the fighter who not only loses, but who also proves himself to be incapable, who is useless for such ends."[169] At the same time one may suspect that in Paul's own mind this term resonated with deeper theological overtones connected to God's final approval of his servants.[170] Thus he closes as he began (cf. verse 23), doing all things, in particular limiting his own freedom for the sake of the gospel, so that he may qualify to share in the blessings of the gospel, the imperishable wreath awarded to successful Christian athletes. The ultimate seriousness of this potential consequence (i.e., salvation itself rather than varied rewards in addition to salvation) will be pressed home in 10:1–13, using the disobedient Israelites as an example of such as fail to please God and provoke the Lord to their own destruction.[171]

This passage confirms the understanding of judgment according to works discovered thus far in Paul's letters. Final enjoyment of the blessings promised in Paul's gospel is dependent upon faithful and enduring submission of oneself to the demands of that same gospel, especially the demands of mutual love. "That is, entry does not in itself guarantee a prize: it does so neither in athletics, nor in

---

[168] μὴ πως ... ἀδόκιμος γένωμαι = a consequence which one fears (Turner, *Syntax*, 99).

[169] Weiß, *Der erste Korintherbrief*, 249. Whether one completes this to mean disqualified "from the race" or "for the prize" (NIV) is immaterial, since they both amount to the same thing.

[170] See Rom. 1:28; 2 Cor. 13:5, 6, 7; also Rom. 14:18; 16:10; 1 Cor. 11:19; 2 Cor. 10:18; 1 Thess. 2:4; 2 Tim. 2:15; 3:8; Titus 1:16; Heb. 6:8. Jas. 1:12 appears to draw on the same tradition: "Blessed is anyone who endures temptation. Such a one has stood the test [δόκιμος γενόμενος] and will receive the crown of life that the Lord has promised to those who love him."

[171] J. Gundry-Volf's interpretation of 1 Cor. 9:24–27 hinges on understanding ἀδόκιμος as "disqualified *from apostolic service*" (*Paul and Perseverance*, 233–237). Though she is doubtless correct that the term is used in many other texts in this fashion, her exegesis fails in my view to take into account adequately that (i) the athletic metaphor applies to Christian existence (both Paul's and the Corinthians'), not just apostolic service, (ii) what Paul will miss if disqualified is the prize, or imperishable wreath (see above), and (iii) the ensuing warning (10:1–12) makes the soteriological significance of disqualification unavoidable (see below).

Christianity."[172] Just as in Romans 6–8 grace does not eliminate
the continuing obligation to obey the Spirit rather than Sin, here
the freedom that belongs already to those who are in the Spirit does
not liberate from the need to "run the race to win." Again, Paul
appears able to speak of future salvation being dependent upon
continued obedience in the present, without thereby feeling any
theological tension with the "already" of justification by faith
alone.

1 Corinthians 10:1–22

Here I wish only to note the way in which Paul uses Israel's history
to warn the proud Corinthians that *entry* into the elect community
does not of itself constitute a guarantee against falling under God's
judgment. The OT people of God are described in verses 1–4 in
terms designed to evoke comparison with Christian baptism and
the Lord's supper. The application to the hearers is made in verses
5–6.

> Nevertheless, God was not pleased with most of them, and
> they were struck down in the wilderness. Now these things
> occurred as examples for us, so that we might not desire
> evil as they did.

This recalls the refusal of the Israelites in Numbers 14 to enter the
land and their rebellion against Moses and God.[173] The result was
God's threat to strike them all with pestilence, to disinherit them,
and to raise up a new nation through Moses (14:12). In response to
Moses' intercession, God relents from his intention to disinherit
Israel completely, but not from his purpose of gradually executing
the sentence of death and destruction upon every individual of the
present rebellious generation, with the exception of Caleb and
Joshua. This annihilation at the hands of the Lord is the expression
of his angry opposition to them as his enemies (Num. 14:34), or as
Paul puts it, "God was not pleased [εὐδόκησεν] with them," he
rejected them as part of his elect people.

Paul then calls upon additional instances of grave disobedience
in Israel's history (verses 7–10) which led to "falling" (Num. 25 =

---

[172] Barrett, *First Epistle to the Corinthians*, 217.
[173] On possible midrashic forerunners to Paul's homily, see W. Meeks, "'And
Rose Up to Play': Midrash and Paraenesis in 1 Corinthians 10:1–22," *JSNT* 16
(1982), 64–78.

divine wrath leading to their death), and to others being "destroyed." The application is worded somewhat differently, but amounts to the same: "So if you think you are standing, watch out that you do not fall," i.e., fall like the disobedient Israelites (verse 12). Neither for the Israelites nor for the Corinthians will the fact that they are baptized, communicant members of God's people protect them from the wrath of God should they persist in rebellion and disobedience. In the case of the Corinthians, their participation in pagan temple feasts amounts to idolatry, something fundamentally incompatible with Christian faith, and which constitutes "provoking the Lord to jealousy" (verses 14–22). It is an unwarranted weakening of the apostle's intention to interpret all of this as anything other than a sharp warning to Christians of the most dire eschatological consequences for persistent disobedience. Such a conclusion is strengthened by the observation that Paul appears to be following a pattern of covenantal judgment thought found elsewhere in Judaism and the NT.

1 Corinthians 11:29–32

Verses 17–34 envision a church gathering, including celebration of the Lord's supper (verses 18, 23–26). In particular it is the abuses on such occasions which Paul wishes to address; abuses which involve disorder (verses 21, 33), drunkenness (verse 21b), and humiliating the socially lower members of the group (verse 22). These have contributed to the "divisions" (verse 18) or "factions" (verse 19) in the church, and their behavior in eating together is termed by Paul "unworthy" (verse 27). He attributes the (recent?) weakness, illness and even death of some members to God's disciplinary judgment (verses 30–32).

My exegesis will focus on two issues: (i) the nature of this judgment, in particular, how disciplinary judgment relates to condemnation (verse 32), and (ii) the basis of judgment (behavior or belief?). Beginning with the latter, the reason for this divine judgment is stated in verse 29 to be "eating and drinking without discerning the body" [μὴ διακρίνων τὸ σῶμα]. A common and ancient interpretation takes "body" here as a reference to the eucharistic "body of Christ."[174] This can appeal to the nearby

---

[174] Apparently so understood by numerous early scribes who added "of the Lord" to "body" in verse 29.

eucharistic reference in verses 23–27, and suggests that the cause of judgment was an undervaluation of the significance of the eucharistic elements (i.e., an issue of belief rather than behavior per se). However, as Barrett notes, "the Corinthians made too much rather than too little of their sacraments."[175]

Instead, Paul's absolute use of "the body" elsewhere in this same passage (verse 17) strongly suggests that he means the church. This same absolute usage ("the body" = the church) occurs in 12:12–27. In addition, the parallel between the wording of verses 29 and 31 (διακρίνειν τὸ σῶμα ... διακρίνειν ἑαυτούς) also supports this meaning; i.e., "the body" = "ourselves," the church. Thus the reference to the elements of the Lord's supper is only a supporting argument for the section ("we who are many are one body, *for* we all partake of the one bread") which revolves around the church-gathering (11:17, 20); the result of such "examination of the body" should be the opposite of "show[ing] contempt for the church" (11:22b). Another strength of this view is its recognition of the fundamentally social nature of the problem, rather than its being primarily a theological-spiritual one.

What then is the failure *"to discern"* the church? On the sacramental interpretation, this means the failure to distinguish between sacred and profane meals or food; i.e., the sin is the profanation of the sacred elements. Again this is unlikely in the light of the magical sacramental views of the Corinthians implied in 10:1–13. Paul is obviously ringing the changes on the stem κριν- in this passage. With the prefix ἀνα- the sense of "distinguish between, discern" often becomes prominent. The problem involves failure to distinguish between (or "discern") the gathering *qua* the body (of Christ) and a gathering *qua* "one's own meal" involving drunkenness and self-centered behavior. That is, the Corinthians are failing to recognize that this is no Greco-Roman *symposion* (drinking party), but the "body" gathered around the Lord's table.[176] This is confirmed by verses 27–28, where the largely synonymous δοκιμά-ζειν [examine, test, prove] is used, referring to a determination of whether or not they are eating and drinking ἀναξίως [in an

---

[175] *First Epistle to the Corinthians*, 275; cf. 10:1–13.

[176] On the relation of the Corinthian problem to such Greco-Roman practices, see esp. P. Lampe, "The Corinthian Eucharistic Dinner Party: Exegesis of a Cultural Context (1 Cor. 11:17–34)," *Affirmation* 4 (1991), 1–15; S. M. Pogoloff, *Logos and Sophia*, 237–271; and G. Theissen, "Social Integration and Sacramental Activity: An Analysis of 1 Cor. 11:17–34," *The Social Setting of Pauline Christianity* (Philadelphia: Fortress Press, 1982), 145–174.

unworthy manner], viz., whether their behavior (not their person) conforms to the character of this gathering. Thus the *reason for God's judgment* is nothing other than the *behavior* spoken of in verses 17–22, 27, 33–34.

What then of the *nature of such judgment?* Such behavior has brought God's judgment [κρίμα] (verse 29), which Paul defines as divine discipline [παιδεύεσθαι] (verse 32a), whose purpose [ἵνα] is to prevent them being "condemned [κατακρίνειν] along with the world" (verse 32b). There are thus three levels of judgment mentioned in the passage.

(1) *Self-judgment*: "But if we judged ourselves" (verse 31a). This does not refer to seeking to be one's own judge regarding status before God or regarding others' consciences (cf. 4:3–5; Rom. 14–15). Rather, as in 5:3, 12–13; and 6:1–6, it refers to the recognition and condemnation of overtly sinful behavior.

(2) *God's disciplinary judgment*: This occurs when individuals or groups fail to exercise the self-judgment just noted, and thus persist in overtly sinful behavior. In this particular instance it has led to sickness and even death (though this should not be construed as teaching that sin will always lead to sickness and death, nor that all such occurrences indicate sin as the cause). Such divine chastisement is meant to function as a *corrective measure*. It is divine παιδεία, a form of divine κρίμα (verse 32), which is only necessary because the Corinthians have failed to judge [διακρίνειν] themselves (verse 31). As we have seen, this refers to their failure to conform their behavior to the recognition of the gathering as the one body of Christ. Thus God's discipline is intended to do what they failed to do for themselves, recognize sin and change behavior. The avoidance of condemnation as the result assumes the acceptance of such discipline (= repentance), which is why Paul closes in verses 33–34a with the admonition which this divine chastisement is intended to press home to them.

This is supported by the understanding of God's chastising punishments in Judaism.[177] God's discipline functions in obvious parallel to human parental discipline, especially in the wisdom literature. Parental discipline protects from death (Prov. 23:13–14) by instructing and correcting the child (1:8; 12:1; 19:20), and thus driving out folly (22:15). Such human discipline certainly does not

---

[177] See G. Bertram, art. παιδεία, *TDNT* V.603–618; Moore, *Judaism*, II.248–256, esp. 255.

prevent death by atoning for sins.[178] God's punishments of his erring people operate in a similar fashion. They can be corrective, functioning to awaken and prompt them to repentance, not to destroy them.[179] However, if not accepted (= no repentance) such chastisement is in vain and will lead to final rejection.[180] This necessity of repentance as the object of chastisement, and as the grounds upon which final condemnation may be avoided, is found in a multitude of texts.[181] As noted in an earlier chapter, such disciplinary judgments are sometimes said to be "in mercy," and are contrasted with the more definitive judgment which is according to deeds.[182]

It has sometimes been suggested that this divine chastisement functions more in terms of *atonement* than correction, in line with later Jewish ideas of atoning suffering in this life substituting for eschatological punishment. While a few texts can be found which may suggest a theology of atoning suffering at this time, this does not seem to be the predominant mode of understanding God's chastisements.[183] Furthermore, the strong hortatory character of the 1 Corinthians passage speaks against this idea; plus the fact that such an atoning suffering (apart from Christ's) is not attested elsewhere in the NT, whereas the corrective chastening is (cf. Heb. 12:5–12; Titus 2:11–12; 1 Tim. 1:20). Thus, it is correct to say that this divine chastising judgment, as well as the self-judgment, preserve from final condemnation; however, they do so not automatically or via atonement, but through their function of leading to repentance.[184] Thus, even here, it remains behavior or deeds which are determinative of the outcome of the final judgment.

---

[178] Not infrequently the organic consequences of one's misdeeds, rather than God, chastise the sinner (cf. Prov. 13:18).

[179] Cf. Hos. 10:9–11:11; see also 2 Macc. 6:12.

[180] Jer. 2:30; 7:27–29. See also the series of corrective punishments in Lev. 26:14–45, each of which is introduced by some form of "but if you still will not repent." If they refuse to repent, God "will destroy them utterly and break [his] covenant with them" (verse 44). Thus, God's disciplinary judgment does not spare Christians automatically from the final condemning judgment (*pace* M. Kinghardt, "Sünde und Gericht von Christen bei Paulus," *ZNW* 88 [1997], 56–80, esp. 64).

[181] Job 5:17; Ps. 94:12–15; Sir. 18:14; 21:6; PssSol. 3:4; 10:1–2; 16:11b. See further pp. 67–68; and in the Qumran literature, see 1QS X,10–13; XI,13 (pp. 102–104 above).

[182] See chap. 1 on Sir. 17 and Ezek. 7:8–9, 27; 24:1–14 (pp. 42–44, 52–54).

[183] PssSol. 9:6–7; 13:10. Nearly all the evidence for this view comes from rabbinic literature; see E. P. Sanders, *PPJ*, 168–172, 397–398; and L. Mattern, *Das Verständnis des Gerichtes*, 30–31.

[184] "Punishments are remedies which believers need, for otherwise they themselves

(3) *Final condemnation*: The language of being "condemned *along with the world*" makes a reference to the eschatological damnation of the non-believing world unavoidable here. Normally, of course, it was only this *massa perditionis* which Paul expected to fall under God's κατάκριμα.[185] However, just as in 3:16–17, 6:9–10, 9:24–27, and 10:1–12, so here failure to repent from such evil behavior will assuredly result in destruction and condemnation by God. Otherwise they will indeed "come together εἰς κρίμα" (11:34). Paul's main thrust is not, in this instance, to threaten the Corinthians with eternal condemnation. However, one element in his persuasive technique is the explanation of current circumstances as expressions of divine judgment, with an accompanying implied threat of worse if they fail to heed the admonition. Such implied threat and ambiguity in the use of judgment language has been seen repeatedly in the Jewish literature studied, with the line separating κρίμα (still reversible) and κατάκριμα never spelled out in order to heighten the sense of danger and the urgency of repentance.

One final question may be permitted: What of those who had already died (verse 30b)? Paul gives no clear indication of their post-mortem fate in this passage. The corrective effect of such deaths will naturally have been upon the still living, as seen in Acts 5:1–11. At the very least the prospect of death under the judgment of God was something to be feared and avoided at all costs, whatever the situation of those who had already died. It is possible that Paul does not mean to imply that only those who were personally sinning in this manner were the ones getting sick and dying; conceivably this was a general community outworking of the judgment of God within the group, and thus not everyone who had died was guilty of the abuses in view.

1 Corinthians 16:22a[186]

The curse [ἀνάθεμα] here pronounced on anyone "who has no love for the Lord" is almost surely a threat of eschatological exclusion

would also rush onwards to eternal destruction, if they were not held in check by temporary punishments" (J. Calvin, *First Corinthians*, 256).

[185] Mattern, *Das Verständnis des Gerichtes*, 59–75.

[186] 1 Cor. 14:38 is taken by some as a prophetic sentence of judgment upon any who fail to heed Paul's letter, and thus as one additional instance of Paul's readiness to tie salvation to behavior (see E. Käsemann, "Sentences," 68–69). However, it is also possible that we have here merely the non-recognition (by the community) of any individual who refuses to recognize Paul's authority (Barrett, *First Epistle to the Corinthians*, 334).

directed against any in the Corinthian community who demonstrate by their actions that their allegiance lies elsewhere, or perhaps who reject obedience to the Lord as now laid out by Paul.[187]

Summary

Outside of chapters 3–4 no additional occurrences of the motif have been discovered in 1 Corinthians. Nevertheless the numerous judgment-related texts in chapters 5–16 confirm my understanding of judgment according to works in the earlier chapters. Paul expected that the believers in Corinth would have to face eschatological judgment issuing in salvation or damnation, the verdict being conditioned upon their behavior. Nowhere does Paul give a hint of theological tension with his doctrine of justification. Judgment functions in many of these texts in a manner quite similar to the OT summons to repentance. A final, irreversible sentence is not being pronounced upon the hopelessly wicked. Instead a warning is uttered against disobedient members of the community, threatening them with what will assuredly occur (not merely a hypothetical possibility) if they do not turn from their disobedience. The precise point at which this conditional threat would become actual condemnation is left ambiguous, perhaps as a means of heightening the motivational force of the warning (i.e., one can never say, "I am still a long way from seriously endangering my covenant status"). Especially in 6:9 and 10:1–22 Paul's language and use of the judgment theme remains firmly rooted in judgment beliefs axiomatic to Judaism, or in related Jewish convictions.

---

[187] See Gal. 1:8–9; (diff. 2 Thess. 3:14–15); also J. Behm, art. ἀνάθεμα, *TDNT* I.354–355; C. Roetzel, *Judgement in the Community*, 142–162.

6

JUDGMENT ACCORDING TO DEEDS IN 2 CORINTHIANS AND COLOSSIANS

2 Corinthians 5:10

For all of us must be made manifest before the judgment seat of Christ, so that each may receive back the things done while in the body according to what each has done, whether good or evil.[1]

2 Corinthians 5:1–10 is a well-known battleground over the precise contours of Paul's eschatology, in particular whether it was subject to development or change, and whether he envisioned an (unclothed?) intermediate state.[2] These debates, however, center almost exclusively on verses 1–8 and may therefore be left to one side. Instead I will focus on sorting through the difficult syntax of verse 10 so as to determine its proximity to the motif tradition thus far traced, and on questions of function and content. It will be my contention that, however unusual the precise wording (some of which will be shown to be dependent on the thrust of Paul's argument), verse 10 is best understood in line with second temple Jewish traditions of equivalent recompense, and is of a piece with Paul's judgment statements in his other letters. Furthermore, as an important aspect of his own motivation, Paul places himself (and all believers) before the universal final judgment issuing in salvation or damnation according to deeds, and this prospect not only coexists with, but actually springs from, his certainty of future glory with Christ (4:16–5:8).

Most are agreed that this verse comes within a larger unit in which Paul is defending his apostolic ministry. However one defines

---

[1] Author's translation.
[2] See R. F. Hettlinger, "2 Cor. 5,1–10," *SJT* 10 (1957), 174–194; F. G. Lang, *2.Korinther 5,1–10 in der neueren Forschung* (BGBE 16; Tübingen: J. C. B. Mohr (Paul Siebeck), 1973).

his opponents, he seems to be answering the question, "Why does this divinely ordained ministry appear in Paul's case so weak and frail?" Thus in 4:7–15 the apostle shows how divine power is revealed paradoxically through weak vessels. In 4:16–5:10, he goes on to explain why this apparent external weakness is not a cause for resignation, nor for the Corinthians to undervalue his apostleship. The reason lies in the new focus of hope on what is unseen rather than seen, on the eternal and heavenly rather than mortal and earthly.

Chapter 5 continues the train of thought started in 4:16–18. In spite of groaning in this earthly tent the apostle's confidence is grounded in the expectation of the resurrection body (verses 1–2) and in the Spirit as current guarantor or pledge of this future hope (verse 5). Verses 6–9 continue the theme of confidence in the face of weakness (esp. verses 6, 8), but introduce as well the thought of "faith versus sight" (verse 7) and a spatial conceptualization, "at home or away." With this note Paul returns to a theme he sounded at the beginning of this defense of his apostolic ministry. "Whether we are at home or away, we make it our aim to please him" (5:9). Paul has been at pains to contrast himself with the false apostles. "For we are not peddlers of God's word like so many; but in Christ we speak as persons of sincerity, as persons sent from God and standing in his presence" (2:17). His sincerity in ministry is motivated by the knowledge that he stands in God's presence, which will now be expanded in 5:10 in terms of appearing before the judgment seat of Christ. Verse 11 will continue this line of thought briefly: "Therefore, knowing the fear of the Lord, we try to persuade others." As for the connection between Paul's apology and the judgment statement in 5:10, "By this means Paul appears as an apostle whose preaching is carried out with integrity because he knows that he is on a path that leads to judgment by Christ."[3]

This contextual overview already reveals a great deal about the *function* of the judgment motif in 5:10. Knowledge of coming judgment motivates Paul (and should motivate others) to sincerity in ministry, to obedience, to "pleasing God." It will remain to be seen to what degree this motivation is tied to the positive promise of reward, or to the negative warning of recompense or punishment for disobedience (cf. 5:11, "knowing the fear of the Lord"), or to

[3] J. Schröter, *Der versöhnte Versöhner: Paulus als unentbehrlicher Mittler im Heilsvorgang zwischen Gott und Gemeinde nach 2 Kor. 2,14–7,4* (TANZ 10; Tübingen: Francke, 1993), 225.

both ("whether good or bad"). This certainty of judgment functions, in turn, within Paul's apology as a further proof of his sincerity and apostolic authenticity since his aim of pleasing God is even now manifest to both God and the Corinthians (verse 11).

Turning now to the motif itself (verse 10b), some troublesome lexical and grammatical issues must first be clarified. The Greek text of this final clause reads, ἵνα κομίσηται ἕκαστος τὰ διὰ τοῦ σώματος πρὸς ἃ ἔπραξεν, εἴτε ἀγαθὸν εἴτε φαῦλον [so that each may receive back the things done while in the body according to what each has done, whether good or evil]. In the middle voice κομίζεσθαι refers to "getting" or "receiving" something, whether wages, letters, crowns, salvation, etc.[4] In most instances this involves receiving *back* or *in return* something which one was owed or previously had. Thus Abraham receives his son back from the dead as it were (Heb. 11:19); the master expects to receive back with interest what was rightfully his own (Matt. 25:27); and Judas Maccabeus' enemy gets back a reward worthy of his impiety (2 Macc. 8:33).[5] Because this verb is used so frequently with wages, it is often translated, with or without contextual pointers to a commercial meaning, "to receive *a recompense for* what one has done."[6] N. Baumert, however, has made a convincing case against this gloss, arguing that any sense of "recompense for" must lie in the context and is not inherent in the word itself.[7] Instead, so Baumert, we have here a Hebraism, which can be found four times in the LXX as a translation of עָוֹן נָשָׂא [= to bear/take back upon oneself (one's own) sin/guilt].[8]

Unfortunately, Baumert gives no serious attention to the concept of organic consequences wherein a deed and its results are intimately tied together. The idea of "taking back one's sins upon oneself" is embedded in this broader way of thinking about deeds

---

[4] References in BAGD, art. κομίζω.

[5] MM argue for this meaning ("receive back, recover") in all NT occurrences (354). See also LSJ, 976 (#8); J. P. Louw and E. A. Nida (eds.), *Greek-English Lexicon of the New Testament Based on Semantic Domains* (2 vols.; New York: UBS, 1988) I.572–573.

[6] BAGD, 442–443.

[7] *Täglich Sterben und Auferstehen: Der Literalsinn von 2 Kor. 4,12–5,10* (SANT 34; Munich: Kösel, 1973), 410–431.

[8] The phrase (κομίζεσθαι ἁμαρτίαν) is found in Lev. 20:17; Ezek. 16:52, 54, 58. Baumert is, however, wrong to isolate the concept of "bearing one's sin (or guilt)" from that of punishment or recompense. This can be seen clearly in Lev. 20:17–21, where "to bear/receive back one's sin" functions as part of the explanation for punishment.

and consequences and provides the clue to the origin of Paul's phrase.⁹ Just as sinners can receive back and bear their own sins, so God can return to them [הֵשִׁיב/שִׁלֵּם] their sins, or their righteous deeds, a concept which found widespread application in the recompense motif.¹⁰ Thus to "receive back one's deed" means "to suffer/ enjoy the consequences." Although κομίζεσθαι is not used for bearing/receiving back one's *good* deeds in the LXX, it is not difficult to construe a development in this direction so that not only sin but also "good" (Eph. 6:8), "good and bad" (2 Cor. 5:10), and even "salvation" (1 Pet. 1:9) can be "received back." This is nothing other than viewing divine recompense ("*God returns* one's good deeds") from the human side ("*we receive back* the good deeds"). As noted previously, the use of this verb in the recompense motif predates Paul.¹¹ Thus whether or not Paul still thought in terms of OT organic consequences, the phrase should be translated "receive back (one's deeds)," and is an especially vivid way of expressing divine recompense according to works.¹²

The phrase τὰ διὰ τοῦ σώματος πρὸς ἃ ἔπραξεν seems to contain a repetition of the object, which led a few later scribes to emend to ἃ διὰ τοῦ σώματος ἔπραξεν [the things he did through the body], thus easing the apparent redundancy.¹³ Actually, however, there is no duplication of the object. Πρός + accus. is not a second object of κομίζεσθαι, but another way of saying "according to" (classical), and thus corresponds to κατά in other motif occurrences.¹⁴ The object of the verb is to be found only in the first phrase, but its meaning depends on how one takes διά¹⁵ + genitive. If

⁹ K. Koch, "Vergeltungsdogma," 1–37. See pp. 26–28 above.
¹⁰ 1 Sam. 25:39; 1 Kgs. 2:44; 8:32; 2 Chr. 6:23; Ezek. 7:3, 4, 8, 9; Hos. 4:9.
¹¹ 1 En. 100:7; cf. p. 72 above. See also the discussion of μισθὸν λαμβάνειν in 1 Cor. 3:8b (pp. 211–213).
¹² See also Col. 3:25; Eph. 6:8; further Heb. 10:35–36; 11:13, 39; 1 Pet. 5:4; 2 Pet. 2:13 v.l.; Barn. 4:12; 2 Clem. 11:5–6; Ign. *Pol.* 6:2. Thus it will hardly do to appeal to 1 Cor. 3:14–15 and interpret κομίζεσθαι at 2 Cor. 5:10 as Hoyt does: "An unfaithful Christian receives the appropriate recompense for that which is worthless, namely, no recompense at all" ("The Negative Aspects of the Christian's Judgment," *BSac* 137 [1980], 128). Receiving (back) one's (evil) deeds has negative consequences in view, not simply the absence of positive rewards. See, for instance, the similarly worded LAB 44:10 ("whatever we ourselves have devised, *these will we receive*").
¹³ The difficulty of these earlier scribes is reflected in modern translations. The NRSV's "what has been done in the body" looks very much like the smoother variant.
¹⁴ BDF 239(8); Turner, *Syntax*, 274. Cf. 1 Cor. 12:7; Luke 12:47. See also 1 En. 100:7, κομιεῖσθε κατὰ τὰ ἔργα ὑμῶν.
¹⁵ An early variant reads τὰ ἴδια τοῦ σώματος (p⁴⁶, *et al.*; "one's own things of the body"), but it seems intrinsically more likely that scribes would emend the difficult

instrumental, it will refer to "the things done through (or by) the body."[16] If temporal, it will refer to "the things done while in the body."[17] One's decision will not have a major impact on the sense. In either case it is human deeds which are meant. However, the temporal meaning has the advantage of alleviating somewhat the stark redundancy inherent in "to receive the things through the body according to what each has done." Taken temporally, the first phrase states that the recompense has reference only to deeds done during this present bodily existence, while the second phrase states the standard of that recompense.

With this stress on deeds done during bodily existence, Paul concludes the line of thought developed in verses 6–9; namely, even though we are currently in the body and thus away from the Lord, it is our aim to please him. He also highlights thereby the eschatological importance of what one does during this present bodily existence away from the Lord. Synofzik is probably correct that the awkwardness of the construction can be explained best by assuming that τὰ διὰ τοῦ σώματος is Paul's own addition to a largely traditional judgment saying, added in order to stress the importance of somatic existence.[18]

As for ἔπραξεν, it overlaps in meaning with ποιεῖν.[19] If one is inclined to see significance here in Paul's choice of the former, perhaps πράσσειν tends to stress the activity itself (= to practice or conduct oneself) more than the product of such activity.[20] Thus Romans 2:25 speaks of "practicing the law," and 4 Maccabees 3:20 can characterize a righteous life as καλῶς πράττειν [to conduct oneself well]. If such a nuance may be assumed here, then Paul is not thinking so much of individual deeds, but of one's life-pattern as a whole. This may also be confirmed by Paul's switch from plural to singular in the following phrase,[21] and would certainly be

τὰ διὰ to τὰ ἴδια than vice versa (contra P. E. Hughes, *The Second Epistle to the Corinthians* [NICNT; Grand Rapids: Eerdmans, 1962], 181, n. 57).

[16] So H. A. W. Meyer (*Critical and Exegetical Handbook to the Epistles to the Corinthians, Vol II (First Epistle, chapters 14–16; Second Epistle)* [trans. D. Hunter (2 Cor. only); MeyerK; Edinburgh: T. & T. Clark, 1879], 271), and the majority of commentators.

[17] So Augustine, *De Civitate Dei*, 17,4; see also R. Bultmann, *The Second Letter to the Corinthians* (trans. R. A. Harrisville; Minneapolis: Augsburg, 1985), 144.

[18] *Die Gerichts- und Vergeltungsaussagen*, 75–76.

[19] See Rom. 2:14, 25; 13:4.

[20] See C. Maurer, art. πράσσω, *TDNT*, VI.632–638.

[21] "The change to the neuter singular [ἀγαθόν/φαῦλον] is significant. It seems to imply that, although persons will be judged one by one and not in groups, yet

supported by the unitary way works were viewed in the motif in Jewish texts.

Finally, εἴτε ἀγαθὸν εἴτε φαῦλον will refer most naturally to πρὸς ἃ ἔπραξεν which immediately precedes it, rather than modifying the more distant κομίσηται ("to receive ... good or evil"). Thus this recompense envisions a dual outcome depending upon whether "the things one has done" are good or bad. It is unlikely that Paul's use of φαῦλος instead of the more usual κακός (cf. Rom. 2:6–10) is anything other than synonymous.[22] He uses this adjective only one other time in the undisputed letters. There it refers to Jacob and Esau who had not yet done anything "good or bad" in order that God's purpose of election might be according to his choice rather than by works (Rom. 9:11). The contrast of ἀγαθός/φαῦλος, like ἀγαθός/κακός, describes the two opposite possibilities for behavior which would characterize a person as either good or bad, i.e., either righteous or unrighteous.[23]

Thus one finds a vivid expression of the traditional recompense motif ("so that each may receive back according to his/her conduct, whether good or evil"), made somewhat awkward by the temporal qualifier ("the things [done] while in the body") added by Paul in order to lay stress on the critical importance of pleasing God in this life (verse 9). As observed elsewhere in Paul's letters, the apostle can take up this fundamental axiom of God's dealing with humanity, shaping its wording and function to suit the particular needs of his argument.

A number of important questions remain, but owing to the typical brevity of Paul's judgment statements they are difficult to answer with certainty. Who are "all of us" in this judgment statement? Throughout 4:16–5:10 Paul has spoken in the first person plural, and in 5:10 adds πάντας [*all* of us]. The use of "we" has been characteristic of the epistle since 2:14, and is generally set over against the Corinthian congregation and/or the false apostles.[24] Although the "we" in 4:16–5:10 could conceivably include Paul's closest co-workers or perhaps apostles (or believers) of the

conduct in each case will be judged as a whole. In other words, it is character rather than separate acts that will be rewarded or punished" (A. Plummer, *Second Epistle of St. Paul to the Corinthians* [ICC; Edinburgh: T. & T. Clark, 1915], 158).

[22] See N. Baumert, *Täglich Sterben und Auferstehen*, 255. Otherwise Hughes, *Second Epistle to the Corinthians*, 181. The strongly attested variant [κακόν] also points in the direction of synonymy.

[23] Cf. also, Titus 2:8; Jas. 3:13–16; John 3:19–21; 5:29.

[24] See 2:17; 3:1; 5:11–12. On the use of "we" in 2 Corinthians, see esp.

New Covenant, a literary "we" (= "I") is to be preferred. This is an apology for Paul's own apostolic ministry, not that of his co-workers nor of all apostles in general. With the addition of πάντας in verse 10, Paul expands the "we," making himself part of a larger whole.[25] He will most likely have "all Christians" primarily in mind at this point,[26] but not to the exclusion of all humanity which forms the larger conceptual backdrop.[27] In the context of Paul's personal apology, this is not meant as a warning to others, but is stated in order to place the apostle within the larger orbit of general Christian (and human) expectations, and thus to support his contention that his actions in the body are undertaken to please his unseen Lord (verse 9).

It is, of course, by no means an assured result of NT scholarship that a universal last judgment forms the backdrop of Paul's statement here. Does this recompense take place immediately after each individual's death, constantly in the present in one's con-science, or at Christ's second advent? Does this judgment issue in salvation/damnation, or in greater or lesser reward(s)?[28]

First of all, this recompense takes place before τὸ βῆμα τοῦ Χριστοῦ [the judgment seat of Christ]. In Romans 14:10, Paul spoke of the final universal judgment of all humanity in similar terms. Although there are a number of differences between these two texts,[29] the recurrence of τὸ βῆμα in this judgment statement

---

N. Baumert, *Täglich Sterben und Auferstehen*, 23–36; and K. Dick, *Der schriftstellerische Plural bei Paulus* (Halle: 1900).

[25] τοὺς πάντας ἡμᾶς = "the sum total of us," contrasting the whole with the part (Turner, *Syntax*, 201).

[26] So most commentators; e.g., R. Martin, *2 Corinthians* (WBC 40; Dallas, TX: Word, 1986), 114; V. P. Furnish, *II Corinthians* (AB 32a; New York: Doubleday, 1984), 275.

[27] See esp. Baumert, *Täglich Sterben und Auferstehen*, 47. Cf. Rom. 14:10 ("We all" = all humanity).

[28] For a vigorous defense of rewards only, not salvation, see Hughes, *Second Epistle to the Corinthians*, 181–183. He bases this largely on (i) the meaning of φαῦλος [= worthless, not wicked or evil], (ii) contradiction with justification by faith, and (iii) 1 Cor. 3:10–15 (believers' works can only determine level of reward, but not affect salvation).

[29] Thus, the fact that it is here Christ who presides in judgment rather than God (Rom. 14:10) does not indicate different judgments (p. 198), but has probably been occasioned by the thrust of Paul's argument. Paul's argument concerns the apostle's relationship to Christ, the Lord, and the fact that in spite of being away from the Lord while in the body, he still makes it his aim to please Christ; and this is then motivated finally by reference to his eschatological appearance before this same Lord Christ at the judgment.

suggests that Paul has the same scenario of universal judgment in mind.[30]

Furthermore, the stress here on the revelatory function of this judgment [φανερωθῆναι δεῖ] argues for a universal eschatological judgment. This is not simply a court "appearance" before the judgment seat (Rom. 14:10); it constitutes a "revealing,"[31] in this case, of the person ("we all must be revealed"). Precisely what is revealed is given in the latter half of verse 10, "what has been done in the body, whether good or bad," which corresponds to one's "work" (1 Cor. 3:13) and the hidden purposes of the heart that shall be made manifest (1 Cor. 4:5; also Rom. 2:16; Eph. 5:13).

Besides the traditional use of this verb for the revelatory character of final judgment, its presence here may also be related to Paul's larger concern in the epistle. His ministry has been described as the "manifestation [φανεροῦντι] of the fragrance of the knowledge of Christ" (2:14), and the Corinthians "manifest" his authenticity as an apostle by being his letter of Christ (3:3). He is particularly concerned to contrast himself with those who practice "shameful things that one hides," who "practice cunning or ... falsify God's word." Instead "by the open statement [τῇ φανερώσει] of the truth we commend ourselves to the conscience of everyone in the sight of God [ἐνώπιον τοῦ θεοῦ]" (4:2; note the same language of "in the sight of [God]"). Immediately following 5:10, Paul will note as well that the God-fearing motivation of his ministry has been manifested (i.e., known) to God, and hopes it shall have been so to the Corinthians' conscience (5:11; cf. also 11:6). Thus, the "manifestation" of Paul's godly motives and methods is a major concern of his apology, and will most likely have influenced his choice of φανερωθῆναι in the judgment context.[32]

[30] K. Prümm, DIAKONIA PNEUMATOS, *Der zweite Korintherbrief als Zugang zur apostolischen Botschaft, Auslegung und Theologie;* Vol. I: Theologische Auslegung des zweiten Korintherbriefes (Rom/Freiburg/Vienna: Herder, 1967), 306. Baumert's failure to consider the use of a judgment seat or throne for eschatological judgment scenes in second temple Judaism weakens his case against universal judgment considerably (see *Täglich Sterben und Auferstehen,* 245–249).

[31] "nonpauline t.t. for eschatological revelation" (E. Synofzik, *Die Gerichts- und Vergeltungsaussagen,* 75). Otherwise C. K. Barrett, *A Commentary on the Second Epistle to the Corinthians* (Black's NT Comm.; London: Adam & Charles Black, 1973), 160. The use of the same verb in verse 11 argues for the revelatory sense rather than that of a court appearance, and the passive "be made manifest" further differentiates this appearance from the active "appearing" of Rom. 14:10 (Baumert, *Täglich Sterben und Auferstehen,* 245).

[32] Martin, *2 Corinthians,* 77–79, 114.

In addition, the motif grounds Paul's desire to please God [εὐάρεστοι αὐτῷ εἶναι, 5:9]. Εὐάρεστος draws upon the slave-master imagery (Rom. 14:18) or perhaps sacrificial imagery (Rom. 12:1–2; Heb. 13:16); that is, a slave pleases (receives the approval of) the master, or a sacrifice is pleasing (= acceptable) to God. In Hebrews it clearly refers to that which is fundamentally acceptable to God, to God's "pleasure" with the one who is characterized by faith and persevering obedience (11:5–6; 12:28; cf. also 1 Thess. 2:15–16; Eph. 5:10). The verb εὐαρεστέω was used consistently in this sense in the LXX version of Genesis to translate הלך (Hith-pael), a term describing the righteous who "walk before God" in contrast to the wicked. "Noah was a righteous man, blameless in his generation; Noah walked with God" [LXX: τῷ θεῷ εὐη-ρέστησεν].[33] Thus this recompense will establish whether Paul has made it his aim to be pleasing to God, and refers to that fundamental acceptance by God of the person, not to varying degrees of "pleasure" on God's part.[34] It is the divine approval of one's service and way of life.[35]

Thus there are strong grounds for perceiving a universal last judgment behind Paul's statement, a perception shared by the entire patristic tradition.[36] It may be noted further: (1) Although a division between the good and the wicked immediately upon death was a prominent feature of the pseudepigraphical writings, a judgment according to deeds was only rarely associated with this post-mortem division, being instead generally reserved for the final universal judgment.[37] (2) The contrast of good/bad was found elsewhere in Paul and the NT to refer to the fundamental distinction between the righteous and the unrighteous, not degrees of righteousness among the saved (see above on κακός/φαῦλος). (3) The use of πράσσειν hints at one's whole pattern of conduct rather than individual deeds. (4) The use of similar language in Colossians

---

[33] Gen. 6:9; cf. also 5:22, 24; 17:1; 24:40; 48:15; Ps. 26:3; 56:13; 116:9; Sir. 44:16. The only occurrences of the *adjective* in the LXX are found in Wis. 4:10; 9:10. Especially in Wis. 4:10–16 the fundamental contrast between those who please God (= the righteous) and the wicked comes out most clearly.

[34] Against L. Mattern, *Das Verständnis des Gerichtes*, 156.

[35] This understanding finds confirmation in a later passage, also a self-defense of Paul's ministry, where he states: "For it is not those who commend themselves that are approved [δόκιμος], but those whom the Lord commends" (10:18). See also Exod. 21:8 (LXX). Further H. Windisch, *Der zweite Korintherbrief* (MeyerK; Göttingen: Vandenhoeck & Ruprecht, 1924), 168–169.

[36] Baumert, *Täglich Sterben und Auferstehen*, 245.

[37] See p. 91–92 above.

3:25 refers to one's eternal inheritance (= life in the age to come). (5) The preponderance of the use of the motif in Paul and second temple Judaism refers to the divine awarding of life or death based upon one's life-pattern of behavior.

Having said this, however, it is only fair to reiterate that such details do not appear to have been central to Paul's concern in citing the motif at this point; rather the bare fact that he and others must have their deeds revealed at the judgment and be recompensed accordingly is sufficient motivation to make it his aim to please the Lord. Thus although 2 Corinthians 5:10 was not intended to teach about details of judgment, it does confirm what we have discovered elsewhere; namely, that Paul expects Christians to face the universal last judgment and there be awarded eternal life or death according to their deeds.

I noted earlier that the motif functions here to defend or explain Paul's own motivation to obey the Lord.[38] The appending of "whether good or bad" indicates that it is not merely the positive encouragement of reward that motivates his behavior, but equally the threat of negative consequences. The precise nature of the motivation is picked up again in the following verse: "Therefore, knowing the fear of the Lord, we try to persuade others" (5:11) This takes up the wisdom theme of the fear of God and uses it in combination with the recompense motif in much the same way as we observed in Ecclesiastes 12:13–14: "The end of the matter; all has been heard. Fear God, and keep his commandments; for that is the whole duty of everyone. For God will bring every deed into judgment, including every secret thing, whether good [ἀγαθόν] or evil [πονηρόν]."[39] The fear of God is not simply terror in the face of God's awful holiness and punishing vengeance, but more broadly the awesome recognition that one's entire life (including supposedly unseen thoughts and actions) is open to God who will deal with one according to deeds.[40] It thus includes both hope of reward and fear of punishment, as it does in both Ecclesiastes 12:13–14 and 2 Corinthians 5:10–11. Paul's use corresponds

---

[38] C. Roetzel thinks Paul is primarily concerned in this text to turn back community judgment (*Judgement in the Community*, 173–175). While this may well be part of Paul's larger concern in the epistle (cf. 6:11–13; 7:2a), the motif functions in this context less to *deny others the right to judge* than to *explain or prove the apostle's own motivation* (cf. verse 9).

[39] See pp. 40–41 above.

[40] See G. A. Lee, art. "Fear," *ISBE* (rev. ed.; 4 vols.; gen. ed. G. W. Bromiley; Grand Rapids, MI: Eerdmans, 1982), 189–192.

closely to what was observed for the motivation-texts in the Jewish Scriptures.

> [The motif] envisions the recompense as undefined sufferings or blessings... It is the *certainty* rather than the precise nature of the reward/punishment which is felt to motivate. There is clearly a *dual recompense* envisioned in these texts (i.e., both reward and punishment), functioning to encourage the righteous to persevere in doing good, and to warn the presumptuous against laxity in obedience. As elsewhere, especially in warning texts, the divine recompense is related to God's omniscience, including knowledge even of hidden deeds.[41]

Even this last element of divine omniscience and hidden deeds is implied in Paul's stress on the revelatory character of this judgment.

Finally, the explicit interplay in this particular passage between the concepts of guarantee, confidence, and faith in regard to his future on the one hand (5:5, 6–8; also 4:16–18), and the sense of fearful responsibility in the face of the coming judgment on the other (5:9–11), are a demonstration of the existential tension typically found in Paul's letters. On the other hand, the transition between verses 8 and 9 gives no indication of any *theological* tension, paradox or dialectic. Rather his faith-confidence in the unseen Lord's preparation of future blessings (verses 6–8) leads naturally into the thought of present responsibility to that same Lord and Judge ("while in the body"). He is confident that future glory is his by faith in Christ, and equally certain that such life in Christ means that all of life now must be aimed at pleasing Christ and must stand up to eschatological scrutiny before the final awarding of salvation will occur.[42] "One's life in the body [σῶμα] is decisive for salvation or damnation, for this is the sphere of περιπατεῖν διὰ πίστεως, οὐ διὰ εἴδους."[43]

---

[41] See p. 44 above.

[42] John Calvin argues from this text "that as evil deeds are punished by God, so also good deeds are rewarded, but for a different reason. Evil deeds are given the punishment they deserve, but in rewarding good deeds God does not have regard to their merit or worth" (*The Second Epistle of Paul the Apostle to the Corinthians* [trans. T. A. Smail; Calvin's Commentaries; Grand Rapids, MI: Eerdmans, 1964 (reprint of 1547 edition)], 71–72). Such a "different reason" can in no wise be drawn from this text which applies the same standard to all works, whether good or bad!

[43] E. Synofzik, *Die Gerichts- und Vergeltungsaussagen*, 77.

2 Corinthians 11:15b

Their end will match their deeds.
[ὧν τὸ τέλος ἔσται κατὰ τὰ ἔργα αὐτῶν]

However one resolves the literary-critical problems,[44] most are agreed that Paul is here engaging in a vigorous defense of his person and gospel, and simultaneously attacking false apostles who have appeared on the scene in Corinth (cf. esp. 11:4–5, 12–15). In verses 13–15 Paul's invective reaches its high point. He unmasks these rivals for those whom he believes they really are: false apostles, deceitful workers, servants of Satan disguising themselves as apostles of Christ. This unmitigated denial of their legitimacy is climaxed by the phrase under consideration.

From the use of similar brief phrases inserted at the end of invective it would appear that Paul was fond of concluding such censure by an appeal to divine judgment.[45] J. Zmijewski has pointed out that this brief concluding word of judgment is analogous to prophetic oracles of judgment. Understood in this way, verses 13–15a bring the accusation or reason for judgment, and verse 15b the sentence of judgment itself.[46]

This particular wording of the motif is not found elsewhere but gives admirable expression to the *lex talionis*, much as in Paul's sharp judgment statement in 1 Corinthians 3:17 – destruction to the destroyer. A similarly constructed judgment statement is found in Romans 3:8 – ὧν τὸ κρίμα ἔνδικόν ἐστιν.[47] The opponents' "end" refers to their "final destiny." The analogy of prophetic judgment oracles and the similar use of τέλος in the invective of Philippians 3:19 ("Their end is destruction") makes it probable that Paul has in mind God's destroying eschatological wrath as their "end."[48] This

---

[44] Chapters 10–13 are generally considered to be part of an originally separate letter since their aggressive and sarcastic tone contrasts markedly with the more conciliatory approach of the earlier chapters. See Martin, *2 Corinthians*, xxxviii–li, 298–301.

[45] See Rom. 3:8; Gal. 5:12; 1 Thess. 2:16; also 2 Tim. 4:14. See esp. Synofzik, *Die Gerichts- und Vergeltungsaussagen*, 31–38.

[46] *Der Stil der paulinischen 'Narrenrede'* (BBB 52; Cologne: Peter Hanstein, 1978), 167, n. 419. See also Westermann, *Grundformen prophetischer Rede*, esp. 57–63.

[47] Note particularly the same opening relative pronoun (ὧν) followed by the article and noun. Not only do τὸ κρίμα [condemnation] and ἔνδικον [just, deserved, based on what is right] correspond *structurally* to τὸ τέλος and κατὰ τὰ ἔργα αὐτῶν, they overlap considerably in meaning as well.

[48] See G. Delling, art. τέλος, *TDNT* VIII.55; also Heb. 6:8; 1 Pet. 4:17.

would correspond to an OT pattern, whereby a sinner's "end" is destruction at the hands of God.[49]

The use of the recompense motif with its stress on "works" may perhaps have been suggested to Paul's mind by his previous designation of these rivals as "deceitful *workers* " (verse 14). It may also be that some irony is intended, since those who "disguise themselves" (verses 13–15a) will be judged not by such appearances, but according to their deeds.

This is one of those rare instances, then, where Paul pronounces a *sentence of judgment* upon specific individuals. There is no summons to repentance; these are enemies of Paul's apostolic calling and gospel, servants of Satan, who shall assuredly face divine wrath. Just as Paul calls down a curse upon those who would preach another gospel in Galatians 1:9, so he does here with other words against those who are in fact preaching another gospel (verse 4).

The ongoing debate as to the particular theology of the opponents here need not detain us.[50] Rather, what is of importance is the fact that nearly all interpreters understand them to be some type of Jewish-*Christian* apostles. It is clear from 11:13–15 that Paul wishes to deny their legitimacy as such (just as they were denying his). However it is equally the fact that they were recognized as genuine followers and representatives of Christ by some (most?) in the early church. Paul is engaged here in a bitter struggle to determine which of two rival Christian apostolates will win out in Corinth.[51] Is Paul then pronouncing a sentence of ultimate condemnation upon other Christians? For Paul the answer will certainly have been 'No.' Regardless of others' opinions of them, for Paul these are traitors to Christ and the gospel.[52] For this reason, the text will yield little regarding the relation of judgment according to works to the justified.

---

[49] See for instance Ps. 73:17–20; also T.Asher 6:4–5 where such destiny is related to the doctrine of the Two Ways (1:3–9); and Philo, *Virtue*, 182.

[50] On the various theories, see esp. J. L. Sumney, *Identifying Paul's Opponents: The Question of Method in 2 Corinthians* (JSNTSup 40; Sheffield: JSOT, 1990), 15–73.

[51] See E. Käsemann, "Die Legitimität des Apostels: Eine Untersuchung zu II Korinther 10–13," *ZNW* 41 (1942), 33–71; C. K. Barrett, "Paul's Opponents in 2 Corinthians," in *Essays on Paul* [Philadelphia: Westminster, 1982], 60–86.

[52] See esp. C. K. Barrett, "ΨΕΥΔΑΠΟΣΤΟΛΟΙ (2 Cor. 11.13)," in *Essays On Paul*, 87–107.

Colossians: introduction

The majority opinion of current scholarship rejects the letter's claim to be from Paul (1:1; 4:18),[53] but there remain troubling doubts about the conclusiveness of the evidence brought against authenticity.[54] Language and style, while different, do not call for another author,[55] particularly in light of the probable use of a secretary in writing the letter (4:18).[56] The theology of such a small piece of literature – not easily discerned even in a more substantial piece – seems Pauline enough to many,[57] and sounds much like the apostle when placed alongside Philemon.[58] Thus, the letter will be treated here as from Paul.

[53] Thus, Hans Hübner can simply make reference to the "assured non-Pauline authorship" of the letter (*An Philemon, An die Kolosser, An die Epheser* [HNT 12; Tübingen: Mohr Siebeck, 1997], 10).

[54] See, for instance, J. Lähnemann, *Der Kolosserbrief: Komposition, Situation und Argumentation* (SNT 3; Gütersloh: Gerd Mohn, 1971). See also the commentaries of Bruce, Dibelius-Greeven, Moule, Michaelis, Merk, and Kuss.

[55] The major stylistic arguments against Pauline authorship can be found in W. Bujard, *Stilanalytische Untersuchungen zum Kolosserbrief als Beitrag zur Methodik von Sprachvergleichen* (Göttingen: Vandenhoeck & Ruprecht, 1973). More recently K. Neumann (*The Authenticity of the Pauline Epistles in the Light of Stylostatistical Analysis* [SBLDS 120; Atlanta: Scholars Press, 1990]) has sought to refine further such stylostatistical analysis, and has come to opposite conclusions. In particular, Bujard's "procedure is limited to the Pauline corpus and does not allow him to test if the differences of Colossians from the rest of Paul are *real* differences [i.e., demonstrating a different author] or insignificant differences. The results of testing various indices by discrimination analysis suggest the differences are insignificant, i.e., the variation is about as great within Paul as it is between Paul and other authors" (214; also 10–13). For further critique of Bujard's "ganzheitliche Betrachtungsweise" [holistic perspective], cf. reviews by G. D. Kilpatrick, *NovT* 20 (1978), 334–336; and R. Kieffer, *TZBa* 31 (1975), 44–45.

[56] See E. R. Richards, *The Secretary in the Letters of Paul* (Tübingen: J. C. B. Mohr, 1991); T. J. Sappington, *Revelation and Redemption at Colossae* (JSNTSup 53; Sheffield: Sheffield Academic Press, 1991), esp. 22–24; and R. N. Longenecker, "Ancient Amanuenses and the Pauline Epistles," in *New Dimensions in New Testament Study* (eds. R. N. Longenecker and M. C. Tenney; Grand Rapids: Zondervan, 1974), 281–297.

[57] See, for instance, G. F. Wessels, "The Eschatology of Colossians and Ephesians" (*Neot* 21 [1987], 186–187); and Sappington, *Revelation and Redemption*, 226–227. For the view that the Colossians theology is too different to be from Paul, see H. E. Lona, *Die Eschatologie im Kolosser- und Epheserbrief* (FB 48; Würzburg: Echter, 1984).

[58] Cf. W. G. Kümmel, *Einleitung in das Neue Testament* (18th edn.; Heidelberg: Quelle & Meyer, 1973), 303–304.

Colossians 3:22–25

(22) Slaves, obey your earthly masters in everything, not only while being watched and in order to please them, but wholeheartedly, fearing the Lord. (23) Whatever your task, put yourselves into it, as done for the Lord and not for your masters, (24) since you know that from the Lord you will receive the inheritance as your reward; you serve the Lord Christ [or: Serve the Lord Christ].[59] (25) For the wrongdoer will be paid back for whatever wrong has been done, and there is no partiality.

This earliest extant Christian *Haustafel* (3:18–4:1) forms a distinct subunit within the letter. A glance at the structure of this unit reveals the disparate emphasis given to the duty of slaves.[60] In the Nestle-Aland Greek text the admonitions to wives, husbands, children and parents take 1½ lines of text each, and to masters 2½ lines, while that addressed to slaves occupies 8½ lines. Each of the paired admonitions consists of a command and a reason (or motivation), and involves a 'weaker' and a 'stronger' partner. The command to the weaker partner in each pair consists of "obedience/submission," but to the slaves this is expanded to 4 lines of Greek text, with each of the phrases in verses 22–23 expanding on the precise nature of this obedience. Likewise the motivation addressed to slaves (verses 24–25) is remarkable for its length and detail.[61]

This is all the more remarkable since research into the development of such household codes has not demonstrated a comparable disproportionate stress on slaves' duties elsewhere, whether in Greek or Hellenistic Jewish sources. In spite of the NT codes' obvious debt to these earlier traditions, the specific Christian form of such codes is now generally attributed to factors within early

---

[59] See note 67 below.

[60] See esp. M. Gielen, *Tradition und Theologie neutestamentlicher Haustafelethik: Ein Beitrag zur Frage einer christlichen Auseinandersetzung mit gesellschaftlichen Normen* (BBB 75; Frankfurt: Anton Hain, 1990), 108–115.

[61] In general the motivational element is more clearly expressed toward the 'weaker' members, where it is consistently christological and/or eschatological. To the 'stronger' this can either be replaced by a reformulation of the command in its negative form (see verse 19), or refer to undesirable natural consequences (see verse 21). Only with reference to masters (4:1) does Paul feel the necessity of a clearly christological/eschatological motivation, perhaps due to the novelty of the relation to a slave/brother (cf. Philemon).

Christianity itself.[62] Thus a number of different causes within the early church have been suggested by scholars as having led to the development of these distinctively Christian codes, and in particular to the disproportionate attention devoted to the duties of slaves.[63] These include, (1) a connection with Onesimus' return to his master, Philemon; (2) the need for such traditional ethical teaching in light of waning expectation of the parousia; and (3) the need to counteract enthusiastic or emancipatory tendencies among slaves and women, possibly occasioned by Paul's own teaching.[64] In addition to the above suggestions, Robert Nash notes that elsewhere in the epistle Paul and his co-workers are portrayed as *servants* in God's household (1:7, 23, 25; 4:7, 9, 13). The instruction to slaves, he suggests, could then function as an *exemplum* of the sort of behavior seen in Paul and expected of all Christians, and thus deserving of more extended treatment.[65]

Slaves are instructed to be obedient "in everything," not superficially but "wholeheartedly." This seemingly conservative ethic is built upon a revolutionary foundation. The earthly master is now qualified as ὁ κατὰ σάρκα κύριος (3:22) who is also subject to the same κύριος ἐν οὐρανῷ (4:1). The slaves' true master is Christ (3:24b), which, far from releasing them from earthly service, commits them to sincere and wholehearted obedience. Already in the terms used to describe this obedience, its fundamental connection to one's relationship to Christ is hinted at.

This obedience is then motivated or reinforced in verses 24–25 by reference to the already known fact of Christ's eschatological

[62] See the helpful summaries of the current state of research provided by G. Strecker ("Die neutestamentlichen Haustafeln (Kol. 3,18–4,1 und Eph. 5,22–6,9)," *Neues Testament und Ethik, für Rudolf Schnackenburg* [Freiburg/Basel/Vienna: Herder, 1989], 349–375, esp. 357–359) and Gielen (*Tradition und Theologie*, 24–67). See also J. E. Crouch, *The Origin and Intention of the Colossian Haustafel* (FRLANT 109; Göttingen: Vandenhoeck & Ruprecht, 1972), 9–31.

[63] Note similar instructions to slaves Eph. 6:5–8; 1 Pet. 2:18–25; also 1 Cor. 7:21–24.

[64] While much can be said for this last explanation (cf. 1 Cor. 7:21–24; Gal. 3:28; Philem. 16; Col. 3:11), there does not appear to be sufficient evidence of such a 'revolutionary' movement among Christian slaves in the first century CE. See S. Bartchy, *MALLON CHRESAI. First Century Slavery and the Interpretation of 1 Corinthians 7:21* (SBLDS 11; Missoula: Scholars Press, 1973); and T. Wiedemann, *Greek and Roman Slavery* (Baltimore: Johns Hopkins University, 1981), 188–223.

[65] "Heuristic Haustafeln: Domestic Codes as Entrance to the Social World of Early Christianity. The Case of Colossians," in *Religious Writings and Religious Systems, II* (eds. J. Neusner, *et al.*, Brown Studies in Religion 2; Atlanta: Scholars Press, 1989) 25–50, esp. p. 44.

rewarding of his servants.[66] The future verbs (ἀπολήμψεσθε, κομίσεται), the content of the recompense ("the inheritance"), and the fact that it will be given by the *heavenly* κύριος in contrast to one's *earthly* master, all point to an eschatological repayment. Both the reward and the rewarder are important as motivational factors in this context. The fact that this rewarding is "from the Lord" [ἀπὸ κυρίου, note the emphatic position] should motivate the kind of obedience [ὡς τῷ κυρίῳ] described in verses 22–23, particularly since slaves could expect no such inheritance as a reward from their earthly masters. This emphasis on the christological basis of obedience is confirmed by the immediately following τῷ κυρίῳ Χριστῷ δουλεύετε.[67] Thus, Christian slaves should obey "as working for the Lord, not for men" (NIV), because it is from the Lord and not from human masters that they expect this inheritance.

Verses 24–25a contain a dual recompense, something already seen elsewhere in Paul's letters. In this instance, however, rather than a single statement referring to a dual recompense, there are two separate motif statements, one strictly positive, the other strictly negative. In both instances, the *function* is the same: to motivate the righteous to obedience. The statement of positive reward (verse 24) grounds the commands to obey and to work (verses 22–23), while the warning of punishment (verse 25) grounds the command to serve (verse 24b). The contrast in forms of address is both instructive and characteristic. The promise of reward takes the form of direct address to the listeners ("you will receive"), since the speaker assumes they belong to the group of those who thus behave and shall receive. The warning, on the other hand, uses the more oblique third person singular ("the wrongdoer will be paid back"), and only applies to the listeners *if* their behavior should

[66] This christological/eschatological motivation is not new with verse 24; cf. "fearing the Lord" (verse 22b), "work as unto the Lord" (verse 23b), which has led some to see verse 24 (εἰδότες ὅτι) as merely a continuation of the imperative. However, comparison with 4:1b (εἰδότες ὅτι) confirms that with verse 24 the motivational element of this form properly begins (so Gnilka; Lähnemann). See Eph. 6:8, 9; and Synofzik, *Die Gerichts- und Vergeltungsaussagen*, 138.

[67] This remains true whether one takes δουλεύετε as an indicative (NRSV) or imperative. Commentators and translations are divided, but the imperative is preferable, since the asyndetic connection to verse 24a reads more easily as a reiteration of the command in verse 23 than as a continuation of verse 24a. This also gives a better connection to verse 25, since otherwise the γάρ of that verse would have to refer back to the imperative in verse 23. The Byzantine addition of γάρ to verse 24b favors the indicative, but is textually inferior.

identify them as belonging to those who are disobedient and unrighteous [ὁ ἀδικῶν].

Most aspects of the wording of these two motif statements have already been covered elsewhere. Thus "you will receive ... reward" [ἀπολήμψεσθε τὴν ἀνταπόδοσιν] is synonymous with "receive reward" [μισθὸν λήμψεσθαι] in 1 Corinthians 3:8b and 14b.[68] Originally a commercial term "for receiving one's pay,"[69] ἀπολαμβάνω came to be associated in Christian literature with eschatological reward.[70] The reward itself [τὴν ἀνταπόδοσιν, NT hapax],[71] is the positive divine "repayment" which the Lord will give his servants for their work. In the LXX the use of both the verbal and nominal forms of δίδωμι and its compounds was found to be quite prevalent in motif occurrences.[72] The content of this reward is nothing other than eschatological salvation [κληρονομία].[73] Paul has already referred to "the inheritance [κλῆρος] of the saints" (1:12), which is equivalent to "the hope laid up for you in heaven" (1:5) and the "life ... hidden with Christ in God" (3:3), and now takes up this term which is elsewhere widely attested in its meaning "salvation as the inheritance of God's children."[74] As Gnilka notes, both these terms stand in starkest contrast to the earthly situation of slaves: here they had neither an inheritance nor any claim to repayment for service.[75] While already qualified to take part in the inheritance of the saints (1:12), Christian slaves have yet to receive this inheritance, conditioned as that is upon steadfast continuance in the faith (1:23) and its concomitant, sanctification (1:22). The absence of an explicit reference to "works" is of little concern. That

[68] See pp. 210–212 above.
[69] Cf. BAGD, 94; Rom. 1:27.
[70] See Luke (16:25); 18:30 (v.l.); 2 John 8. Patristic sources refer to "receiving" the promise, eternal life, the future age, etc. (references in BAGD, 94). Gal. 4:5 speaks of "receiving the adoption as children," which is, however, an eschatological gift received already by faith.
[71] This older form ending in -σις later yielded to the equivalent ἀνταπόδομα (BDF, §109.2,4) which is found in Luke 14:12 and Rom. 11:9 (punishment as mostly in LXX). Positive "repayment" is found in Rom. 11:35.
[72] See pp. 22–23 above.
[73] Lit. "the reward of the inheritance," and best taken as a genitive of content (= the repayment consisting of the inheritance); cf. BDF, §167. See also 2 Cor. 5:5 (τὸν ἀρραβῶνα τοῦ πνεύματος) for a similar genitive of content. Thus the NRSV is quite correct to make "inheritance" the object of the verb ("you will receive the inheritance as your reward").
[74] Cf. Gal. 3:18; Eph. 1:14,18; 5:5; Heb. 9:15; Acts 20:32; 1 Pet. 1:4. For the rich OT and Jewish background with the same meaning, see J. Eichler, *NIDNTT*, II.295–303.
[75] *Der Kolosserbrief* (HTKNT 10/1; Freiburg/Basel/Vienna: Herder, 1980), 222.

such are in view is clear enough from the immediate context;[76] and the use of nouns of "repayment" as the object of the verb in the motif can make a reference to "works" superfluous.[77] This absence and the initial "from the Lord" combine to shift attention away from the correspondence between deed and reward, and toward the one who rewards and the certainty of his repayment.

If Paul perhaps showed some hesitation in Romans in applying terms such as "wage" [μισθός, 4:4] and "pay" [ὀψώνιον, 6:23] to the realm of salvation by grace, here he clearly utilizes the commercial language of "receiving repayment" for the reception of the Christians' inheritance. The Romans passages just noted show well enough that Paul was sensitive to potential abuses of recompense concepts in the direction of merit theology (also Rom. 11:35). However, a text like Colossians 3:24–25 shows equally well that recompense terminology did not automatically bring merit theology to Paul's mind.[78] The history of the motif in second temple Jewish literature certainly yielded little evidence of a tendency toward a supposed merit theology.[79]

The negative counterpoint to this promise of reward is found in the threat of judgment in verse 25. The wording here reads literally: "the one who does wrong will receive what he/she has done wrong" [ὁ ἀδικῶν κομίσεται ὃ ἠδίκησεν], and has verbal similarities to the motif expression in 2 Corinthians 5:10. As determined in my discussion of this last-named text, this formulation is reminiscent of the OT concept of a person's deeds returning upon one's head.[80] Unlike the dual thrust of 2 Corinthians 5:10 ("whether good or bad") Colossians 3:25 speaks only of the wrongdoers receiving back their unrighteous deeds. The nature of this wrongdoing [ἀδικεῖν] is not specified.

Some interpreters can perceive no direct application to slaves in verse 25, and thus understand it as addressed to both slaves and masters, but primarily warning masters against "mistreating" their

---

[76] Ἐργάζεσθε (verse 23); ὃ ἠδίκησεν (verse 25).

[77] See LXX Ps. 27:4d; 93:2b; Isa. 59:18; 66:6b; Jer. 28:6b (= MT 51:6b); Lam. 3:64; Joel 4:4, 7; Sir. 17:23.

[78] See also my discussion of Rom. 2:6–11; 1 Cor. 3:5–17; 9:24–27 (salvation as a prize to be won by endurance); cf. also Phil. 3:14.

[79] Failure to note this fact leads a commentator like Hans Hübner to call Col. 3:25 "nothing but works-righteousness [*Werkgerechtigkeit in Reinkultur*]" (*An Philemon*, 113).

[80] See pp. 262–263 above. Some think this is another sentence of holy law (Gnilka, *Kolosserbrief*, 223).

slaves (cf. Eph. 6:9).[81] Structurally, however, the admonition to masters begins only at 4:1, while verse 25 is clearly meant to be a continuation of the admonition to slaves.[82] The immediate context suggests that the failure to obey one's master "in everything," "wholeheartedly," "as done for the Lord," constitutes this ἀδικεῖν. Was there, perhaps, a temptation for slaves to do wrong under pressure of mistreatment (1 Pet. 2:18–25)? Whatever the social-historical occasion, Paul's choice of this verb will have been influenced primarily by the thought of wrongdoing against one's true master, Christ (verse 24b). Refusal to obey one's earthly master is in fact wrongdoing against Christ.[83] It is also possible, as in Revelation 22:11, that the use of ὁ ἀδικῶν stems from Jewish or early Christian hortatory tradition in which "the wrongdoer" = the sinner, the ungodly.[84]

Thus Paul concludes his exhortation to obedience by a warning of God's impartial recompense of deeds upon wrongdoers. Christian slaves who resist obedience to Christ (= submission to earthly masters) are in danger of falling under the condemnation of the unrighteous, thus providing the contrasting parallel to the positive eschatological statement in verse 24. The similarity with 2 Corinthians 5:10, which likewise speaks of eschatological judgment upon the doers of good or evil, supports this understanding.

The associated reference to divine impartiality (verse 25b) has been found in other motif occurrences, and supports the contention that God's judgment is here in view.[85] In this instance its inclusion may also reflect a tendency on the part of Christian slaves to excuse disobedience on the basis of extenuating circumstances such as the limitations of a slave's position or the new relation to the master as brother or sister. In any case Christian slaves should be obedient and not wrongdoers, both because Christ is their true master, and because their recompense (both as eschatological reward and as punishment) is tied to this behavior.

The possible reasons for an expanded *admonition* to slaves in Christian household codes were discussed above. A similar question

[81] See Ralph P. Martin, *Colossians and Philemon* (NCB; Grand Rapids: Eerdmans, 1981), 123–124. This interpretation can appeal to the common usage of ἀδικεῖν for mistreatment of others.

[82] M. Gielen, *Haustafelethik*, 195–198.

[83] Ibid., 192–193.

[84] E. Lohmeyer, *Die Offenbarung des Johannes* (HNT 16; Tübingen: J. C. B. Mohr (Paul Siebeck), 1926), 176.

[85] See Rom. 2:6–11; Eph. 6:8–9; further references on p. 156, n. 41.

may be posed in regard to the expanded *eschatological motivation* for slaves' obedience. Comparison with other NT and post-apostolic household codes does not support the idea that an eschatological reward as motivation was a traditional element in this particular form of ethical instruction to slaves. Since this eschatological expansion cannot be adequately explained via adoption of a pre-Christian tradition, several other influences may help to explain its presence in Colossians 3:22–25. (1) In popular Greek ethical teaching, "some discussions of household management recommended motivating slaves by holding out various rewards, for example, more praise, more food, better clothing, and shoes."[86] (2) The servant-master analogy itself suggested quite naturally issues of reward and punishment, which for Paul meant normally eschatological reward and punishment.[87] (3) In general, eschatological motivation is of central importance in Paul's ethical teaching.[88]

It remains now to mention briefly several additional texts in Colossians which contain possible reference to the future judgment of believers.[89]

Colossians 1:22–23a, 28

> (22) he has now reconciled [you] in his fleshly body through death, so as to present you holy and blameless and irreproachable before him (23) provided that you continue securely established and steadfast in the faith... (28) It is he whom we proclaim, warning everyone and teaching everyone in all wisdom, so that we may present everyone mature in Christ.

Although "holy" [ἅγιος] and "blameless" [ἄμωμος] are cultic-

---

[86] A. Lincoln, *Ephesians* (WBC 42; Dallas, TX: Word, 1990), 422 (citing Xenophon, *Oeconomicus* 13.9–12). Also Gielen, *Tradition und Theologie*, 162–166.

[87] See Rom. 6:23; 14:1–12; 1 Cor. 3:5–15; 4:1–5; 9:15–27.

[88] D. A. Low, *Apocalyptic Motivation in Pauline Paraenesis* (unpub. diss.; The Southern Baptist Theological Seminary, 1988), esp. 6 and 24.

[89] Although some translations refer to the loss of one's heavenly "prize" in Col. 2:18 ("Do not let anyone ... disqualify you for the prize," NIV; "beguile you of your reward," KJV), the verb in question [καταβραβεύω] means simply to "victimize, mistreat, bring under accusation" or "disadvantage" someone (so NRSV, RSV, NEB, JB). In context this warns the hearers against losing their freedom in Christ by submitting to the judgments of visionary false teachers ("do not let anyone condemn you," 2:16a). See F. Field, *Notes on the Translation of the New Testament* (Cambridge: Cambridge University Press, 1899), 196–197.

sacrificial terms describing an unblemished animal set apart for God, they here seem to be pressed into the service of a judicial scene. "Irreproachable" [ἀνέγκλητος] describes those against whom no charge or accusation can be pressed when they are "presented" before the court.[90] This goal of the reconciliation via Christ's death is clearly conditioned upon continuance in the faith.[91]

Thus, just as the result of their former alienation from God was "evil deeds" (1:21), so now, in total contrast, the aim of reconciliation is that believers be irreproachable at the judgment seat of God. This is likewise the aim of Paul's ministry (verse 28), using now the concept of "maturity/perfection" [τέλειος]. While an ethical component is unmistakable in this word, it does not imply sinless moral perfection.[92] Rather its focus is on "wholeness," "completeness" or "maturity" in line with Jewish and Hellenistic parallels, and "he is 'perfect' who inwardly and in the manifestation of his life has appropriated the content of the Christian faith in the right way."[93] That Paul views this as taking place at the eschatological judgment is indicated again by the verb "that we may present" [παραστήσωμεν], and suggested by the preceding reference to "Christ in you, the hope of glory." Hence, this text would seem to testify to Paul's expectation that believers will meet the requirements of a coming judgment according to works.

Colossians 3:6

On account of these the wrath of God is coming [on those who are disobedient].[94]

---

[90] Although παραστῆσαι can be used for presenting a sacrifice, this meaning is excluded by ἀνέγκλητος. The judicial usage is common: 1 Cor. 8:8; 2 Cor. 4:14; 11:2; Rom. 14:10; 2 Tim. 2:15. See further, W. Grundmann, *TDNT* I.356.

[91] Εἰ γε = if indeed.

[92] "One does not find in the NT any understanding of the adjective in terms of a gradual advance of the Christian to moral perfection nor in terms of a two-graded ideal of ethical perfection" (G. Delling, *TDNT* VIII.77).

[93] H. Ridderbos, *Paul: An Outline of His Theology* (trans. J. R. DeWitt; Grand Rapids: Eerdmans, 1975), 271. See also P. J. Du Plessis, *Teleios. The Idea of Perfection in the New Testament* (Kampen: J. H. Kok, 1959); and H. K. La Rondelle, *Perfection and Perfectionism: A Dogmatic-ethical Study of Biblical Perfection and Phenomenal Perfectionism* (Andrews University Monographs 3; Berrien Springs, MI: Andrews University Press, 1971).

[94] The bracketed phrase is textually suspect (B. Metzger, *Textual Commentary*, 624–625).

The coming divine wrath is directed against practices associated with "whatever in you is earthly" (3:5), such as sexual immorality, greed and idolatry. These are practices which characterized the "old self" (3:9), and which once characterized believers (3:7), but should do so no longer (3:3, 8–10). Although believers have died to such things in Christ (3:3), they are still required to put them to death and to rid themselves of such evil behavior, instead putting on the new self, which is being renewed in knowledge in the image of its Creator (3:5, 10). There may be an implied warning should believers fail to heed this admonition, but if so it is left non-explicit.

7

PAUL AND A JEWISH MOTIF: CONCLUSIONS

My aim in this concluding chapter is two-fold: to summarize the key findings regarding the character and use of the motif in second temple Judaism and in Paul, and to explore briefly the ramifications of this study for the perennial issue of judgment and justification in Paul. While the first aim derives directly from the analysis of the motif-texts in the previous chapters, the second remains more tentative, since it must rest on a text-basis much broader than those passages containing the motif.

In Judaism the motif is surprisingly widespread. It possesses the character of a fundamental theological axiom which does not appear to have been tied to any single OT text or texts and could be applied to a wide variety of rhetorical situations. This increases the probability that NT authors, when employing the motif of divine judgment (or recompense) according to deeds, are not citing or alluding to specific Scripture passages, but are drawing upon this common body of fundamental theological conviction.

Although certain authors may have preferred particular modes of expression, the literature as a whole evinces no formulaic rigidity. What most likely began as divine *recompense* of (or according to) deeds, with closer affinity to organic and talionic conceptions, evolved into divine *judgment* according to deeds, and in later texts was almost always conceived as a part of the larger topic of divine judgment. The range of terminological possibilities remains large throughout the period studied. I have suggested certain semantic criteria by which to identify the motif, a task to which little attention has been given in previous studies; but it must still be admitted that the boundaries between this motif and related concepts such as the *lex talionis*, organic consequences, or blood-guilt, remain fluid.

The functional typology has proven useful, pointing up both continuity and development in the rhetorical use of the motif. The chief functions in Judaism are:

- to motivate the righteous to obedience (through both threat and promise),
- to comfort godly sufferers,
- to pronounce sentence upon the disobedient and summon the wayward to repentance, and
- to praise God and justify his actions toward humanity.

The use as an appeal to God to intervene on behalf of the righteous (either to bless them according to their righteousness or punish their enemies according to their wickedness) was strongly present in the Jewish Scriptures, but nearly absent thereafter. This probably has a theological explanation, since such appeals were not infrequently based upon the supplicant's righteousness.[1] Later writings tend to stress human inability and sinfulness and attribute all blessings to God's gracious initiative, thus making an appeal to one's own righteousness in this context seem somewhat out of place.

The increasing fragmentation in second temple Judaism led to two further developments in the use of the motif. Although present to some degree in the OT prophets, the use of the motif to distinguish between true and false Jews gains considerably in prominence. Completely new is the use as a theological warrant against intra-community judgment. Both of these developments will leave their mark on the NT.

Considerable attention was given in part one to tracing the continuity and development in the understanding of the motif within the larger pattern of soteriology found in the Jewish documents. In particular, two conceptual aspects were found again and again to be characteristic of this motif throughout the period studied. First, when it is said that individuals will be recompensed or judged "according to their deeds," this presumes a holistic or unitary view of human works. It is not a deed for deed inspection, but rather one's entire pattern of life is in view, one's "way." Not even all one's deeds in a lifetime need be considered, since repentance and forgiveness could eliminate the relevance of past misdeeds and mark the beginning of a new way. Nor does this life-pattern demand flawlessly perfect obedience. Thus there is precious little evidence of the "Jewish atomization" of deeds and ethics which has formed the backdrop to many studies of Paul.

---

[1] See esp. 1 Kgs. 8:32; also Ps .18:20, 24.

Second, the understanding of this motif in Judaism was set squarely within the framework of covenantal nomism, not legalism.[2] The invitation to, and the provision for, life within God's covenant favor and protection (= salvation) proceeds solely from God's grace. This *sola gratia* becomes even more pronounced in the Qumran literature. However, entry into and continuance in this gracious covenantal relationship requires accepting and walking in God's ways. This is not seen as *earning* a covenant status one did not yet have, but as the only proper response of love and trust toward the covenant God who had already bestowed life. One's works of obedience are not viewed as *merits*, each to be recompensed in atomistic fashion, but instead are the observable manifestations of the covenant loyalty of the unseen heart. One's deeds are a single whole, the *way* upon which one is walking, and it is this which normally forms the basis or standard for the divine recompense. Behavior demonstrating this fundamental inward disposition of covenant loyalty brings the promise of continued participation in the covenant blessings; consistently disloyal behavior brings God's wrath. Faith and works are not competing criteria of judgment, but represent two sides of the single coin of human response in the light of God's gracious covenantal arrangement. The boundary between apostasy and fidelity is seldom legislated in unambiguous fashion, since it is a matter not of legal boundaries but of the human heart and of sovereign divine freedom. Questions as to the *quantity* of transgressions or righteous deeds are pointless. There is thus in this literature ultimately no tension or paradox between salvation by grace and judgment according to deeds. One "gets in" (to use Sanders' terms) by covenantal grace, and "stays in" by not abandoning the covenant and its required obedience. This is equally true in sectarian circles such as Qumran, in which case, however, covenant grace is no longer manifested to all Israel through the Torah, but is channeled more narrowly through the revelation and interpretations given to the sect. Within this framework of covenantal nomism, divine judgment according to works functions to confirm or reveal one's fundamental loyalty to God

[2] This is not, of course, to claim that my study has established covenantal nomism as the soteriological pattern of second temple Judaism. It is, rather, to suggest that the understanding of the recompense motif found in these texts supports at crucial points covenantal nomism instead of legalism. Particularly in chapters 2–3, the attempt was made to draw in a larger body of textual evidence in order to lend strength to this suggestion.

and his covenant. One does not *become* righteous at this judgment, but one's righteousness is revealed or confirmed.

Alongside these two elements common to all the writings studied, there are also a number of developments which occur. The historical eschatology of the Jewish Scriptures gives way more and more to an apocalyptic or transcendental eschatology, so that judgment according to deeds occurs post-mortem and often in the context of an apocalyptic universal last judgment. Reflections on post-mortem existence open the door to an increasing individualization of judgment. Also, as mentioned above, there is an increasing use of the motif for the purposes of distinguishing "true Jews" in a sectarian sense. Alongside this development is a growing dichotomy between God's treatment of the righteous (who are promised mercy and no judgment) and the wicked (who will be judged without mercy). This is often used to distinguish between God's treatment of Jews and Gentiles respectively, but more and more the line between the righteous and the wicked tends to run right through the larger body of Jews. Only true Jews (i.e., faithful members of a particular sect or party) need not fear the judgment, while Jews outside the sect will suffer the fate of the Gentiles. Even in such cases, however, the partiality shown to community insiders is contingent upon their continued faithfulness, rather than constituting a privileged immunity. Finally, there is a decreasing use of the motif for the reward of the righteous. The stronger emphasis on human sinfulness apparently made "reward according to deeds" seem less appropriate (though the belief in Israel's "reward" per se remained strong).

As for Paul, in spite of limited use of the motif his writings testify to the fact that judgment according to deeds remains a fundamental and living axiom in Judaism of the first century CE.[3] He does not appear to be citing any set form of the motif or authoritative text(s), but is appealing to a fundamental conviction of practically all Jews. His wording of the motif shows the influence of Jewish tradition. There is no formulaic hardening, and new terminological expressions are still being crafted.

Paul's use also demonstrates the continuing variety of function and conceptual development of the motif. In terms of the functional typology he employs it as a call to repentance (Rom. 2:6), motiva-

---

[3] The motif occurs in Rom. 2:6; 1 Cor. 3:8b; 2 Cor. 5:10; 11:15b; and Col. 3:24–25.

tion to obedience (2 Cor. 5:10; Col. 3:24–25), a sentence upon the disobedient (2 Cor. 11:15b), and as the theological basis against intra-community judgment (1 Cor. 3:8b). In broadening the investigation to include related judgment texts, the situations of conflict and intra-Jewish debate reflected in Paul's letters have highlighted the importance of the judgment theme in arguments over who is a "true Jew" and as a warrant against intra-community conflict. Also of interest is the seeming renaissance of "reward according to deeds" in Paul's writings, something that will flower in rabbinic writings, but had nearly died out in the last two centuries of the pre-Christian era.

Alongside this Jewish rebirth of judgment according to deeds, Paul is a witness to the developments in the understanding of the motif which were noted above in Jewish texts. Even where recompense terminology is employed, this is clearly a part of an *eschatological* judgment scenario. Thus Romans 2:6 speaks of divine recompense according to deeds, but as an expansion upon the "righteous judgment" of God which will occur on the eschatological "day of wrath" (2:5). Though collective aspects are not eliminated, it is particularly *individual* accountability which is now stressed most strongly (see esp. 1 Cor. 3:8b; Rom. 14:10–12). I have already mentioned his use of the motif to *distinguish the "true Jew."* In addition, Paul continues the *dichotomy in the treatment of the wicked versus the righteous.* The ones will be "the objects of wrath ... made for destruction," the others "the objects of mercy ... prepared beforehand for glory" (Rom. 9:22–23). For Paul, however, it is not the distinction between Jew and Gentile which makes a difference, but between Christians and the rest of humanity. Thus the whole world, both Jew and Gentile, stands under the wrath of God (Romans 1–3) and vengeance awaits the enemies of the gospel (2 Thess. 1:6–10), whereas "God has destined us [Christians] not for wrath, but for obtaining salvation" (1 Thess. 5:9; also 1:10).[4]

However, just as the line dividing mercy and wrath could run right through the Jewish community, so in Paul it could run through the midst of the Christian congregation and did not constitute for community members a blanket immunity from divine

---

[4] On this dichotomy in Paul, see Wetter, *Der Vergeltungsgedanke bei Paulus*, 16–85; and esp. Mattern, *Das Verständnis der Gerichtes*, 59–111. As is typical of many, however, Mattern misconstrues this dichotomy in terms of an immunity for Christians from judgment (= condemnation) in spite of sins (98–111).

judgment. The exegesis has demonstrated at numerous points that Paul was fully prepared to threaten persistently sinful Christians with divine destruction,[5] and the same is true for leaders or teachers within the community who departed from his apostolic message.[6] Thus, as generally in second temple Judaism, Paul's promise of mercy and no judgment was actually directed only to the genuinely faithful within the community, which corresponds precisely to the line of demarcation that will be revealed at the judgment according to deeds.

Paul not only demonstrates solidarity with the tradition-historical *developments* in the motif, but, even more importantly for my interpretation of his judgment statements, *he is also at one with second temple Judaism regarding the two fundamental areas of continuity* identified above. NT scholars are generally perfectly ready to argue that Paul held to a *holistic* or *unitary view of human* (or at least of Christians') *works*. Where they have sometimes erred is in asserting an essential discontinuity between Paul and Judaism at this point, based upon their misreading of the latter as a religion which fragments and atomizes.[7] If my reading of Jewish texts in part one is correct at this point, then judgment according to deeds in Paul stands much closer to the understanding of the same in Judaism than has commonly been allowed.

Second, I have maintained that *Paul understands the significance of this judgment within a larger soteriological framework remarkably similar to the covenantal nomism of part one.*[8] In short, one "enters" the sphere of salvation (or is counted a participant among those who are the saved) by God's grace and election. One "stays in" by obedience; or in more Pauline terms, by "living in the Spirit." The judgment of those saved by grace will be according to their deeds.

[5] E.g., 1 Cor. 3:16–17; 6:9–10; 10:1–12; 11:29–34; 16:22a; Col. 3:25.

[6] 1 Cor. 3:16–17; 2 Cor. 11:15b; Gal. 1:9.

[7] "It is common to distinguish between the supposed Jewish legalistic view that one is righteoused and judged on the basis of the sum of individual deeds and Paul's view that behavior is conceived as a whole" (Sanders, *PLJP*, 113, and n. 77 for references).

[8] The caveat issued above applies here as well (n. 2), since a demonstration of this thesis would require a much more thorough analysis of topics such as justification by faith, election, and the Law in Paul's letters. Nevertheless, at quite a number of points judgment texts have also touched explicitly on these issues, so that this suggestion is certainly not without textual warrant. For a recent voice supporting general continuity, and based upon a notoriously thorny text, see Scott J. Hafemann, *Paul, Moses, and the History of Israel: The Letter/Spirit Contrast and the Argument from Scripture in 2 Corinthians 3* (WUNT 81; Tübingen: J.C.B. Mohr (Paul Siebeck) 1995).

While the *term* "covenantal nomism" may not be particularly appropriate for Paul, the fundamental structure of grace and works, election and obedience, salvation and judgment, remains the same.[9] Certain differences are, of course, evident. The Christ-event replaces the giving of the Torah as the defining event of electing grace, and it is no longer relation to the Torah but to Christ which defines membership in the people of God. Thus it is no longer a specifically *Jewish* covenantal nomism which Paul presents, a fact which was perceived in his treatment of the "works of the law" and in his radical soteriological equality between Jew and Gentile. Further, the role of the Spirit in enabling obedience, while not absent in Judaism, is certainly heightened significantly in Paul.[10] Nevertheless, in both patterns salvation is not earned by human initiative, but is given by God's grace; *and* it is contingent upon continuance in the faith and obedience which are required by that relationship.[11] Such obedience remains a *condition* for the main-tenance of righteousness and for final justification. More precisely,

[9] Here siding with M. Hooker ("Paul and Covenantal Nomism," *Paul and Paulinism: Essays in Honour of C. K. Barrett* [London: SPCK, 1982], 47–56).

[10] This is one of Sanders' main reasons for rejecting covenantal nomism as a description of Paul's pattern of religion. "In Pauline theory, deeds ... flow from the Spirit, not from commandments" (*PLJP*, 208). Yet elsewhere, against those who would put too much distance between Spirit and Law in Paul, he can say, "there is no distinction between the manner in which Christians are to fulfill Paul's require-ments – whether Paul calls those requirements "the law" or not – and the manner in which Jews traditionally observe the Mosaic law" (113).

[11] R. H. Gundry insists there *is* a fundamental difference. "Paul's un-Jewish extension of faith and grace to staying in makes good works *evidential* of having received grace through faith, *not instrumental* in keeping grace through works." "The evidence Sanders cites from Palestinian Jewish literature shows overwhelmingly that good works are a *condition* as well as a sign of staying in. It appears, however, that for Paul good works are *only* (but not unimportantly) *a sign* of staying in, faith being the necessary and sufficient condition of staying in as well as of getting in" ("Grace, Works, and Staying Saved in Paul," 11, 35). This comparison appears biased in my opinion. When Paul says, "So let us not grow weary in doing what is right, for we will reap [i.e., eternal life, v. 8b] at harvest time, *if we do not give up*" (Gal. 6:9), he makes continuance in "doing what is right" a *condition* for reaping eternal life exactly as in Judaism (see further the statements in Rom. 11:22; 1 Cor. 6:9–10; Gal. 5:21; and Col. 1:22–23). In Paul and in Judaism, "Loss and commendation ... are both earned in the sense of "deserved," but salvation itself is not earned by enumerating deeds or balancing them against one another" (Sanders, *PLJP*, 111). That is, if one defines "condition" as the necessity of *congruence* to a given behavioral norm (i.e., only the righteous shall enter the kingdom of God), then both Paul and Judaism make salvation conditional. If "condition" is defined more *instrumentally* (i.e., by doing this one obtains what one formerly lacked), then neither should be called conditional.

it remains the *necessary manifestation* of that which has already been obtained and assured through faith.[12]

Finally, I am now in a position to make a suggestion regarding the traditionally asserted tension or paradox in Paul between justification by faith alone and judgment according to deeds. As has become clear in part two, Paul's letters give no evidence of such a tension in Paul's own mind.[13] He uses the judgment motif, both for reward and punishment, without apology and with no seeming fear of misunderstanding. This is easily explainable when one realizes that the apostle has inherited a way of speaking and thinking about divine judgment according to deeds which itself felt no such tension. Those who had already been justified by grace through faith in Christ were expected (by God's grace and the Holy Spirit, of course) to live righteous lives as well. That is, their righteousness by faith would manifest itself in obedience, in works; though not necessarily in sinless perfection. Their obedience is a consistent and wholehearted conformity to God's will, with provision made for unintentional sins, temporary backsliding, and restoration. Thus, there is no tension in saying that the status of righteousness is conferred solely by means of faith in Christ, and that all (including the righteous) will be judged according to their deeds. This is not a second justification, nor does it somehow place one's present justification (by faith) in doubt. It is the standard Jewish expectation that one's outward behavior (one's *works* or *way*) will correspond to, and be a visible manifestation of, inward reality. The eschatological recompense according to deeds *confirms*, on the basis of deeds, one's justification. For the justified, that is for those who are in Christ by faith and therefore are walking in or according to Christ's Spirit, this future judgment causes no *theolo-*

---

[12] In spite of the previous note, *condition* can, perhaps, be too easily misunderstood in the sense of an entry requirement which must be met *before* or *in order that* one may obtain something. For Paul, the crucial *condition* in this sense has already been fulfilled (Rom. 5:1 = faith), yet without rendering the manifestation of that ongoing reality in any way superfluous. It goes without saying that faith for Paul, as for Judaism, is more than any single (one-time) act of assent to the truth, commitment to God, etc., being instead one's life-long stance toward God and the truth (cf. H. Ridderbos; = "the new mode of existence"; *Paul*, 231–252).

[13] James Dunn stresses Paul's affirmation of a "tension . . . between God's saving righteousness and his wrath, between the grace/faith nexus of salvation and the moral outworkings of human choice" (*The Theology of Paul the Apostle* [Grand Rapids: Eerdmans, 1998], 490), but seems to mean primarily an *eschatological* tension (497, see also the heading of §18, "The Eschatological Tension"), rather than a *theological* one (see also 41–42, 133–137, 365, 490–492).

gical tension or paradox vis-à-vis their already assured justification by faith.

There is a remaining tension, but it is *existential* rather than theological. Those who would depart from the gospel and from Christ, who would walk according to the flesh rather than the Spirit, will be judged to be unrighteous according to their deeds. In Paul's letters this warning is made applicable repeatedly to his Christian audiences, and no less to the apostle himself. This impossible possibility does create an existential dynamic which permits the assurance of present and future justification by faith while denying any sort of unconditional guarantee or immunity. For all humanity, the righteous as well as the unrighteous, the believer as well as the unbeliever, it shall be "to each according to deeds."

Appendices

APPENDIX 1

MOTIF-TEXTS IN THE JEWISH SCRIPTURES

	Hebrew verb	Greek verb	Hebrew noun*	Greek noun*
Judg 1:7	שלם	ἀνταποδίδωμι	[כאשר עשיתי]	[καθὼς ἐποίησα]
Ruth 2:12	שלם	ἀποτείσαι	פעל (sg.)	ἐργασία (sg.)
	[היה שלמה]	[γένοιτο πλήρης]	משכרת (sg.)	μισθός (sg.)
1 Sam 25:39	שוב	ἀποστρέφω	רעה (sg.)	κακία (sg.)
2 Sam 3:39	שלם	ἀνταποδίδωμι	רעה (sg.)	κακία (sg.)
2 Sam 22:21	גמל	ἀνταποδίδωμι	צדקה (sg.)	δικαιοσύνη (sg.)
	שוב	ἀνταποδίδωμι	בר ידי	καθαριότητα τῶν χειρῶν
2 Sam 22:25	שוב	ἀποδίδωμι	צדקה (sg.)	δικαιοσύνη (sg.)
	—	—	בר (sg.)	καθαριότητα τῶν χειρῶν
1 Kgs 2:44	שוב	ἀνταποδίδωμι	רעה (sg.)	κακία (sg.)
1 Kgs 8:32	נתן	δίδωμι	דרך (sg.)	ὁδός (sg.)
	נתן	δίδωμι	צדקה (sg.)	δικαιοσύνη (sg.)
2 Chr 6:23	נתן	ἀποδίδωμι	דרך (sg.)	ὁδός (pl.)
	נתן	ἀποδίδωμι	צדקה (sg.)	δικαιοσύνη (sg.)
Job 34:11	שלם	ἀποδίδωμι	פעל (sg.)	[καθὰ ποιεῖ]
	מצע	—	ארח (sg.)	—
Ps 18:20[1]	גמל	ἀνταποδίδωμι	צדק (sg.)	δικαιοσύνη (sg.)
	שוב	ἀνταποδίδωμι	בר ידי	καθαριότητα τῶν χειρῶν
Ps 18:24[2]	שוב	ἀνταποδίδωμι	צדק (sg.)	δικαιοσύνη (sg.)
	—	—	בר ידי	καθαριότητα τῶν χειρῶν

* If underlined, the noun is used as a *standard* ("according to …").

[1] MT = 18:21; LXX = 17:21.
[2] MT = 19:25; LXX = 17:25.

Ps 28:4[3]	נתן	δίδωμι	פֹּעַל (sg.)	ἔργον (pl.)
—	—		רע מעלל (sg.)	πόνηρα τ.ἐπιτηδευμάτων (sg.)
	נתן	δίδωμι	מעשה ידי (sg.)	ἔργον τ.χειρῶν (pl.)
	שוב	ἀποδίδωμι	גמול (sg.)	ἀνταπόδομα (sg.)
Ps 62:12[4]	שלם	ἀποδίδωμι	מעשה (sg.)	ἔργον (pl.)
Ps 94:2[5]	שוב	ἀποδίδωμι	גמול (sg.)	ἀνταπόδομα (sg.)
Ps 94:23[6]	שוב	ἀποδίδωμι	און (sg.)	ἀνομία (sg.)
	צמה	ἀφανιῶ	רעה (sg.) + ב	πονηρία (sg.)
Ps 103:10[7]	עשׂה	ποιέω	חטא (pl.)	ἁμαρτία (pl.)
	גמל	ἀνταποδίδωμι	עון (pl.)	ἀνομία (pl.)
Prov 19:17	שלם	ἀνταποδίδωμι	גמול (sg.)	δόμα (sg.)
Prov 24:12	שוב	ἀποδίδωμι	פֹּעַל (sg.)	ἔργον (pl.)
Eccl 12:14	[יבא במשפט]	[ἄξει ἐν κρίσει]	מעשׂה (sg.)	ποίημα (sg.)
Isa 59:18	שלם	ἀνταποδίδωμι	גמלה (pl.)	ἀνταπόδοσις (sg.)
	שלם	—[8]	גמול (sg.)	—
Isa 66:6	שלם	ἀνταποδίδωμι	גמול (sg.)	ἀνταπόδομα (sg.)
Jer 16:18	שלם	ἀνταποδίδωμι	עון/חטאת (sg.)	ἀδικία/ἁμαρτία (pl.)
Jer 17:10	נתן	δίδωμι	דרך (pl.)	ὁδός (pl.)
			פרי מעלל	καρπὸς τ.ἐπιτηδευμάτων (pl.)
Jer 21:14	פקד	—[9]	פרי מעלל	—[10]
Jer 23:2	פקד	ἐκδικέω	רע מעלל (sg.)	τ.πονηρὰ ἐπιτηδεύματα (pl.)
Jer 25:14	שלם	—	פֹּעַל (sg.)	—
Jer 32:19[11]	נתן	δίδωμι	דרך (pl.)	ὁδός (sg.)
			פרי מעלל	
Jer 51:6[12]	שלם	ἀνταποδίδωμι	גמול (sg.)	ἀνταπόδομα (sg.)

[3] LXX = 27:4.
[4] LXX = 61:13.
[5] LXX = 93:2.
[6] LXX = 93:23.
[7] LXX = 102:10.
[8] See the recensions of Lucian and Origen.
[9] Hexapla, Aquila & Theodotion: ἐπισκέψομαι.
[10] Hexapla, Aquila & Theodotion: Τὰ πονηρὰ ἐπιτηδεύματα (pl.).
[11] LXX = 39:19.
[12] LXX = 28:6.

Jer 51:24[13]	שלם	ἀνταποδίδωμι	רעה (sg.)	κακία (pl.)
Lam 3:64	שוב	ἀποδίδωμι	גמול (sg.)	ἀνταπόδομα (sg.)
			מעשה ידי (sg.)	ἔργον τ.χειρῶν (pl.)
Ezek 7:3[14]	שפט	ἐκδικέω	דרך (pl.)	ὁδός (pl.) + ἐν
	נתן	δίδωμι	תועבות (pl.)	βδέλυγμα (pl.)
Ezek 7:4[15]	נתן	δίδωμι	רדך (pl.)	ὁδός (sg.)
	היה	εἰμί	תועבות (pl.)	βδέλυγμα (pl.)
Ezek 7:8[16]	שפט	κρίνω	רדך (pl.)	ὁδός (pl.) + ἐν
	נתן	δίδωμι	תועבות (pl.)	βδέλυγμα (pl.)
Ezek 7:9[17]	נתן	δίδωμι	רדך (pl.)	ὁδός (pl.)
	היה	εἰμί	תועבות (pl.)	βδέλυγμα (pl.)
Ezek 7:27	עשה	ποιέω	מ + (sg.) דרך	ὁδός (pl.)
Ezek 18:30	שפט	κρίνω	דרך (pl.)	ὁδός (sg.)
Ezek 24:14	שפט	κρίνω	דרך (pl.)	ὁδός (pl.)
			עלילה (pl.)	ὁδός (pl.)
	—	κρίνω	—	αἷμα (pl.)
	—	κρίνω	—	ἐνθύμημα (pl.)
Ezek 33:20	שפט	κρίνω	דרך (pl.)	ὁδός (pl.) + ἐν
Ezek 36:19	שפט	κρίνω	דרך (sg.)	ὁδός (sg.)
			עלילה (pl.)	ἁμαρτία (sg.)
Hos 4:9	פקד	ἐκδικέω	דרך (pl.)	ὁδός (pl.)
	שוב	ἀνταποδίδωμι	מעלל (pl.)	διαβούλια (pl.)
Hos 12:2[18]	פקד	ἐκδικέω	דרך (pl.)	ὁδός (pl.)
	שוב	ἀνταποδίδωμι	מעלל (pl.)	ἐπιτήδευμα (pl.)
Hos 12:14[19]	נטש	ἐκχέω	דם (pl.)	αἷμα (sg.)
	שוב	ἀνταποδίδωμι	חרפה (sg.)	ὀνείδισμος (sg.)
Joel 3:4[20]	שוב	ἀνταποδίδωμι	גמול (sg.)	ἀνταπόδομα (sg.)
Joel 3:7[21]	שוב	ἀνταποδίδωμι	גמול (sg.)	ἀνταπόδομα (sg.)

[13] LXX = 28:24.
[14] LXX = 7:7.
[15] LXX = 7:8.
[16] LXX = 7:5.
[17] LXX = 7:6.
[18] MT/LXX =12:3.
[19] MT/LXX = 12:15.
[20] MT/LXX = 4:4.
[21] MT/LXX = 4:7.

Zech 1:6	עשׂה	ποιέω	דרך (pl.)	ὁδός (pl.)	
			מעלל (pl.)	ἐπιτήδευμα (pl.)	
Sir 11:26	שׁוב	ἀποδίδωμι	דרך (pl.)	ὁδός (pl.)	
Sir 16:12	שׁפט	κρίνω	מפעליו (pl.)	ἔργον (pl.)	
Sir 16:14	מצא	εὑρήσει	מעשׂה (pl.)	ἔργον (pl.)	
Sir 17:23	—[22]	ἀποδίδωμι		ἀνταπόδομα (sg.)	
Sir 35:23a[23]		ἀνταποδίδωμι		ἐκδίκησις (sg.)	
Sir 35:24[24]	שׁוב	ἀνταποδίδωμι	פעל (sg.)	πρᾶξις (pl.)	
			גמול (sg.)	ἔργον (pl.)	
			מזמה (pl.)	ἐνθυμήματα (pl.)	
1 Macc 7:42		κρίνω		κακία (sg.)	

[22] No extant Hebrew text.
[23] LXX = 35:20b.
[24] LXX = 35:22.

APPENDIX II

MOTIF-TEXTS IN THE OLD TESTAMENT PSEUDEPIGRAPHA

Text		*Function*[25]
Jub	5:11	J/M
	5:15	M
1 En	95:5	C/S
	100:7	C/S
PssSol	2:7	J
	2:16	J
	(2:25)	A
	2:34–35	P
	17:8–9	P/(J)
JosAsen	28:3	C
LAB	3:10	M
2 Bar	54:21	M

[25] *P* = Praise; *J* = Justification; *A* = Appeal; *M* = Motivation (for the righteous) to obedience; *C* = Comfort; *S* = Sentence/threat of condemnation; *B* = Theological Basis against inter-personal retribution. Cf. pp. 29, 104–106 above.

APPENDIX III

MOTIF-TEXTS IN THE QUMRAN LITERATURE

	Function[26]	Verb	Object/Standard	Ind. Object
1QS II,7–8	S	(ארור)	כחושך מעשיכה (sg.-pl.)	
1QS X,11	J	יכח משפט	כנעחיתי (pl.)	
1QS X,17–18	B	שלם	גמול (sg.)	לאיש
1QH IV, 18–19	S/P	שפט	כרוב פשעיהם/כגלוליהם (pl./sg.-pl.)	
1QH V,5–6	C	שפט (לוא)	כאשמתי (sg.)	
1QH XIV, 24	P	פקד	עון רשעים (sg.)	[עליהם]
1QM VI,6	P	שלם	גמול רעתם (sg.)	לכול גוי הבל
1QM XI,13–14	P(M/J)	השיב	גמול רשעים (sg.)	בראש אויביכם
1QM XVIII,14	P(M)	השיב	גמול רשעים (sg.)	לאויביכה
CD III,4–5	M	ענש	לפי משגותם (pl.)	
CD V,15–16	M	פקד	מעשיהם (pl.)	
CD VII,9 (=XIX,6)	M	השיב	גמול רשעים (sg.)	עליהם
1QpHab XII,2–3	M	שלם	גמול (sg.)	לו
4QpPs37 IV,9	C	שלם	גמול (sg.)	

[26] See previous note.

BIBLIOGRAPHY

This selective bibliography includes generally only those works which have significance for the issue of judgment in second temple Judaism or Paul. Thus, there are few commentaries, reference works of a more general nature, or works dealing with only a single text or document, although quite a number of these have been cited in the footnotes.

Andre, G. *Determining the Destiny, PQD in the Old Testament.* ConB OTSeries, vol. 19. Lund: Gleerup, 1980.

Aono, T. *Die Entwicklung des paulinischen Gerichtsgedankens bei den apostolischen Vätern.* Europäische Hochschulschriften, vol. 23, no. 137. Bern: n.p. 1979.

Bassler, Jouette M. "Divine Impartiality in Paul's Letter to the Romans." *NovT* 26, no. 1 (1984): 43–48.

Divine Impartiality: Paul and a Theological Axiom. SBLDS, vol. 59. Chico, CA: Scholars Press, 1982.

Baus, Karl. *Der Kranz in Antike und Christentum.* Bonn: Peter Hanstein, 1940.

Beardslee, W. A. *Human Achievement and Divine Vocation in the Message of Paul.* London: SCM, 1961.

Becker, Jürgen. *Das Heil Gottes: Heils- und Sündenbegriffe in den Qumrantexten und im Neuen Testament.* SUNT 3. Göttingen: Vandenhoeck & Ruprecht, 1964.

Beilner, Wolfgang. "Weltgericht und Weltvollendung bei Paulus." In *Weltgericht und Weltvollendung: Zukunftsbilder im Neuen Testament.* ed. Hans-Josef Klauck, 85–105. Quaestiones Disputatae 150. Freiburg/Basel/Vienna: Herder, 1994.

Beker, J. Christiaan. *Paul the Apostle: The Triumph of God in Life and Thought.* Edinburgh: T & T Clark Ltd., 1980.

Berger, Klaus. "Zu den sogenannten Sätzen Heiligen Rechtes." *NTS* 17 (1970): 10–40.

Bornkamm, G. *Paul.* New York: Harper & Row, 1971.

Bousset, Wilhelm, and H. Gressmann. *Die Religion des Judentums im späthellenistischen Zeitalter.* 3rd ed. HNT. Tübingen: J. C. B. Mohr, 1926.

Brandenburger, Egon. "Gerichtskonzeptionen im Urchristentum und ihre

Voraussetzungen." In *Studien zum Neuen Testament und seiner Umwelt 16*, 5–54. Linz: n.p., 1991.

Brandon, S. G. F. *The Judgment of the Dead: The Idea of Life After Death in the Major Religions*. New York: Scribner, 1969.

Braun, Herbert, *Gerichtsgedanke und Rechtfertigungslehre bei Paulus*. UNT. Leipzig: J. C. Hinrich'sche, 1930.

Qumran und das Neue Testament. 2 vols. Tübingen: J. C. B. Mohr (Paul Siebeck), 1966.

"Vom Erbarmen Gottes über den Gerechten: Zur Theologie der Psalmen Salomos." In *Gesammelte Studien zum Neuen Testament und seiner Umwelt*, 8–69. Tübingen: J. C. B. Mohr, 1971 [= *ZNW* 43 (1950/ 1951): 1–54].

Brocke, M. "Tun und Lohn im nachbiblischen Judentum: Ein Diskussionsbeitrag." *BibLeb* 8 (1967): 166–178.

Broer, Ingo, "Das Ius Talionis im Neuen Testament." *NTS* 40, no. 1 (1994): 1–21.

Brun, L. *Segen und Fluch im Urchristentum*. Oslo: Dybwad, 1932.

Büchler, Adolph. *Types of Jewish-Palestinian Piety from 70 B.C.E. to 70 C.E.* New York: KTAV, 1922 [repr. 1968].

Bultmann, Rudolf. *Theologie des Neuen Testaments* 8th ed. Uni-Taschenbücher 630. Tübingen: J. C. B. Mohr (Paul Siebeck), 1980.

Carson, D. A. *Divine Sovereignty and Human Responsibility: Biblical Perspectives in Tension*. New Foundations Theological Library. London: Marshall, Morgan & Scott, 1981.

Charette, Blaine B. *The Theme of Recompense in Matthew's Gospel* JSNTSupp, vol. 79. Sheffield: JSOT, 1992.

Charles, R. H. *A Critical History of the Doctrine of Future Life in Israel, in Judaism, and in Christianity*. London, 1899 [repr. *Eschatology: The Doctrine of a Future Life in Israel, Judaism and Christianity (a Critical History)*. New York: Schoken Books, 1963].

Collins, R. F. "The Berith-Notion of the Cairo Damascus Covenant and Its Comparison with the NT." *ETL* 39 (1963): 555–594.

Conzelmann, Hans. *Grundriss der Theologie des Neuen Testaments*. 2nd ed. EETh 2. Munich: Kaiser, 1968.

Cosgrove, Charles H. "Justification in Paul: A Linguistic and Theological Reflection." *JBL* 106 (1987): 653–670.

Cossmann, W. *Die Entwicklung des Gerichtsgedankens bei den alttestamentlichen Propheten* BZAW 29. Gießen: A. Töpelmann, 1915.

Cranfield, C. E. B. "'The Works of the Law' in the Epistle to the Romans." *JSNT* 43 (1991): 89–101.

Davies, Glenn N. *Faith and Obedience in Romans: A Study in Romans 1–4*. JSOTSupp, vol. 39. Sheffield: Sheffield Academic Press, 1990.

Davies, Philip R. "Eschatology at Qumran." *JBL* 104, no. 1 (1985): 39–55.

Davies, William D. *Jewish and Pauline Studies*. Philadelphia: Fortress Press, 1984.

Paul and Rabbinic Judaism: Some Rabbinic Elements in Pauline Theology. 4th ed. Philadelphia: Fortress Press, 1980.

Devor, Richard C. *The Concept of Judgment in the Epistles of Paul*. Ph.D. Diss., Drew University, 1959.

Disley, E. "Degrees of Glory: Protestant Doctrine and the Concept of Rewards Hereafter." *JTS* n.s., 42, no. 1 (1991): 77–105.

Donfried, Karl P. "Justification and Last Judgment in Paul," *Int* 30 (1976): 140–152.

Du Toit, Andreas B. "Faith and Obedience in Paul." *Neotestamentica Pretoria* 25, no. 1 (1991): 65–74.

Dunn, James D. G. "Echoes of Intra-Jewish Polemic in Paul's Letter to the Galatians." *JBL* 112, no. 3 (1993): 459–477.

Jesus, Paul and the Law: Studies in Mark and Galatians. London/Louisville: SPCK/Westminster, 1990.

"The New Perspective on Paul." *BJRL* 65, no. 2 (1983): 95–122.

The Theology of Paul the Apostle. Grand Rapids: Eerdmans, 1998.

"Works of the Law and the Curse of the Law (Galatians 3.10–14)." *NTS* 31 (1985): 523–542.

"Yet Once More – 'The Works of the Law': A Response." *JSNT* 46 (1992): 99–117.

Eichrodt, Walther. *Theology of the Old Testament*, trans. J. A. Baker. 2 vols. OTL. Philadelphia: Westminster, 1961 [= *Theologie des Alten Testaments*. 6th ed., 1959].

Eisenbeis, Walter. *Die Wurzel shlm im Alten Testament*. BZAW, vol. 113. Berlin: Walter de Gruyter & Co., 1969.

Elliott, Neil. *The Rhetoric of Romans: Argumentative Constraint and Strategy in Paul's Dialogue with Judaism*. JSNTSupp, vol. 45. Sheffield: Sheffield Academic Press, 1990.

Fabrega, Valentin. "Eschatologische Vernichtung bei Paulus: Ein Beitrag zur Erhellung des apokalyptisch-rabbinischen Hintergrunds." In *Jahrbuch für Antike und Christentum, Jahrgang 15, 1972*, 37–65. Münster: Aschendorffsche Verlagsbuchhandlung, 1973.

Fabry, Heinz-Josef. *Die Wurzel ŠÛB in der Qumran-Literatur*. BBB. Cologne/Bonn: Peter Hanstein, 1975.

Filson, Floyd. *St. Paul's Conception of Recompense*. UNT 21. Leipzig: J. C. Hinrichs'sche, 1931.

Fischer, Ulrich. *Eschatologie und Jenseitserwartung im hellenistischen Diasporajudentum*. BZNW. Berlin: Walter de Gruyter, 1978.

Flusser, David. "The Dead Sea Sect and Pre-pauline Christianity." In *Aspects of the Dead Sea Scrolls*, eds. C. Rabin and Y. Yadin, *Scripta Hierosolymitana*, vol. 4., 215–266. Jerusalem: Magnes, 1965.

Freed, Edwin D. *The Apostle Paul, Christian Jew: Faithfulness and Law*. Lanham/New York/London: University Press of America, 1984.

Fuller, Ruth Marion. *A Pauline Understanding of Rewards: Its Background and Expression in First Corinthians*. Ph.D. Diss., Fuller Theological Seminary, 1991.

Gammie, John G. "The Theology of Retribution in the Book of Deuteronomy." *CBQ* 32, no. 1 (1970): 1–12.

Garlington, Don B. *Faith, Obedience, and Perseverance: Aspects of Paul's Letters to the Romans*. WUNT. vol. 79. Tübingen: J. C. B. Mohr (Paul Siebeck), 1994.

"The Obedience of Faith in the Letter to the Romans. Part I: The

Meaning of 'ΥΠΑΚΟΗ ΠΙΣΤΕΩΣ (Rom 1:5; 16:26)." *WTJ* 52 (1990): 202–224.

"The Obedience of Faith in the Letter to the Romans: Part II, The Obedience of Faith and Judgment by Works." *WTJ* 53 (1991): 47–72.

Garnet, Paul. "Qumran Light on Pauline Soteriology." In *Pauline Studies: Essays Presented to Professor F. F. Bruce on His 70th Birthday*, 19–32. Exeter: Paternoster, 1980.

Salvation and Atonement in the Qumran Scrolls. WUNT 2nd ser., vol. 3. Tübingen: J. C. B. Mohr (Paul Siebeck), 1977.

Gaston, Lloyd. *Paul and the Torah*. Vancouver (BC): University of British Columbia, 1987.

Green, W. S., ed. *Approaches to Ancient Judaism: Theory and Practice*. BJS, vol. 1. Missoula: Scholars Press, 1978.

Griffiths, J. Gwyn. *The Divine Verdict: A Study of Divine Judgement in the Ancient Religions*. Studies in the History of Religions, NumenSup 52. Leiden: E. J. Brill, 1991.

Gundry, Robert H. "Grace, Works, and Staying Saved in Paul." *Bib* 66 (1985): 1–38.

Gundry-Volf, Judith M. *Paul and Perseverance*. WUNT, vol. 2/37. Tübingen: J. C. B. Mohr, 1990.

Gunkel, Hermann. "Vergeltung im Alten Testament." In *Um das Prinzip der Vergeltung in Religion und Recht des Alten Testaments*, ed. Klaus Koch, 1–7. Wege der Forschung. Darmstadt: Wissenschaftliche Buchgesellschaft, 1972. [= *RGG*. 2nd ed., vol. 5, 1931, cols. 1529–1533].

Harris, J. G. "The Covenant Concept Among the Qumran Sectaries." *EQ* 39 (1967): 86–92.

Haufe, Christoph. *Die sittliche Rechtfertigungslehre des Paulus*. Halle: VEB Max Neimeyer, 1957.

Hays, Richard B. *Echoes of Scripture in the Letters of Paul*. New Haven and London: Yale University Press, 1989.

Heiligenthal, Roman. "Soziologische Implikationen der Paulinischen Rechtfertigungslehre im Galaterbrief am Beispiel der 'Werke des Gesetzes.' Beobachtungen zur Identitätsfindung einer frühchristlichen Gemeinde." *Kairos* 26 (1984): 38–53.

Werke als Zeichen, Untersuchungen zur Bedeutung der menschlichen Taten im Frühjudentum, neuen Testament und Frühchristentum. WUNT, vol. 2/9. Tübingen: J. C. B. Mohr, 1983.

Hengel, Martin. *Judentum und Hellenismus: Studien zu ihrer Begegnung unter besonderer Berücksichtigung Palästinas bis zur Mitte des 2.Jh.s v. Chr.* WUNT 10. Tübingen: J. C. B. Mohr (Paul Siebeck), 1988.

Hooker, Morna D. "Paul and Covenantal Nomism." In *Paul and Paulinism: Essays in Honour of C. K. Barrett*, eds. Morna D. Hooker and S. G. Wilson, 47–56. London: SPCK, 1982.

Hoyt, Samuel L. "The Judgment Seat of Christ and Unconfessed Sins." *BSac* 137 (1980): 32–40.

"The Negative Aspects of the Christian's Judgment." *BSac* 137 (1980): 125–132.

Hübner, Hans. "Gal 3:10–12 und die Herkunft des Paulus." *KuD* 19 (1973): 215–231.

"Pauli Theologiae Proprium." *NTS* 26 (1980): 445–473.

"Was heißt bei Paulus 'Werke des Gesetzes'?" In *Glaube und Eschatologie, FS Werner Georg Kümmel zum 80.Geburtstag*, eds. E. Gräßer and O. Merk, 123–133. Tübingen: J. C. B. Mohr (Paul Siebeck), 1985.

Huntjens, Johannes A. "Contrasting Notions of Covenant and Law in the Texts from Qumran." *RQ* 8 (1974): 361–380.

Jewett, Robert. *Paul's Anthropological Terms: A Study of Their Use in Conflict Settings*. AGJU, vol. 10. Leiden: E. J. Brill, 1971.

Karner, F. K. *Die Bedeutung des Vergeltungsgedankens für die Ethik Jesu, dargestellt im Anschluss an die synoptischen Evangelien*. Oedenburg-Sopron: n.p., 1927.

Käsemann, Ernst, "Gottesgerechtigkeit bei Paulus." In *Exegetische Versuche und Besinnungen*, 181–193. Göttingen: Vandenhoeck & Ruprecht, 1964 [= *ZTK* 58 (1961): 367–378].

"Sätze Heiligen Rechtes im Neuen Testament." In *Exegetische Versuche und Besinnungen*, 69–82. Göttingen: Vandenhoeck & Ruprecht, 1964 [= *NTS* 1 (1954/55): 248–60. ET: "Sentences of Holy Law." in *New Testament Questions of Today*, 66–81. Philadelphia: Fortress Press, 1969].

Kinghardt, Matthias. "Sünde und Gericht von Christen bei Paulus." *ZNW* 88 (1997): 56–80.

Klostermann, Ernst. "Die adäquate Vergeltung in Rm. 1:22–31." *ZNW* 32 (1933): 1–6.

Koch, Klaus. "Gibt es ein Vergeltungsdogma im Alten Testament?" *ZTK* 52 (1955): 1–42.

"Der Spruch 'Sein Blut bleibe auf seinem Haupt'." In *Um das Prinzip der Vergeltung in Religion und Recht des Alten Testaments*, ed. Klaus Koch, 432–456. Wege der Forschung. Darmstadt: Wissenschaftliche Buchgesellschaft, 1972 [= *VT*, vol. 12 (1962): 396–416].

Kuck, David W. *Judgment and Community Conflict: Paul's Use of Apocalyptic Judgment Language in 1 Corinthians 3:5–4:4*. NovTSup, vol. 66. Leiden: E. J. Brill, 1992.

Kühl, D. Ernst. *Rechtfertigung auf Grund Glaubens und Gericht nach den Werken bei Paulus*. Königsberg i. Pr.: Wilh. Koch, 1904.

Kuhn, Heinz-Wolfgang. "Die Bedeutung der Qumrantexte für das Verständnis des Galaterbriefes." In *New Qumran Texts and Studies: Proceedings of the First Meeting of the International Organization for Qumran Studies, Paris 1992*, ed. George J. Brooke, 169–221. Leiden/ New York/Cologne: E. J. Brill, 1994.

"The Impact of the Qumran Scrolls on the Understanding of Paul." In *The Dead Sea Scrolls: Forty Years of Research*, eds. Devorah Dimant and Uriel Rappaport, 327–339. STDJ 10. Leiden: E. J. Brill, 1992.

Kuntz, J. Kenneth. "The Retribution Motif in Psalmic Wisdom." *ZAW* 89 (1971): 223–233.

La Rondelle, H. K. *Perfection and Perfectionism: A Dogmatic-ethical Study of Biblical Perfection and Phenomenal Perfectionism.* Andrews University Monographs, vol. 3. Berrien Springs, MI: Andrews University Press, 1971.

Laato, Timo. *Paul and Judaism: An Anthropological Approach,* trans. T. McElwain. South Florida Studies in the History of Judaism, vol. 115. Atlanta: Scholars Press, 1995.

Licht, J. "The Doctrine of the Thanksgiving Scroll." *IEJ* 6, no. 1 (1956): 1–13, 89–101.

Lincoln, Andrew T. "From Wrath to Justification: Tradition, Gospel and Audience in the Theology of Romans 1:18–4:25." In *SBL Seminar Papers 1993,* ed. E. H. Lovering, Jr., 194–226. SBLSPS 32. Atlanta: Scholars Press, 1993.

Lindars, Barnabas. "Ezekiel and Individual Responsibility." *VT* 15 (1965): 452–467.

Lohmeyer, Ernst. "Gesetzeswerke." In *Probleme Paulinischer Theologie,* 31–74. Stuttgart: Kohlhammer, n.d.

Low, Douglas, A. *Apocalyptic Motivation in Pauline Paraenesis.* Ph.D. Diss., Southern Baptist Theological Seminary, 1988.

Lund, N. W. *Chiasmus in the New Testament.* Chapel Hill: University of North Carolina Press, 1942.

Luz, Ulrich. *Das Geschichtsverständnis des Paulus.* Munich: Kaiser, 1968.

Maier, Gerhard. *Mensch und freier Wille: Nach den jüdischen Religionsparteien zwischen Ben Sira und Paulus.* WUNT. Tübingen: J. C. B. Mohr (Paul Siebeck), 1971.

Malherbe, Abraham J. *Social Aspects of Early Christianity.* Baton Rouge and London: Louisiana State University Press, 1977.

Mattern, Luise. *Das Verständnis des Gerichtes bei Paulus.* ATANT, vol. 47. Zürich and Stuttgart: Zwingli, 1966.

Meeks, Wayne, *The First Urban Christians.* New Haven: Yale University Press, 1983.

———. "Judgement and the Brother: Romans 14, 1 – 15, 13." In *Tradition and Interpretation in the New Testament: Essays in Honor of E. Earle Ellis,* ed. Gerald Hawthorne, 290–300. Grand Rapids: Eerdmans, 1987.

Melinek, A. "The Doctrine of Reward and Punishment in Biblical and Early Rabbinic Writings." In *Essays Presented to Chief Rabbi Israel Brodie,* ed. H. J. Zimmiels, 275–290. London: n.p., 1967.

Michel, Otto, "Der Lohngedanke in der Verkündigung Jesu." *ZST* 9 (1932): 47–54.

Miller, Patrick D., Jr. *Sin and Judgment in the Prophets: A Stylistic and Theological Analysis.* SBLMS. Chico, CA: Scholars Press, 1982.

Minear, Paul S. *The Obedience of Faith: The Purposes of Paul in the Epistle to the Romans.* SBT (2nd ser.) 19. Naperville, IL: Alec R. Allenson, Inc., 1971.

Moo, Douglas, *The Epistle to the Romans.* NICNT. Grand Rapids: Eerdmans, 1996.

———. "'Law,' 'Works of the Law,' and Legalism in Paul." *WTJ* 45 (1983): 73–100.

———. "Romans 2: Saved Apart from the Gospel?" In *Through No Fault of*

Their Own? The Fate of Those Who Have Never Heard, eds. Wm. V. Crockett and James G. Sigountos, 137–145. Grand Rapids: Baker, 1991.

Moore, George Foot. *Judaism in the First Centuries of the Christian Era, the Age of the Tannaim.* 3 vols. Cambridge: Cambridge University Press, 1954.

Morris, Leon. *The Biblical Doctrine of Judgment.* London: Tyndale, n.d.

Moule, C. F. D. "Jesus, Judaism, and Paul." In *Tradition and Interpretation in the New Testament: Essays in Honor of E. Earle Ellis*, ed. Gerald Hawthorne, 43–52. Grand Rapids: Eerdmans, 1987.

Müller, Karlheinz. "Gott als Richter und die Erscheinungsweisen seiner Gerichte in den Schriften des Frühjudentums." In *Weltgericht und Weltvollendung: Zukunftsbilder im Neuen Testament*, ed. Hans-Josef Klauck, 23–53. Quaestiones Disputatae 150. Freiburg: Herder, 1994.

Münchow, Christoph von. *Ethik und Eschatologie: Ein Beitrag zum Verständnis der frühjüdischen Apokalyptik mit einem Ausblick auf das Neue Testament.* Göttingen: Vandenhoeck & Ruprecht, 1981.

Nicholson, Ernest W. *God and His People: Covenant and Theology in the OT.* Oxford: Clarendon, 1986.

Nickelsburg, George W. E., Jr. *Resurrection, Immortality, and Eternal Life in Intertestamental Judaism.* HTS. Cambridge: Harvard University Press, 1972.

Nickelsburg, George W. E., Jr. and Michael E. Stone, comps. *Faith and Piety in Early Judaism: Texts and Documents.* Philadelphia: Fortress Press, 1983.

Nötscher, Friedrich. *Zur Theologischen Terminologie der Qumran-Texte.* BBB 10. Bonn: Peter Hanstein, 1956.

Pesch, Wilhelm. *Der Lohngedanke in der Lehre Jesu, verglichen mit der religiösen Lohnlehre des Spätjudentums.* Münchener Theologische Studien, vol. 1/7. Munich: Zink, 1955.

"Der Sonderlohn für die Verkündiger des Evangeliums." In *Festschrift für J. Schmid: Neutestamentliche Aufsätze*, eds. J. Blinzler and Otto Kuss, 199–206. Regensburg, 1963.

Preuß, Horst Dietrich, ed. *Eschatologie im Alten Testament.* Wege der Forschung. Darmstadt: Wissenschaftliche Buchgesellschaft, 1978.

Pryke, John. "Eschatology in the Dead Sea Scrolls." In *The Scrolls and Christianity*, ed. Matthew Black, 45–57. Theological Collections II. London: SPCK, 1969.

Rad, Gerhard von. *Theologie des Alten Testaments.* 2 vols. Einführung in die evangelische Theologie, vol. 1. Munich: Kaiser, 1957.

Räisänen, Heikki. *Paul and the Law.* 2nd ed. WUNT, vol. 29. Tübingen: J. C. B. Mohr (Paul Siebeck), 1987.

Raitt, T. M. "The Prophetic Summons to Repentance." *ZAW* 83 (1971): 30–49.

Reiser, Marius. *Jesus and Judgment: The Eschatological Proclamation in Its Jewish Context*, trans. Linda M. Maloney. Minneapolis: Fortress Press, 1997.

Reventlow, H. Graf. "Sein Blut komme ueber sein Haupt." In *Um das Prinzip der Vergeltung in Religion und Recht des Alten Testaments*, ed.

Klaus Koch, 412–431. Wege der Forschung. Darmstadt: Wissenschaft-liche Buchgesellschaft, 1972 [= *VT* 10 (1960): 311–327].

Rhyne, Clyde T. *Faith Establishes the Law: A Study on the Continuity Between Judaism and Christianity: Romans 3:31*. Ph.D. Diss., Union Theological Seminary, 1979.

Ridderbos, Hermann. *Paul: An Outline of His Theology*, trans. J. R. DeWitt. Grand Rapids: Eerdmans, 1975.

Ringgren, Helmer. *The Faith of Qumran*, trans. Emilie T. Sander. Philadel-phia: Fortress Press, 1963.

Roetzel, Calvin J. *Judgement in the Community: A Study of the Relationship Between Eschatology and Ecclesiology in Paul*. Leiden: E. J. Brill, 1972.

Sanders, E. P. *Judaism: Practice and Belief, 63 BCE–66 CE*. London/ Philadelphia: SCM/Trinity, 1992.

"On the Question of Fulfilling the Law in Paul and Rabbinic Judaism." In *Donum Gentilicum: New Testament Studies in Honour of David Daube*, eds. E. Bammel, Charles K. Barrett, and W. D. Davies, 103–126. Oxford: Clarendon, 1977.

"Patterns of Religion in Paul and Rabbinic Judaism: A Holistic Method of Comparison." *HTR* 66 (1973): 455–478.

Paul and Palestinian Judaism: A Comparison of Patterns of Religion. Philadelphia: Fortress Press, 1977.

Paul, the Law and the Jewish People. Philadelphia: Fortress Press, 1983.

Scharbert, Josef, "SHLM im Alten Testament." In *Um das Prinzip der Vergeltung in Religion und Recht des Alten Testaments*, ed. Klaus Koch, 300–324. Wege der Forschung. Darmstadt: Wissenschaftliche Buchgesellschaft, 1972.

"Das Verbum PQD in der Theologie des Alten Testaments." Idem., 278–299 [= *BZ* 4 (1960): 209–226].

Schoeps, Hans Joachim. *Paul: The Theology of the Apostle in the Light of Jewish Religious History*, trans. H. Knight. Philadelphia: Westminster, 1961.

Schreiner, Thomas R. "Is Perfect Obedience to the Law Possible? A Re-Examination of Galatians 3:10." *JETS* 27, no. 2 (1984): 151–160.

The Law and Its Fulfillment: A Pauline Theology of Law. Grand Rapids: Baker, 1993.

"Paul and Perfect Obedience to the Law: An Evaluation of the View of E. P. Sanders." *WTJ* 47 (1985): 245–278.

" 'Works of Law' in Paul." *NovT* 33, no. 3 (1991): 217–244.

Schuster, Hermann. "Rechtfertigung und Gericht bei Paulus." In *Stat Crux Dum Volvitur Orbis: Eine Festschrift für Landesbischof D. Hanns Lilje*, eds. Georg Hoffmann and Karl Heinrich Rengstorf, 57–67. Berlin: Lutherisches Verlagshaus, 1959.

Scott, James M. " 'FOR AS MANY AS ARE OF WORKS OF THE LAW ARE UNDER A CURSE' (Galatians 3.10)." In *Paul and the Scriptures of Israel*, eds. Craig A. Evans and James A. Sanders, 187–221. JSNTSup 83. Sheffield: JSOT, 1993.

Seifrid, Mark. *Justification by Faith: The Origin and Development of a Central Pauline Theme*. NovTSup, vol. 68. Leiden: E. J. Brill, 1992.

Sloan, R. B. "Paul and the Law: Why the Law Cannot Save." *NovT* 33, no. 1 (1991): 35–60.

Snodgrass, Klyne R. "Justification by Grace – to the Doers: An Analysis of the Place of Romans 2 in the Theology of Paul." *NTS* 32 (1986): 72–93.

Stendahl, Krister. "The Apostle Paul and the Introspective Conscience of the West." *HTR* 56 (1963): 199–215.

Stowers, Stanley K. *The Diatribe and Paul's Letter to the Romans*. SBLDS, vol. 57. Chico, CA: Scholars Press, 1981.

Synofzik, Ernst. *Die Gerichts- und Vergeltungsaussagen bei Paulus: Eine traditionsgeschichtliche Untersuchung*. Göttingen: Vandenhoeck & Ruprecht, 1977.

Theissen, Gerd. *The Social Setting of Pauline Christianity*, ed. and trans. J. H. Schütz. Philadelphia: Fortress Press, 1982.

Thielman, Frank. *From Plight to Solution, a Jewish Framework for Understanding Paul's View of the Law in Galatians and Romans*. NovTSup, vol. 61. Leiden: E. J. Brill, 1989.

Paul and the Law: A Contextual Approach. Downers Grove, IL: IVP, 1994.

Thiselton, Anthony C. "The Meaning of SARX in 1 Corinthians 5:5, a Fresh Approach in the Light of Logical and Semantic Factors." *SJT* 26 (1973): 204–228.

Towner, W. Sibley. "Retributional Theology in the Apocalyptic Setting." *USQR* 26 (1971): 203–214.

Travis, Steven H. *Christ and the Judgment of God, Divine Retribution in the New Testament*. Foundations for Faith. Basingstoke: Marshall, Morgan and Scott, 1986.

Tyson, Joseph B. "'Works of Law' in Galatians." *JBL* 92 (1973): 423–431.

Volz, Paul. *Die Eschatologie der jüdischen Gemeinde*. Hildesheim: Georg Olms Verlagsbuchhandlung, 1966 [orig. *Jüdische Eschatologie von Daniel bis Akiba*. 2nd ed. Tübingen: J. C. B. Mohr, 1934].

Wacker, M.-T. *Weltordnung und Weltgericht: Studien zu I Henoch 22*. Würzburg: Echter, 1982.

Walter, Nikolaus. "Die Botschaft vom Jüngsten Gericht im Neuen Testament." In *Eschatologie und Jüngstes Gericht*, eds. N. Walter, G. Wenz, and O. Bayer, 10–48. Fuldaer Hefte 32. Hannover: Lutherisches Verlagshaus, 1991.

Watson, Francis. *Paul, Judaism and the Gentiles*. Cambridge: Cambridge University Press, 1986.

Watson, Nigel M. "Justified by Faith; Judged by Works – an Antinomy?" *NTS* 29 (1983): 209–221.

Weber, Ferdinand W. *Jüdische Theologie auf Grund des Talmud und verwandter Schriften*. 2nd ed. Leipzig: Dörffling & Franke, 1897.

Westerholm, Stephen. *Israel's Law and the Church's Faith: Paul and His Recent Interpreters*. Grand Rapids: Eerdmans, 1988.

Wetter, Gillis P. *Der Vergeltungsgedanke bei Paulus: Eine Studie zur Religion des Apostels*. Göttingen: Vandenhoeck & Rupprecht, 1912.

Wilckens, Ulrich. "Was heißt bei Paulus: 'Aus Werken des Gesetzes wird kein Mensch gerecht'?" In *Rechtfertigung als Freiheit: Paulusstudien*, 81–104. Neukirchen-Vluyn: Neukirchener, 1974.

Wright, Nicholas Thomas. *The New Testament and the People of God*. Christian Origins and the Question of God, vol. 1. Minneapolis: Fortress Press, 1992.

Würthwein, Ernst. "The Old Testament Belief in Recompense." In *TDNT*, ed. G. Kittel, trans. G. Bromiley, vol. IV, 706–712. Grand Rapids: Eerdmans, 1967.

Ziesler, J. A. *The Meaning of Righteousness in Paul*. Cambridge: Cambridge University Press, 1972.

SUBJECT INDEX

INDEX OF PASSAGES